Book Typography
1815—1965

Book Typography
1815–1965

In Europe and the
United States of America

Edited with
an Introduction by
KENNETH DAY

THE UNIVERSITY OF CHICAGO PRESS

First published 1965, in the Netherlands, by
NV Drukkerij G. J. Thieme, Nijmegen,
under the title
Anderhalve Eeuw Boektypografie
1815–1965

Library of Congress Catalog Card Number: 66–13864

The University of Chicago Press, Chicago 60637
Ernest Benn Limited, Bouverie House, London E.C.4
English translation © 1966 by Ernest Benn Limited
Original © 1965 by Koninklijke Drukkerij G. J. Thieme NV
Printed in the Netherlands

Preface

This volume first appeared, as the bibliographical note records, under the imprint of NV Drukkerij G. J. Thieme, Nijmegen, whose one hundred and fiftieth anniversary its publication was timed to celebrate. As the introduction to the Dutch edition pointed out, the history of this printing firm has always been closely connected with that of the book. In the period covered, the transition from the nineteenth to the twentieth century, more than one revolution occurred in printing, but literature recording this history has until now remained comparatively scarce. Therefore it appeared to the present publishers that here was a contribution which should be translated into English.

It seemed to the Directors of Thieme an opportunity to provide a new assessment, and following the advice of Stanley Morison and Jan Tschichold the team of contributors was assembled and to them all thanks are due for their collaboration in the original conception: Fernand Baudin, typographic adviser to the Etablissements Plantin Limited of Brussels; Gérard Blanchard and Maximilien Vox of Paris; Dr. Georg Kurt Schauer of the Deutsche Bibliothek, Frankfurt and Secretary of Die Schönsten deutschen Bücher; Miss P. M. Handover of The Times Publishing Company, London; Franco Riva of the Biblioteca Civica, Verona; Dr. G. W. Ovink, adviser to Lettergieterij 'Amsterdam'; Dr. Willy Rotzler, editor of *Du*, Zurich; and James M. Wells, The Newberry Library, Chicago. Thanks are also due to Jan Vermeulen, teacher at the Academy of Design and Applied Art, Arnhem, who was responsible for the typography and design retained in this edition.

In the preparation of the English edition with its somewhat larger area of circulation certain modifications have been made. Most of the footnotes and references have been retained but incorporated in the text; the selection of plates whilst remaining the same in total has been re-arranged to provide a more equitable balance; the order of presentation has been made alphabetical by the countries described; the endeavour has been to introduce a greater degree of uniformity especially in references to common factors, for example Art Nouveau has been used consistently, the only exception being the retention of Jugendstil where the German term seemed more applicable.

The contributors each interpreted their brief in their own way, and it seemed therefore wise to retain the non-uniformity of titles to the sections, thus emphasising this difference of approach. Finally, the full list of illustrations has been added for the convenience of readers and librarians as a ready reference, and the index has been completely recast, and considerably extended.

The English and American publishers join with their Dutch colleagues in expressing the hope that here has been provided a welcome contribution to international history in the field of typography and book printing.

Contents

CONTENTS

viii

Introduction

Printing has always been prepared to let its face speak for itself. The outward image its mechanical processes presented has for long periods of the five hundred years of its existence been the only evidence of its slow evolution. Very little new research has been done, and none on a systematic basis, to cover the history of this vast subject although many delightful byways have been explored, some perhaps to exhaustion. Tracing the growth of mechanisation and illustrating the changing patterns of the machines themselves would provide an immense field for investigation.

The story, from the hand-press through its practical improvements to the first mechanical press; again the stage of improvement and refinement leading to rotary presses; the intervention of new production processes making some further variants, to first tackle lithography, then offset it; to command gravure in such a way as to make it a mass production operation; the revolution in harnessing photography to many stages of all processes, hastening them and at the same time giving them greater precision. All this and one has only begun to cover one aspect, the actual multiplication of the printed image in numbers great or small. The camera, and the growing use of photographic, and more recently electronic, means to produce the printing surfaces, are again a fruitful field for historical exploration. There is a paradox here, as there has been some documentation of the early pioneers of photography, yet little on those equally inventive in the days before photography was born. The wider use of colour has followed progressively the improvements in photographic transfer and separation. The nineteenth century saw colour gathering weigh but only today has it really taken hold—particularly in the educational sphere—and the full flood doubtless still to come.

How much of the history of book-binding has been fully recorded? Most of the research has been confined to studies of individuals and their work in divergent periods. The craft of hand-binding, the growth of design for decoration, and information on content after the onset of publishers' edition binding, the high speed of multiplication at all stages of book-making from the sheet stage, all need recording in order to fill the wide gaps in such knowledge as has been so far provided within limited and scattered areas. The processes of gilding and blocking; the formulation of new foils and inks to suit new methods and materials provide copy for a book on their own. Materials too, in a wider sense; the paper, but here there are a number of historical works giving a wide coverage, if not always as detailed as some would wish; printing inks, too, have been little studied. Then again the changing patterns of publishing, especially during the last seventy-five years, and nearer today, even more so in the last twenty, have of themselves dictated changes in materials and mechanics to cope with larger impressions and ephemeral bindings—hence the paperbacks of today.

Perhaps of even greater interest to a widening public is the history and evolution of letter-forms and their use, which we call typography. Here is where printing has always proved itself most eloquent—at least its advocates and devotees have found more to say about this aspect. Modern uses for print have produced cycles of fashion: modes have commanded designers and typographers in greater numbers, thus encouraging a language of criticism and a growing literature.

The least ephemeral form of print today, as when printing in the western world began, has always been the Book. It is satisfactory to find, therefore, that the first international symposium of its kind to appear for many years is devoted to Book Typography. It is a happy coincidence that the celebration of a leading Dutch printer of its 150th birthday means we have a span 1815–1965 that covers the major revolutions in the growth of printing, typography, type design and the presentation of the book. The opportunity, presented so aptly to G. J. Thieme, was seized avidly with the results now seen in this volume. Truly a veritable mine of information, much of it hitherto unpublished, in which sociologists and historians of the future may well quarry to follow new lodes and build even more complete pictures of the past, both in printing and the overall sociological pattern of evolving society. The Industrial Revolution was largely borne on the back of the printing trade, which provided the necessary means of transition from street ballads to manuals of instruction, cheap reprints of the classics, and the wide homilectic literature so characteristic of the Victorian Age.

One of the most fascinating periods was the twenty years spanning the turn of the century. Preceding and influencing these was the towering figure of William Morris. The contributors to this collection of studies, from their differing geographical concepts, all pay tribute to the significance of this one man and his ideals—ideals partially or more fully implemented in widely divergent circumstances and climates. Morris has devotees today who will find herein a due recording to their satisfaction: not mere adulatory comment but reasoned assessment of his influence and tradition. To set against this great Englishman, there is at least one corresponding continental who adopted and adapted the Master's teaching, Henry Van de Velde, whose influence was widespread—in the van of the Art Nouveau movement and the founder of the Weimar school that was to become the first Bauhaus established by Walter Gropius. Here the reader may see Van de Velde set in historical context from several angles. To follow and to match Morris and Van de Velde, here are newly recorded accounts of P.J.H. Cuypers in the Netherlands, and Rudolf Koch in Germany. The roll widens in scope, and increases in numbers, as one advances further into the twentieth century.

Another coincidence of publishing—and publishing has shown throughout its history an aptitude for happy coincidences—is that at a time when there is growing evidence that the Art Nouveau movement is undergoing a reassessment and a resuscitation in several fields, here are series of threads running through the contributions, weaving the pattern that was Art Nouveau and tracing in some detail its birth, rapid growth and sudden demise in the countries represented. Whether or not one is in sympathy with the essence of Art Nouveau, and whether or not a renaissance will be of any lasting value, or enjoy a new life of any span, there is much of interest in the historical picture. There are in particular new pointers to the effects of the movement on letterforms of the time.

In all, this collection by the several authorities helps to present a more balanced view of printing and typography, mainly as related to the book, although there is naturally some detail on the inter-relation with the growing Press of the late nineteenth century, and to put in possibly better perspective than hitherto those 150 years we are covering. The present-day pre-occupation with the welding of good design to mass-production versus the craftsmanship of the individual producer, has here a background to make much of the reasoning more coherent. Whatever one says about the printed word and its presentation, we have to bear in mind that it echoes the human voice, however polyglot the family from which it springs. Doubtless books about books fall into a special category, but they are nonetheless governed by the same production and publishing factors as all books wherever produced. This 'international' undertaking has been fraught with some language difficulties, but it is to be hoped that the published version offends none—contributors or readers—and succeeds in pleasing most.

The familiar quotation from Ecclesiastes:

> 'of making many books there is no end;
> and much study is a weariness of the flesh'

will be viewed and judged according to the tastes of the reader and student, but those who have the good fortune to enjoy some part, if not all, of the present volume will more aptly echo the Latin author who said:

> 'Pro captu lectoris habent sua fata libelli
> (The fate of books depends on the capacity of the reader).'

LONDON 1966   K.D.

List of Illustrations

GERMANY (between pages 112 & 113)

GREAT BRITAIN (between pages 160 & 161)

THE NETHERLANDS (between pages 256 & 257)

SWITZERLAND (between pages 304 & 305)

Fernand Baudin

BOOKS IN BELGIUM

It is less than one hundred and fifty years since Belgium came into existence, at least in the political sense and under that name. The real beginning of the history of the modern book in Belgium goes back to the time when she was still part of the Low Countries under William I of Orange, and we must start there, if we are to arrive at a just estimate of typographical production in Belgium. The hundred and fifty years or so of Belgium's existence can be roughly divided into three periods. In the first, from 1814 to 1860, Belgium, which had been reduced by her successive rulers to a sort of Northern Boeotia, was slowly recovering, renewing her links with her past, and building up vast publishing enterprises before even acquiring a literature of her own. Then came a brilliant period, up to the turn of the century, when the country's literary and artistic production tended more and more to merge with those of France and Holland. Then, after 1910 and on through the testing time of the First World War, Belgian book production led its own more discretely national existence.

What is there of typographical interest here? These being things that are intimately connected, there are again three distinct phases to be seen. In the first, books in Belgium, as everywhere on the Continent, followed the Didot style. The Didots in France and Bodoni in Italy had effected a revolution in typographic style comparable, in its own dimension, to the change in ideas and manners brought in by the French Revolution.

Consumer goods were not more changed by the industrial revolution than was typography by the work of the Didots and Bodoni. The then recent invention of lithography and the needs of the equally new technique of advertising set their mark above all on the printed word. This was followed by a period of general decadence, that plunged Belgium into the same poverty of typographical and other ideas, as prevailed in England and elsewhere on the Continent. This, in its turn, led to a reaction, in which Belgium herself played a conspicuous part. At this time, Van de Velde, Horta, Hankar, Serrurier-Bovy were winning fame in architecture and the decorative arts, and so were Lemmen, Deman, Van Rysselberghe, and the same Van de Velde, in typography, this, a difficult new departure occasioned by the introduction of the ideas of William Morris on the one hand and the types of the Dutch foundries, on the other. Neither, however, could bring about the birth of a national style to counter that which De Roos and others started in Holland.

In Belgium, no concerted attempt in this direction on any large scale was made before the foundation by Henry van de Velde in 1927 of the Institut Supérieur des Arts Decoratifs (ISAD) in the abbey of la Cambre. Further credit is due to the printing press of Saint-Augustin at Bruges, the publishing houses of *De Sikkel* at Antwerp, Manteau at Brussels and Lannoo at Thielt. Their current production is of a typographic quality that has been exceptional in Belgium since about 1910, while, following William Morris's example, it tended to be more and more widespread in the current production of other countries. Typographic quality, by the way, is not chiefly dependent on the excellence of the material used. Neither the literary merit of the texts, nor the quality of the illustrations, where there are any, can redeem the weaknesses of composition and printing. Good composition is no more a luxury than impeccable machining. They are necessities in any book intended to be read, however modest. Care for good composition should not be confined to the title-page and the hierarchy and proportions of the various parts of the book. Spacing, leading out, balance of margins, necessitate the same care throughout the body of the text.

There has always been a need for de-luxe editions and the ordinary book has never suffered because of it. Such discrimination was necessary at a time of general decadence; but it would be an obstacle now, not to our returning to a glorious past, but to the development of the country's graphic arts and industries on the scale of the Common Market.

(From the point of view adopted here, which is that more or less of typographic perfection, Bodoni's work, for all its genius, can be used as an illustration of the faults that are inherent in the publishing of what we now call coffee-table books and the production of private presses. The interest in these books is often as limited as the size of their editions. The value of Bodoni's publications was often further lessened by carelessness, mistakes in the text and by

4

the lack of any critical apparatus. Here, Bodoni is like the worst amateur. The Didots were quite different. They showed a real respect for their texts, which they knew how to choose so as to keep the interest of scholars and of the general public. What is more, they developed the commercial methods of reproduction, notably by the invention of the stereotype.)

TYPEFOUNDRIES IN BELGIUM

In 1927, Henry van de Velde wrote: 'The efforts of Belgium's artists are still too new to have been able to induce our printers to make the sacrifices that have to be made to create modern Belgian type faces.' This prompted Bertrand Guégan to write, in *Arts et Métiers Graphiques* 1931 No. 26, 14, that Belgium could still have fine books without these. Bertrand Guégan was right, though that does not mean that H. van de Velde was altogether wrong. It is quite true that one can have fine printing, even a form of printing that in the long run can take on a national character, without having national type faces. It is only that there is more risk of being superficial. It is also quite true that nowhere are books more original typographically than in the countries which do their own letter-cutting, so this is an element that ought to be taken into consideration.

In 1815, Belgium no more had its own letter-cutting than it had a literature of its own. It was soon to have a literature in the French idiom and one in the Dutch idiom, but it seems that it was not to do any letter-cutting of its own during the period under consideration. Before this time Belgium had had Jacques-François Rosart. Born in Namur, he emigrated to meet with ill-fortune in Egmont-Binnen and in Haarlem where his rival with the Enschedé's was no less than J. M. Fleischman. He finally set up in Brussels where, under the patronage of Charles de Lorraine he quickly (between 1761 and 1777) acquired an international reputation. His son, Matthias, even less fortunate than his father, and probably less gifted as well, worked for J.-L. de Boubers, a Lille-born publisher, printer and typefounder who surely was the last to have old style faces cut in Belgium. During the occupation of the country by the armies of the Republic, however, his type soon disappeared from printers' cases, where their place was taken by those of Didot. The work of René Ponot has shown that the purely aesthetic success of Didot's type faces was reinforced by the equally great success of the Didot system. This system meant that having once chosen Didot you had to stick to it. You could not

5

use old style along with new style. (*See* Charles Enschedé: *Les Fonderies de Caractères et leur Matériel dans les Pays-Bas du XVe au XIXe siècle*, Haarlem 1908, and Fernand Baudin: *J.-F. Rosart, graveur et fondeur typographique Belge* in Cahiers Bruxellois, Vol. 2, No. 3).

Sufficient justice has not been paid to the enlightened efforts of William I to restore our country's economy. We no longer know to what extent he innovated and to what extent he took up plans that others had already laid. Perhaps, one day we shall learn of previous plans that events had thwarted, and which he implemented or took up again. At all events, instead of calling in Dutch engravers and typefounders, it was French material, that of Jules Didot, that he had installed to the considerable disgruntlement of his compatriots, when, in 1829, he set up the Fonderie et Imprimerie Normales in Brussels.

This was not the only foundry in the southern provinces. Since 1820, there had also been those of Delemer, Gando, Foudriat, Dumont, Pennequin, Vaultier-Bonnard, Conard and Joniau, and Clément; but typefoundry does not necessarily mean that there was letter-cutting as well. Of these typefounders, those who were also letter-cutters, the Delemers and the Gandos, were French, as was their equipment. The others, as far as one knows, used foreign, mostly French, matrices. To this extent, we certainly cannot say that we lacked typefoundries; and, indeed, the big printing-works that produced the so-called pirated editions, to which we shall come shortly, cast type for their own requirements, which were considerable.

After the revolution of 1830, the big names are those of Dumont and Charles Pennequin, who have already been mentioned, and also that of Vanderborght; while in the second half of the century they were to be Carabin-Schildknecht and Van Loey-Noury. Charles Pennequin and Vanderborght both had businesses of considerable scope. Perhaps the only one to have new types cut was Vanderborght. His assurances in this respect are unambiguous; but he was the only one to have boasted of his types being original. The others used the type faces of the Didots, Derriey, Mayeur, Schelter-Giesecke, etc. and, in fact, sometimes presented them as such.

It has been proved that there were typographic engravers in Belgium in the days of William I and even later, but whether they possessed originality of talent is not so evident. If they only cut type on large bodies, display letters and a few ornaments or borders of no great merit, they would naturally not be remembered. What would be surprising, would be if their contemporaries and also the historians and critics had failed to notice anything as unusual as the cutting of type, let alone a whole fount, of any originality and merit.

For us, the question is no longer one of knowing whether Belgian artists were ready for the creation of a *national* type; nor whether that would have been a useful or desirable thing to have had, but whether such a thing was itself possible. The answer to this question necessarily involves the whole art of book production in Belgium.

The creation of a letter is both the fruit and the seed of a considerable typographic sensibility. In this sense, Van de Velde's wish to have a Belgian-designed type was more justified than ever. And, as such, it was not impossible. What is doubtful, is whether this hypothetical type could be called Belgian. Whatever the geographical frontiers or political definition given to Belgium, as a country and a nation, it has always included two distinct linguistic communities. That which speaks French has always been Latin, while those who speak Dutch have always belonged to the Germanic world. Obviously, no artistic or intellectual product can be placed in a compartment as distinctly delimited as the political and geographical boundaries of a country, and it is nonsense to hope that it could be otherwise where typography in Belgium was concerned. In Belgium, books have never been able to be anything but French or Dutch. Either of our linguistic communities can give a particular accent, good or bad, to their local products in any particular field; but it is neither likely, nor desirable, that they would ever deliberately together give rise to a hybrid, Belgian product. Finally, the verifiable evidence as well as the essentially social character of typography invite a remark which may well be conclusive. Art for art's sake has been practiced with typography as with any other art. Several types were cut deliberately—by Grasset and Auriol in France, and by Eckmann in Germany—in an attempt to give typographic expression to Modern Style. These are far from lacking artistic merit, but they did not last and were perhaps used less than other expressions of this style. After that, what could be the chances of a specifically Belgian type being successful, especially now when people are seriously considering universal types?

THE SO-CALLED BELGIAN CONTREFAÇON

Having suppressed the liberty of the press in the rest of France, Napoleon I was not going to make an exception of the Belgian departments. The result of his régime, which was more rigorous than any that had preceded it, was that in 1814 there were only a few working presses left in Belgium and no typefoundry. These presses, perhaps, were mostly working for the needs of the administration.

On 23 September 1814, William I by decree took up the defence of the interests of literature and the book trade in the Low Countries. He deprived foreign authors of any rights and this, it is considered, gave birth to what is conventionally called Belgian Contrefaçon. Like everything else, this contrefaçon is capable of several interpretations. The most malicious is not necessarily the true one. The word 'Contrefaçon' is itself misleading: it implies fraud and clandestine activities. It is, however, a question of re-issuing, a practice that was certainly not new then and certainly did not originate in Belgium any more than anywhere else. This contrefaçon was in fact a common practice, time-honoured and grown universal. According to a contemporary writer (Eugene Robin: 'De la Contrefaçon belge' in *Revue des deux Mondes*, 15 January, 1844, quoted in H. Dopp: *La Contrefaçon des livres français en Belgique, 1815–1852*.): 'Each country has its own workshop for re-issuing foreign works. Books by Piedmontese, Lombardian, Roman authors do not create literary property other than within the confines of the political divisions in which they have seen the light of day, and they have been re-issued without more ado throughout the rest of Italy. It was the same in Germany some years ago, before the establishment of the Prussian union. The works of Italian, Spanish and German writers are re-issued more or less everywhere, and that is even more true of the English and French... English books are re-issued in Leipzig for the German market; in Paris by two publishers who profit considerably by the proximity of the English market.'

What was this contrefaçon? 'The open reproduction of the whole of a book, without imitating format, character, paper etc. for the purpose of selling it to the consumer under the imprint of a different publisher or printer.' That, at least, is what the Belgian publishers did, and they did it very well. So well, indeed, that they did more to spread French literature in the world than the French publishers themselves, and despite the fact that at that time, a single French printer in Tours possessed as many presses as there were in the nine southern provinces of the united Low Countries. As a matter of fact the Dutch literature of that period enjoyed no flowering nor, accordingly, any degree of interest comparable with the French one. Therefore there is little talk of any re-issuing of Dutch books in Belgium. Yet, here also, Belgian printer-publishers apparently took their advantage and provoked all but friendly reactions—Van Dieren for one, then as now publisher in Antwerp, enjoyed both experiences with more than common success!

This distinction between contrefaçon and re-issuing is not just a legal one. There is a typographical aspect, too. Counterfeit proper is typographical plagiarism as well as literary piracy. The printed copy would be re-set (in France this was called 'Belgian copy') copying even the typographical form of the first edition. This was never at any time done by Belgian publishers or printers. To have done so would have been a blunder. It would have perpetuated the faults of the censorship in France, when censorship had been suppressed in the Low Countries, and also those of the French publishers' policy, which for fifty years had been a stubborn insistence, despite repeated, general complaints, on high prices. On the contrary, the Belgian re-issues were as different from the French originals as it was in those days possible for books to be. Characteristic of French books, the types of which had been copied more or less everywhere, were their large format and text composed in a large type-body, with wide margins and generous leading. By this method, French publishers could make the shortest novel into four volumes. In Paris, each volume cost Frs. 7.50, an enormous price for those days. Think what it must have cost those who wanted to read French authors in French editions! The Belgian reprints were in a much smaller format, instead of large octavo, 16mo or 18mo, and instead of four volumes only one, which cost Frs. 3.00 without the quality of the paper being in any way inferior. The text was set in a small type-body. The margins and leading were generous compared to those of present-day pocket books. Composition was generally neat and just as elegant as that of the French editions. The Belgian reprints even imitated the layout of the title-pages with their characteristic mixing of Didot type set off by a line in Gothic and perhaps a vignette; the whole being aligned along a central axis, symmetrical, in the romantic style that was to become 'classical' in the eyes of all typographers of subsequent generations. Such a transposition seems quite simple and natural to those who have never attempted it. Those who adhere to the myth of the racial inferiority of Belgian printers and publishers, like to emphasise that the Belgian printing-works were managed by Frenchmen. Apart from the rash and hasty nature of any such generalisation, it would seem a lack of intelligence and of that professional conscience, which is at all times so desirable, to make racial discrimination where skilled manpower is concerned. At any rate, this is what *Revue Britannique* (quoted, without date, by H. Dopp *idem* who remarks that the British writer's sympathies had certainly not been won for Belgian re-issuing) had to say on the subject:

'The (Belgian) publishing houses have raised the art of printing; they have obtained elegant types, have built magnificent works, which house everything needed for book production, they have bought a lot of plant and their work is now superior to that of the French publishers.'

Gachard, who was a Frenchman, said that Belgian printing had never failed to advance: 'Our printers today can compete with those of Paris, where beauty and clearness of impression are concerned.' (*Rapport du jury sur les produits de l'industrie belge exposés à Bruxelles dans les mois de septembre et d'octobre 1835*, Edited by the Royal Archivist, Gachard. Bruxelles 1836. Quoted by H. Dopp.)

This praise is due especially to J. E. Buschmann, Adolphe Wahlen and Alexandre Jamar, whose work marks the apogee of romantic typography in Belgium. (Where romantic illustration in Belgium is concerned, we cannot do better than refer the reader to the excellently documented work of Dr. J. H. Van der Marck: *Romantische Boekillustratie in België*, Roermond, 1956. A résumé in French, an index and a chronological table make this work of value even to those who do not read Dutch.)

Auguste Wahlen had taken over a printing works founded at the beginning of the century, which had already been managed by Balleroy, Wodon and Méline. In 1834, his son, Adolphe Wahlen, turned it into a limited partnership: Adolphe Wahlen & Cie. This was the first in Belgium to use mechanical steam presses, with speeds of 1000 to 2000 an hour. Later, it passed into the hands of De Mat, Tallois, Stapleaux and Eugène Guyot, whose name since 1856 has been the official one of this considerable concern. Wahlen gave his business a definitely industrial bias, but this did not mean that he neglected the quality of its work. In the eyes of Dr. Van der Marck, Octave Delepierre's *La Chronique des Faits et Gestes admirables de Maximilien I durant son mariage avec Marie de Bourgogne*, one of those printed by Wahlen for the Société des Beaux-Arts, is a model in this respect that has rarely been equalled. Let me add here that the volumes of Théodore Juste's *L'Histoire Moderne* which Wahlen printed for the Société pour l'Emancipation intellectuelle, that is for the publisher A. Jamar, are no better than those which Delevigne et Callewaert produced for this same publisher's Bibliothèque Nationale. The name of Alexandre Jamar is associated with two of the largest 'national' series: the Panthéon National and Bibliothèque Nationale. The many volumes that they comprise are, where composition of the page, leading and register are concerned, among the best that we have seen produced in 'Charpentier format' since its introduction. (This format in 18mo is still the most usual in French book production. It is at least tempting to regard Charpentier, who introduced it into France, as the first French publisher to follow the example of his Belgian competitors and reduce his prices by reducing the format of his books.) Where illustration is concerned, the pick of Belgian illustrators and engravers were used for the forty-eight volumes of the Bibliothèque Nationale, which was subsidised by the State. Each volume cost Frs. 1.25 and the series was sold by subscription only. On at least one occasion Alexandre Jamar used J. E. Buschmann, who printed the former's edition of H. Conscience's *De Geschiedenis van België*.

The name of Buschmann is so well-known because it has persisted in the title of the firm he founded in 1842. J. E. Buschmann (1814–1852) was a poet and one of the foremost Belgian writers of his day, who turned printer. His work recalls that of Christophe Plantin, inasfar as that is possible in romantic printing in Belgium, and at Antwerp. The best of his work owed something to French inspiration—he did in fact take his degree in Paris. His prestige was so great that it brought his descendants their clientèle of authors and publishers of de-luxe editions. From our point of view, his greatest service is that which he rendered to popular literature. This he produced in a more convenient format (16mo) with more readable type and good illustrations. He was Henri Conscience's first publisher—in the series *Nederduitsche Kunstbibliotheek voor lezende huisgezinnen*—though Conscience then went to Van Dieren.

The worth of the albums of lithographs by Antoine Dewasme, Jobard and Pierre Simonau depends, by definition, on the quality of the work of the artists. Books illustrated with wood-cuts were admittedly the most suitable in letterpress-printed books, and here Dewasme produced for the Société des Beaux-Arts the best of Belgium's romantic books. Silvio Pellico's *Mes Prisons* (1839) was illustrated by Jos Coomans, the wood-engravings being by Brown and Pannemaker, two Belgian engravers who acquired an international reputation. Octave Delepierre's *Les Aventures de Tiel Ulenspiegel* and Louis Desnoyer's *Aventures de Jean-Paul Choppart* were illustrated in 1840, by Paul Lauters, with wood-engravings by the pupils of the Ecole Royale de Gravure, under the direction of Henry Brown.

THE PUBLISHING HOUSES

These Belgian re-issues were sometimes faulty where spelling was concerned, but they redeemed this shortcoming through the fact that they were the only ones in which one could always be sure of finding the whole text. They restored every passage that the censorship had suppressed in the French editions. Not only novels, but works of all kinds were re-issued in this way, and the fact relieves us from the necessity of giving a list of names that would, at the best, be summary. The authors of the books thus re-issued were divided in their attitude. Their ideas of literary property had nothing in common with ours today, and the diversity in them was dictated by motives, which can be reduced to two main concepts: some were conscious above all of how convenient these Belgian re-issues were for spreading ideas, while others could not forget that they earned nothing from them. Stendhal regarded every Belgian 'contrefacteur' as a benefactor, but it was the contrary opinion that prevailed.

This contrefaçon as it has been called, contrary to the facts, lasted, in Belgium, from 1815–1852. The historian of these thirty-seven years, H. Dopp, divides them into three periods: a beginning (1815–1830), a golden age (1830–1845) and a decline (1845–1852). What we have already said of it from the typographical point of view refers above all to the first two periods.

In 1836, La Société Typographique Belge d'Adolphe Wahlen & Cie was founded with a capital of one million gold francs. It lasted twenty years. In the same year was founded La Société de Librairie, Imprimerie et Fonderie de Caractères Meline, Cans & Cie, with a capital of two and a half million francs, and this lasted for the same period. 1836 also saw the establishment of La Société Belge de Librairie et Papeterie Hauman Cattoir & Cie. Two years later, La Société Nationale pour la propagation des bons livres was set up for a period of twenty years with a capital of four million gold francs. Finally, in 1847, came La Société pour la fabrication et le commerce des papiers with a capital of three million.

These are just some names, the most important of a great number. These huge enterprises ended wretchedly, when, after years of bickering on the question of literary property, France and Belgium reached an agreement in 1852. For reasons largely of policy, the policy of Napoleon III, all contrefaçon was simply suppressed. The printing, typefounding and paper industry then comprised 142 enterprises of an industrial character and a further 611 of a private character, and employed 5,575 people. To be truthful, it must be pointed out that it would have come to an end anyway, for the mad competition between these huge Belgian reprint houses had already bankrupted most of them. Their financial ruin was preceded by a decline in the literary and typographic value of their books. Their endeavours and enormous resources helped to disseminate what was worth-while, but also what was not: Paul de Cock as well as Victor Hugo, not only in Belgium, but throughout the civilised world, because they had branches everywhere chiefly in Leipzig and in Livorno. This is, perhaps, the best point at which to conclude this chapter. Scarcely had Belgium recovered her liberty of economic activity, than she hastened to take up again her traditionally international vocation. And she made no bad showing at a moment when the West, by way of the French Revolution, and the industrial revolution, was entering upon an age which now appears more and more decisive not only for our national cultures, but also for the civilisation of the world.

Obviously the development of the publishing trade is narrowly linked with the mechanisation and industrialisation of the printing process. To expatiate on this is not our task. Let us, however, point to the fact that the enormous output of the Belgian publishing companies, together with a growing steel industry combined to favour the rise of press manufacturing. The only surviving name in this context is Henry Jullien. His plant, founded in the second half of the nineteenth century, lasted until late into the twentieth. Yet he was by no means the first to launch such a venture. From the very beginning of the nineteenth century, several names could be recounted: Uyterelst, Gouy, Sacré, Wasseige; not to forget Vanderborght who perfected the type-casting machines. A. W. Sijthoff, Leiden, bought in Belgium from Delcambre, Cruys & Co, one of the very first typesetting machines ever invented by Young & Delcambre in 1840.

The Belgian paper industry of this period is also wanting an historian. He would find more evidence for the real significance of the Belgian 'contre-façon'.

There are, nonetheless, some survivors from those stormy days: L'Office de Publicité, founded by Alphonse Lebègue in 1843 and the firm of Veuve Monnom, founded by Delevigne & Callewaert in 1834, have only just closed down. Les Etablissements Bruylant (1847), Lesigne (1840), Mertens (1847, now EGI, Ets Généraux d'Imprimerie), Vaillant-Carmanne (1838) and Guyot, already mentioned, are still active concerns. There are, besides, the concerns of Weissenbruch, Desoer, Brepols, Casterman, Wesmael-Charlier, all of which were founded in the nineteenth century and among the oldest publishing and printing houses in Belgium.

TRAINING AND CUSTOMERS

The art of book-making is a faithful mirror of the culture and civilisation that it serves, and to that extent presupposes a degree of training and instruction in its skills that will normally be determined as much by the customers the presses supply as by the industry as such or by the authorities. It is of greater interest to examine this aspect of the question, than to attempt to draw a parallel between Belgian and French illustrators, engravers and printers. Suffice it to say that Baugniet and Madou devoted themselves to lithography in Paris, as did Pannemaker who, after Pisan, was perhaps the best engraver of Doré; that Haghe went to London and there, in association with William Day, founded the city's best lithographic works, and that Ghemar did the same in Edinburgh; while, for all their talent, the work of Stroobant, Fourmois, Verboeckhoven, Hendrickx and all the others, taken as a whole, could not make Belgian production appear other than provincial in comparison with that of Paris—which in no way means that it was without merit.

Let us rather consider for a moment two men who deserve more than a mere mention: Antoine Dewasme and Philippe Vandermaelen. Neither was an artist; but both played essential parts, the one as businessman, the other as scholar and businessman, in that they trained their people in a way that appears exemplary to us today, when training especially for careers in the book trade, printing, publishing and book design, are presenting problems in more than one country. Even though it can be said that their methods are now outmoded, they still deserve the credit of having been active, practical and efficient, while present-day business men are generally indifferent or critical.

Antoine Dewasme (1798–1851) originally came from Tournai. He was one of the first lithographic printers to set up in Belgium, first in his home town, then in Brussels. He showed as much flair in choosing his associates as in assessing public taste, and he proved to be one of the most far-sighted printers in the country, if not of his day. He had an ambition to revive a national art and conceived the idea of a school of engraving. Having with no little difficulty, overcome official mistrust and objections, he obtained a government subsidy with which, in 1836, he founded the Ecole Royale de Gravure in Brussels. Here, lithography, engraving on wood and copper were taught. In return, its pupils undertook to work for nothing for the school for a period of four years. As soon as their services had commercial value, they were allowed to work on orders received from publishers, that is to say reproduction by gravure of the work of the publishers' illustrators. An Englishman, Henry

Brown, was brought from Paris to teach wood-engraving, and an Italian, Calamatta, taught copper-engraving, while lithography was taught by Lauters, a Belgian. (In 1840 Brown was appointed head of the Koninklijke Graveerschool newly founded in The Hague by William I. His brother, William Brown, also English-bred, took his place at the Brussels school where, accordingly, no loss was felt.)

One of the school's customers, of course, was La Société des Beaux-Arts, which was managed by Dewasme himself. The Ecole Royale excelled in wood-engraving, at any rate until 1848, in which year the Prix de Rome for engraving was won by a pupil of the unsubsidised Académie d'Anvers. This blow was fatal to the Brussels Ecole and to wood-engraving in Belgium.

Philippe Vandermaelen (1795–1869) was a man endowed with unusual energy and possessed of considerable private means. Charles Senefelder, brother of the inventor of lithography, lived in Brussels, and Vandermaelen realised the advantage of this new process for cartography, in which he was very interested. With the encouragement of William I, he founded the Etablissement Géographique in 1825 and had soon acquired the reputation of being the greatest cartographer of the nineteenth century, which he himself called the century of Humboldt. His *Atlas Universal* (1830) of 400 sheets, though out-of-date, is still one of the greatest monuments to the science of geography. The typography of his scientific works, such as his *Dictionnaire Géographique*, is of such quality as many works of today could envy. (This refers mostly to the printers of his earlier works, for his later works are marred by a certain degree of typographic decadence.) What concerns us here is that at his institute, which was not subsidised, he too started free courses for students of between fourteen and eighteen years of age, at which they received instruction in drawing on stone and in cartography, but also a general scientific grounding. Between 1838 and 1845, he even provided the elements of higher training. Several of his pupils and collaborators became members of the Académie de Belgique. As well as this, he also financed several scientific missions. The business declined after his death.

Perhaps the best patrons of the Belgian printing industry were the country's horticulturalists of the second half of the nineteenth century. Those of Brussels, Ghent and Liège were everywhere known and admired for their love of their plants, grain and flowers, and for the way in which they grew and sold them. Verschaffelt, Van Houtte, Linden, Morren, François Vandermaelen (brother of Philippe) and others commissioned drawings and printed de-luxe editions and periodicals in chromo-lithography, which defy modern competition, even though our offset printers today are among the best in the Common Market. All this was assuredly promoted by the direct contact with the Dutch and, through them, with the exotic flora of their overseas territories. Yet, while a Dutchman, Frans Kierdorf, may be said to have taught many a Belgian colleague, it is no less true that Desguerrois, a famous Dutch publisher, was instructed in lithography by Jobard, in Brussels. Later, Desguerrois had Madou come over to Amsterdam in order to show a few painters what a really good lithographer could do. (*See L'Orchidée en Belgique*. Catalogue of an exhibition held at the Bibliothèque Albert I, Brussels, July/September 1961, 77 pages with 9 plates in colour and 12 in black and white).

These examples were not immediately followed. Proper typographical instruction, organised and supported by the Government, the industry and the trade unions, had to wait for the foundation of the Brussels Ecole Typographique in 1888, till which time all apprenticeship had been empirical. (*See La Typographie à Bruxelles au début du XXe Siècle* by J. Laurent M. Perquy.) The interests of the public and the industry's customers were necessarily divided. The country being swamped by French books published by the contrefacteurs, the appeal of a literature that was nationalistic rather than national could not long be anything but patriotic. It thus began to rely on copious illustration or low prices made possible by government subsidies given to such enterprises as Jamar's Bibliothèque Nationale. It is not surprising that, under such conditions, the art of bookmaking could not achieve a distinct, national character, but soon sank into the nondescript, in Belgium, as, to a certain extent, everywhere.

What were the reasons for this general decline? We know that William Morris attributed the decline in the standards of printing as much to the poverty of type design as to the absurdity and bad taste of the ornaments that were borrowed without discrimination from all old styles. What strikes one most when looking through the catalogues of the typefounders of the middle and end of the nineteenth century, is the contrast between the thickness of the bold-faced types intended for titling and display, and the thinness of the letters on a small body intended for the composing of text matter. As well, one almost always finds several bold faces among the intermediate sizes intended for sub-titles, paragraphs, indented lines and for titling advertisements and announcements. All this admittedly for use in bookwork. In fact they tended to confuse books and periodicals. The latter underwent considerable development during the nineteenth century. They had long been set by hand, before mechanical setting came in, and it is tempting, to say the least of it, to suppose that many of the types were there to answer the needs of journalism rather than those of belles lettres. And as the majority of authors, whether novelists or learned writers, had long been uninterested in fact, if not in theory, in the so-called technical aspects of the reproduction of their books, it is not surprising to find that the composing-room foremen were mostly concerned to display the wealth of type in their cases and their own virtuosity in juggling with the greatest possible number of sizes, faces, bodies and over-runs. They used the need to emphasise every subdivision in the copy as a pretext for adding all the ornaments and printing in as many colours as the budget allowed.

That, of course, does not explain everything. Lithography, which had come into being more or less simultaneously with the industrial revolution, was splendidly suited to the insatiable thirst for showy ornamentation of a new clientèle which had nothing in common with the old leisured classes with their insistence on elegance and refinement. To satisfy them, the type designers vied with each other, the foundries competed in patience and ingenuity in order to supply the ornamental letters, borders, rules and head- and tail-pieces. More than one letterpress printer added a lithography section to his works, hence the wealth of extraordinary material that today tempts the collector of typographic curiosities; hence, too, the fashion for the romantic novel to have a paper cover decorated with lithographic ornaments. The total effect could not fail to disgust first the veteran trained in the equilibrium and ascetic severity of pure Didot typography, then the pioneers of art nouveau, to which we shall be coming later.

AFTER THE CONTREFAÇON

The contrefaçon was abolished in 1852, on the eve of the Prince-Président's coup d'état and a few days before he made himself Napoleon III. It was, of course, a serious blow to the Belgian printing industry; yet the subsequent crisis was not wholly attributable to the literary convention made with France. The political situation also played a part, as did the competition between the country's printer-publishers. The increased productivity due to improvements in mechanical reproduction was itself an aggravating factor. Even so, the slump did not last long. The proscribed and others whom the coup d'état had sent into voluntary exile in Belgium, did not confine themselves to words: they wrote and published, though scarcely enough to feed the presses accustomed to the volume of business of the contrefaçon. While this practice as regards French authors found a new home in Germany, various international publishing enterprises were set up in Brussels, such as Kiesling and Schnee et Cie. Hetzel was publishing George Sand and Victor Hugo from Belgium; and when he felt that *Les Misérables* was too big an undertaking for him, he entrusted it to Lacroix et Verboeckhoven, who were Belgian.

Then, at last, came the first blossoming of a budding Literature. But our authors insisted in wanting to be national—and thus remained provincial. Each of our literary languages had its writer of some greatness: French had Octave Pirmez and, especially, Charles de Coster; and Flemish had Henri Conscience, who was translated into French and enjoyed success in France, as well as in Belgium. The needs of Belgium's expanding industries, of a national legal system, of our scientists and scholars—think of Quételet, Fetis, the Vandermaelens, of our learned societies and academies, found expression in a variety of works that swelled the number of those by French authors who had reason to fear the imperial censorship in France. All that for the profit not only of the printers and authors, both Belgian and French, but also for the benefit of far greater numbers, for what is published is in fact displayed, offered to anyone who might be interested or curious.

'Blessed be the country, where the most conscientious works of the intellect are not exposed to the rigours of a touchy administration, where thought is not lightly punished with ostracism or where for a few sentiments displeasing to a minister's ears a writer is forced to lose the fruits of long and painful labour. Happy Belgium! In this little corner of Europe there is more dignity and true greatness than in another country, the extent of whose territories and size of whose armies place it in the forefront of the nations.' (Thus Poulet-Malassis in his preface to *Marie La Sanglante*, a history of the great Catholic reaction under Mary Tudor, preceded by an essay on the fall of Catholicism in England. No date, but later than his *Histoire de Saint-Just* which was published in 1859.) And there is Charles Baudelaire to confirm that they were writing of the same culture, or lack of it, using a common typography. Too many people know the text of his 'amenities'—addressed to the Belgians, yet never published by him—without apparently having any idea of the context, that is to say, of his attitude of mind not towards the Belgians only, but really towards the whole of the world. This is what he wrote to M. Ancelle on 13 November 1864:

'Neither the (Belgian) ministers and deputies, nor those in charge of the country's gravest concerns, know the meaning of words or how to spell them, or the logical construction of a French or Latin phrase. It is true that in France they know no more... This book on Belgium is, as I have told you, a trial of my talent. I will make use of it later on France. I shall explain patiently all my reasons for my loathing of the human race'. (Charles Baudelaire: *Lettres 1841–1866*, Mercure de France, 1907.)

The human race, however, and especially the French and the Belgians, whose language was French or Flemish, wrote a sufficient number of works of varying types and sizes to keep the Belgian presses working, and this branch of industry was soon on its feet again. Around 1866, there were 500 printing presses in Belgium. Brussels alone had 250, of which seventy-five were mechanical. The Vanderborght foundry supplied the country's printers with their type and material and was soon to enjoy a considerable international business. The war of 1870 provoked a fresh and even shorter crisis, which was soon followed by a period of extraordinary prosperity. By 1880, the year of the industrial census, the number of mechanical presses had risen to 125—having been twelve in 1852 and seventy-five in 1866.

This year also saw what the textbooks of our literary history call the '1880 Awakening'. What was it to which the writers of *La Jeune Belgique* and shortly afterwards the symbolists awoke after so many years of reaching out after a national literature? Despite all such slogans as 'Soyons nous', —and how they must have made the French camp smile!—they woke up to find themselves part of an international literature the medium of which was French. What was really characteristic of the work and lives of Belgian writers of those days was that the best among them were growing more and more identical with the writers of France, and more specifically of Paris. The original editions of Lautréamont and Rimbaud are typical; they bear the imprint of a printer or publisher who may be Belgian or French, depending on the copy. Belgians wrote in France and published in Paris or Brussels indiscriminately; and so did the French in Belgium. Little reviews proliferated in Brussels and Liège, as they did in Paris. Mallarmé and Valéry contributed to *La Wallonie*. Different people have interpreted this differently at different times, it is true. Félix Fénéon, who can be seen in a famous painting which shows him beside Gide in a group listening to a reading of Verhaeren by the author, wrote:

'About 1882 Parisian Gaul was invaded by the Atrébates, Bellovaques, Véliocasses and Aulètes, brandishing fat manuscripts and marching with heavy tread. Covering and, if need be, uncovering the rear, came Aug. Brancart, Lucien-Charles Hochsteyn and Kistemaekers. Camille Lemonnier,

Edmond Picard and Cladel, the deserter, were the front-rank men; Emile Verhaeren, George Eeckhoud, Khnopff, Ivan Gilkin, Albert Giraud, Max Waller, Théodore Hannon, G. Rodenbach and Henri Nizet, the second file men. They pillaged the states of Zola, Barbey d'Aurevilly and Verlaine. But discord scattered their numbers, and they were thrust back towards the Escaut, the Lys and the Meuse... Calm and serene, the Manneken-Pis watered the combatants. The prosperity of Ostend dates from that time.' (Félix Fénéon, Œuvres, Paris 1948.)

How different was the tone of Remy de Gourmont in his La Belgique Littéraire (Crès & Cie 1916), but to quote here briefly would be useless, and properly, too long.

But what of the typographical aspect? In our eyes, as in those of the more indulgent Henri Liebrecht, the only difference between French and Belgian editions was one of degree of badness. Yet Octave Uzanne could write (Nos Amis les Livres, Paris 1886):

'The art of producing beautiful books, is the only one that the foreigners have not been able to imitate. Essentially, it is a purely French art and one could parody Villon and say: 'Il n'est bon livre que de Paris!'

'Printing, illustration, stitching, binding make us the absolute superior of all others in Europe or America, and this applies to everything, not only to the talent of our artists, but to the eye and perfect taste of our main publishers.'

It is, of course, true that it was no use our Belgian publisher, or those who published in Belgium, thinking of beating the French publishers at their own game. Kistemaekers and even Gay & Doucé had to yield points to Lemerre, Quantin and others, where choice of type went and even in subtle make-up and gradation along a central axis balanced with the inevitable vignette. Then, in 1884, des Esseintes thought of something absolutely different in concept, so different that there was nothing comparable until the Bauhaus and the ultra-American and Germanic experimental typographies: '...In order to introduce a little variety into his collections, on several occasions he obtained from London flock-papers, linen woves and such-like, and, to help show his contempt for the bibliophiles, a Lubeck merchant made him an improved grease-proof paper, blued, crackly, and rather brittle, the coating of which contained gold-spangles, like those you get in Dantziger Goldwasser, instead of straw. In this way, he made books that were unique and for which he used unusual formats...' (J.-K. Huysmans, A Rebours, Paris 1883.)

These imaginary solutions, worthy of Dr. Faustroll, were not then, unless I am mistaken, more than a sort of teething-ring, so let us rather look at what effective achievements there were. There is no doubt that both French and Belgian publishers wrangled over Félicien Rops's frontispieces. Baudelaire, one knows, considered him a genius, or very nearly one; yet by 1930 Claude-Roger Marx could see no more in the 'strappings' of this 'Belgian by a Hungarian' than another example of Belgian counterfeit, this time of the Baudelairian idea. Which is in no way contradictory. Quite different again is the importance attached to him by Madame Roswitha Riegger-Baurmann in 1958 'Schrift im Jugendstil', in *Börsenblatt des deutschen Buchhandels*, Frankfurter Ausgabe, 21 April 1958. A detailed analysis of the lettering of two of the frontispieces (1870–71) of which Rops did so many, led her to regard them as foreshadowing Jugendstil and as a contribution to it that exceeds in importance anything in this line done in France. Claude-Roger Marx would scarcely dispute that.

In what way did Rops anticipate Jugendstil? Not so much in the form or over-elaborate line of his lettering, which were rather borrowed from the draughtsman's store of accessories and romantic bric-à-brac, as in the way in which, instead of laying them anyhow above or around a vignette, Rops made his letters an integral part of the composition, to the extent that you cannot separate the two, cannot detach the letters without, so to speak, tearing off the paper behind them. In fact, looked at in that way, Rops, as an illustrator, was more horribly Jugendstil than that other Belgian who was able to give a very personal, if not national, appearance to his books, Edmond Deman.

Deman published mostly the work of his friend, Emile Verhaeren. He published three volumes of Mallarmé (*L'Après-midi d'un Faune*, 1876, *Pages*, 1891 and *Les Poésies d'Edgar Poe*, 1888) three by Verhaeren (*Les Soirs*, 1887, *Les Flambeaux Noirs* 1888, *Les Débâcles*, 1888) in the unusually large format for those days of quarto. Despite the dullness of their typography, the text drowning in too much white, they are sought after today for their frontispieces, floral ornaments, pendants and culs-de-lampe by Manet, Whistler, Renoir and Redon. Deman later adopted a more elegant format, perhaps at the suggestion of Théo Van Rysselberghe, but however that may be, the volumes he produced with discreet floral ornamentation by the latter, printed in pale, decadent tints, are undoubtedly among the most restrained examples of what goes under the label of Art Nouveau. In their relative discretion they are comparable to Horta's façades, which, though no more discreet, are less massive and more elegant than those of Van de Velde. The typography, in romans or italics, is crystal clear, discreet, but no longer dull. And, in addition, the imposition is fine. As a tribute to Villiers de l'Isle-Adam, Deman published a selection of his tales under the title, *Histoires Souveraines*. With its quarto format, its layout and ornamentation done by Théo Van Rysselberghe, it is one of the most sumptuous books he produced. In 1895, the same Théo was commissioned by Dietrich & Cie to adorn an *Almanach*, of which the text had been written by Verhaeren. This also, in point of lettering as well as ornament, is a very fine example of Art Nouveau in the Belgian book production.

HENRY VAN DE VELDE

The decade 1890–1900 was a decisive one for modern art. In England, France, Germany and elsewhere, a number of artists who had received a strictly academic grounding, felt a 'violent and irresistible' repulsion against the ugliness to which such training had given rise during the second half of the nineteenth century. 'This ugliness was the result of the constant repetition, less and less intelligent and progressively less careful, of the models of former styles.' These artists wanted something new, at any price, at all costs! And they wanted it so badly that they made it. There are some Belgian ones among the names now inseparably linked with the beginning of this new era in architecture, decoration and commercial art: those of Serrurier–Bovy, Hankar and Horta will be found in all books dealing with these subjects; but it was the name of Henry Van de Velde (1863–1957) which was best known outside his country. He made himself the apostle of the new style both in his many works of architecture, decoration and industrial design (a phrase then still unknown) and in his numerous theoretical writings. It was not his fault—nor that of Horta or Hankar—that what the Germans were soon to call the 'Veldescher Style' did not become a Belgian one (*See* H. Fierens-Gevaert, *Nouveaux Essais sur l'Art Contemporaines*, Paris 1903). We know that, after being subjected to ridicule in Paris as in Brussels, he met with such success in Germany that he went there to work. The reputation he acquired there, and in Holland, as well as in Switzerland was so great that it is well to remember that he spent nearly sixty years of his long life—he lived to the age of ninety-four—in Belgium, and that his worth was recognised there at least by his equals. The Vingtistes took him into their group (1889), which comprised an international élite, whose artistic worth is well established, as is the historical rôle they have played.

Throughout his long career, Henry Van de Velde took an active interest in typography, yet, despite his forceful personality, his teaching and example, he was not able to create a national style in this field. He was never able to do in his own country what William Morris, de Roos and Van Royen did in theirs. It is at least probable that the fault lay more with the indifference of public opinion and its makers, than with Van de Velde himself. That makes it all the more wrong to confuse his typographic work with that of his contemporaries and compatriots. We have already quoted him in order to emphasise the important part a typefoundry and, above all, a type designer can play in the national character of book production. Surely he was right to consider these as determining factors. Yet somehow that is not enough. One needs the additional personal intervention of someone who *knew* and in a position to set the fashion during a period long enough to bring about a national trend. Here Holland was in a triply fortunate position: De Roos had a long career at the Lettergieterij Amsterdam, the letter-cutting programme of which he altered completely, himself designing all its printed matter, which served as models for a whole generation of printers. Van Krimpen did the same with Joh. Enschedé & Zonen, and Van Royen who had a private press, for which he got De Roos to cut him a type, also had charge of the postal services of the Low Countries, where he made all the printed matter of his department conform to his own style. The influence of William Morris—which will take us back to Van de Velde, though not directly, was so far-reaching, that I may be permitted to dwell on it briefly, although it is really outside the scope given me.

Though various countries have *their* own pioneers in architecture, the decorative arts and commercial art, William Morris is universally recognised as *the* pioneer in typography in all countries—France being the only one where his influence on printing as a whole was negligible. Yet there is a paradox here, because his influence did not lead to imitation of what he had done, because it was too personal to be imitated, but worked through the contagious influence of the true principles of good typographic composition. Morris had rediscovered these principles through the study, and practice, of calligraphy and of Italian Renaissance printing. This is important not only in itself, but also because it is by the light of these principles which he rediscovered, that most critics and experts anxious to maintain quality, today judge the worth of what is printed (other than experimental work) and why they are so severe in their judgement of nineteenth-century production. It is undoubtedly worthwhile recalling them, as Morris himself expressed them:

'I found I had to consider chiefly the following things: the paper, the form of the type, the relative spacing of the letters, the words and the lines; lastly the position of the printed matter on the page... Next as to type...and here what I wanted was letter pure in form; severe, without needless excrescences; solid, without the thickening and thinning of the line, which is the essential form of the ordinary modern type, and which makes it difficult to read; and not compressed laterally, as all later type has grown to be owing to commercial exigencies.'

Where spacing is concerned, he wanted—with every justification—to see words far closer together than was the custom then—and all too often is so today.

Completely orientated towards the past, on which he claimed to be remodelling the society of his own day, he gave his letters and decorations and the books he designed such a Gothic look that they could not have any direct imitators even among his most ardent admirers. It was only his principles that were accepted and triumphant, while his application of them was too 'ill-timed', in fact anachronistic. These principles infected all those we have named so far: De Roos, Van Krimpen, Van Royen and many others, as far away as Germany and America.

Van de Velde was not the last to know and admire the work of William Morris. He at once regarded him as one of his great masters and precursors. He took a lesson from his work and made it the theme of the lectures he gave after 1889 at the academy in his native city of Antwerp, where he himself had studied, obtaining its diploma in painting. Great as was his admiration, it did not prevent him separating grain and chaff. He himself was not oriented towards the past, at least not in the same way as Morris. He liked referring back to history, even to prehistory, where he found examples of what he understood by style and tradition, but he certainly did not hold these up as models to be copied. In fact, here he shunned the very idea, as he was to show in the books that he designed. It was not till 1892 that he first turned his attention to the art of book production, typographic composition and book embellishment.

One of his friends, August Vermeylen, was planning a literary magazine in Dutch with the object of raising Flemish literature from its provincial rut and putting it on the international level of the Belgian reviews being published in French. He got together an editorial team of both Dutch and Belgian writers and poets, and asked Van de Velde if he would take charge of the layout and ornamentation of *Van Nu en Straks*. Van de Velde accepted, though with reservations dictated by the lessons he had learned from the work and writings of William Morris and some of his own conclusions drawn from them. He began by telling Vermeylen that book-production had never reached such a low level in England as it had in Belgium, and also that he knew of no artist in their group capable of designing a new type face nor of any printer prepared to have one cut and cast; thus necessarily all that he could do would be to produce a make-up using existing material. Having said this, he consulted various printers in order to make sure that his fears were justified, as, indeed, they were. And more than that, he was horrified to find that they all had the same anaemic types, a watering-down of the old that his century had only made more insipid and uninteresting. They had nothing that could be compared to the pure italics and romans of Jenson and Garamond. All this was horribly true. He forgets to mention in his memoirs whether he ever consulted a typefounder, or whether any printer ever suggested him doing this. Must one assume that it just never occurred to him? If it did, we shall never know now, why he did not do so. He has not told us either from which printer he obtained the Caslon that he used for the charming little collection of poems, *Six chansons du pauvre homme pour célébrer la semaine de Flandre* (1895), which he printed on a hand-press. The poems and ornaments were the work of his friend, Max Elskamp. Remy de Gourmont paid it this tribute in his *Le Livre des Masques* (1924): 'J'aime que les poètes aient le goût de la beauté extérieure et qu'ils vêtent de grâces réelles leurs grâces rêvées: mais que nul ne veuille la pureté d'art des *Six chansons du pauvre homme*; il ne saurait,—car la semaine est finie...'

This little book and *Triptyque de louange à la vie, selon l'amour, l'espérance et la foi* (which consisted of *Dominical, Salutations, dont d'Angéliques* and *En symbole vers l'Apostolat*)were produced in 1895; before that he had already done the layout for *Van Nu en Straks* (1893) and the two editions of *Déblaiement d'Art* (1894). For the review he adopted the unusual format of grand quarto and gave it sumptuous margins which were given up after its second year. The square format of the first edition of *Déblaiement d'Art* was just as unusual though inevitably more discreet. For the second edition, he altered the text, the format, type area, ornaments and the margins, to such an extent as to make it quite a different book, one that had gained both in elegance and size. But what gives this revue and his books historical value are the ornaments and initials that he designed and cut for them. These were the product of a theory of his own and, in direct opposition to William Morris's Gothicism, the floralia of Art Nouveau and to the whole gallery of traditional ornament of his day. They may well present the very first deliberate attempt at abstract ornament in contemporary art; while the title-page to *Dominical* shows one of the first, if not the very first asymmetric layouts in book-typography. The most interesting here are the *bandeaux* that ornament *Van Nu en Straks* and *Dominical*. The abstraction of these is closer to the non-figurative, lyrical sense that we give the word today. They proclaim a deliberate desire to break with the traditional repertoire of decorative forms, with everything borrowed from the past, and from all direct representation of natural shapes. The foam on the waves and the marks left on the sand by the ebbing tide are, by Van de Velde's own admission, the only figurative reminiscences to be discovered there. On the covers for *En Symbole* and *Salutations* the rhythm of the lines is more compact, more controlled and symmetrical. The contrast between the two kinds is all the more striking, because they are contemporary and because, to put it briefly, it was the more regular style that prevailed. This, of course, agrees perfectly with his wish for rationality.

This serves to focus attention on an aspect of his personality that can at times (he had then entered his thirties) be disconcerting. There is no doubt that the contradictions inevitable in the artist sometimes proved an embarrassment to him, as the man of theory. They were present in his writings and work. He was well aware of this, as witness Jacques Mesnil's introduction which Van de Velde added to the third edition of his *Formules d'une Esthétique Moderne* and the foreword to his essay *La Colonne* (Van de Velde, ISAD 1943). The first edition was published by the Cranach Presse, Weimar, and is dated 1916–1917; the second by l'Equerre, Liège 1927, and the third is that of ISAD, Brussels, no date.

His initials are no less interesting. Their design was obviously dictated by a desire for ornament. That is their function. Thus, they conform to the theory that he was to hold right up to the end. He was always to incline towards pure form, and, where he was concerned, this never implied the suppression of all ornamentation, but merely of all borrowed ornament. Ornament should grow out of the graphic context and not be imposed on it from outside. His initials, like his scrolls, owe nothing to anyone nor to any known decorative theme, but were governed and animated by what Van de Velde called the dynamism proper to the line, the form and movement of which can only be determined by the personality and taste of the artist. If the initials in *Van Nu en Straks* and *Déblaiement d'Art* bear the stamp of their age as well as his, that is due as much to the brush with which he painted them, before cutting them, as to the *Zeitgeist*. They are demonstrably not drawn with a pen, but painted—and not with a flat brush, such as the sign-writer uses, but the pointed brush used for wash and gouache. Many letters were created in this way at the time, which was also that of Auriol in France and Eckmann in Germany.

He had to wait several more years before achieving a book designed as he really wanted it, that is to say: starting with the type, which, like Morris, he considered the base of everything; that is, type not designed from the point of view of its decorative function, but from that of having to be read. This opportunity was given him by a German friend, Count Harry Kessler, and the Insel-Verlag.

During his time in Germany, Van de Velde worked with the greatest artists and printers of the day on the graphic presentation of the Insel-Verlag's books, not to mention his own writings on the subject which were published by such people as Bruno and Paul Cassirer. Especially *Renaissance in Kunstgewerbe* which consisted of the text of several lectures he gave in 1900 at the house of Frau Corn. Richter. For a time he also managed the Cranach Presse for Count Kessler. Those who brought the influence of 'Arts & Crafts' to bear on the typographic renaissance in Germany were Edward Johnston, Anna Simons (who translated Johnston into German), Emery Walker and Graily Hewitt. Germany did not lack its own national talent in this field, where Count Kessler acted as a sort of international catalyst.

Van de Velde's veneration for Friedrich Nietzsche prompted him to publish *Ecce Homo* and *Also Sprach Zarathustra* under the Insel-Verlag imprint. His *Zarathustra* is undoubtedly one of the most important books in the Art Nouveau style—as opposed to modern style. (In the public opinion the difference is slight, but the term 'modern style' had a nasty sound in Van de Velde's ears.) The book appeared in 1908 in an edition of 530 copies printed by Drugulin-Presse of Leipzig, then one of the most outstanding printers in Germany. The type was designed, as early as 1900, by a Belgian, Georges Lemmen, one of the most representative painters, decorators and poster-designers of the period. The colophon states that it was cut (in 10 pt and 12 pt) on the initiative of Count Kessler. Though the type-cutter in all probability was German, Lemmen's letters show an anglo-saxon influence. They can be compared, for example, to a type face used by Lucien Pissaro in the books put out by his Eragny Press. Van de Velde, who was in touch with Charles Ricketts, another owner of a private press, as he was with L. Pissarro, cannot have been ignorant of their elaboration. It should be noted that he did not design the type himself. He often designed letters that were ornamental, but not ornate, especially for his publicity layout and jobbing work. He himself drew the letters for the title page of *Ecce Homo*, as well as those which provide the principal motif of the ornamentation of several bindings. On the other hand, when he died, his papers were found to include a draft alphabet very like an attempt at a type face for titling, which he would presumably have called modern. It would appear, however, that nothing more came of it. This still-born attempt is of course not Van de Velde's main contribution to book production at the turn of the century. This should rather be looked for in his management and ornamentation of the book as a whole.

He designed the bastard-title, title-page and make-up of *Zarathustra*. The ornaments, printed in gold, which head the pages and serve as line-endings are distinctly his. He also designed the binding. The whole is undeniably monumental and has the same massive, spontaneous appearance as have his architectural works. His *Zarathustra* is an excellent example of where he was inspired by William Morris and where he deviates from him. He followed him to the extent that he too conceived the book as an architectonic unit; in it he followed Morris's typographical prescriptions and also designed all its ornaments himself: end-papers and title-pages, and even the text, are some-what congested with them. He parted company with Morris in that he turned his back on the past as well, renewing from beginning to end his entire reper-toire of ornaments, and in wanting a 'modern' form of decoration, what we would call Art Nouveau, but he would have corrected us and called them ab-stract in contrast to the floral decorations that abounded in other books of the day without equalling, in his eyes, the advantages obtained from it by Gothic artists.

This, perhaps, is the place to state that despite this complete replacement of ornaments and the acquisition of Lemmen's type, Van de Velde never departed in essence from the means (line-endings) nor the page layouts used by the artists of the Middle Ages and Renaissance. For thirty years now, our page layout and our illustrations have been changed as much by new possi-bilities afforded by technical progress, and by the influence of poets, the cine-ma and painting, as by the express wishes of any individual typographer. Van de Velde would scarcely have denied this.

Van de Velde returned to Belgium in 1925. Thanks to the support of his friend, Camille Huysmans, who was then a member of the government, he was able to found the Institut Supérieur des Arts Décoratifs (ISAD, in the Abbey of la Cambre). This filled an undoubted gap in Belgian education and enabled him to try to do for his country what, at Weimar, he had done for German art and, indirectly, for international art (through the agency of Walter Gropius whom he had appointed to succeed him and who was inspired by his principles and methods in opening the Bauhaus.)

One of Van de Velde's first concerns as director of ISAD was to instal a printing-shop, which was soon producing a series of works by Belgian authors designed by himself, with the help of Fernand Geersens. The catalogue of types he acquired is an important indication of the orientation he intended giving to the institute's typographic experiments. Originally, there were six bodies of Indépendant (a display type, designed in 1930 by two Belgian commercial artists, G. Colette and J. Dufour. Indépendant is even more geometric and black than Paul Renner's own Futura Black, 1929), five bodies of an Antique (actually a normande), five of Garamond, eight of Futura light, seven of Futura semi-bold, followed by four pages of Futura ornaments. Later, ten bodies of Erasmus Roman and seven of italic, ten of Grotius, two of Erasmus black initials and two of light initials, were added to the Lemmen. This was all presented in a large volume of oblong format; surrounded with rules of different thicknesses printed in vivid colour, and divided into sections by leaves of brightly coloured paper.

The production of this press was not large, except relatively, in relation to the small numbers of those who worked there and to the criterion that quality was all-important on which Van de Velde insisted. Anyhow, it is not possible to say exactly how many titles it did put out, for even the collection kept at la Cambre is incomplete. Also, they are not all dated. Whatever the importance we think should be accorded to them, there can be no question of discussing each of those we know of.

Most, if not all, were financed by 'Les Amis de l'Institut Supérieur des Arts Décoratifs' who wished to 'make it possible for the Institute to devote itself to these publications without having to consider anything but perfection. All the volumes in this remarkable series were produced under the supervision of Henry Van de Velde.' (Catalogue Général de la Nouvelle Société d'Editions, Brussels 1933).

Let it be said straightaway that these books comply with Morris's standards of quality in all respects: paper, printing, composition, layout and illustration, though still differing in every aspect from the products of the Kelmscott Press.

After that, the first distinction to make, and the most important, because it is so striking and also far-reaching, is that between the books composed in Futura and the others. Van de Velde was almost certainly the first, at any rate in Belgium, to use Futura for setting literary texts, both for ornamentation and the body of the text, which was the use intended for it by its designer Paul Renner. He procured it as soon as it appeared—the first publications of the ISAD are dated 1927 to 1930. The fount he used has certain letters, especially g, m, n and r, which were subsequently modified. Here again, the original use he made of Futura ornaments for the composition of his initial letters, shows how he was searching for new ways. Otherwise, the layout proper is traditional. According to the late M. Verwilghen, Professor of Architecture at the ISAD from 1930 to 1946, Van de Velde resorted to a pair of compasses when applying the golden section to the apportionment of margins and text, which is in the pure Renaissance tradition—though I do not mean that in any way as a reproach!

Van de Velde explained his reasons for buying Futura in a lecture he gave on Letters, the historical part of which was taken from F. Thibaudeau's *La Lettre d'Imprimerie*. (Paris 1921 and 1924. Van de Velde's lecture has not been published. I am indebted to M. Verwilghen for allowing me to see the MS of Van de Velde's notes.) In order to avoid a long quotation, let me summarise his reasons: Futura reflects the new direction taken by industrial arts. It shows greater conformity between the materials and the techniques used. It gets away at last from the aberrant imitation, which consists of laborious reproduction by means of a burin of the expressive movements of handwriting. It does away with all traces of the downstrokes and upstrokes reminiscent of the pen and thus has an international character that is welcome in printing as everywhere else.

Van de Velde also had recourse to Garamond. Here, he broke the composition with semi-thick vertical rules printed in red. He also used Lemmen. It is surprising that he should have encouraged two practices that are doubtful to say the least of it: one, a German practice, that of spacing out the lowercase instead of using italics; and the other, that of composing titles in 'a lump', a thing just excusable in an architect who never bothered about 'mere' typography.

As well as these works (the greater number) which, square and massive, bear the undoubted stamp of Van de Velde, there are others (notably *Syrinx* which was designed by Josef Cantré) which show distinct affinities with the Dutch manner of Charles Nypels and, especially, Stols. As to the illustrations, one could not say more than that they are by Joris Minne, Masereel and Cantré. One last observation about format. It is obvious that where Van de Velde was concerned, the idea of a 'series' did not imply uniformity of format. No two of these books have the same dimensions, and about the only thing to indicate that they belong to a series, 'Auteurs Belges' for example, is that they are numbered. This, of course, was only in line with the spirit of the research and deliberate experiment that Van de Velde wanted to provoke and encourage. Each work, of course, has its own harmony.

BELGIAN BOOKS IN DUTCH

This account of Van de Velde's work has upset the chronology of our story, rather as he stepped out of line to give Germany and Holland a quicker rate of clearing out and renovation in the commercial arts than his own country had. We must now go back to where we were, in 1893. Here, our main concern is with the factors that gave rise to the difference, which will become greater later, between Belgian books in Dutch and those in French. This difference was partly due to the contact with Dutch men of letters and Dutch publishers like Van Dishoeck, of Bussum, maintained about this time by August Vermeylen—for the sake of his revue *Van Nu en Straks*—and Herman Teirlinck. It was, too, due in part to the propaganda that Emmanuel de Bom and Prosper Verheyden never stopped making for the theories and practices of William Morris, and which led Julius de Praetere to go so far as to set up a private press at Laethem St. Martin, though without designing new letters. This press produced a number of books by H. Teirlinck, Styn Streuvels, Guido Gezelle and Karel Van de Woestijne, before de Praetere went to Zürich to found the school of Graphic Arts that has since become famous. He too was in touch with Holland, and his books were distributed there by an Amsterdam publisher, L. J. Veen. In 1894, with Edmond Van Offel and Charles Doudelet, he re-designed the review *De Vlaamse School*. In 1904, Max Rooses, first curator of the new Musée Plantin-Moretus, arranged an exhibition of modern books in it. All countries were represented. Emmanuel de Bom gave a lecture on William Morris and his influence on book-typography, which was subsequently published and, later, in 1910, re-issued in Amsterdam by Ipenbuur & Van Seldam, the layout being made by S. H. De Roos. (*See* pp. 261-2). Rooses thus started a tradition that has made the Museum the centre for those interested in typography that it still is (it now lends part of its space to a College of Graphic Arts).

Several periodicals also helped to accentuate the originality of publishing in Dutch, as opposed to French, in Belgium. One was *Tijdschrift voor Boek- en Bibliotheekwezen* founded in 1903 by Emmanuel de Bom as a counterpart to *Le Bibliophile Belge*, which had been started in 1845 by Baron de Reiffenberg, director of the Bibliothèque Royale de Belgique; *Het Boek*, published since

31

1912 by C. P. Burger and V. A. de la Montagne; the illustrated *Onze Kunst*, printed and published at Antwerp by Paul Buschmann with the assistance of L. J. Veen of Amsterdam. In a lighter vein there were the humorous albums, *Scalden*, printed by Buschmann for a group of bibliophiles. These were scarcely in line with the austere opinions and example of Morris!

As well as the influence of William Morris's ideas, which was indirect as we have already noted, and these contacts with Dutch men of letters, the pressure of the competition of Dutch printers and publishers drove Belgian publishers of books in Dutch to make their books more and more different from Belgian books published in French. This difference did not become absolute until after the First World War, as witness the annual exhibitions from 1927 on, of the Vereeniging ter Bevordering van het Vlaamsche Boekwezen, and soon the books published by Eugène de Bock under the imprint *De Sikkel*, by L. J. Krijn, De Standaard, Lannoo, Manteau and Nederlandsche Boekhandel, were on a level with the best Dutch production.

Special mention should be made of Jos Léonard. Associated first with Willy Godenne, the printer, under the style *Studio Novio*, then as the collaborator of Etablissements Plantin, then being run by Peter Oly, he was undoubtedly the first to set up in Belgium as an independent book designer and typographer—about the same time as Van de Velde founded la Cambre. If he did not enjoy the material success that he undoubtedly deserved, he at least had the honour of being invited by Van de Velde, along with Willy Godenne, to be an adjudicator for his book courses.

BELGIAN BOOKS IN FRENCH

At the beginning of 1911, the Chambre Syndicale des Imprimeurs de Bruxelles published a special number of its monthly bulletin devoted to the Universal Exhibition that was held in Brussels in 1910. This included two reports, one by Remy Havermans on the graphic arts in general and from the technical point of view; and another by Emile Gevaert on the aesthetic of books. Both were appalled at the wretched showing made by the Belgian submissions compared with the work of the foreign printers and publishers.

Remy Havermans: 'In general, we found that it was above all the actual impression our typographers were most interested in. So much so, that some of the show-cases, some of the make-ups, made one almost feel that one was at an exhibition of process-engravers, not of typographers.'

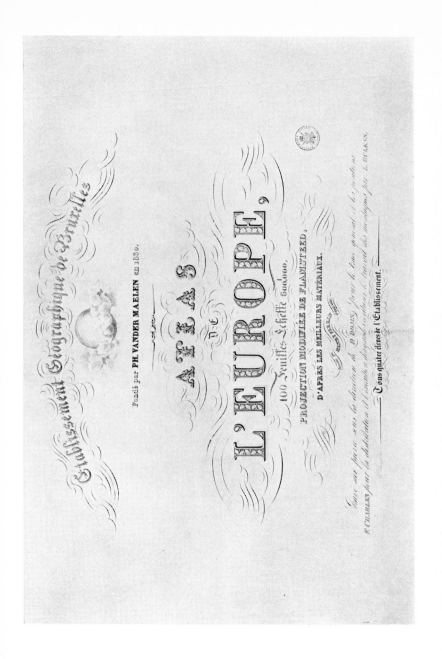

1. Philipe Vandermaelen: *Atlas de l'Europe*, Etablissement Géographique de Bruxelles, Brussels (1829–30)

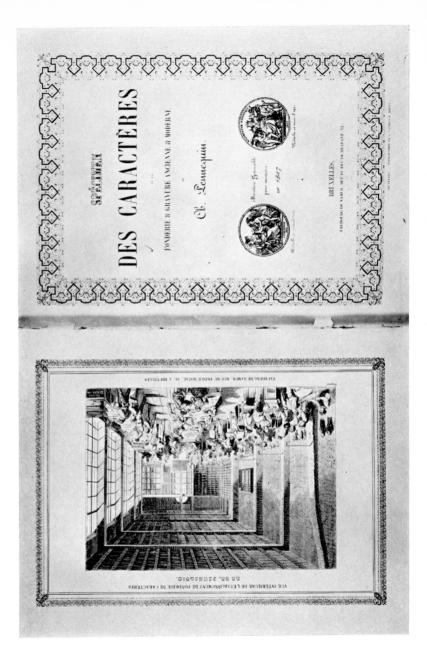

2. Type Specimen Book of Charles Pennequin, printed by Van Buggen-
houdt, Brussels (1839–52). Woodcut frontispiece by Pannemaker

LES PARENTS PAUVRES.

LE COUSIN PONS

Par H. DE BALZAC.

TOME PREMIER.

BRUXELLES,
ALPH. LEBÈGUE ET SACRÉ FILS,
IMPRIMEURS-ÉDITEURS.

1847

3. Honoré de Balzac: *Le Cousin Pons*, Alph. Lebègue & Sacré Fils, Brussels (1847). Title-page of first unauthorised edition

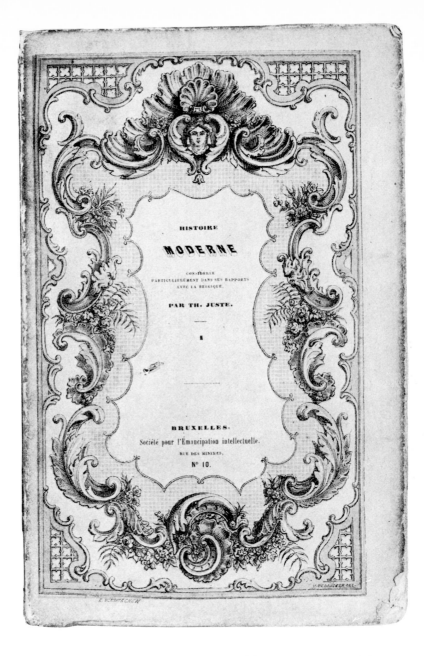

4. Théodore Juste: *Histoire Moderne*, A. Wahlen & A. Jamar, Société pour l'Emancipation intellectuelle, Brussels (1847). Cover

LES

MISÉRABLES

PAR

VICTOR HUGO

PREMIÈRE PARTIE — FANTINE

Tome Premier

BRUXELLES

A. LACROIX, VERBOECKHOVEN & Cᵉ, ÉDITEURS

RUE ROYALE, 3, IMPASSE DU PARC

M DCCC LXII
Droits de traduction et de reproduction réservés.

5. Victor Hugo: *Les Misérables*, A. Lacroix, Verboeckhoven & Cie, Brussels (1862). Title-page of first authorised edition

6. Charles Baudelaire: *Les Epaves*, Brussels (1874). Frontispiece
by Félicien Rops

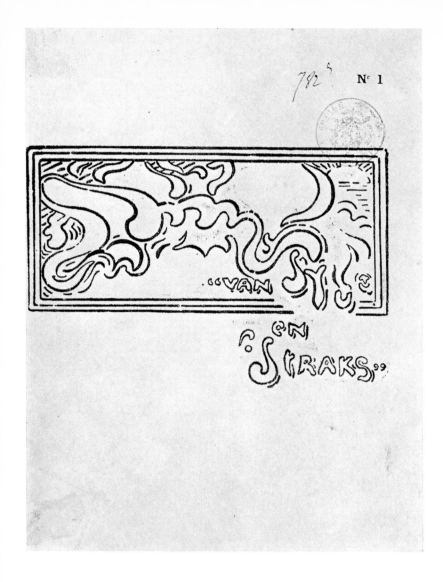

7. August Vermeylen (*ed.*): *Van Nu en Straks*, First Series (1892). Title-page by Henry van de Velde

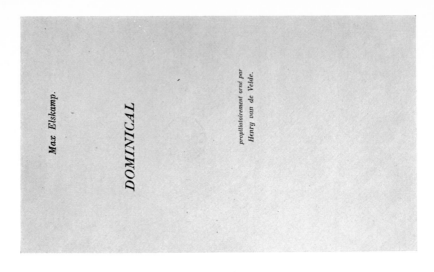

8. Max Elskamp: *Dominical*, Lacomblez, Brussels (1892). Cover and title-page by Henry van de Velde

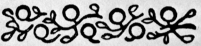

SIX CHANSONS DE PAU-
VRE HOMME POUR CE-
LEBRER LA SEMAINE DE
FLANDRE. PAR MAX ELS-
KAMP.

IMPRIME CHEZ HENRY
VAN DE VELDE POUR P.
LACOMBLEZ, EDITEUR A
BRUXELLES. MDCCCXCV

9. Max Elskamp: *Six Chansons de Pauvre Homme, etc.*, Lacomblez, Brussels
(1895). Designed and printed by hand by Henry van de Velde

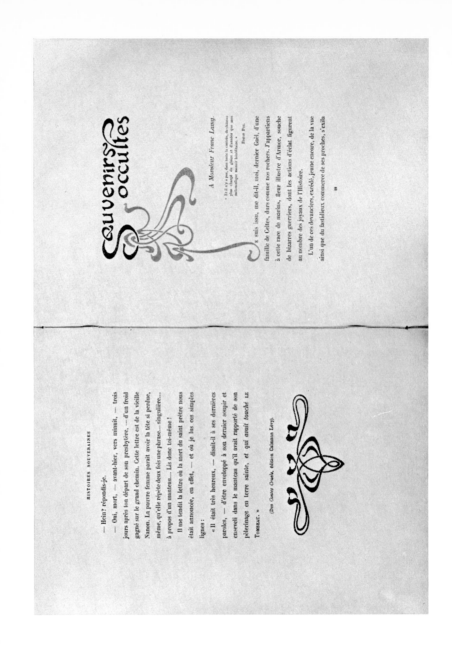

10. G. Villiers de l'Isle-Adam: *Histoires Souveraines*, Edmond Deman, Brussels (1899). Two-page opening with ornaments by Théo van Rijsselberghe

11. Emile Verhaeren: *Almanach*, Dietrich & Co, Brussels (1905). Ornaments
by Théo van Rijsselberghe

12. Friedrich Nietzsche: *Also sprach Zarathustra*, Insel-Verlag, Leipzig (1907). Two-page opening, type designed by George Lemmen, typography and ornaments by Henry van de Velde

13. Max Elskamp: *Les Sept Notre-Dame des plus beaux métiers*, printed by Buschmann, Antwerp (1923). Two-page opening, woodcut illustrations and ornaments by Max Elskamp

■ 1er Réchant :

Ah! Prométhée, nous écoutons ta voix toute gonflée de son délire et nous craignons qu'elle appelle le malheur! N'évo-que pas tant de forces perfides; tu succomberais à leur malice. Quel jeu joues-tu dans lequel tu t'acharnes à mettre aux mains de tes ennemis les armes les mieux aiguisées?

Prométhée :

Je sais quelle victoire je poursuis. Je sais son exigence et sa haine du médiocre. Ses appels se répètent et ses pas me tellement si ma passion de la servir un instant s'est suspendue.
Je connais sa morsure. S'il m'arrive d'oublier de quelle bouche elle me presse une cendre m'envahit, un froid mortel qui touche au désespoir.

■■ 2e Réchant :

Ah! Prométhée, vais-je voir changer le sens de mes pen-sées? Vont-elles consacrer une vaine erreur j'ignorais? Il me semble qu'elles au choc de tes paroles, soudain mon esprit va répondre, qu'elles résonnent en lui comme elles frouaient sous des voûtes.

Prométhée :

à ta victoire, tu sembles la connaître, c'est donc que souvent tu t'es approché d'elle, que souvent tu l'as interrogée?

Je ne sais si jamais aucune persévérance est tellement récompensée, ni si jamais aucune question reçoit la réponse qu'elle veut. Mais j'éprouve parfois une douceur étrange à bien saisir la tourment que je porte.
Réalité qu'il m'arrive d'approcher, je me découvre de toi vers moi qu'une piste à peine soupçonnée! Mais si fin que soit le fil, il m'attache mieux qu'une chaîne; si discrète que soit la contrainte elle ne m'adresse que des ordres.
Comment lutter avec cette vivante, quand toujours elle dé-mine l'excuse de mes doutes, quand les contradictions lui servent à me guider, les espérances à m'entraîner, les mai-sons de m'espérer pas à m'entraîner plus loin encore?
Elle s'est assurée de moi jusqu'en ces confusions où je vois les preuves de sa fidélité.
Comment veux-tu que je te porte d'elle? Comment te dé-signer mes seuls mystérieuses? Vives et lependes comme les vents de la nuit rien d'elles ne se captive.

20

■ 1er Réchant :

Si vraiment tu crois m'entendre mieux comprends que ma voix ne peut pas te rejoindre, qu'elle ne peut pas me quitter à ce point, n'être plus ce qu'elle était en moi. Homme in-quiet, tu n'es pas Prométhée et sa porche entière n'est pas faite pour toi. Cesse de m'interroger. Mes réponses ne sont pas des présents sûrs. Laisse-moi.

■ Réchant :

Le jour déjà nous a quittés. Les brouillards, que la terre gardait se sont échappés d'elle. Partout ils se déploient et recouvrent le sol pour y former ces froids et mols tissus dont se vêtent les ombres.

■■■ Réchant :

Hélas! le jour n'est plus. Je suis baigné des noirceurs de la nuit!

Prométhée :

Bientôt vont jaillir ces voix dont je crains la puissance. Bientôt va s'éveiller en moi le désir dont le bec me fouille.

■ Réchant :

Toute chose n'est plus que le reflet d'elle-même. Il n'est plus qu'une lueur, qu'une aigrette à la pointe d'un coq! O Terre où les hommes s'étendent, ou brusquement mûris-sent le sommeil et les songes, nous ne partageons pas ton repos.
Nous sommes criblés des trois qu'une troupe de fantômes sans cesse nous destine. Elle nous essouffle et peu à peu nous vaine. Et pourtant nous suivons sans arrêt une curio-sité qu'aucun échec ne lasse. Nous épions Prométhée.
Nous questionnons sa voix et les rumeurs du monde qu'il habite.
Déjà n'y a-t-il pas d'un frur de plus sensibles vibrations et le présage d'un raisonnement prochain? Le silence ne va-t-il éclater comme l'an l'écorce sous la poussée du jet?

■■■ Réchant :

Ne t'éloigne pas de moi! Je ne sais quel effroi m'agite quand je vois s'effacer les couleurs de la terre et la nuit accabler un homme qui ne trouve en elle aucun repos. J'entends bouger les ombres. Je les sais pleines de sug-

21

14. H. H. Dubois: *Prométhée*, Institut Supérieur des Arts Décoratifs, Brussels (1929). Two-page opening, designed by Henry van de Velde, set in Futura

HET NAJAAR.

De weide is gansch omringd met hooge boomen,
Die roerloos in den achternoene droomen
En lange schaaûwen teeknen op den grond.
Benauwde najaarsmadelieven vlijen
Hun kroontjen in het gras, en kijken blije
En hoopvol naar den zonlach omme en rond.

Drij koeien grazen rustig in de weide,
En Zale zit bezij den barm te breiden
In 't loover. 't Kind, dat met zijn oogjes dicht,
Op haren breeden schoot te wiegen ligt,
Heft soms zijn handjes naar heur borst omhooge,
En als een kittelend vliegsken altemet
Zich op zijn blanke voorhoofd nederzet,
Ontluikt geduldig zijne droomende oogen.

Terwijl nog de andere om en weere gaan

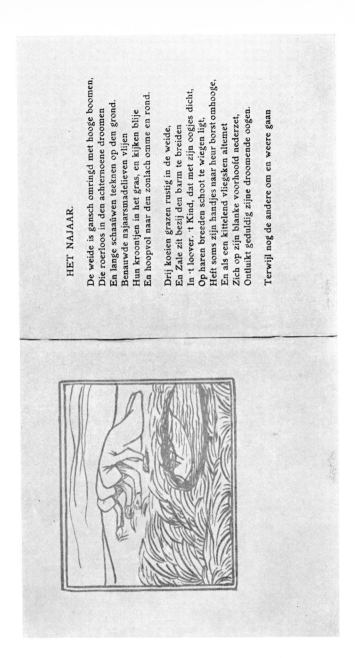

15. Herman Teirlinck: *Verzen*, Sint Martens-Laethem (n.d.). Two-page
opening, illustrated and privately printed by hand by Juul de Praetere

Zij kwam, en zij ging in huis, en hij zag,
en hij stapted heur achternaar:
zij klom en hij klom, en zij lag en hij lag,
en zij loeg,... en hij loeg op haar.

En zeider daar eene: «Ei, hij lacht! hij
Wat heeft er med' hem geweest!‖lacht!
Wat doet hij nu, dat hij nog nooit en placht:
ons broeder, ai Heere, hij geneest?»

«Ah,» zeider daar toen nog eene andere
«dat was mij een aardige lach!‖vrouw,
Zoe loeg hij, wanneer dat hij sterven zou,
mijn areme man en hij... ach!»

De schrik kwam in huis, en elk beefde en
en elk vloog, alhier, aldaar:‖elk sprong
en 't klopte op den torre, en de belle klonk,
en 't brandede een keerse klaar.

16. Guido Gezelle: *Het Kindeke van de Dood*, Institut Supérieur des Arts
Décoratifs, Brussels (1938). Woodcuts by Joris Minne

Emile Gevaert, after recalling the merits of the old, somewhat antiquated St. Augustin Society founded in 1877 by the Desclées, ended his exordium thus: 'The fact still remains that in 1910 Belgium has no typography of her own. We have not wished to pay attention to the lessons given us at home, and we have been blind to the progress made abroad.' (Chambre Syndicale des Imprimeurs de Bruxelles. *Bulletin Mensuel.* Numéro spécial. Deuxième année. Nos. 9–10. Mars-Avril 1911. The third report by Albert Delstanche, was very short and concerned solely with Belgian engraving in the seventeenth century.)

Haverman's indictment is accompanied by the supporting evidence of some reproductions of work submitted by printer-publishers Lamberty, Lesigne, Bulens, Xhavier Havermans, Buschmann, Lebègue, Lamertin and the art-publisher Van Oest. To support his condemnation, Gevaert gives examples from abroad exclusively.

The conclusion they both arrived at was: a bitter lesson. Let's hope it has effect.

And afterwards? What happened after this?

1910 saw the foundation in Brussels of the Société des Bibliophiles et des Iconophiles de Belgique, which is still far more energetic than the two older societies, Bibliophiles Belges séant à Mons (1836) and Société des Bibliophiles Liégeois (1863). In 1923 it started *L'Œuvre Nationale pour la Reproduction de Manuscrits & Miniatures de Belgique* which filled a real need and established the reputation of Malvaux, the photo-engravers, and of Goossens printing works. 'Les Cinquante', incorporated in 1913, were unable to produce anything until 1920. In 1927, L'Union Liégeoise du Livre et de l'Estampe, started its section of modern books. Max Rooses founded 'Les Bibliophiles Anversois' in 1877, and since 1923 their bulletin, *De Gulden Passer*, has been a welcome publication. They have also published a number of learned works.

Apart from the work of these learned societies, there was a considerable activity in the field of the de-luxe and near-de-luxe edition that would have sufficed to earn that decade the description, 'the roaring twenties'. There was scarcely a printer or publisher of any (or no) importance in Brussels or the provinces, who did not in addition to his normal production occasionally produce a de-luxe or super-de-luxe edition of greater or lesser sumptuousness, or some experimental work, all in very small editions, and mostly in very large format.

In Liège, three printer-publishers, Mawet, Thone and La Printing, stuck to Belgian authors and illustrators. 'La Lampe d'Alladin' chose French authors

and a French printer, M. Audin, or a Dutch printer, Charles Nypels. 'Le Balan-
cier' had only French authors and a Dutch printer, Ch. Nypels or Enschedé.
The 'Cygne Noir' sang twice and died. 'Les Editions Aryennes' did not survive
the publication of *Douze Chansons* by Maeterlinck. 'Vigie 30' and 'L'Enseigne
du Clinfoc' have long since disappeared.

Though both were Dutch, Ch. Nypels and A. A. M. Stols have enriched
Belgian (and foreign) libraries with several volumes printed in Belgium,
though they did not start a fashion there.

At Antwerp, Roger Avermaete, founder and inspirer of the Lumière
Group, vied with Eugène de Bock, director of *De Sikkel*, in using the talents
of the 'Flemish expressionists'. Here, Avermaete's production is more experimental and *avant garde*.

In Brussels, *La Vache Rose, Le Journal des Poètes, La Lanterne Sourde, Le
Thyrse*, some of which no longer exist, have or still do publish 'slim volumes'.
La Nouvelle Equipe reflected the 'new typography' of Jan Tschichold and Paul
Renner. There are others, but, to my shame be it said, I have forgotten them.
But there was Isi Collin's *L'Almanach de Compère Guilleri* with illustrations by
Suzanne Cox, published by *L'Eglantine*, to which we are also indebted for
Petite Fresque des Arts et des Lettres dans la Belgique d'Aujourd'hui by R. Aver-
maete with ornamental letters by Joris Minne (1929).

All this and more was known to H. Liebrecht when writing the sixth and
last part of *L'Histoire du livre et de l'Imprimerie en Belgique des origines à nos jours*
for the *Musée du Livre* (1923–1934). What did he have to say about it? Note
first of all that in his opinion Emile Gevaert was too severe in his condemnation. Here, then, are some of Liebrecht's pronouncements:

'The development of Belgian publishing, especially of illustrated books,
has never been large enough to form a school of illustration... The last decades of the nineteenth century was not one of the most attractive periods in
the evolution of the book. Both in printing and illustration, all respect for
the best traditions and most necessary rules seem to have been lost... All in all,
Belgian printers did not specialise in books. We have no big printers concentrating entirely on the production of books in series, as they have in Holland
and France, the material for which is designed for the swift, cheap production
of books of all prices. The technical aspects of typography have never been
the subject of original research here in Belgium. In other words, there is no
Belgian style in the field of the graphic arts.'

This 'monument set up to the glory of the book in Belgium' ends with a
wishful sigh: 'May the future bring about that fortunate set of circumstances

that will develop here in Belgium the taste for books and the art of book-making...'

Until 1940, nothing happened that would allow one to modify Liebrecht's judgements. We ought, however, to mention two publishers, Raymond Dupriez and Georges Hoyoux, who gave De Smet-Verteneuil, opportunities to prove that he really was a master printer.

To us, it seems all too evident that from 1910 to 1940, neither the serious pre-occupations of the learned, nor the most pleasing and surprising pursuits of the poets, painters and fantasts, had any effect on contemporary book production. Maybe they could not, should not have done so. Mistakes were possible, but now the test has been made. Even Paul Van Ostayen's *Bezette Stad* for example, however experimental it was, has left no traceable influence in our book production—nor, for that matter, in our advertising output.

Neither warnings, prophecies nor imprecations have troubled the serenity of our printers and publishers, whose numbers are always growing and who find business worse and worse. Or do they? Perhaps their profits, too, are growing, despite raised eyebrows and frowns.

CONCLUSION

The years of the German Occupation were by no means years of idleness, at least not for all printers and publishers. Altered though working conditions may have been, the changes had no lasting effect. It was only after the War that the real changes began. To begin with, no one could think of anything but renewing his plant and stock, then of developing along established lines, with known methods. Yet the first prerequisite is still largely lacking: to wit a new outlook. A new organisation of the production is all well and good. But what about the first principles of typography? Industrialisation has dispelled many false notions about would-be fine typography and so-called bibliophily. De-Luxe editions and nationalistic tendencies no longer obsess our commercial printers and publishers. Only, what the vast majority of them apparently fail to see is that printed matter is a consumer-good admitting of an industrial aesthetic, that is to say, subject to rational preparation with a view to mass production on the international level. The most striking example of this is the pocket book. The production of pocket books certainly does not satisfy the criteria of the private press, and equally certainly the criteria specifically applicable to them do admit of a considerable margin between the better and the worse, so considerable that in the last resort, there are even common features between the various pocket books of a country that allow one to distinguish between those published in France and Belgium and those that are of Dutch, English or American origin.

Scientific and art books can also be produced on a commercial basis with varying degrees of efficiency and care. Here our printing presses of St. Augustin, Leemans & Loiseau and the photo-engravers De Schutter uphold the honour of Belgium. In fact, conditions today are ideal for producing good work in all fields, because we have got rid of the perverse idea that one could to some extent atone—in whose eyes?—for the abominations one was producing by losing money on the production, as a side-line, of a freak, which would have 'beauty' by virtue of its cost. We have had only too many such freaks, which have been costly, but not fine.

Morris's principles of typography, if not his methods, still apply today, allowances being made for other needs of production. They are currently applied by several very large concerns, ranging from foundries by way of publishers to printers. Abroad, their application has long been entrusted in general to specialists, commercial designers of books and print, who are recruited from outside the ranks of the professional typographers. The intensive training required presents a problem in more than one country, and nowhere more than in Belgium, where Count de Villegas de Clercamp has instituted a prize, Prix Graphica Belgica, with the object of encouraging the training and employment of the talents of the professional typographer.

We have several times spoken of the influence of William Morris and more frequently of the typographic work of Van de Velde. We shall be asked what was the influence of this latter? A question in which there might be more malice than there is in the reply, which is that his influence was nil. There is no trace of it in contemporary Belgian books whether printed in Dutch or Flemish. But the fact that an example has not been followed, does not entitle one to conclude that it was bad or inadequate. Everyone knows that there is more justification for assuming the contrary!

Van de Velde's teachings and example no longer need justifying. They will bear fruit now, as they have in the past, in Belgium as well as in other countries, as the industrialists of the book trade rediscover, as other industrialists are doing, the essential importance and value of what today is called 'industrial design'.

Gérard Blanchard

THE TYPOGRAPHY
OF THE FRENCH BOOK
1800—1914

The aesthetic of the printed character is as much a function of an age's intellectual and commercial organisation, as of its technical progress. 'In typography', Charles Peignot wrote in *Caractère* (December 1953), 'there are laws whose slow evolution has followed that of our civilisations and cultures. Each epoch has had its form of typographic expression: there is a "graphism" of the Middle Ages, a "typo-graphism" of the Renaissance, of the eighteenth century, and of the Revolution.' The beginning of the nineteenth century is marked by the supremacy of the Didot type faces.

The universality of the use of Didot meant, as René Ponot pointed out in *Caractère Noël* (1962), that it was no longer possible to use earlier types based on the Fournier point system. On the other hand, the quick multiplication of an extensive range of type that had become possible enabled one to replace the old by the new. Garamond, 'which had reigned supreme from Jenson to Fournier, or for more than four centuries,' vanished almost overnight into the pots of the foundries.

The history of typography is not just that of the various creations of the engraver's tool. Characters are nothing unless they are used, and for several centuries books were the unrivalled form in which they found their true expression. By the nineteenth century this was no longer the case. Printing had developed and people had become aware of the variety of possibilities it offered; so that nineteenth-century printing is dominated throughout by the pictorial element introduced by the incredible development of wood-engraving, of the press and printing machinery, and by the growth of advertising.

The history of the printed word that achieved wide circulation, put out in instalments bound in cheap paper-boards, is linked with these developments.

What is meant by 'book' in the nineteenth century is radically different from what had been understood by the term hitherto. The concept of typography was also to evolve considerably. Didot was the final synthesised expression of a civilisation that was already cracking under the influence of the graphic phantasy that romanticism had introduced into the composition of its texts and display.

Publishers reacted to the confusion subsequent to the end of romanticism by creating their own style; this coincided with the Elzévirian renaissance of 1869, when Lemerre adopted Perrin's 'Augustaux' and Plon made use of variations on traditional Didots, when Motteroz created a separate type face for his own use, etc. These were the signs that heralded the 'creative typography' that 1900 was to start in France, and whose book-types were to be renewed with splendid regularity, ('1900, continuing the haphazard research of the romantic 19th century, introduces the "creative typography", in which the rhythm of re-equipment allowed by industrial potential was fundamentally different from that we had known hitherto.' Charles Peignot). Pelletan, able to select from the wide choice of type faces available to him, was to initiate the practice of adapting a particular type face to each text. The new century inaugurated the era of great discoveries, in which a variety of foreign influences played a part and out of which grew the first 'imaginative' popular synthesis of knowledge. This exaggerated socialism, born of the Revolution, was to resolve into a profound individualism, from which we are even now scarcely beginning to free ourselves. Books were to be the evidence of this.

The enterprise of the Didots was to set its mark on the early part of the new century. Their printing works became a strict school that enjoyed official favour. Their type, logical development of the evolution of characters and their shapes, was to be widely adopted with its variants by publishers. The nineteenth century is the century of Didot.

Printing of this century was characterised by the use of Didot types right up to 1869, which saw a return to Elzévir. In its delicacy of engraving, Didot —a further refinement of the attainments of Grandjean (1702), Fournier (1742) and Baskerville (1757)—pushed differentiation between ascending and descending strokes to the extreme, almost in imitation of the letters of copperplate. This extreme fineness of upstroke is also to be found in the ornaments and corners of the frames used during the Empire. Progress in the technique of engraving together with fashion allowed this, and it persisted throughout the nineteenth century. Closely related to the 'pen strokes' engraved on copper and steel and soon to be lithographed, typographic pen-strokes were soon surrounding initial letters and headings.

Geometrical abstraction, advocated by the Jaugeon report (1694–1719), is here applied to its utter logical conclusion. At the same time, in Italy, Bodoni had arrived at similar conclusions. Printing in Didot provides a multiplicity of fine variations. A whole family of printers and typefounders worked un-remittingly to make it the most flexible instrument for solving all problems of typographical arrangement of those days, in accordance with the canons of classical beauty dictated by the school of J.-L. David.

Pierre Didot, l'Aîné, states at the beginning of his *Spécimens des nouveaux caractères* (1819): 'For ten consecutive years I have spent with fair regularity more or less three hours every day on this work (of perfecting) with Monsieur Vibert, who is without doubt one of our most skilful engravers of letters or line.' It was in 1797 that Pierre Didot l'Aîné, son of François Ambroise, trans-ferred his presses to the Louvre. There he produced, amongst other works, the three volumes of *Racine* (in type engraved and cast by his brother Firmin) which at the exhibition of French industrial products held in 1801 were adjudg-ed 'the most perfect printing of all ages'.

It was, in fact, Firmin Didot who cast the type that made the name of Didot famous. In 1811, Napoleon appointed him head of the Imperial Foundry, and, between 1812 and 1815, he had thirteen bodies of Roman and Italic of so-called *millimetric type* cast there, this being officially destined to replace the *types du Roi* engraved by Grandjean. In 1805, Firmin Didot had perfected an *anglaise* type—a cursive imitating the fashionable handwriting of the day, which was a miracle of precision. Cast on inclined body, justified by quadrats at right angles, their jointures remaining invisible thanks to a system of 'bi-grammes' and cuts in the very interior of the letters, where the eye was not accustomed to look for them. (As well as for *anglaise* we are indebted to the Didots for several scripts, a Gothic, in 1825, and a curious microscopic letter used for Jules Didot the Elder's (1819–1827) *Voltaire*, which he dedicated to lovers of typography.) Firmin Didot, engraver, founder, printer, bookseller, paper-manufacturer, and author of two tragedies, was also the inventor of a stereotyping process. After setting from type, a mould was taken and into this metal was run. 'This process,' he wrote, 'should multiply at little cost many good works that have been printed with elegance and care with the added pleasure of a convenient format.' The Didot brothers did, in fact, put on the market plates of their stereotype edition of the classics. 'The Didots' books', wrote Marius Audin, 'are sober and hidebound, of implacable rectitude; in

41

them everything is subordinated strictly to the typographic discipline that they have imposed upon themselves and which can be compared only with that of the work of Bodoni and Baskerville; this, I believe, is due as much to the austerity of the age as to the principles of these magnificent typographers.'

Completed in 1805 L'Oraison Dominicale en 150 Langues is one of the most important products of the Imprimerie Nationale (then Imprimerie Impériale) in the field of foreign language printing, the credit for which is due to Marcellin Legrand and his engravers. This was the age of archaeological discovery and its publication.

'In 1805, on the occasion of His Holiness Pius VII's visit to the Imprimerie Impériale, Monsieur Marcel, as the Director, received the Pontiff and in his presence had *L'Oraison Dominicale* printed in 150 languages. While His Holiness watched, each of the Imprimerie Impériale's presses in turn printed a separate sheet of this wonderful polyglot book, set in the type peculiar to that language; and Pius VII as he went along received from each machine-minder a perfect sheet of this remarkable work printed before his very eyes. When the Holy Father reached the last press, the printing of the book was finished, and, when he then went on to the bindery, the book was bound almost at once by a special process.' (Review by Belin in *Journal Asiatique* 1854.) The Imprimerie (Impériale) was indeed a good advertisement for the emperor; it printed the *Code Napoléon* in 1807 and *Le Sacre* in 1812 using the Firmin Didot's *millimetric*. Under the management of J. J. Marcel it developed further, increasing the number of presses from eighty to 150. The number of foreign types increased—especially because of the Egyptian Campaign—the country's orientalists collaborating in this with the engravers Delafond, Ramé (père), Lœuillet and, especially, Marcellin Legrand.

Legrand, during his twenty-seven years of service, engraved more than twenty types. (Didot was to give rise to a whole series of similar type faces. Already by 1818, Jacquemin of the Imprimerie Nationale had cut his type which, while retaining the extreme thinness of the Didot ascenders, appreciably thickened the strokes. After the Restauration, Marcellin Legrand, Henri Didot's nephew, was put in charge of the royal typography, like Grandjean and Didot in their day. Between 1825 and 1832 he furnished it with thirty-two romans and italics of a variant, narrower than Didot, which were called 'Charles X's type'. These he modified in 1847. At the same time as working at the Imprimerie Nationale Marcellin Legrand ran Henri Didot's *fonderie polyamatype* in Rue de Vaugirard, where he and his nephews, Christian and Ferdinand Virey, aimed at reducing the boldness of the compact letters in vogue at the time and setting up their elegance and variety to compete with the monotony of the English type that had invaded the country.) 'I devoted more than ten years to the preparation of Chinese type with movable characters to take the place of the wooden characters used hitherto in Europe and even in China. I have used this to print elementary primers for the study of Chinese; and already two printing works in China are using my type with great success.' (Letter addressed to the Director of the Imprimerie Nationale, 9 June 1852).

With great perseverance, throughout the century, the catalogue of foreign types, ranging from Renard's Kufic Arabic (1806) to Henaff's Memphitic Coptic (1898) was completed. 'If one consults the Imprimerie Nationale's specimen of inscriptional Greek,' states René Ponot, 'one can at once recognise the principal forms of our lineals...' ('Origine des Linéales' in *Le Courrier Graphique*.)

It is the small printers who are producing the little 'novelty' books with vignettes which are paving the way for the great renaissance of wood-engraving, to meet the demand —and to merit the prize of the Société d'Encouragement pour l'Industrie Nationale— the typefounders are multiplying their attempts at engraving 'in the English manner'.

While the 'official houses' were devoting themselves to an enormous scientific task, the Didots firmly became established with a near-monopoly of printing the classics. The Didots considered typographic ornaments heresy and would make the concession to the fashion for illustration of using scrolls or inset plates in their books, like the Louvre *Racine* or the neo-classics of the Abbé Delille.

The wonderful little composite vignettes of Fournier, his open-face letters or 'decorated', which had conquered eighteenth-century printing, were now forgotten and repudiated. All that was still to be found in the printers' cases were some vignettes of the Revolution, worn and on their last legs. The great renaissance of the romantic vignette was being prepared by the small publishers, like Alexandre Desenne, who produced the light reading (*see* Michelet below) that appealed to the customers of the shops in the Palais Royal. (In 1810, when a large number of printing works had been closed by order of Napoleon: 'We had debts,' wrote Jules Michelet, 'and the only way of paying them was to print for our creditors certain works belonging to my father. We no longer had any employees, so we did the work ourselves. My father, who was attending to outside affairs, was unable to help. My mother stitched, folded and cut. I, still a child, was compositor. My grandfather, very old and weak, took on the hard work of the press and, hands trembling, did the printing. The futility of these books that we printed then and which sold quite well, was in strange contrast to the tragedy of those years of immense destruction. There was nothing in them, just little parlour games, charades, acrostics, nothing to feed the mind or soul of a young compositor. However, the very dullness and emptiness of them left me all the freer, and I do not think I have ever travelled so far in imagination as while I stood there at the case. The more alive my own imaginings, the quicker my hand worked and my stick filled.')

In 1805, the Société d'Encouragement pour l'Industrie Nationale set up a prize for the best illustrative vignettes of the kind that were then used in large numbers in the English books that were beginning to be sold in Paris. After Duplat's experiments in engraving in relief on stone and those of Bougon, on wood, and of Besnard on copper in the style of the wood-engraving (for Besnard had told the Society that the English vignettes engraved on wood cut across the grain), Gaspard Gillé, typefounder, produced the first catalogues of typographical vignettes of the nineteenth century, which he sold as polytypes to publishers who could not afford the illustration of a book with newly commissioned plates. In his prospectus of 1809, Gillé says: 'The art of printing, like the Fine Arts, must make itself worthy of a great future, such as France is preparing elsewhere... Yet the Dutch, German and English engravers have shown us what one ought to expect from sustained rational work in this field: in France, Papillon, Caron, Millière, Beugnet have distinguished themselves here... In 1789 the country's printing works possessed 80,000 ornaments engraved on wood. I have the collection of them in eight folio volumes, which were known as culs-de-lampe vignettes. Many of these have been lost or become unusable. Those are our losses: we ought to make them good, because we ought to do honour to our century. I wish for the success of printing in general and wood-engraving in particular. *Note:* this new collection first undertaken twelve years ago and which has won awards at various exhibitions of the products of French industry—ought to support the opinion of those who encourage me in my zeal to the extent of giving me the means of successfully providing vignettes and ornaments for their publications, seeing that I shall have the backing of the premier artists in the Capital.'

Up to the advent of the romantic illustrated book in 1830, printers used passe-partout vignettes from the foundries which dealt in polytypes. Collections like Balzac's catalogue are few and far between.

44

1808 Recueil des divers caractères, vignettes et ornements de la fonderie et imprimerie de *J. G. Gillé*—gravures de Besnard, Beugnet, Bougon, Lafond.

1809 Prospectus de nouvelles gravures sur bois, desquelles on se procure des polytypages en métal, tels que sujets de religion, sciences exactes, paysages, ornements d'un goût recherché. Chez *Gillé*.

1810 Spécimen de vignettes typographiques multipliées au moyen du polytypage, commandés par *Didot* à Gubitz de Berlin.

1819 Vignettes et Fleurons de la Fonderie *Firmin Didot*. Gravures de Andrieu et Thompson.

1822 Épreuves de divers ornements typographiques gravés sur bois et polytypes de la collection P. Durouchail. Bois de Godard d'Alençon, Lafond, Bougon, Durouchail chez *Didot l'Aîné* (917 articles).

1827 Collection de polytypages de *Gallay*.

1828 Ornaments typographiques. Recueil de vignettes gravées sur bois et polytypées par Thompson. (thirty clichés de 464 exemples) *Imprimerie Pinard*.

1828 Spécimen de divers caractères, vignettes et ornements typographiques de la Fonderie Laurent et De Berny. Vignettes de Duplat et Dugourc, Thompson, Leloir, Durouchail, Godard d'Alençon, Lafond et Bougon, Besnard. Dessins de Monnier, Devéria, Dugourc. *Imprimerie de H. Balzac.* (Pour la plus grande partie de *Gillé*).

Gillé was the first to try to introduce the taste for wood-engraving in the English manner into France. But the Didots did not want to be left behind. In 1817, they obtained Professor Gubitz's woodcuts from Prussia to illustrate Camoëns and that same year they got Thompson, Bewick's young pupil, to come to Paris. (In France wood-engraving had been more or less confined to using the work of Jean-Baptiste Michel Papillon, to whom Gillé pays tribute, who in the previous century (1698–1768) was a prolific engraver of *bois-de-fil* vignettes. A theoretician as much as an expert craftsman, he wrote a 'treatise on engraving' which he illustrated. He is representative of a whole line of unappreciated vignettists of the eighteenth century. An excellent technician, he was always seeking ways of improving the craft; for example, he invented the idea of lowering certain parts of his blocks in order to produce grey tints (grisaille). Although he knew of Foy's experiments in engraving on blocks cut across the grain, he remained vainly faithful to with-the-grain and so missed the chance of 'becoming the French Thomas Bewick and the real precursor of the romantic engravers'.)

In 1775, in London, Thomas Bewick (1753–1828) was awarded a prize for

45

his wood-engraving of a gun-dog, which he had engraved on end-wood. 'By end-wood we understand a block sawn in discs across the grain. In that way you obtain the heart which can be cut like metal, in all directions. While grain-wood is cut with a gouge or penknife, end-wood is cut with a burin, like metal; the size of the line is proportionate to the width of the belly of the burin and the angle at which it is held.' (Pierre Gusman: *La Gravure sur Bois du XIVe au XXe siècle*, Paris 1926.)

Thomas Bewick wrote his memoirs towards the end of his life and in them he tells of his great love of Nature which helped him to observe and impart life to his work. He drew and engraved both his *General History of Quadrupeds* (1790), and *History of British Birds* (in 1797 the *Land Birds* and in 1804 *Water Birds*).

As well as French production 'blocks and matrices of whole collections of Empire ornaments were imported wholesale from Germany. These used the Greco-Roman motifs of Percier, which foreign engravers had reproduced and which now returned home in catalogues with a French text.' (F. Thibaudeau: *La Lettre d'Imprimerie*, Paris 1921.)

The nineteenth century can be said to be the century of end-wood-engraving, and the success of this was to bring about a radical change in the appearance of books.

Romantic publishing was chiefly influenced by the wood-engravings, which, being incorporated into the text, obliged publishers to refashion the traditional make-up of their books. Printing was equally influenced by the growth of lithography. Voyages Pittoresques dans l'ancienne France, *as will be seen, followed the fashion set by the albums of artist's lithographs. In one way, Goethe's* Faust *translated by Stapfer and illustrated by Delacroix is the* Préface de Cromwell *of romantic illustration. Lithographers of texts were soon to influence typefounders by the great freedom and wealth of ornament in their work.*

In 1796, after five years of research, a Bavarian, Aloïs Senefelder, perfected lithographic printing. In 1797 he invented the first litho press and, in 1798, engraving on stone (incised litho) and transfer. In 1800, he went from Vienna to London, then to Paris where he set up a lithography works in rue Servandoni, remaining there for two years, after which he returned to Vienna. (Apart from his own productions, Senefelder was very successful in selling in Paris a lithographic set costing 300 francs, which consisted of a portable lithographic press in a box, boards covered with a chalky coating and called 'stone-paper', various accessories and instructions on how to use it all.) Two young imperial officers, Baron Lejeune and Colonel Lomet, had seen Senefelder in Munich and worked with him prior to 1806, and, in Paris, they started a craze for this new form of expression. By 1809, the Director of Museums, Vivant Denon, was teaching ladies of fashion how to do lithography. ('Vivant Denon's lithographs are some of the portents of this new genre. This was its fashionable period, when in France, England and Germany, amateurs, great lords, the Duchess of Berry, Bath's "gentleman artists", amused themselves with crayons and lithographic stones; the future king of Bavaria wrote that lithography was one of the most important discoveries of the nineteenth century; but the works of the illustrious amateurs allow one to doubt that.' Jean Adhémar: *La Lithographie en France au XIXe siècle*). It was the fashion then to draw portraits of your friends in crayon on stone. While Charles de Lasteyrie was duplicating police announcements, the painters of the day, especially the romantic painters, Charlet, Géricault, Delacroix—adopted the process and made fortunes by it. In 1820, Charles Nodier and Baron Taylor began publication of twenty-five volumes of lithographs by Bonington and Isabey: *Voyages Pittoresques dans l'ancienne France*. (Aubert, printer-lithographer, became the specialist in these albums, *croquis*, *macédoines*, oblong collections rather like the albums of artist's sketches which became fashionable about 1830.) Originally planned as a richly illustrated book, it quickly became a series of albums of pictures of crumbling towers, Gothic ruins, medieval churches, ancient manors, tilled fields and landscapes dominated by the towers of some age-old town.

In 1827, the English players put on Shakespeare at the Odéon. (At the time of these performances, an album of twelve lithographs coloured by Devéria and Louis Boulanger was published under the title *Souvenirs du Théâtre Anglais*. In 1843 Delacroix published thirteen lithographs for *Hamlet* which he had made between 1834 and 1843. These 'series' of engravings, mostly on copper, were the fashion then. Their format was that usual for the copies of Corneille, Cervantes, Lesage, Rabelais, and Voltaire which the well-to-do used to grangerise.) 'Young France' was there: Victor Hugo, Delacroix, Nerval, Berlioz, Vigny, Gauthier, Sainte-Beuve, Dumas. 1827 was the year of *Préface de Cromwell* which was to act as banner for the new school: 'eyes fixed', as Victor Hugo wrote, 'on events that were both laughable and fearsome, under the influence of this spirit of Christian melancholy and philosophical criticism, poetry was to take a great, decisive stride forward, that, like an earthquake, was to change the face of the intellectual world. Henceforth it was to do as Nature did and in its creations mix, though without confusing them, shade and light, the grotes-

47

que and the sublime, in other words giving a body to the soul, a head to the spirit.'

The equivalent of Hugo's *Préface de Cromwell* for romantic illustration appeared that same year, when Delacroix drew and incised on stone the illustrations intended for Goethe's *Faust*, (which Gérard de Nerval had just translated and which was to appear in 1828). In them, the grotesque gesticulations of Mephistopholes and Faust contrast with the sensibility of those of Marguerite at her spinning wheel, against a dramatic background in which chiaroscuro drowns the décor, objects and scenes of murder, gallows and witches' sabbath. '...the strangeness of the plates which were the object of caricatures, established me more and more as one of the leaders of the school of the ugly'. (Delacroix: *Correspondance*.)

'The invention of lithography,' wrote Walter Leonhard, 'fundamentally modified a tradition more than three centuries old, that of printing... Letterlithographers soon saw the possibilities their pens and gravers afforded. The collection of models of the early nineteenth century was technically perfect and comparable to the calligraphs of former centuries. Now, artists began breaking new ground designing their own letters, bold or light, wide or narrow. Egyptian and Italian were the first creations of lithographers' imagination; they are found beside tall, slender shaped arabesques... The joy experienced in composition and their manifest wealth of ideas led them to a diversity of solutions—plastic reliefs, shaded letters, letters in the form of ribbands, branches—or flowers—often characterised by the unexpected or by humour, though also by impossible ornaments, borrowed from the whole universe. This privilege of the lithographers was soon disputed by the printers... today, we are more and more attracted by these works.'

At the beginning of the nineteenth century the market for books was largely that of the Reading Room. The romantic publishers' dream of making books popular would never have been fulfilled had it not been for two things: the continuing assault of the Press which created, expanded and transformed this clientèle, and the irresistible attraction of illustrated books.

According to *Bibliographie de la France* the number of literary publications quadrupled in France between 1814 and 1828, and doubled again between 1826 and 1835—thanks to the invention of the mechanical press and other improvements. And yet... the part played by the Reading Room, to which one could go to read the newspapers or books of the hour, was an important one.

From 1820 to 1835, publishers (Renduel, Mame, Gosselin, Fournier) provided for the Reading Room, and one saw more and more books printed in several volumes with small type areas and plenty of white space. From 400–500 pages, the average size shrank to 300; and the page was reduced from 25 to 30 lines of 40 ems to 15 or 18 lines of 25 ems. Books were not reprinted and the average edition was 1000 copies. (Quoted by Jean-Alexis Neret in *Histoire illustrée de la Librairie*, Paris, 1953.) The book-lenders complained that books could be read too quickly and that they could not put up the price of an hour's reading, which was high already. The appearance of the serial story dealt a mortal blow to the Reading Room, which stagnated until 1848, when the laws of censorship put an end to it.

The classical leather binding disappeared with the Revolution, its place being taken by paper-covers. About 1810, it became the fashion to repeat the title-page on the cover with a double rule or border round it, an ornament at each corner and a vignette in the middle. This kind of cover was still being used in 1828, but was slowly changing into the picture-cover thanks to the craze for polychrome paper-boards, a shoddy innovation. Usually, books for Reading Rooms were supplied with a blank paper cover.

Did Honoré Balzac set up as a printer too soon, or was he, perhaps, not cut out for that profession? Far from earning him a fortune, his idea of compact editions of the classics encumbered him with the debts, which, according to legend, we have to thank for the prodigious quantity of his writings.

Balzac was twenty-seven in 1826, when he gave up writing pot-boilers for the Reading Rooms under his two pseudonyms of Horace de Saint-Aubin and Lord R'Hoone, and obtained a printer's certificate thanks to the support of Monsieur De Berny, husband of his mistress. 'Madame De B..., though married, has been like a god to me: she has been a mother, a girl-friend, a family, a friend and counsellor; she has made me a writer, consoled me as a young man, created my taste, she has wept like a sister, laughed. She came every day like kindly sleep to lull my pains and grief.' ('Lettre à l'étrangère', Coll. Lovenyoul, quoted by Gabriel Hanoteaux and Georges Vicaire in: *La Jeunesse de Balzac; Balzac imprimeur; Balzac et Madame De Berny*, Paris 1921.)

Urbain Canel, the publisher, had asked Balzac to write a preface for a double-column edition of La Fontaine to be printed in minion (7 point) on paper made by M. Montgolfier d'Annonay and illustrated with thirty vignettes by Devéria, engraved by Thompson. The edition, which was to be of 3000 copies, was to be sold in parts at five francs each. Balzac obtained some money from his parents and his mistress and put it into the project, with the object of extending this idea of a 'compact' edition into a whole collection of French classics. La Fontaine was followed by a Molière, but in one year not twenty copies were sold. 'There were at that time,' he wrote, 'twenty new booksellers, who judged books by the layout of the title (page).' The letters were too fine, the engravings mediocre and the price high. But Balzac wanted to be in business: he bought Laurent's printing works; then, his blood up, he turned typefounder, acquiring the old-established Gillé foundry. He incurred debts. He produced the works of Volney, Ducis, La Harpe, Béranger in pocket format, but he also had to print prospectuses and trash, until he was as well-known for his 'way of wearing his tie' as for 'his way of paying his debts and satisfying his creditors without forking out a sou', which did not prevent him from contracting the enormous debt to which he was to remain shackled all his life.

The end came in 1829. He fled from Paris and started writing again. *Le Lys dans la Vallée* and *Les Illusions Perdues* were the echoes of those first years of discovery. He believed in progress through machines: he dreamed of mechanically-made paper, of rolls of plastic paste, printing from stereotypes. He makes someone say to Père Séchard of *Les Illusions Perdues:* 'Ha, ha! my boy, the provinces are the provinces and Paris is Paris. If a man from l'Houmeau comes to you for his wedding announcement and you print it without a Cupid and garlands, he won't consider himself married, and he'll bring it back if he sees only one M; as you do with the Didots who are the glory of typography, but whose inventions won't be taken up in the provinces for another hundred years.'

Before he gave up, Balzac, in 1828, printed his Specimen des divers caractères, vignettes et ornamens typographiques de la Fonderie de Laurent et De Berny, *which allows us to plot book-types before the 1830's. The 1828 specimen is one of the last things Balzac printed. By publishing the catalogue of Gillé and Laurent he gave us a complete list of the typographic material used by the printers of the day.*

The most striking thing about the specimen book of the Laurent and De Berny foundry, as printed, is the wealth of ornamental borders it contains: each page—of oblong format—has two or three surrounds depending on whether the type body is large, medium or small. Empire or Restauration framing-borders: from the simple rule with a 60 pt body to the background lines for tarot cards, there are nearly 400 different ones. 'Borders in 12mo and 8vo,' the advertisement says, 'made up of movable type, that frame the specimens of each character have been polytyped and mounted on wood; they are sold for 15 francs each and cannot be divided. The large surrounds of movable ornaments have not been polytyped.' The characters, apart from the classic range of Didot book types, comprise some bold-faced ones like Vibert, romans and italics, under the heading of poster letters. The Egyptians, romans and italics, engraved and shaded, ornate, sundries engraved in wood. The Egyptians are either of French pattern with sharp angles, or variants of the English form (like Clarendon) in which angles are reduced by a slight inner rounding. There are also bold-faced Didots ornamented or shaded.

The section of titling and title-pages contains a large selection of Didots of all kinds (bold, bold-shaded, ornamented, hatched, some even being treated like the open letters of Fournier in roman and italic), French Egyptian and ornamental Tuscans, (strange letters with split or splayed serifs which Thibaudeau refused to admit as being a category of its own). Another section contains the Gothics and Greek and the *civilité* types: rondes, cursives, open Gothics and light-faced *anglaise* types.

With about forty light-faced rules and eighteen waved rules (fashionable then) the whole catalogue gives a pretty fair idea of the material available to the printer of 1828, and its exact uses.

The second half of the catalogue consists of eighty-six pages of vignettes, most from the old Gillé foundry. These range in style from the emblematical baldness of the First Empire to the vignettes of Duplat, Besnard and Bougon, the imitations of Bewick, the charming little works of Devéria, forerunners of the great romantic blossoming.

Though the catalogue contains some Egyptians—characteristic of the nineteenth century—there are no lineals (sans serifs). In his handbook, Thibaudeau vainly tries to persuade us that Egyptian is a lineal crossed 'at the top and bottom of its descenders by a stroke of the same strength as that of the body of the letter'. Comparison with extra-bold Didots leads us rather to think, as did René Ponot, that the latter cannot have been without influence on the creation of the 'fat face'. As for the lineals—just as characteristic of the nineteenth century—there is no proof of their alleged lithographic origin. They are to be found in the catalogues of the London typefounders from 1816 onwards. The Nationale's engravers cut Etruscan and Greek alphabets in sans. There are numerous series modified in all ways: light, bold, elongated, condensed, even italic or inclined. The absence of them from Balzac's catalogue merely shows that mechanistics (Clarendons, etc.) were in use before, which does not mean lineals were not cast and used in 1828. (*See* p. 94.)

Another case of publishers suffering misfortune was that of the brothers Delangle, who ruined themselves publishing Charles Nodier's Histoire du Roi de Bohême et de ses sept châteaux. *In 1800 Charles Nodier was twenty. He was thus a child of the nineteenth century. Of the romantic 'coteries', the Arsenal salon played a considerable part in the conception and spreading of new ideas.*

Nodier, the dreamer was an enthusiastic admirer of 'this Germanic school where, twenty-five years ago, the last fertile germs of imaginative literature and, if you like, of imaginary love, were still alive,' and he deflected French romanticism towards the irrational. ('Nodier et les rêves' in P. J. Castex: *Le conte fantastique en France de Nodier à Maupassant*, Paris 1962.) He wrote as early as 1818 that 'the subject of romantic poetry consists of the still unperceived aspects of a thing, an order of perception new enough often to be bizarre...' Strangely akin to that genius Nerval, he praised dreams as a source of knowledge: 'Sleep is not only the most powerful, but also the most lucid state of thinking, if not in the fleeting illusions in which it envelopes one, at least in the perception that comes from it.' (It was Nodier who turned Nerval's attention to semantics, folklore, and the experience and theory of dreams.) Nodier's *Histoire du Roi de Bohême et de ses sept châteaux*, which Delangle published in 1830, is a milestone in the history of the book in France in the nineteenth century. (The brothers Delangle started the day of the great illustrateds with their *Histoire du Roi de Bohême*, 'this romantic folly'. Tony Johannot revolutionised book illustration by replacing the copperplate engraving, Restauration style, with the 'romantic' wood-engraving, the quality of engraving of his early wood-blocks was inferior to that he subsequently attained.) In *Histoire du Roi de Bohême*, is the charming poet who is also linguist, philologist, entomologist and archaeologist, a great reader who parodies himself and his own erudition; there is the librarian who is also an ardent collector and great connoisseur of the art and of the history of bookmaking. ('Nodier, a man of wit, warmth and perfect taste, preached love of books and knew how to make people appreciate and love old books, rather in the way that Chateaubriand revived admiration for Gothic cathedrals among his own contemporaries. In the early nineteenth century Nodier was the prince of bibliophiles and reviver of the love of books.' Jean Marchand: *Etrennes à un ami bibliophile*.) In the chapter entitled 'Combustion' he reviews the fires that have destroyed famous libraries and, after invoking Gutenberg, Coster, Jenson, Aldus, Tory, etc. 'the over-riding need to humour my printer by presenting you with a *specimen* of a fount that would make Sanlecque and Garamond turn in their graves, decided me to cast before your eyes, in the order in which they came to hand, these few words that have escaped the flames and the critics, *combusti membra poetae!*'

Then follows a chapter entitled 'Exhibition' consisting of a single page framed, like a Bible, with a vibrant wood-engraving depicting a confusion of monsters, serpents, angels, cupids and Venuses beneath a bower of roses, with twenty-two words set in Egyptian bold. There are other examples in this book of parodic 'typographical jokes', for example: the resurrection of the Alexandrine 'calligrams' which you can find in Rabelais's *Dive Bouteille* (one of Nodier's bedside books) or of Panard (1674–1765) before Apollinaire. A figurative layout suggests: a stairway, pipes of Pan or 'his parallelogramatic-box'. When he uses typographic artifice as a means of illustration, he underlines it ironically and after a 'motto in large capitals' WHAT DOES THAT MATTER TO ME? (occupying half a page), a discourse of six lines of full points and the 'distraction' of three inverted lines (Nicholas Cirier was probably to remember it when producing the typographic ravings of his pamphlets, 1839, 1840, 1850. *See* Queneau: *Bâtons chiffres et lettres*, Paris 1950: 'Romanticism and the schools that followed it evidently found matter from which to draw dreams and suggestions in the mere fact of being printed), he ends with: Breloque was about to begin, when the positive and calculating fingers of my publisher who has given me only 387 pages of white wove to fill, put in shaded 22-point initials at the foot of the page I had finished, the monosyllable END.'

He began with a double title-page, the two being separated by several pages and the second being a 'romantic' parody of the first's classical layout in Didot, set in Gothic, shaded Egyptian and with a truly dreadful vignette. His liking for the wood-engravings of the books published in the sixteenth century (the last story, *Franciscus Columna*, is a bibliophile's tale about *Le songe de Poliphile*, which few people bothered about then), sent him to Tony Johannot, a frequent visitor, with whose help he established the first romantic illustrated book: 'This first experiment with wood-engravings scattered about the text, making moderate use of hatching, like free-hand pen sketches', (Aristide Marie: *Alfred et Tony Johannot*, Paris 1925), paved the way, and brilliant use of this idea was to be made later by Gigoux in his *Gil Blas* (1835) and by the same Tony Johannot in his Molière (1835), Cervantes (1836), Prévost (*Manon Lescaut*, 1839), Lesage (*Le Diable Boiteux*, 1840), Jules Janin (*L'Âne mort*, 1842), J. Hetzel (*Voyage où il vous plaira*, 1843), and Ariosto (*Roland furieux*, 1844).

Then there were the light vignettes of *Roi de Bohême* which started the fashion for preliminary wood-blocks ornamenting title-pages and covers. The closing-down of the Reading Rooms forced publishers to attract readers with the tempting advertisement of these little pictures.

The big early volumes of romanticism were often illustrated with only a title-page: Célestin Nanteuil was the favourite artist of this new school. The letters of these title-pages are engraved with a graphic freedom that became more and more accentuated.

In 1830, *Revue des Deux Mondes* appeared with a new sign engraved on wood by Tony Johannot showing a young half-naked savage girl—made fashionable by Chateaubriand—holding out a bough to a pale medieval maiden in front of a tombstone overgrown with foliage.

Célestin Nanteuil was undoubtedly the champion artist of these romantic title-pages. 'Rejecting the systematic patterns and the regular cut of the cold soft burin of the Davidian illustrators, Nanteuil produced plates in which the biting was energetic yet clumsy. His was a naïve, inspired art that sought to translate a literary emotion, he dreamed of headings that would be graphic symphonies summarising both the major theme of the book and its chief subject matter...' (Aristide Marie: *Célestin Nanteuil*, 1925.) On these title-pages there then began to appear painter's lettering, drawn with passion and imagination—and this lasted until the day of the delectable blunders of Lautrec, the poster-designer, or of Bonnard of the *Revue Blanche*—which were to be the delight of Victor Hugo and the despair of the classifier. These title-pages and letters were to books what Delacroix's *Faust* was to the art of illustration: they ushered in an age that turned its back on the fair beauty of the calligrapher on steel.

About 1820 British publishers began producing for the Christmas market small gift books illustrated with steel engravings, keepsakes, which were a great success. The engravings were very fine and used a process discovered in 1816 by which the metal could be softened and re-tempered after it had been worked. The process was widely used during the Restauration, everything English being very fashionable at the time. The important thing about these keepsakes was their charming pictures, the plates of which, or copies, crossed the Channel, so that they served alternately for the English and French editions. These gift books contained short easy texts. Théophile Gautier, who did work for them, said, 'The usual thing was to ask writers for a piece of verse or prose to act as text to these splendid illustrations by Robinson, Cousins, Finden and Prout.' Though they were called *Album Britannique, Beautés de Shakespeare,*

Fleurs, Emeraudes, Ecrins, and *Diamante,* they were really the old eighteenth-century almanacks in a new garb, and inherited the latter's paper-board binding, now sometimes decorated with ornamental borders and gold-tooling, sometimes not.

Louis Janet, who specialised in Christmas gift books after 1814, was one of the most important manufacturers of keepsakes ornamented by the 'best artists of London'. The typography of the texts, sometimes framed in a rule of a different colour, is severe and unimaginative, while the engraved title-pages—doubling the typographical ones—contain blackletters, light-faced letters, ornamental outline letters, in the middle of calligraphic ornamentation worthy of George Bickham's *The Universal Penman* (London 1741). Starting in 1830, the keepsakes had disappeared by 1842—though this type of book illustrated with steel-engraved plates and woodcuts in the text survived in such publications as Jules Janin's *Un Été à Paris* until 1843. In 1850, a publisher called Mandeville, tried to make them the fashion again, but failed.

The early magazines—an import from England—used the book publisher's method of publication in parts, and, like books, were bound up at the end of the year. There was no clear dividing line between publications, the encyclopedic subject matter of which owed much to the social ideas of the most advanced thinkers of the day, and the big romantic illustrateds. Many illustrations incorporated into the text made them veritable 'visuals'. The most important of these was Magasin Pittoresque which was the Paris-Match of the nineteenth century.

'The fact that we were the first to venture to import into France—without patrons or prospectus—the idea of providing a varied text interspersed with engravings, divided into parts at a most modest price, is solely due to our knowing of the success enjoyed by magazines in England and especially by the miscellany published in London, under lofty guidance, by Mr. Charles Knight, a writer and distinguished economist, whose kindly relations with us have helped to make the early difficulties of our enterprise less discouraging.'

Thus Edouard Charton in the preface to the bound volume of the first fifty-two numbers of *Magasin Pittoresque* in 1833.

Le Magasin Universel which appeared that same year also confessed its English origin and in the preface to the second volume, says: '...among the many engravings that accompany most of our articles and which will stand comparison with those of other two-sou publications, a large number are of interest either by the very nature of the subject or by the way the artist has handled his burin; but many of them are well above the level of the others we print... We owe these engravings to the first directors of the *Magasin Universel* who went to England to buy them; and to sell them cheaply would be to impose too heavy an expenditure on our enterprise.'

By 1835 England's influence was a thing of the past. At the end of the third volume of *Musée des Familles*, one can read the following: 'Great progress has been made towards perfecting our engravings some of which can rival the loveliest steel engravings published by the English in their rich keepsakes. Commissioned from the most celebrated black and white artists of Paris, they have been engraved by the most able artists of Paris and London.' And in the same magazine's 'News for Families': 'One cannot deny that where luxury of presentation goes, *Musée des Familles* has left the *Penny Magazine* and our translation of it, *Magasin Pittoresque*, far behind. This simple fact shows that the French only require will and perseverance to surpass the English, even in the care they take over the material execution of things.'

The issue of the first number of *Magasin Pittoresque* in 1833 was a real event. It caused a sensation and was a great success. Founded and published by La Chevardière, it was managed by Edouard Charton, a Saint-Simonian—which fact is not without its significance.

Its social investigations, its scientific articles, its pedagogic and didactic endeavours, even its self-imposed aim of giving room to the human and the picturesque, were undoubtedly inspired by Saint-Simon. (In 1831, 'Father' Enfantin was already having congregations of more than 1500 faithful, many of whom were working men. At the reunions, Charton was able to meet Franz Liszt, Sainte-Beuve and the Péreires as well.)

'Determination to be universal but only in the framework of our choosing,' Charton continued, 'we have wanted especially to get close to that sphere of education which you might almost call luxury education, which, being addressed to the heart, the imagination and the taste, aims chiefly at enriching the leisure of our readers with pure and instructive hobbies for themselves and their families, whether rich or poor.'

The *Magasin Pittoresque* most of whose illustrations at first were English plates from the London magazines, after its second year used Andrew, Best and Lenoir (the first two coming from England), the celebrated A. B. L. trio of engravers, who engraved both on copper 'in the style of woodcuts' and on actual boxwood.

In the intellectual field, the *Magasin Pittoresque* sought to satisfy, using the media of the printing press that was being continually improved, people's need to know, their thirst for what was new, unpublished and exotic; the need to learn what was behind the great archeological expeditions and the more than numerous descriptions of travel. ('What will remain of these journeyings... integrally, I suppose, two books rather different in inspiration, illumination and style: *Trois ans en Asie* by the author of the *Pléiades*, and Nerval's *Le Voyage en Orient*,' wrote Gilbert Rouger in his introduction to the reissue of this book (Librairies associés, 1955). 'Here he demonstrates all that Nerval took from others and grafted on to his own impressions, the strangest being the help he found in the many engravings that inspired him or which he simply describes.')

It was the century of the great spread of education, the century that invented visualisation of print, which is still in full swing. In the technical field 'the cross-grain wood-engraving which was to take the place of the woodcut,' Maximilien Vox writes, 'up to the end of the century, spread into those pages where the text was still carefully divided into two columns and had titles set in Didot. But, in the hands of the artists, art, scenery, science, etc., were all re-interpreted, re-invented... the first *imaginary museums* were those of these early magazines which reduced painting and sculpture to diagrams of "thin" outline drawings. It took a whole evolution,' wrote René Huyghe 'before anyone thought of asking gravure and photogravure to render the values; the convention was for black and white which took one half-way towards sensorial truth, and it took the twentieth century to make colour a normal requirement.' (*Dialogue avec le visible.*)

(Wood-blocks were relatively expensive, so one should not be surprised to see them used again to illustrate books or to find that they had been taken from books. This apart from the illustration blocks that publishers sometimes assembled in a catalogue of polytypes, like that curious, undated 'Curmer', *Fantaisies parisiennes, album d'artistes en tous genres* which contained this strange 'Note' I cannot resist the pleasure of quoting: 'This artists' caravanserai, this Parisian imagery, is addressed to the foreigner to inform him of our manners, to the person of quality to enjoy in the hour of his *dolce far niente*, to the mother of a family as well as to the fashionable lady because of its delightful assortment of ornaments, flowers, monograms for tapestry, embroidery, scarves and handkerchiefs; to artists and engravers on metal and wood, to sculptors, lithographic writers, designers of shawls and embroidery, manufactuers of blinds, coloured papers, embossers; this pictorial museum is suited to the whole great family of Paris which makes so many lovely things. Because of the immense variety of subjects in it, it will be useful to their arts, and here, tossed higgledy-piggledy into a hurly-burly mosaic, their expert taste will guide them; here, like the poet, they will have flowers in bloom always at hand: briefly, if Alembert's *Encyclopédie* was for the learned, this is an encyclopaedia of imagery for persons of quality and artists of all kinds.')

Between 1833 and 1893 you could follow the different phases of the evolution in the pages of the pictorial magazines. The magazine gave place to the 'illustrateds'. *L'Illustration* dates from 1843—but there were *Journal illustré, Le Monde illustré, Paris illustré, La Semaine illustrée, L'Année illustrée*, etc. as well and in 1860 Edouard Charton began publishing with Lahure the *Tour du Monde* 'a new journal of travel, illustrated by our most celebrated artists'.

In 1835 publishing entered upon the positive age of its production. Paulin made a fortune with Gil Blas *illustrated by Jean Gigoux. He used an enormous number of woodcuts incorporated in the text. Layout was not yet going in for decorative excrescences, but in the many initial letters, the draughtsmen gave much play to their invention, departing entirely from tradition and introducing the romantic initial.*

The single title vignette or printer's flower on the cover, a Nanteuil title-page which had been enough for Renduel's books were no longer enough for Paulin, who, engaged Jean Gigoux to illustrate Lazarille de Tormès' *Gil Blas de Santillane*, translated by Viardot. (Renduel was the publisher of the outstanding writers of Romanticism, Hugo, Gauthier, Vigny, Nodier, Gozlan, Sainte-Beuve, Borel, of 'Bousingo' and the 'jeunes Frances'. He was a lover of books and had copies specially printed for himself on pink or green paper.)

This was the development and exploitation of the principle of the romantic illustrated book initiated in 1830 by *Histoire du Roi de Bohême*: it had ornamental bandeaux for each chapter starting with initial letters inspired by a variety of things ranging from medieval MSS, oriental carpets, Gothic cathedrals, Arabic motifs, wrought-iron, grasses, or initials ornamented with foliated scrolls, crowned with vine-tendrils, flowers and butterflies, intertwined with grasses. The text, still in neo-Didot and each page soberly headed, was studded with engravings with type run round them and with vignette tailpieces. There were no plates except large full-length portraits of the hero and of the author, and a frontispiece. It had 600 vignettes. (*Gil Blas* showed Tony Johannot the way. His reply to it was *Don Quichotte* which Dubochet published in 1836. In it the text is framed with a double rule. The illustrations in the text are not run round, but have the whole width of the type area. The initials, some of them figured, are mostly scenes in which the letter occupies a corner left free by the design. For all its good qualities, Johannot's book is not the equal of Gigoux's.)

Fifteen thousand were sold in a few years. This was the book that did most to restore the wood-engraving to favour for illustrations. Paulin was to be followed by Curmer, Perrotin, Hetzel, etc. Boudin, who published books illustrated by Johannot, Nanteuil, Raffet, Meissonier, Grandville, Daumier, and Gavarni, often collaborating to illustrate the same work. In fact, Gavarni, Johannot and Grandville were the only ones to illustrate a whole book alone.

These big romantic illustrated works were not books for collectors. They were sold in the first place in parts in large impressions, then the parts were bound up together in one volume in paper boards and sold as a Christmas gift.

The economic state of France after the wars of the Restauration and the Revolutions of 1793 and 1830 was very precarious. There were no more than 2000 persons with a private income exceeding 2000 francs. Publishers thus looked for their customers among the broad masses; full leather binding that had been used earlier was now too expensive and was dropped in favour of the paperboards that publishers used right up to the end of the Second Empire, becoming more and more elaborate until you got the red and gold pastrycook's blocking of the 'Hetzels' of our childhood. (Fouquet, whose employment Renduel entered in 1821, was preparing a new edition of Voltaire in seventy-five volumes. Wanting to reach all classes of society, he was planning to publish it in four editions, each with a different quality of paper depending on its intended destination: the *Voltaire* 'for the people of small means', the *Voltaire* 'for those in commerce and trade', a *Voltaire* 'for the propertied' and, lastly, a 'cottage' *Voltaire*. From J. R. Thomé: *Le Courrier Graphique*.)

The books were in a way cheap luxury books and they enjoyed the same degree of success as the crystal balls 'à mille fleurs' about 1845.

Curmer deserved the title of the romantic publisher, even more than Renduel with his romantic writers. His sympathies with the social ideas of the time, his continual experiment in his profession, made him very much a man 'of his day' and a model of what a publisher-book designer should be.

Henri Léon Curmer, born in 1804 in Paris, was an enthusiastic supporter of Saint-Simon, Augustin Thierry, Auguste Comte and 'Father' Enfantin. He entered publishing in order to spread among the masses those new ideas which were to lead to the revolution of 1848. His social and humanitarian ideals led him—and a number of his contemporaries—to dream of producing cheap books. His liking for avant-garde philosophy went well with his taste for the work of the young writers of his day. Balzac, Gauthier, Lamartine, Vigny, Hugo, Musset, Janin were his masters. 'If a publisher is to play a worthy part,' he wrote, 'he must be a man of learning and upright judgement, aware of the social trend and ideas of his day. If he wishes to concern himself with contemporary writers instead of choosing from among established literature the books in favour with the public, he must be even more if he is to fulfil his mission.'

Curmer regarded it as both a duty and a mission to be of his day. In 1835—the year of Gigoux's *Gil Blas*—he published *L'Histoire de l'Ancien et du Nouveau Testament* with 700 wood-engravings: 'We think that we have thus raised a monument to wood-engraving: it is easy to see the resources offered by this too-long neglected art.'

He also insisted on informing any who might be interested—like the credits in a film—of the names of his collaborators, artists and engravers, which he did opposite each of the engraved plates. He had a great idea of his role as instigator and maker of books, which he thus financed, designed and saw through the press. He not only exploited wood-engraving to the limits of its possibilities, but also experimented successfully with transfers of copperplate engravings on to lithographic stones, and he was one of the first to use chromolithography (for reproducing ancient MSS) and used 'photographic illustrations' for a translation of Horace, went in for stereotyping and polytyping, and started a foundry. He died in 1870.

The chef d'œuvre of the big romantic illustrated books is Curmer's Paul et Virginie, in which text, initials and illustrations together present a synthesis of the 'visualist' research of the period.

In Curmer's own copy there is this inscription in his hand: 'Well, my dear book, here you are in the garb I wanted; for ten years I have dreamed of the glory of this, and, after ten years of trouble, work and joy, too, I have reached my goal.... thanks to you, my dear book, I have studied typography and I have been fortunate enough to advance it somewhat. I have put paper-making on a new track; I have brought about a revolution in the handling of printer's ink; wood-engraving had never before ventured what it has done for this book. And, too, what drawings or, rather, what masterpieces! It is with this book that Français and Meissonier founded their reputations.... May you fall into the hands of a long dynasty of intelligent amateurs who will appreciate you and put you in the limelight as you deserve. May they cherish you and love you.'

The book itself is dedicated 'to the artists who have raised this typographic monument to the memory of J. H. Bernardin de Saint-Pierre'.

Paul et Virginie was published in thirty parts, each of 16 pages with ten engravings and one inset plate. Each part cost 1.25 fr. in Paris and 1.50 fr. in the provinces. 10,000 sets costing 45 fr. each were sold in ten years. Altogether there were 450 vignettes on cross-grained wood in the text (Meissonier drew 130 of them), 7 portraits on chinese paper engraved on steel, and a map.

It achieved an excellent balance between text and illustration. You can see that this was a constant aim. From one page to another is a succession of initials, scrolls, vignette tail-pieces in great exuberance. ('The wood-engravings of the romantic period between 1825 and 1845, of which *Paul et Virginie* is the most eminent example, were made in two styles, which often went together: one was the sketch, picturesque in treatment, its line amusing and subtle, based, in principle, on outline, the engraving being facsimile. In the other, the design and outline were used jointly with a tone, somewhat after the manner of the English wood-engravings, which themselves borrowed the formula of the burin on steel, with its characteristic vermiculated cutting and flat tints.' Pierre Gusman: *La Gravure sur Bois*.) Nowhere, perhaps, than here are we more aware of the dynamism of the adolescent baroque that romanticism was. Eugenie d'Ors, in his *Du Baroque*, had already noticed this connection between Bernardin de Saint-Pierre's text and baroque (and how much more true that is when applied to the pictures in Curmer's edition): 'The baroque which was then becoming part and parcel of romanticism, received the delightful group of Paul and Virginie with open arms and adored it as much for its novelty as for its eternal image: widowed mothers and splendid Negroes, balanced by their own suffering, in the cradle of a hot climate, under a canopy of a stately palm and meteors. French literary fashion took up the Tropics and Negroes. In *Atala* they became Indians and virgin forest. A great victory for the exalted and for sensibility... Atala is a Werther in a savage setting.' *Paul et Virginie* was published in 1787, *Atala* in 1801. The 'vegetable awareness' of which d'Ors speaks is everywhere evident in the subjects and the technique of the illustrations in Curmer's edition of it. The 'flora' of *Paul et Virginie* and of the Indian cabin, given in a sequence of initials, is almost a quintessence of this. In these initials, motif and letter are completely fused without the letter thereby becoming illegible. If there are a few bold Egyptians open and shadowed, the text itself is set in Didot type letters, bold, open or shaded, unlike *Gil Blas* which had Didot, Gothic *fantasie* (lots of them); Egyptians, open, shaded, etc.

Figurative letters (a serpent for an S or a crescent moon for a C) which were exceptional in *Paul et Virginie*, abound in *La Chaumière indienne* which followed it. These fantastic letters though not new in themselves, since you can find them in medieval MSS and the early woodcuts, are characteristic of the romantic period. At first amusing, by sheer repetition they end by stimulating the imagination. The Second Empire was to take this up again and expand it systematically into a whole alphabet, which is charming because it has freshness of invention and the element of surprise. The illustrators went beyond the tradition of the ornamental letter, a permanent feature of the romantic book —first on the title-pages, then on the margins, and you cannot condemn this, when it is successful in its way. Nor should one extend to the whole of the *Chaumière indienne*, which has ninety-seven pages, the principle of drawn margins used in the nine pages of line-for-line illustrations which follow, step by step, the peregrinations through the world of the learned doctor of some Academy in London on his search for the recipe of happiness.

The aesthetics of romanticism were in violent conflict with the academism of Didot. Now books had become 'visuals' almost in the modern sense—typographers having discovered how to run type round in such a way as to facilitate optical transition between image and text. The text was composed in a nice, very legible Didot with wide leads except for the six pages of Virginie's letter to her mother which was set (as a cut) in Firmin Didot's *anglaise*, framed with foliated scrolls.

Thus the balance in books changed, and they gradually assumed the appearance which we now regard as characteristic of the period.

In his Les Français peints par eux-mêmes, *1841, Curmer produced a moral encyclopedia of the nineteenth century, based on the concept of the little 'physiologies' which were enjoying such great success at the time.*

'Between 1840 and 1842 the counters of the bookshops were invaded by dozens of small illustrated books describing professions, institutions and types. Most were published by Aubert and Lavigne, they were called *Physiologies* and the public snatched them up.' (R. Picard and J. Adhémar, 1960.)

These little pocket books in 18mo, of 124 pages, illustrated with wood-engravings by Gavarni, Daumier, Trimolet, Monnier, and Traviès were put out by the publishers of the Palais Royal. Their humorous texts were written by journalists now forgotten, the best of whom, perhaps, was Philipon, editor of *Charivari*. Balzac contributed a *Physiology of Marriage* in 1829.

The covers of these physiologies consisted of a jumble of letters surmounting an engraving. The ornamental letters used a variety of motifs; the centres of the blank spaces at the ends of chapters are occupied with a tail-piece as in the heyday of Fournier. Some have typographic or engraved bands, where renaissance ornaments rub shoulders with floral tracery and still life.

Les Français peints par eux-mêmes was the largest of the works published by Curmer in 1841–42. It comprises 422 parts which made up nine volumes. In actual fact it is a series of 'physiologies' which sets itself up to be a moral encyclopedia of the nineteenth century.

In his introduction to it, Jules Janin emphasises the peculiar nature of compound works like this: 'In the time of La Bruyère, making a book was a craft like making a clock: but it is worse than that today: it is more like mending old shoes. In the day of La Bruyère, no one had ever seen a chef-d'œuvre that was the work of several hands: that has come about in our day. La Bruyère allowed the critic no other right than that of informing the public that the book was well bound, printed on good paper and sold at such and such a price; if he were alive today, La Bruyère would assuredly be the foremost of the critics he despised so greatly. In the day of La Bruyère, literary life had scarcely begun and we are not altogether sure that it has even done so today. What will it be like in a hundred years time?'

Each part was illustrated with an inset plate of an ornamental letter that was also a picture, with a head-band and several engravings in the text. In the ninth volume, *Le Prisme*, however, there are no inset plates. Daumier now made his appearance, the greatest of the romantic painters, the celebrated lithographer-caricaturist, the unrecognised wood-engraver. Ornamental rules, like those in which the Deriez foundry was to specialise, and the innumerable vignettes that were usual in books like *Le Diable à Paris* or *Paris et les Parisiens*, were used in whole pages, one after the other, in the spirit of the Journal.

Les Français was followed—from another publisher—by *Les Etrangers à Paris*, 1844, to which Gavarni contributed some plates.

The romantic book in its final stage was characterised by the use made of rule-boxes. Célestin Nanteuil and others designed veritable frontispieces for chapter-beginnings. In this way whole or half-pages of the text were filled with wood-engravings or ornaments in the style of the old missals, but with their aesthetic values changed to suit the sentimentality of the age.

In *Les Etrangers à Paris*, for example, the title-pages of the early days of romanticism are used again, but now engraved on wood for each of the chapters. Following the principle of Célestin Nanteuil, this book, too, attempts to synthesise the text in a series of linked medallions. The jointures—found in the old Gothic cathedral façades which used to frame the pages—are now more subtle and bear witness to genuine graphic inventiveness.

In Nodier and Lurine's *Les Environs de Paris* which Boizard published that same year, each chapter opening has a wood-block elegantly surrounded by print. After this you begin to find in this kind of illustration, sophisticated vistas, distances cleverly brought up close, which are a complete re-invention of the Gothic frames, the taste for which had been started by the troubadour fashion. Célestin Nanteuil also contributed to this with his *Les Rues de Paris*, which Kugelmann published.

One of the works, where rule-boxes were used more than for just the title-page and chapter beginnings, was Count de Laborde's *Versailles ancien et moderne*, which Everat published in 1839.

Under Louis-Philippe, the taste for ornamentation was indulged to a degree that some find excessive. Copying Fournier in the way they placed vignettes inside rule-boxes, the compositors of those days mixed ornaments of different kinds in the same way as they mixed different kinds of letters. Rules, culs-de-lampe, and borders abound along with a thirty-year accumulation of capitals, pediments, columns, rosettes mingled with pearls, fan-palms, scrolls, flowers and penstrokes. In the somewhat contestable opinion of Thibaudeau: 'One remains purely romantic, that is to say what is achieved is a complacent décor for naive souls, which, besides, could not survive this imaginative period with its spectral visions which it loved to place in a monarchial setting, because from antique Art one is suddenly switched to evocation of the Middle Ages.' The end of it was a typically baroque surfeit of ornamentation, the ornaments being multiplied to the extent of cancelling each other out, and providing a surface that is in constant motion such as one gets in medieval Gothic, in the Italianised France of Fontainebleau and above all in Germany, Austria, the Portugal of Emmanuel and Spain (with its Latin-American derivatives) and, of course, the countries of Islam.

The Jardin des Plantes *of 1842 draws one's attention to the innumerable scientific publications which, up to the end of the century, proved the excellence of the wood-engraving when used in scientific documents.*

64

1842 is the year which saw Dubochet publish Boitard's *Jardin des Plantes* and Curmer his *Jardin des Plantes* by Lamaout, Bernard, Couailhac and Gervais.

Typographically, the two works offer nothing new, but where engraving is concerned, the wood-blocks are little masterpieces and remind one that, at the beginning of the century, in England, Thomas Bewick had produced his last book on water birds, following a long series of engravings of animals. In France, the different magazines had had natural history sections in which were reproduced engravings from which one can follow the development both of the art of illustration and its technique. In the *Jardins des Plantes* of 1842 a sort of perfection is attained, and the quality of engraving found there was to be maintained in a large number of scientific works, *L'Air et le Monde aérien, Le Désert et le Monde sauvage, Les Mystères de l'Océan, Les Montagnes, Le Monde végétal, Zoologie, La Forêt, Le Monde de La Mer, Les Volcans*, etc., in which you would often see the same engravings repeated on the exchange principle that had long been practised in the trade.

1843 was the year in which Victor Hugo's Les Burgraves *failed.*

Its red waistcoats—the Teddy Boys of those days—were no longer so young: 'Young people,' Nanteuil said before the première, 'but they no longer have youth!' The young people of ten years before were tired of applauding fine sonorous verse and of being moved by passion of spectacular extremes. The failure of *Les Burgraves* was the death knell of romanticism.

Before 1848, publishers had done nothing but affirm the lines which the coming years were to take; without renewing anything, they had just been content to exploit their successes.

The real source of influence during the Second Empire was to be that of the newspaper. The whole nineteenth century was marked by the Press; not so much where graphic innovation went, as in the field of competition. The real Press as such was to be born with the revolution of 1848 and the one-sou newspaper of Emile de Girardin.

Wood-engraving, in its turn, began a fresh evolution with Gustave Doré, while typography marked time until 1869, when Lemerre took up the Elzévirian typography of Perrin and made it that of the poets of the new symbolist school. (Gustave Doré (1833–1883) was the most forceful illustrator of the century. Realist in his *Voyage en Espagne* or *Londres*, caricaturist of Philipon's 'funny magazines', he was also a visionary who illustrated great works of the mind by Dante, Milton, Rabelais, Ariosto, and the Bible. He and Pisan invent-

65

ed tint engraving and interpretation woodcuts. Working swiftly, he delivered woodcuts drawn for tints, and his engravers had to interpret his tints in a system of closer or more open hatching.)

1843 was the year of first publication of L'Illustration-journal universel. *In reproducing part of its declaration of intent we will see both the way the press was tending towards 'visualisation', which we have already noted in the field of books, and also what this formula owed and brought to that of the magazines, in particular, by the introduction of pictorial reportage.*

'As the taste of the century has seized upon the word *illustration*, let us take it and use it to characterise the new fashion in the news-giving Press.

'Is there, though, no way in which the Press (which so well fills the want of the public for swift information) could enrich itself and so better achieve its aim? Yes, there is: a very ancient one, long neglected, but heroic; and it is this that we intend to use: reader, you have just mentioned wood-engraving. The extraordinary advance in the last few years in the use of this kind of illustration would seem to indicate that an immense future awaits it. The function of print is not just to multiply texts: it is expected at the same time to depict that about which it writes. Books speak with only half a voice, if the genius of the artist inspired by that of the writer does not translate their accounts into brilliant images for us, and henceforth people will say that all descriptive literature is like that of the theatre. You cannot know it well till you have seen it acted.

'Why should not illustration go outside books? Has it not already begun to do so in the miscellanies, which have been given the name *Pittoresques*? We are thus only continuing this process, though giving it a new direction... These picturesque miscellanies are really only books made up of different articles published together... further we have the newspapers which know how to catch the eye with attractive art forms.

'... We will complement our text with maps, wherever these will be useful: but that is not enough. The reports of our correspondents and travellers will, where necessary, be supported by views of cities, marching armies, fleets, battles... The life we are living abounds with events that come within this scope; without even mentioning the extraordinary and unusual, the things of every day are quite enough... Who would not have liked to have seen the terrible river Rhône filling the plain of Tarrascon like a lake in motion, and transforming Lyons into a Venice? Who would not like to see the sea depicted during one of those furious hurricanes beneath which the ports all groan; the stranded ships, the rescues, the desolation of the shore? And how can all that be depicted here? Voyages of discovery, scenery of distant lands, the colonies, studios of the great, even the railways that are going to be opened and the construction of which we shall follow carefully in all points where it offers sights worth seeing. Let it not be thought that we shall not also introduce our readers to painting exhibitions, for it is there that we shall triumph, the theatre, fashion... etc.'

The date was Saturday 4 March 1843. The type was three narrow columns of Didot; the titles in 'fat face', later in Egyptian. The third issue announced the publication by Hetzel of *Voyage où il vous plaira*, illustrated by Tony Johannot; No. 4 contained an article on The 'Invention of Mechanical Printing'; No. 5 announced *Un autre Monde* by Grandville as a serial; No. 6 printed sketches and diagrams of Mr. Henson's 'steam-driven aerial machine', the publication of drawing-room ballads was the start of the great vogue this was to enjoy under the Second Empire, when they were lithographed. There were also a serial, picture puzzle, caricatures, advertisements, including one announcing the publication of Balzac's *Comédie Humaine* in twelve 8vo volumes, illustrated. (After 1840, *L'Echo des Feuilletons* specialised in reissuing the stories which Dumas, Hipp. Estiennez, and Maria d'Anspach, had serialised in various journals, in volumes illustrated with woodcuts and steel-engravings.)

The nineteenth century saw the creation of the Press as we understand the term today. Expensive and at first reserved to the limited clientèle of subscribers, the general public was content with popular broadsheets. Emile de Girardin extended his network by starting La Presse *in 1836. The one-sou newspaper of 1836 thus achieved its vulgarisation. The other newspapers had to follow suit.*

In his *Le Diable à Paris*, Gérard de Nerval wrote: 'It was an age when newspapers had not yet been invented... then, the broadsheet took the place of the journal. Politics were of little interest for those who lived in villages and the countryside; the Hydra of anarchy, the ship of state, popular storms were not yet ideas capable of stirring the passions of those who knew them not; their attention was given rather to less academic fictions: the were-wolf, the hobgoblin, the beast of Gévaudan: those were the chief subjects that engravings, captions and ballad undertook to immortalise.'

The 'occasionals' were a sort of special printing of information already published, intended for the mass of Frenchmen who did not subscribe to a newspaper (Jean-Pierre Seguin: *Nouvelles à Sensation: canards du XIXe siècle*). Various details of politics, crime and scandal, true or false, provided the master—

67

more like the coloured sheet than anything—of the broadsheet, which was the real one-sou paper before its invention in 1863. Newspapers, of course, did exist, but they were expensive and sent only to subscribers. It was not till 1863 that you had the newspaper sold by the issue; and after that the broadsheet gradually disappeared, though the pictures and ballads went on until about 1909.

Emile de Girardin was the one who first thought of seeking a clientèle for newspapers among the masses. To do this, he thought it necessary to lower its price, do away with the ties of subsidies and subsist on a larger readership and the advertising that depends on their number. At the time, this was a novel idea and it was opposed by the establishment, which was afraid of the development of that formidable force, public opinion. Emile de Girardin struggled for five years, starting more and more new newspapers. Then, on Tuesday, 15 June 1836, he founded *La Presse*, the subscription to which cost 40 francs instead of the usual 80. His collaborator, Dutacq, left him to found on similar lines *Le Siècle*. 'It was certainly not Girardin who invented the changes that were to come,' wrote Charles Ledré (*Histoire de la Presse*, Paris 1958). 'He had no more headlines than the others, no longer reports, or proper layout. But he had imagination, which though sometimes a little careless, went hand in hand in those uniformly pale columns with genuine seriousness.' The tone of *La Presse* is shown by its choice of contributors: Hugo, Gauthier, Balzac, Dumas, and Scribe. It was during the revolution of 1848 that Girardin's *La Presse* was first printed by perfecting machines using the Taylor system patented in 1822.

In 1863, Polydore Millaud's *Le Petit Journal* sold for one sou. 'The pricing of the newspaper at one sou was made possible by the industrialisation of our most daring and rich enterprises. The invention of the rotary press and the Linotype enabled them to apply Girardin's formula: sell cheaply to sell much.' (Raymond Manevy: *L'Evolution des Formules de Présentation de la Presse quotidienne*, 1956.)

The Second Empire was a period that lived on the momentum of the preceding period without innovating anything in the field of typography. It is the age of the historical romance and of the 'pink library'.

After the feverish swashbuckling of the historical romances, heroes were tired, and ahead lay the no man's land of the Second Empire.

It was a great period—for the *café concert* and children's books. Popular literature, alive, alert, in demand, became a separate branch, detached from the dead tree of official literature that persecuted *Les Fleurs du Mal* and *Madame*

Bovary and condemned *Maldoror*, Verlaine and Rimbaud. The success of Victor Hugo's *Les Misérables* (1857) was the last big success in which the two genres were united. The 'serial' gave rise to the dramatic novel and the tales of sword and derring-do. This was the age of *Rocambole, Bossu* and of Dentu's cheap editions that sold in the arcades of the Palais Royal. Then biographies took the place of 'physiologies', but that was also the time when children's books, either for entertainment or as gift books, came into being as such. The Countess de Ségur made Hachette's fortune, while Hetzel was publishing Jules Verne, at first in parts, then in glowing red and golden covers. Gradually the pink library replaced the blue one of colportage. You could now buy the poems of Victor Hugo for ten centimes. In 1852, Chaix started his Railway Library and in 1862 Pierre Larousse began publishing his *Dictionnaire Universel*.

The cross-grain wood-engraving, in colour, illustrated most books of the Second Empire. Lithography, in colour or monochrome, was also used for inset plates.

'Less drastic than nitric acid and more transparent than aquatinting, not so dry as the woodcut and more expressive than the steel-engraving,' wrote Aristide Marie, 'lithography, with its velvety softness like that of grease-paint, is certainly the best accompaniment for vague poetic or musical fantasies, the misty sort of illustration for the ballad or the romance.'

Invented to facilitate the reproduction of musical scores, it was to enjoy a great vogue among publishers of the popular novels, which were in full development during the Second Empire. Their title-pages, like the trade circulars, show a wonderful range of letters more or less ornate, more or less fantastic, which sometimes put the founder's type book in the shade.

The Second Empire exploited—rather indifferently the technical successes of the preceding period, without initiating anything. The Didots, like everybody else, printed books in the taste of the period and Curmer devoted himself to chromo-lithography.

Louis Perrin, a printer in Lyons, was the only innovator of the Second Empire. He designed the 'Augustaux' from the lapidary examples given him by Alphonse de Boissieu, author of Inscriptions Antiques de Lyon *(1846). The lower case that was added subsequently was the beginning of 'Elzévir' types, the efficacy of which was first made apparent by Lemerre's revival of 1869.*

Louis Perrin, was probably in no different case from many of his fellow provincial printers who, depending on their orders, oscillated between the wish to be up-to-date and thus 'romantic' and revert to the classical Didot, symbolic of traditional printing, in which there were no surprises and which, in its abstract severity, was well suited to the requirements of the printer's craft (the rest being decoration). But Louis Perrin was also the cutter of the 'Augustaux' or rather the 'Augustales', the incised capitals that were the precursors of the recent creations of Pascal and Optima.

Perrin's contribution is well described by de Boissieu (quoted by René Ponot in his article, *Caractère Noël*, 1962, where he discusses the position of Louis Perrin's *Augustaux*) in his preface to his book *Inscriptions Antiques de Lyon* (1846): 'It is thanks to the ready and faithful burin of M. Louis Perrin, who has been kind enough to devote to the production of our joint work new methods in an art, all the resources of which are known to him, that I have been able to depict the existing monuments in engravings which are accurate and scrupulously exact and thus to reproduce, as far as possible, the state of preservation, the style and form of the lettering... antique remains to which I am calling attention ... the scrupulous care with which I have revised and corrected both the original drawings and the first proofs (of these engravings), guarantee the exactitude of the text ... the generous and enlightened assistance of M. Perrin aiding me yet again, I have been enabled to reproduce them (the inscriptions) with the true antique character of the best period of the art... This innovation, with which my subject allowed me to experiment and the honour for which is all due to this skilful, intelligent man and distinguished artist, who agreed to help me in my work, deserves the attention and encouragement of all people of taste. When one sees all the transformations to which fashion, whim, charlatanism and bad taste have subjected letters, making them giant, dwarf, elongated, flattened, skeleton, microscopic, grotesque or misshapen, it is astonishing that no one ever thought of reproducing the lovely letters of antiquity with their happy and cleverly matched proportions.'

Perrin's 'Augustaux' were thus used for setting the classical quotations, the text of the book itself being set in Didot. It was not till about 1855 (the date given by R. Ponot) that Perrin thought of adding a lower case to these capitals, for which there was no employment, and so designed one, though probably modelling it on an old design used by François Rey, another Lyons printer, and thus produced the 'Augustaux' fount.

Bereft of the guidance of the specialist in inscriptions and having to rely on his own taste, Perrin resuscitated an old 'Roman' which he arbitrarily put with his capitals. (Arbitrarily: the capitals were the 'incised' type and the lower case 'réale' or 'transitional'.) By doing this, Perrin broke with the all-powerful forms of Didot and, rather prematurely, gave the signal for the Elzévirian revival. (Oblong format, box-frames à la Geoffroy Tory or vignette bands in the Italian style, wide margins, open-lettered title-pages, vignettes few and light, decorated capitals, such were the elements of the books printed by Perrin towards the end of his life.)

Théophile Beaudoire, gave a definite form to the modern Elzévir, and Alphonse Lemerre, taking up Perrin's type once more, created an 'Elzévirian' style that was to become that of the poets of Parnasse Contemporaire.

Beaudoire, a Paris typefounder, launched his Elzévir in 1857, the name he chose as an act of homage to the celebrated Dutch publishers who had made the types of Garamond, Le Bé and Sanlecque so widely known. Though the capitals are close to Perrin's, the lower case demonstrates its originality; and instead of the greyness that Perrin gives the pages, his print was less pale and the colour of the letters was definitely accentuated.

'The letters that we have had cut are not an exact copy of any type of that age; they have the double advantage of being elegant and easy to read: and it is because of this and not from an affectation for the archaic, that we have adopted them. We do not share the view held by certain people that they are not admissible except for reprinting old authors. On the contrary, we think that their shape, being more picturesque and artistic, makes them ideal for deluxe works, and we feel that it is a good thing that there should be a kind of letter that may serve as the hallmark of the bibliophile's book.' Thus the learned Jouaust, publisher-printer and creator of the *Cabinet du Bibliophile*.

Alphonse Lemerre bought the matrices of the 'Augustaux' from Perrin's son, who had hung on to them after his father's bankruptcy about 1880. If he did not anticipate Jouaust, his work is of greater importance, because he made his shop in Passage Choiseul the rendezvous of the young Parnassian School. Grouped round Leconte de Lisle, you would see there Villiers de l'Isle-Adam, Mallarmé, Mendès, Sully Prudhomme, Copée, Hérédia, Verlaine and even old Barbey d'Aurevilly. Lemerre loved poetry. He started his Petite Bibliothèque Littéraire and published poetry. He was to the Parnassians what Renduel was to the Romantics. (In 1868, Alphonse Lemerre published a new edition set in Elzévir of *Paul et Virginie*, the book which had made Curmer famous. What a difference between the two! Useless wide margins, tedious repetition of the same light ruled borders printed in mauve, wood-engravings by La Charlerie, quite without poetry or invention. Lemerre, publisher of poets, here at least showed that he was no poet in books: he was a man of taste, not of imagination.)

There were several kinds of Elzévir. Of these the antique roman of Aubert and Huchet used by Deberny (1910) and that of Mayeur (1883) were the most interesting. The Didot faces made a final bid with Le Raçon of about 1850 (narrow, in the English style) and Le Plon in 1852 (with its strange rounding-off instead of angularity).

The fashion for Elzévir re-introduced Italian Renaissance niello as an ornament: frames and bands were brought back again. Once again one saw cherubs and satyrs in scrolls, grimacing masks in the scrolls of rolled leather and open letters on a tracery of flowers and foliage. Others revived the ornaments of Geoffroy Tory and Aldus Manutius.

It was then that whole series of ornamental by-products (of all kinds: medieval, Renaissance, etc.) were imported from Germany. Characteristic of these was the starkness of their engraving and their lack of typographic invention. Such material was in practically every printers' at the end of the century.

The printing industry at that time found itself in a state of expansion and utter confusion. The birth of photography and thus of process blocks opened up possibilities that the industry had difficulty in assimilating. The design of letters was more and more subordinated to the 'artistic' taste of the age. The development of advertising made people want to create new forms—Motteroz became the champion of baroque typography that, though out-of-date, was inventive.

In 1876, *Les Travailleurs de la Mer* appeared in the *Librairie du Victor Hugo Illustré*, printed by Motteroz and illustrated with drawings by Victor Hugo and Daniel Vierge. (With Daniel Vierge came the last new step in the evolution of the tint engraving: the wood-blocks were cut by engravers—especially Lepère, like brush strokes. Gradually the parallel cuts of the last works of Doré were discarded, thus allowing a greater and hitherto unsuspected freedom.)

'If he had not been a poet, Victor Hugo would have been a first-class painter', Théophile Gautier wrote, 'in his sombre, wild fantasies he excelled in mingling the chiaroscuro effects of Goya with the architectural terror of Piranesi.' Hugo, alone of his illustrator friends: Devéria, Boulanger, Nanteuil, Delacroix, had no out-of-date sentimentality in his form of expression. Here he was better than Delacroix the lithographer, the 'ideal' great romantic illustrator. Hugo, the writer, had a feeling for lettering, drawn, perhaps rather than printed. He wrote some strange things about the figurative import of letters.

'Have you noticed how picturesque a letter Y is, and how numerous its significations? A tree is a Y; the fork of a road is a Y, the confluence of two rivers is a Y, the head of a donkey or bullock is a Y, a glass on its foot is a Y, a candelabrum on its stem is a Y; a suppliant with arms raised to Heaven is a Y. This sort of observation can be extended to all the elements of writing. Everything in demotic writing has been put there by hieratic language. The hieroglyph is the necessary root of the written character. Every letter started by being a sign and every sign started as an image. All society, the world, mankind is in the alphabet. Building, astronomy, philosophy, all the sciences have their point of departure there, perhaps imperceptible, but real; and that is as it should be. The alphabet is a spring: A is the roof, the gable-end with its cross-piece, the arch *arx;* or it is the accolade of two friends embracing and shaking hands; D is the back; B is the D on the D, the back on the back, the hump; C is the crescent, the moon; E is the basement, the right foot, the bracket and the architrave, the whole architecture of the ceiling in a single letter; F is the jib, the fork, *furca;* G is the hunting horn; H the façade with its twin towers; I is the war-machine launching its projectile; J is the ploughshare and the cornucopia; K is the angle of reflection equal to the angle of incidence, one of the keys to geometry; L is the leg and the foot; M is the mountains or a camp with adjacent tents; N is the door closed with its diagonal bar; O is the sun; P is the porter with a burden on his back; Q is the rump and tail; R is repose, the porter leaning on his stick; S is the serpent; T is the hammer; U is the urn; V is the vase (which is why they are often confused); I have already said what Y is; X is the crossed swords of combat: who will win? No one knows: the hermetics took X as the sign of destiny, the algebraists as the symbol of the unknown; Z is the flash of lightning, God. Thus, first you get man's house and its architecture; then his body its structure and deformities; then justice, music, the church, war, grape harvest, geometry, the mountains, nomadic and cloistered life, astronomy, work and rest, the horse, the serpent, the hammer and the urn, which, if you reverse it and join its ends you can make into the bell, the trees, rivers, roads; finally destiny and God—that is what you get in the alphabet.'

The title-pages added to Paul Meurice's copies, for example, or that of *Les Travailleurs*, use letters drawn with a single stroke of the brush. The titles—which were not by Hugo—placed at the beginning of the different parts, gave a foretaste of the fascinating aberrations of Art Nouveau. Motteroz had been in good hands, and he was the publisher-printer of the illustrated Hugo.

73

Jean-Claude Motteroz was born in Romanèche (Saône et Loire) in 1830. He became in turn embosser, wire-drawer, joiner, locksmith, silver-washer, mason. He learned how to set type with Théollier in Saint-Etienne, became a compositor there, then at Lyons, went to Paris and became a lithographer, then a pressman at Dijon. When about thirty-five years of age, he definitely took up printing and became a head machine-minder, got his technical certificate, helped to start a printing trade journal, worked for Marinoni and finally started his own works in rue Visconti (the old Rue des Fossés St. Germain); then, in 1897, he became managing director of the Librairies-Imprimeries Réunies. 'Motteroz' chief title to fame,' wrote F. Thibaudeau, who was one of his pupils, 'is that of having really been the printer of his day... creating the art of making a text speak, of illustrating an advertisement, a catalogue, a circular, a prospectus and getting it read, advertisement though it might be, just as much as any fashionable job-work.'

His excessive honesty in business reduced him after fame and fortune, to poverty. On his death, his books and chattels were auctioned. The printer of the *Victor Hugo Illustré* was also a great user of romantic material, the last apostle of romanticism. He was both the last of his kind and in more than one way the herald and influencer of Art Nouveau.

In the title-pages of his books you will find the curved composition which he was to use above all in publicity matter. Motteroz was, in fact, the first to make advertising dummies. He sought originality at any price and he successfully mixed type faces and used diagonal, curved, asymmetrical, lopsided compositions, justification of ornamental initials, used along with all sorts of bookwork. He made himself the champion of French material (he used much of the remains of romantic ornamentation) opposing the importation of the foreign material. He pushed the use of whole lines in bold type to the uttermost limit. Marius Audin mentions a type that Motteroz designed about 1876 –1880 in *Le Livre*, 1924. This type is also mentioned by F. Thibaudeau, who devotes several pages to Motteroz in his *La Lettre d'Imprimerie* and *L'Annuaire Graphique* 1910–1911. This was one among many variants of a Didot face, in which Motteroz has lessened the contrast between the descending and ascending strokes and accentuated the jointures according to the Elzévirian formula. (He arrived at these solutions after 'very extensive comparative studies of the question of legibility.') His capitals are very square.

Motteroz took part in the preparation of the catalogue of the exhibition of the 'Cercle de la Librairie' in 1880. (Motteroz specialised in catalogues for stores, seasonal gifts, publishers, and so on.) 'This catalogue, the printing of which was shared out among the chief establishments of Paris, gives one a most comprehensive specimen that can be consulted for judging and comparing the printing of the age...' wrote Thibaudeau. 'One must confess that in this catalogue Motteroz's pages eclipse all those round them.'

Motteroz, crazy, yet the perfect technician, was one of those baroque geniuses who blossom into excess, yet from their excesses draw a little art, whereas the mediocre will do no more than make themselves ridiculous. He anticipated the typography of the Dadaist school not with any lyrical purpose, but as the result of the logical analysis of a commercial text which he applied without formulating it. 'I have had a many imitators,' Motteroz wrote, 'of my freakish settings, of which, by the way, I have published none, as the supporters of my systems of making-ready, that have been described so often, are few and far between.'

Stéphane Mallarmé's work ran counter to the current of contemporary ideas and was met with indifference, except by his disciples and the faithful who attended his Mondays in Rue de Rome. In 1897, after a lengthy period of gestation, he published Un Coup de Dés... *which raised printing to the rank of a privileged means of expression. Here, for the first time, the white of the paper played not only an aesthetic part, but was a constituent of the poetry itself.*

The first version of Un coup de Dés jamais n'abolira le Hasard appeared in the revue *Cosmopolis*, laid out by Stéphane Mallarmé, in May 1897. Its twenty-odd pages are more important in the history of book printing than many of the volumes published at the time. *Un Coup de Dés* was only the draft of the big book he was planning. (1897 was the year of the publication of *L'Image* by La Corporation Française des Graveurs sur Bois. In this all the great illustrators and engravers of the day tried—and often succeeded—to show that their virtuosity was able to translate everything: from sketch to lithograph and painting, on to wood.)

'...quite simply a book,' he wrote in a letter to Verlaine, 'in many volumes a book that will be architectural and premeditated, not a collection of chance inspirations however wonderful they may be... I would go further and say: *the* book, because I am convinced that fundamentally there is only one, whatever the writer, the genius even attempting the orphic explanation of the earth. This is the sole duty of the poet and the literary game par excellence, because then the very rhythm of the book, impersonal and alive, even in its pagination, can be joined with the equations of this dream or ode. There, I have

75

confessed my vice, bared it a thousand times I have rejected it, when feeling battered in mind or weary, but it possesses me and I shall succeed perhaps not in making the whole book (it would take I do not know who to do that!) but in showing a fragment of it ready, letting its glorious authenticity sparkle and indicate what the whole, which would take more than one life-time, would be like. Thereby proving that the book exists and that I know it, but have not been able to achieve it.'

In 1898, Mallarmé wrote in *Mercure de France*: 'I am not in favour of any illustration, because all the conjuring up a book does ought to be in the mind of the reader: if you substitute photography, why not go straight to the cinema and let its reels take the place of picture and text, as you could with advantage in the case of many books.' For Mallarmé, in the audio-visual society in which the vehicle of information and entertainment would be the image, books were to be the province of pure thought.

For Mallarmé, *Coup de Dés...* was the first of several similar poems which together formed the cycle of his 'book'. His preface explains what he was getting at:

'I would prefer it, if people would not read this note, or, that they would forget it, when they have; it will tell the intelligent reader little that he cannot see for himself, yet may confuse the unsophisticated who has to set his eyes on the first words of the poem if the subsequent ones, arranged as they are, are to conduct him to the last, all without novelty other than the spacing of the reading matter. The "white" is, in fact, of importance and the first thing to strike one: versification requires to have it, like silence around it, and, ordinarily, a piece, lyrical or of just a few feet, occupies in the centre about one third of the page: I am not exceeding that measure, only spreading it. The paper comes in between each time an image stops or reappears, accepting the succession of others, and, as it is not then or ever a question of regular sonorous features or verse—but rather of prismatic subdivisions of the Idea, the moment when they appear and for how long, in what exact intellectual setting, how near or far in verisimilitude from the latent conductor-thread, is determined by the text. The literary advantages, if I am entitled to say so, of this distance whereby groups of words or individual words are mentally separated, is that it seems now to accelerate, now to slow down the movement, scanning it, intimating, giving formal notice in accordance with the simultaneous vision of the page: the latter taken as a unit as is the verse or finished line...

'Let me add that this bare use of thought with retreats, extensions, flights, or its design, turns it into a musical score for those who wish to read it aloud.

Differences in type used for the major motif, the secondary and the subsidiary ones, dictate their importance when spoken, while their position in the middle, at the top or bottom of the page, shows whether the intonation should go up or down...

'This Poem (a work without precedent) presents a "state" which does not break everywhere with tradition; in its presentation I have in many ways not pushed it far enough forward to shock, yet enough to open people's eyes. Today, without presuming that it will have a future, we can certainly say that the attempt participates in the special, cherished pursuits of the day: free verse and the prose poem. They have been brought together under an influence, admittedly foreign, that of music heard at a concert: you will find in it several means that seemed to me to belong to letters and I took them up. May it become a form like the symphony...'

This invention, repeatedly used in advertising today by those who do not know its origin, is the logical consequence of Mallarmé's reflections on books and printing. From newspapers ('...what does the newspaper, this scrap, lack in order to wipe out books: nothing or almost...') he borrowed the boldness of titling. 'Judging by the extraordinary present over-production, with the press yielding its means intelligently, the prevailing impression is of something very decisive building up: like the start of an era, a competition for the foundation of the popular modern poem, at the least, or innumerable *Arabian Nights* to dazzle a suddenly invented literate majority; from now on you will witness the perils of this crushing accomplishment!' and: '...the press limited to advertisement, it seems, art left out.' (Mallarmé: *Etalage*.) He had composed the first type-score where white/silence plays the part in the space/page of punctuation; where the position of the words (after the fashion of their place in many of his MSS) approximates to that which they occupy in the development of the idea. The only copy of *Lahure*, which was never published, annotated in his hand, shows a care for typographic exactitude pushed to the extreme. (*See* Jacques Shérer: *Le Livre*, Paris 1957, on Stéphane Mallarmé's work with the same title. This is an important study.) 'He sought,' wrote Valéry, one of Mallarmé's disciples, in *Variété II*, 'to elevate the page to the status of the starry heavens. There its constellation will, in accordance with precise laws and to the extent allowed by a printed text, inevitably make it an album of constellations.' (Mallarmé, letter to André Gide.)

Book printing in France between 1900 and 1914 was influenced by Georges Peignot, the typefounder, who completely changed our printers' material by calling upon the services of such remarkable artists as Grasset, Auriol and Naudin and by having the Garamont and Cochin series cut.

Georges Peignot prefaced a brochure publicising the types chosen for the 1900 Exhibition with a declaration of faith: '...create new letters and ornaments suited to modern taste... This taste and the public's search for a new formula are encouraging the industry to experiment with more or less happy results; and this state of mind is today so strong that industrialists themselves have become more persevering... After this how could an art that calls itself the painter of the spirit and which invests all science with its spirit and which has already been defined as the "Art of all the Arts", how could it fail to follow this development? In our industry, it is true, the problem is perhaps more abstract than in others: but it is no less tempting, even absorbing, because of that, and I felt that one did not have the right in our day and age to be content with the letters we have.'

Georges Peignot lived largely among artists. From 1895 onward he worked with Eugène Grasset, the stage-designer, on a letter that was used—in 1899— in *Les Aventures merveilleuses de Huon de Bordeaux*. (Eugène Grasset also did the illustrations for *Quatre Fils Aymon* published by Launette in 1883, colour photogravure by Charles Gillot. This book is the flashy herald of the entry of photo-mechanical processes into colour illustration for books.) M. Charles Peignot wrote recently: 'Personally, I think that Grasset goes somewhat beyond the idea of value relative to its age. Because Grasset is no more and no less of its age than Fournier was of its own age. Once it is freed, as it is beginning to be, of the dust of the 1900's and people stop thinking of fashion and think of style instead, then one will discover solid virtues in Grasset, which make it no fancy type, but a book text. Its early critics actually reproached it for being an imitation of the fifteenth century!' ('Georges Peignot, créateur français de typographie moderne' in *Caractère* 1961. Grasset was unjustly accused of copying a 1530 character of Gryphius.)

In 1902, wrote Anatole France of Auriol, 'very ornamental and yet very legible, is the letter of 1900 par excellence.' Designed to be up-to-date, in it the poet Georges Auriol replaced the traditional serif of the Latin letter with the little drop of ink—borrowed from Japanese calligraphers—which preserved the legibility of the small-bodied letter without it being tiring. Satisfying the needs of advertising, Auriol had from the start a complete range that included, as well as the first book sizes, a narrow (elongated), a thin (light), an open and a bold, the Robur.

In a way Auriol was the Cheltenham of French publicity work. M. Charles Peignot has emphasised that it was for Auriol that his father, Georges Peignot, issued the first presentation brochure. It was a great success.

In 1912, Georges Peignot, with the support of the *Gazette du Bon Ton*, launched the Cochins a face, which had links with the great ones of the eighteenth century engraved on copper. At the same time he recast the Fournier ornaments. 'Cochin was really the greatest success of world printing, being sold everywhere. This success encouraged its author to continue in this art; so, considering that the Imprimerie Nationale had a sort of monopoly of Garamond, he decided that he would provide a Garamond that was in the public domain.' (Charles Peignot, *idem.*)

Naudin, the career of which was halted by the 1914 war, was in the line of the Cochins. It was made in the first place for an illustrated edition of François Villon with illustrations by Bernard Naudin.

The Peignot brothers (there were four of them) disappeared in the turmoil of war and the last page was turned of the history of nineteenth-century typography, which overlaps slightly into the twentieth century.

*Pelletan, the publisher, was the one who started the typography of expression, using, according to the text, either old founts still available at the foundries or the newest creations. He published one after the other—before the First World War—*Livre d'Artiste *and* Livre de Peintre *which set a new trend in illustrated books.*

'The day that Charpentier invented the cheap book by combining compact text, small format and paper without picture or weight, the book trade had its '89... The day has gone, when one can publish the collected works of a famous author in twenty volumes with any chance of success. We need a great variety of reading matter...' (Charles Peignot, *idem.*)

So there was Pelletan who, during the sixteen years between 1896 and 1912, at much labour and for little reward, published his fifty-eight volumes which, in our eyes, are both new and ambitious, in that in them he has sought to adapt the character of a fount to that of a text in a layout the look of which would reveal the deeper significance of the work. The end of this century was a period, when bad taste triumphed. As a sort of reaction against romanticism, bibliophiles rejected Doré or Daniel Vierge and would only buy works that imitated the past. The pastiche was in favour and eighteenth-century nonsense fashionable. *Les Mémoires du Comte de Grammont*, which obtained a prize of honour at the 1889 Exhibition, is a typical example.

79

'At a time,' wrote Clément Janin, 'when others only thought of the image, he thought only of the text. Thinking only of the text, he thought only of the type which would be its outward form.'

Pelletan set forth his own views on this in his *Lettre aux Bibliophiles:* 'Since Buffon, texts have their own personality. The black on white ought to have its own personality independent of the illustration... One must find the type of letter for each work. One could not allow Mathurin Régnier to be printed in the same type as Verlaine or Flaubert... The type ought to recall the epoch just like the illustrations and the binding, though without going as far as imitation.' (He printed *La Mandragore* in black and red Gothic; *L'Affaire Crainquebille* in lower case Grasset; *Les Nuits* in Raçon, *Les Ballades de Villon* in Deberny, antique, etc. Raymond Hesse in *Le livre d'Art du XIXe siècle à nos jours,* Paris 1927, gives a bibliography of Pelletan's chief books, which, though not works of art, show the considerable influence Pelletan had on book production.)

He tried to achieve the same synthesis in illustration and for preference used wood-engravings. 'The dominant factor in a book,' he insisted, 'is its letterpress and it is important that the pictures do not encroach upon the text. If they are allowed inadvertently to come into the foreground, if, on thumbing through the book, you get the impression that the book has been made for the illustrations, that is a mistake and the book is a failure.'

Pelletan's efforts bore fruit with the generation of bibliophiles, educated before the war of 1914, who became the book-buyers of 1920.

Alongside the production of the publishers, there now appeared the artist's book: chosen, arranged, and decorated by an artist at his own risk and peril. A typical example is Huysman's *A Rebours* illustrated by the engraver-painter Auguste Lepère and set by him in Auriol light in 1903.

Ambroise Vollard, a picture dealer, started the first artist's books, a sort of reaction to those of the professional illustrators. In 1893 there was André Gide's *Le Voyage d'Urien* illustrated with lithographs by Maurice Denis and in 1899 Jules Renard's *Histoires Naturelles* illustrated with lithographs by Toulouse-Lautrec. Pierre Bonnard composed a number of light lithographs for Paul Verlaine's *Parallèlement* in 1900 and for Longus's *Daphnis und Cloe* in 1902, which were the forerunners of the many artist's books published after the war. They were printed by Imprimerie Nationale.

Thus, on the threshold of the war, ended a great epoch in the history of the book, which after many vicissitudes was to see a new typographic awareness come into being, of which today's generation is the last and the remote heir.

OEUVRES

DE

JEAN RACINE.

TOME PREMIER.

À PARIS,

DE L'IMPRIMERIE DE PIERRE DIDOT L'AÎNÉ,

AU PALAIS NATIONAL DES SCIENCES ET ARTS.

AN IX; M. DCCCI.

1. Jean Racine: *Œuvres*, Pierre Didot l'Aîné, Paris (1801). Title-page

ANDROMAQUE,
TRAGÉDIE.

ACTE PREMIER.

SCENE I.
ORESTE, PYLADE.

ORESTE.

Oui, puisque je retrouve un ami si fidele,
Ma fortune va prendre une face nouvelle;
Et déja son courroux semble s'être adouci
Depuis qu'elle a pris soin de nous rejoindre ici.
Qui l'eût dit, qu'un rivage à mes vœux si funeste
Présenteroit d'abord Pylade aux yeux d'Oreste;
Qu'après plus de six mois que je l'avois perdu,
A la cour de Pyrrhus tu me serois rendu?

PYLADE.
J'en rends graces au ciel, qui m'arrêtant sans cesse
Sembloit m'avoir fermé le chemin de la Grece.

2. Jean Racine: *Œuvres*, Pierre Didot l'Aîné, Paris (1801). Two-page opening

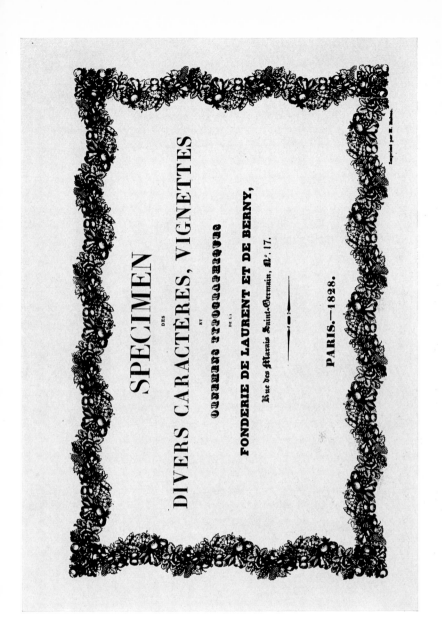

3. Type Specimen Book of Laurent & De Berny, printed by Honoré de
Balzac, Paris (1828). Title-page

4. Type Specimen Book of Laurent & De Berny, printed by Honoré de Balzac, Paris (1828). Vignettes by Besnard and Duplat

LOISIRS

D'UN

ANACHORÈTE;

Par M. Adolphe De Chesnel.

» J'effleure à peine le sentier : laissez-moi passer. »

1830.

5. Adolphe De Chesnel: *Loisirs d'un Anachorète* (1830). Title-page with vignette by Durouchail

HISTOIRE
DU
ROI DE BOHÊME
ET
DE SES SEPT CHATEAUX.

Il y avoit une fois un roi de Bohême
qui avoit sept châteaux. TRIBRU.

PARIS.
DELANGLE FRÈRES,
ÉDITEURS-LIBRAIRES,
PLACE DE LA BOURSE.

M DCCC XXX.

6. Charles Nodier: *Histoire du Roi de Bohême*. Paris (1830). First title-page
with vignette by Tony Johannot

Histoire
du
Roi de Bohême
et
de ses sept châteaux.

PASTICHE.

O imitatores, servum pecus !
HORAT., *Epist.* I. XIX, 19.

PARIS.

CHEZ LES LIBRAIRES
QUI NE VENDENT PAS DE NOUVEAUTÉS.

3.

7. Charles Nodier: *Histoire du Roi de Bohême*, Paris (1830). Second title-page
with vignette by Tony Johannot

« nétrant au fond de mon ame d'un regard acéré;
« et je consens à satisfaire votre curiosité, car je
« sais, à vous voir, que nous suivons la même
« route... »

Et pendant qu'il prononçoit ces paroles, il
avoit saisi le bridon de mon cheval, et il m'em-
portoit dans la course du sien avec une rapidité
dont aucun des souvenirs de notre vie terrestre
ne peut donner l'idée, mais qui avoit cela d'é-
trange que je n'en éprouvois pas même le mouvement, et que je me demandai un instant si
ce n'étoit pas le désert, le fleuve et le ciel, qui
fuyoient.

8. Charles Nodier: *Histoire du Roi de Bohême*, Paris (1830). Text page with
vignette by Tony Johannot

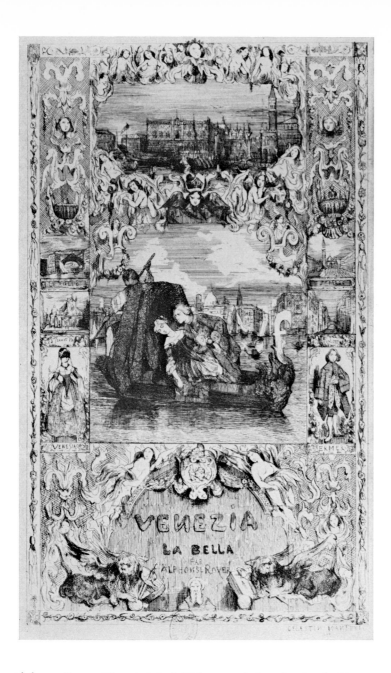

9. Alphonse Royer: *Venezia* (1833). Title-page designed and etched in copper
by Célestin Nanteuil

LE BOA CONSTRICTOR.

LE LAPIN ET LE BOA. — FESTIN DU BOA. — SA BEAUTÉ.
— ADORATION DU BOA EN DIVERS PAYS.

Dans le dessin qui précède, la nature a été prise sur le fait, et reproduite par un artiste qui a vu le boa dans cette attitude pittoresque. Le serpent était sous un grillage; on lui avait jeté un lapin vers l'époque de son repas mensuel, et plusieurs jours s'étaient passés sans accident, de façon que le pauvre petit animal s'était familiarisé avec son ennemi. Tout-à-coup le monstre se dresse, ouvre sa gueule effroyable, et, prompt comme la foudre, se lance vers le lapin!... Puis... était-ce compassion, ou nonchalance d'un appétit mal éveillé? il recule, achève son bâillement énorme, et se rendort. Pauvre lapin! la mort vient de t'effleurer, et dans ton innocence tu recommences à jouer dans les replis écailleux de ton dangereux camarade; mais sa miséricorde ne durera qu'un jour, demain tu seras englouti sans remords.

Le singe, dans un coin du tableau, considère ce spectacle avec une face diabolique, comme s'il était le mauvais génie du lapin; il ricane à son aise parce qu'il est à l'abri; mais dans les forêts quelqu'un de sa famille fournit souvent aux frais du festin. Le boa atteint les branches les plus élevées, en roulant son corps autour de l'arbre avec autant de rapidité qu'une lanière se roule autour des cornes d'un taureau lorsqu'elle est armée de deux balles de plomb, et lancée avec raideur. Les fleu-

ves ne sont qu'un faible refuge contre le monstre, qui poursuit sa victime au milieu des ondes agitées.

Quand il lutte contre un ennemi digne de lui, il l'enveloppe dans mille nœuds, lui fait craquer les os avec un fracas retentissant, et l'étouffe. Il se roule ensuite avec sa proie contre un tronc d'arbre dont il se sert comme d'un levier pour triturer tout ensemble les os concassés et les chairs meurtries; il pétrit, il alonge cette masse informe, l'inonde de son infecte bave, et l'engloutit dans son gosier dilaté. Quelquefois le festin, trop considérable, ne peut être terminé en une séance; le boa n'avale alors, et ne digère que par parties; la gueule horriblement ouverte, et remplie d'une proie à demi dévorée, il demeure dans la torpeur pendant le pénible travail de sa digestion.

On peut suivre au travers de la peau du boa les cornes d'un animal englouti, qui parcourt toute la longueur du serpent, en marquant successivement sur son passage une hideuse tuméfaction.

Mais si le boa se présente ainsi sous une apparence horrible, il est superbe lorsque, plein d'une vie active, il parcourt la campagne. On le voit, en Afrique, s'avancer au milieu des herbes hautes et des broussailles, semblable à une gigantesque poutre qu'on remuerait avec vitesse; les plantes s'inclinent sur son passage, et laissent voir le sillon que tracent les ondulations de son corps; devant lui fuient des troupeaux de gazelles; et le

11. *Paul et Virginie* and *La Chaumière indienne*, Curmer, Paris (1838). Frontispiece engraved on wood by Français

eau, ceux dont les graines sont faites pour flotter. Ainsi, chaque végétal croissait dans son site propre, et chaque site recevait de son végétal sa parure naturelle. Les eaux qui descendent du sommet de ces roches formaient, au fond du vallon, ici des fontaines, là de larges miroirs, qui répétaient, au milieu de la verdure, les arbres en fleurs, les rochers et l'azur des cieux.

algré la grande irrégularité de ce terrain, toutes ces plantations étaient pour la plupart aussi accessibles au toucher qu'à la vue. A la vérité, nous l'aidions tous de nos conseils et de nos secours pour en venir à bout. Il avait pratiqué un sentier qui tournait autour de ce bassin, et dont

Il avait disposé ces végétaux de manière qu'on pouvait jouir de leur vue d'un seul coup d'œil. Il avait planté au milieu de ce bassin les herbes qui s'élèvent peu, ensuite les arbrisseaux, puis les arbres moyens, et enfin les grands arbres qui en bordaient la circonférence; de sorte que ce vaste enclos paraissait, de son centre, comme un amphithéâtre de verdure, de fruits et de fleurs, renfermant des plantes potagères, des lisières de prairies et des champs de riz et de blé. Mais, en assujettissant ces végétaux à son plan, il ne s'était pas écarté de celui de la nature : guidé par ses indications, il avait mis dans les lieux élevés ceux dont les semences sont volatiles, et sur le bord des

12. *Paul et Virginie* (1838). Two-page opening, set in Didot with illustrations by Marville and Meissonier

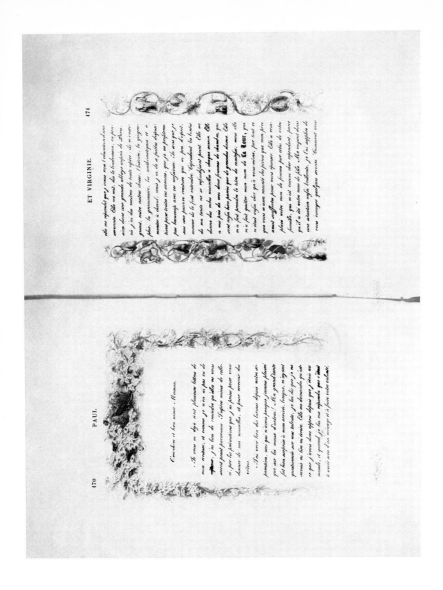

13. *Paul et Virginie* (1838). Two-page opening, set in the *anglaise* of Firmin Didot with decorations by Français

14. *La Chaumière indienne* (1838). Two-page opening, set in Didot with illustrations by Meissonier

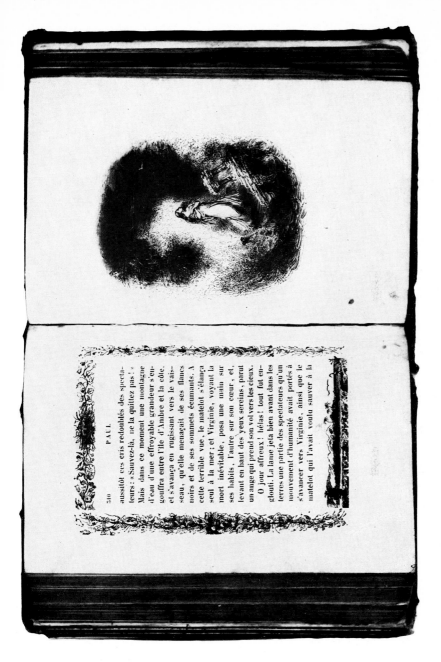

PAUL

aussitôt ces cris redoublés des spectateurs : « Sauvez-la, ne la quittez pas! »
Mais dans ce moment une montagne
d'eau d'une effroyable grandeur s'en-
gouffra entre l'île d'Ambre et la côte,
et s'avança en rugissant vers le vais-
seau, qu'elle menaçait de ses flancs
noirs et de ses sommets écumants. À
cette terrible vue, le matelot s'élança
seul à la mer; et Virginie, voyant la
mort inévitable, posa une main sur
ses habits, l'autre sur son cœur, et,
levant en haut des yeux sereins, parut
un ange qui prend son vol vers les cieux.
O jour affreux! hélas! tout fut englouti. La lame jeta bien avant dans les
terres une partie des spectateurs qu'un
mouvement d'humanité avait portés à
s'avancer vers Virginie, ainsi que le
matelot qui l'avait voulu sauver à la

15. Miniature book, Masson fils (1839). Two-page opening with illustration by Laville

16. 'Physiology', Paris (c. 1840). Cover with illustration by Honoré Daumier

LES DIVERTISSEMENTS TYPOGRAPHIQUES

PUBLIÉS SOUS LA DIRECTION DE MAXIMILIEN VOX

PAR

DEBERNY ET PEIGNOT

L ES "Divertissements" font désormais partie de l'actualité typographique française et étrangère; les deux premiers fascicules ont, comme nous l'espérions, été favorablement accueillis par les Imprimeurs des deux mondes. Ce troisième numéro vise à simplifier davantage encore leur travail, en démontrant les multiples ressources à tirer des FILETS, et les effets variés, non seulement de cadres, mais de jeux de fonds, de vignettes et d'illustrations qu'il est possible d'en obtenir. Nous avons joint un extrait de notre spécimen FILETS, présentant sous une forme logique les séries spécialement utiles.

Série 16, c. 18

27. *Les Divertissements Typographiques*, Deberny & Peignot (1930). Opening page of number three

SCÊNE IV.

RENAUD *endormi, une* NAÏADE *qui sort du fleuve, troupes de* NIMPHES, *de* BERGERS *et de* BERGERES.

LA *N A Ï A D E.*

AU tems heureux où l'on sait plaire,
Qu'il est doux d'aimer tendrement!

Pourquoi dans les périls, avec empressement,
Chercher d'un vain honneur l'éclat imaginaire?
Pour une trompeuse chimere
Faut-il quitter un bien charmant?

Au tems heureux où l'on sait plaire,
Qu'il est doux d'aimer tendrement!

LE *C H Œ U R.*

Ah! quelle erreur, quelle folie
De ne pas jouir de la vie!
C'est aux jeux, c'est aux amours,
Qu'il faut donner les beaux jours.

(Les Démons, sous la figure des NIMPHES, *des* BERGERS *et des* BERGERES, *enchantent* RENAUD, *et l'enchaînent durant son sommeil avec des guirlandes de fleurs.)* D ij

---

28. *Les Divertissements Typographiques*, Deberny & Peignot (1930). Specimen
page from early number

Maximilien Vox

THE HALF CENTURY
1914—1964

In France, the 'cultural century' has always lagged fifteen years behind the 'historical century'; and our twentieth century has proved no exception. In reality, this began with the great break in everything made by the 1914–1918 War. The outbreak of the First World War put an end to an epoch, and the prodigious nineteenth century, which gave us life, movement and being, really only ended with it.

The writer—by the nature of things—has a certain perspective by which to measure the fifty years and more of the century so far. What exactly has happened since the date, up to which my brilliant young friend Gérard Blanchard brought us in the preceding pages? Can one discern any general line in the evolution of the book trade in France at half-century, when one searches among one's memories, inevitably personal, of what has taken place?

First, a little chronology: if one schematises, one can distinguish certain stages which, to borrow the terminology of the cinema, may be called 'the nine waves'.

1. Modern Style or Art Nouveau, at its most successful about 1900, then in decline from about 1910 onwards, after giving us its chef d'œuvre, the type of Georges Auriol, charming and functional in that it corresponded to the sensibility of the day, which was a perfectly valid fashion and which perfectly well may come into its own again one day, if only as a reaction.

2. The launching of this national, not to say nationalist rocket of ours included the explosion of the squib of Cochin style, the creation of a typefounder of genius, Georges Peignot, which was taken up by Lucien Vogel's *Gazette du Bon Ton*. Despite the brutal interruption of the War, the waves set up by Cochin continued to spread until about 1930.

3. The reflux, which began about 1916–17, was the neo-romanticism of the Classic blackletters: normandes, Vibert, Thorowgood, which were returned to favour in a sombre revolution carried out by the poets and artists who had escaped the shells and bullets of war to group round Blaise Cendrars and Editions de la Sirène. This was at its height about 1924.

4. The waters of the fourth wave are still mixed up with the undertow of the waves that broke after it, for it brought with it one of the permanent features of French typo-graphism: a superb eclecticism that drew on everything and was more keen on creating new images than new types, constantly playing personal taste against amused indulgence of the public... This was the 1925 School, whose debt to Picasso, the Cocteau of *Le Bœuf-sur-le-Toit* and to the painters of the Paris School is only now being discovered. The years 1925–30 with Grasset's jackets, Deberny-Peignot's *Divertissements Typographiques*, the periodical *Arts et Métiers Graphiques*, the posters by Cassandre, Colin, Carlu, the weekly *Vu* and the revelation of the photo-image, mark its apogee.

5. The fifth wave came as a shock like that of a cold shower. While we were out for a good time, across the Rhine, Dessau's Bauhaus was stolidly hacking out the purified forms of functional futurism. Paul Renner's Europe (ex-Futura) appeared on the French market (1931) as a revolution and was given an enthusiastic reception, for that was a time when new creations were few and far between. When they finally did come, it was with the Exhibition of 1937 in the daring experiment of Peignot-Cassandre, which was an attempt to combine authentic modernity with a return to the uncial.

6. The debate was not resumed after the interruption of the Second 'last war'. Printing was in a bad way. Then, at last, momentum was imparted again by books, that is the book clubs. In contrast to British book clubs, the aim was revolution: young designers were granted free play for their explosive experiments which included all preceding ones, heated red hot by the ardour of the self-taught. This calmed down after 1950, but the ice was broken: French publishing had consented to evolve.

7. The lettering artist in his turn was now coming into his own once more, in what was a more or less conscious revival of the baroque that is always latent in our Latin script. The rising generation was being given a Mediterranean stamp by the teaching of Jean Garcia and others who matured in P.O.W. camps, by the arabesques of Crous-Vidal who carried on the work of the late Gaudi of Barcelona; and, above all, by the penetrating work being done at the Olive foundry by Roger Excoffon, perhaps our most complete graphic artist.

8. This wave was better placed to stand up to the counter-offensive—at the same time as taking part in it—of the old Bauhaus—banished by politics to Switzerland, whence it began conquering Paris despite its ultra-summary doctrine; this it did thanks to the keenness and above all the professional training of the artists representing Swiss printing or 'Grotesque printing', which, going back beyond the sans-serifs of 1930, dreamed of having one character only: the ancient Antique of the nineteenth-century railways, conceived as the only democratic, rational one. The movement began in the magazines and in advertising, and critics who favour abstract art welcomed this 'new wave'.

9. This, however, was to disregard the public, for whom, especially in France, the thousand-year old habit of reading had become second nature, a habit which it insists on indulging. The more the block-letter multiplied, the more the eye of the reader rediscovered (from 1960 on) the visual comfort of Clarendon, Scotch, Caslon, the types 'of the transition,' to which (a form of hidden persuasion) the labour of the 'legibility' group of the Press had accustomed it. In this way, the optic wave is leading us—as one could have foreseen as soon as photo-composition became imminent—to a letter that neither has nor does not have serifs (which the beam of the photo-setter risks cutting off), to the long stagnant formula of the incised, derived from the ancient Latin letters. The first manifestations of this are Albertus, Pascal, Optima near-lineals with their extremities reinforced and squared.

Ahead lies the three-dimensional letter, a true leap into the unknown. Successful or not, the next stage will be to tackle the third dimension.

This, then, would be the right time to attempt a conspectus: the printer-publisher who wants to be up to date can start now. The quite recent past is on the point of becoming History and we already know the values of tomorrow.

Of course, the evolution of the letter (and its usage) is not confined to print, but in the eyes of the public as of the artist, the publisher and the book-buyer, print is the visible part of it. Up till about 1950, neither the advances made in printing machinery nor the development of processes like heliogravure and offset, not even of mechanical setting, had any appreciable effect on the general appearance of printed matter in France. Everything went on as if in all essentials neither rules nor regulations had evolved more than just a little over the last five centuries and not at all during the last hundred years.

It is only the imminence of photo-composition that has made it urgent to reassess values. The catchword 'Mort de Gutenberg' was considered slightly scandalous when we let it loose twenty years ago, yet today everybody understands it in the sense of there being a need to re-think the norms of composition, now that it no longer depends on a weighty mass of metal, but on an electronic beam acting on a film. What are the rules we must keep and preserve because they are absolute, and which are the new conditions going to alter?

At the time at which this brief survey starts, neither of these questions had presented itself. The main mechanical processes were already in use: rotary presses and photogravure and typesetting machines (Linotype, Monotype); but the foundry type and hand-composition were to continue for a long time as the working basis of the small and medium-sized printing works, which were, and are, the majority. Grasset and Auriol have not suffered from not being used for mechanical setting, for they nonetheless dominate the early part of the century; their competitor Cheltenham has become to such an extent part of the national routine that only four years ago an important firm of printers was all but prevented from replacing this item of outmoded material with the universal Times.

Let us go back to the series of tendencies we tried to isolate earlier, and see what thread of continuity unites these aspects, sometimes concomitant, of the French printing industry of yesterday and the day before yesterday.

The fuss and commotion of 'Cochin printing' in 1912–13 was not solely a manifestation of the letter, but also the expression of a moment of civilisation: as Georges Peignot and his brothers had always wanted and tried to achieve, assisted by Thibaudeau the typographer (author of a valuable encyclopedic manual that is now impossible to find), and by such hand engravers as Bourreau, Malin, Parmentier and those of the artists and writers of their day as had a marked sense of elegance in its various forms, Cochin style was in no way a restoration of something archaic, but a resumption of a tradition, obviously linked with Anatole France and Henri de Régnier, deeper down with Bergson and Proust, then not yet published, P. J. Toulet and young Giraudoux.

Psychologically, the sharper, more audacious twin variety of Nicolas-Cochin is bound up with the Ballets Russes, Paul Poiret dresses and Iribe's drawings; but above all, as we have already said, with what at the time was a charmingly modern enterprise, *La Gazette du Bon Ton* edited by Lucien Vogel (who later started *Vu* and *Jardin des Modes*) a man who put life into publishing at a time of great publishers: Pierre Laffitte, Alfred Tolmer, then Bernard Grasset, Pierre Lazareff, and lots of others.

Psychologically—that was the word. In no other country than France could the psychology of Print have played as important a part. Without being pedantic, what is *la couture* of Paris, but a subtle use of psychology? Those pre-war years are in their way pathetic: sensitive and serious, they drafted a whole world of new concepts and advanced ideas, which could have taken shape by a process of transition, without violence or disturbance, and which were not realised until after the slaughter, by battered survivors who had lost the best of their companions.

Among these latter were the four brothers Peignot, who fell on the field of battle, an irreparable loss for mid-century French printing. Their line ran parallel, though without duplication, with that of the great British creations especially of the Monotype Corporation under the wise and steady guidance of Stanley Morison, an authority of the kind that we miss over here. But, while Monotype was continentalising (that is to say: universalising) its production by reviving the famous basic forms of the sixteenth and eighteenth century, the Peignots' programme had consisted of making French type faces outstanding in a way that was both traditional and forward-looking. When taken up again, ten years later, those which appeared were only half successful: the 'transitional' character, which reproduced the graphic of Bernard Naudin, the designer; Doric, a Calvinistic Didonic of Carlègle and Leon Pichon; an unborn Guy Arnoux.

Astrée, designed by Robert Girard, who succeeded Charles Tuleu at Balzac's old foundry, Deberny, was more fortunate. It was launched at the time when two famous foundries were being merged thanks to the initiative of a young man, Charles Peignot, who was to become a leading figure of the École de 1925.

Looking back, those who shared that great adventure with him will wonder with a tinge of melancholy at the brilliance of that short period of hopes, so many of which have as yet been only half-fulfilled.

Perhaps we owe more to the past and less to the claims of the future than we were inclined to believe at the time. The black reaction of *bois-de-fil* (woodcuts) and normandes was shifted in a 'Coquemer' style, called after the commercial printer who started the idea of doing without capitals—to the indignation of Clement Vautel, daily moraliser in *Le Journal*. Books put on a new appearance, using the whole range of types for their jackets. Following the example of Apollinaire, Dadaists and Surrealists learned to toy with typography, not without some solemnity. One journalist, Roger Dévigne, who had a basement in Ile St-Louis, installed a Stanhope hand-press there. *Les Nouvelles*

Littéraires (1924) started a new type of literary weekly. The company's first chairman was Charles Peignot.

Peignot, however, heir and rival of a gifted dynasty, had ambitions, which, though not irreconcilable, were divergent: one was to prolong and continue the family tradition, the other to accomplish something that owed nothing to that tradition.

Sensitive to the movement of ideas, to a degree of modishness, clever at discovering people and temperaments even in the heart of *la dolce vita*, a prudent man of business where one would have expected to encounter the artist, Peignot's doctrine was infectious—and profitable to all—in the immediate part to be played by 'la typographie' in France.

He engaged, I thankfully remember, an artist as art director, and commissioned type from Cassandre.

It is worth while analysing this Deberny-Peignot duality, because—apart from certain eddies—it conditioned the atmosphere of French printing between the wars. The other typefounders, the printers (apart from Draeger) and even the advertising people made no attempt deliberately to influence the typographic conscience of their day. Deberny-Peignot, alone conducted in a tempo close to that of Cocteau at *Le Bœuf-sur-le-Toit*, the noisy but effective offensive which has resulted in making Print part of the Parisian scene, a vital thing of the day.

The first of his two *larrons*, as they were called, was met by Peignot when in charge of the production of Bernard Grasset books. The designer of the covers for that famous firm had just been awarded a prized and lucrative artistic distinction, the Prix Blumenthal, a biennial award from the Fondation Américaine pour l'Art et la Pensée Française, together with André Chamson (for Literature), Planson (for Painting), Arbus (for Architecture), Delannoy (for Music) and by thus distinguishing the only typographer then employed as such in France, the Foundation recognised typography as a major decorative art.

Not only had Grasset, in a stroke of genius, used press advertising to sell the 'just out', but by changing the 'conditioning' of his goods, the presentation of which had been utterly neglected till then, he revolutionised the appearance of bookshop windows, veritable temples of mediocrity and ennui.

The four M's, Mauriac, Maurois, Morand, Montherlant, were now dressed, as though by a couturier, in the firm's jackets. Pure type, hard and bare, played the publicity packaging role that today has been restored to colour.

The Blumenthal award of 1926, itself a consecration, marks an epoch. (Since then two other typographers have received it: Maurice Frédéric in 1949 and Gérard Blanchard in 1956.) Deberny-Peignot then entrusted the recipient, to whom they gave the grandiloquent title of engineer-typographer, with designing the booklets of type display, the compilation of a monumental catalogue, and their *Divertissements Typographiques*, 'a collection of models and examples' the purpose of which was to demonstrate the resources and richness of available founts—in the absence of unpublished novelties—and this proved a revelation to outsiders revealing to designers such as Marcel Jacno and Jean Garcia where their vocation lay.

Public opinion had been prepared by then by the new so-called demi-luxe editions of modern works, usually in demy format in editions of about 1000, profusely illustrated with wood-engravings with stencil-plate underlay, subsequently with lithographs and dry-points, which between 1922 and the 1930 crisis found a considerable number of purchasers among those unable to obtain the official luxury editions of the big bibliophile clubs or of such artist-publishers as F. L. Schmied, Daragnès, Sylvain Sauvage. The most famous name of that period was Henri Jonquières, whose romantic typography started a whole school and attracted round him most of our cleverest draughtsmen: Falké, Chas Laborde, Pascin, Dignimont, Hermine David...

After 1925, various popular series (Livre de Demain, Livre Moderne) took up wood-engraving and brought it into disrepute by obliging the artists concerned to work hurriedly. As for the 'ordinary' book, now with its cover revolutionised, it remained inside, at the lowest price, the same mediocre object, sections of coarse paper carelessly printed and roughly stitched, as the Bibliothèque Charpentier had been in the days of Zola and Alphonse Daudet.

One had to wait till after the next war before, after the manner of what had happened in the Anglo-Saxon countries, the present situation burst upon us. As the clever observer had anticipated, the 'normal' French book was shunted (to the surprise of our publishers) on to two easily predictable lines: the cloth-bound book, product of the book clubs, and the pocket book, the prototype of which is the Penguin.

Lastly, as a final extension, the traditional limited edition book, has been superseded, at an unspecified number of copies, by the facsimile reproduction: Maurice Robert of the Union Latine launched the Jacomet style of illustration, the 'illusion of the original'; with Vox's Molière and Beaumarchais; the Dante, Shakespeare, and Bible by Edy Legrand; Don Quixote by Berthold Mahn.

89

In order to keep up with these various pressures, and the parallel growth in the use of poster, catalogue and photography, Charles Peignot started the irreplaceable *Arts et Métiers Graphiques* in 1927. But there remained the essential part of his programme, the real feat, that of producing 'the letter of our time' for which everyone was hoping and which no one had produced.

Garamont, put in hand by Georges Peignot in 1913 and launched in 1921, could hardly be the answer, though this admirable face—most typically French—was superior to all the world's more-or-less Garamonds and destined to be used widely by printers who set by hand.

Nor could Futura serve, unprecedented though its sale had been. Designed by Paul Renner of the Bauhaus, this was released in Germany at the same time as Monotype put out Gill Sans. With this wave of more or less international lineals, accepted and exploited, the aim now was to add to them, even to set up against them, some innovation that would reverse the trend.

This was the role intended for the Cassandre type face (which became 'Peignot' after it was launched in 1936), a reflection of the abstract, trenchant intelligence of the man who spectacularly revolutionised the modern poster, by adapting cubism to commercial taste, Adolphe Mouron-Cassandre. A franco-slav blend of the Latin and Cyrillic alphabets, it demonstrated the possibility, more the necessity, for an alphabet to borrow from the uncials of the pre-carolingian epoch the mixture of shapes today differentiated by lower case (Caroline) and upper case (Trajan), to retrace one's steps through a thousand years of civilisation and reading, five centuries of printing and legibility.

Would it be possible to get the public and the trade, ever conservative, to accept so gratuitous a shock? Ten years of gestation is nowadays more than long enough for conditions to change; thus Peignot, broadcast on the occasion of the Paris Exhibition of 1937, used in Paul Valéry's inscriptions—by the French Railways and in advertising—has not crossed the demarcation line into the public domain, at least where its lower case is concerned. It has not yet said its last word, unless this was said in 1929 with Bifur Cassandre. This pushes didonic logic to actual decomposition of the letter into two flats, of which only the black counts, a solitary fingerpost, prototype of what will be the photo-composition of tomorrow (on which today's photo-composition still has its back turned).

Bifur remains an unexploded bomb.

After 1925, heliogravure, though changing nothing in typography, made a great appeal to publishers. One of the managers of Néogravure, Jacques Lagrange, from being a printer, turned client and risked his money in publishing. He met a great success with a series of books of photographs *Visage de la France*, printed by heliogravure, an idea that has been used over and over again since. The album of *Arts et Métiers Graphiques* publish the world's great photographers. In 1933, *Tout est Foutu*, the cruel little classic by Vox and Carlo Rim, started the idea of confrontation of images, a new form of pamphlet.

No parallel progress has been made in the world of the daily press; technical upheavals (newspapers are still awaiting), easier to conceive than to put into practice, which may produce great transformations in this sector, pari passu with large investments. Printed on the same presses, the political or literary weeklies are in the same boat, despite the hopes offered by offset, that active rival of letterpress.

The stagnation due to the war and the Occupation was relieved only by the activities of the clandestine press, the Vichy publications, and some luxury editions, which cashed in on an untimely taste for the book beautiful—and the profits of the Black Market.

The revitalisation of public opinion in 1944 aggravated the shortage of paper, that prop of liberty, which became almost impossible to get. Those who were temporarily in charge of the publishing houses which had been sequestrated, will remember the illegal expedients to which they had to have recourse in order to do their job.

It was as an offshoot of one of these managed firms that the first idea of the book club was born, that is of publishing cloth-bound books, carefully printed by offset and because sold direct, costing no more than the ordinary publisher's book of bad quality. The ball was set rolling by Jean de la Varende's *Guillaume-le-Conquérant*, printed and bound in Alsace with 'salvaged' equipment. It had a classical appearance, but the formula was revolutionary.

The movement of the book club, a child of restrictions, of suppressed young artists weary of conforming, also of lack of imagination on the part of official publishers and book shops, extended the market for books to include hundreds of thousands of new purchasers. Taken up by the old organisations and the big printers, this phenomenon has done a lot to launch French production on the international dual line of cloth bound book plus pocket book. Offset has come into its own here and allowed the 'liberated' writers (Sartre, Camus, Vercors, Triolet, Eluard) to achieve parity.

From the typographic point of view page-composition, though it has thus freed itself of the servitude of the old constraints and routines, has acquired

91

fresh, reputedly 'modern' ones, such as that of doing away with the white quadrat at indented lines, the subversion in margins, and the invasion of lineals (or antiques) into book work to the detriment of readability. This tendency is not accepted everywhere: in other countries the exclusive use of 'grotesques' has become a tidal wave. There is no common-sense justification for the reduction of print to one single style of block-letter: the least legible of all, according to Cyril Burt's report; nor can the reader be expected to make the extra effort necessary to decipher letters deliberately made less distinguishable one from another just for the sake of greater harmony and the homogeneity of the printed page. It is an unforeseen return to the aesthetic heresy of the books.

Even in advertising, where it is an element of legibility, lineal on its own introduces a feeling of monotony that fails to arouse curiosity. Made for other languages than French, languages in which each syllable as it is 'decoded' adds to the total comprehension, so-called functional grotesque runs upstream against the current mass-usage.

Nonetheless, it remains indispensable for various kinds of individual uses, especially where there is need for a sort of anonymous cement. All the world's typefounders have sought to meet this need, at the same time. The most complete version consists of a graduated range of twenty-one series and can be regarded as definitive. Designed in Paris by the Swiss artist, Frutiger, this Univers is put out both by Deberny-Peignot and Monotype. It looks like becoming international.

The slow return towards the baroque, the romantic, even the Victorian, which is affecting all the arts today, is here, as elsewhere, acting as a counterbalance to the theories inspired by Mondrian and Le Corbusier. The latest reaction in France is a Clarendon craze.

This quick round-tour of French printing would be incomplete without an effort to look ahead and ask what is likely to be the effect on the printing industry in the second half-century of the accession of photo-composition to the rank of normative technique.

First, some facts:

1. At the moment, there is no one style that would allow you to speak of specifically French printing, but there is a complex of tendencies.

2. During the period under consideration, there has been no new book-type absolutely Gallic, as were Garamont, Didot, even the Cochins, except Vendôme, designed by F. Ganeau, the designer of the Festival d'Aix; limited to hand-setting, it is therefore hardly available for mass publishing. This ex-

plains and justifies the growing use of the remarkable neo-Roman Times, the last in chronology, of the great classical types, the extensive range of which makes up for an unmistakably British undertone.

3. There is some hope, however, that the keyboards will soon have to deal with the exigencies of a government-inspired typography 'à la française', calling for material adapted to a specific national style. (The Société Nationale des Chemins de Fers Français in 1943 published a *Standard Typographique*, which had the status of an official instruction book, laying down rules and providing examples of the procedure to be followed for all printing orders given by its purchasing department. This brought about a remarkable purification of the presentation (logical and aesthetic) of the railway's printed matter. Their example was followed in 1945 by the Ministry of Finance.)

4. Each new basic type face ought to take account of photo-electric realities and not shut its eyes to the fact that light really can etch like an acid, and that thus one has to anticipate points of intensification, not only for reasons of esthetics or legibility, but as a physico-chemical necessity. This will inevitably give rise to new structural concepts and fresh interpretation of the everlasting theme of the Latin alphabet.

5. Photo-composing machines, which one imagined as likely to be first used for all sorts of tricks hitherto impossible, are proving to be most efficient for placards, column and tabular work.

6. One still cannot measure the part to be played by 'photo-lettering', and photo-setting: 'Artist's lettering' is going to experience a revival.

7. In France, typographical criticism is swiftly developing into an independent art. Till now, the only means of information having been the lush but far from impartial publicity of the typefounders themselves.

This being so, it would appear that the present role of French typography is to preach a spirit of keeping within bounds, attempting to isolate certain primordial rules of clarity and rightness and have them respected, leaving a free field to all that is spontaneous, providing that it is also beautiful and graceful.

But we must also go thoroughly into the principles of the printed language, re-defining its permanent disciplines, (one could indeed speak of a philosophy of media), entrusting them to the care, as well as of artists and those professionally interested, of the Universities, predestined guardians of the printed word as they were at the time of the Renaissance. As a first step in this direction, the Faculté des Lettres et Sciences Humaines of Aix-Marseille has started a course in '*psychologie de la Lettre*', on the model of what is being done in the Netherlands.

INTERNATIONAL CLASSIFICATION OF PRINTER'S CHARACTERS

GROUP	FRENCH	ENGLISH	GERMAN	DUTCH
I	Humane	Humanistic	Venezianische Renaissance-Antiqua	Humanen
2	Garalde	Garaldic	Französische Renaissance-Antiqua	Garalden
3	Réale	Transitional	Barock-Antiqua	Realen
4	Didone	Didonic	Klassizistische-Antiqua	Didonen
5	Mécane	Mechanistic	Serifenbetonte Linear-Antiqua	Mechanen
6	Linéale	Lineal	Serifenlose Linear-Antiqua	Linearen
7	Incise	Incised	Antiqua Varianten	Inciezen
8	Scripte	Script	Schreibschriften	Scripten
9	Manuaire	Manual	Handschriftliche Antiqua	Manuaren

A characteristic symptom of this trend of the French intellectual conscience is the annual meeting of typographers, designers, technicians and writers known as *Ecole de Lure*, held among the ruins of the old village of Lurs-en-Provence and attended from all over the world. Here they study their problems in the light of modern conditions and future prospects.

This has resulted, amongst other reforms, in a classification of types, a thing that had never been done before, despite its obvious usefulness. This is now in general use in France, used in most other countries, and has been adopted officially in Germany (DIN 16518) and by Association Typographique Internationale, which Charles Peignot founded to defend the moral interests and ethics of the printing world.

The Lure classification takes the place of the over 'Cartesian' system taught in France under the name of Thibaudeau's principle (wholly based on the serif) just as well as it replaces the vague, empirical terminology used in English. It is based on the biological concept that each living being (thus each character) has a dual origin and that two family names may be necessary to locate a given character exactly.

These families, of which there are nine, have both a historical past, a personality in the present and the faculty of generation in the future. In French, they had been given vaguely suggestive poetic names. But each language has been free to adapt them to its own terminology. The main thing was to have common concepts and similar methods of discriminating.

PORTUGUESE	SPANISH	LATIN	EXAMPLE
Humanos	Humanos	Humana	Dutch Medieval, Palatino
Garaldos	Garaldos	Garalda	Garamond, Caslon, Romulus
Reais	Reales	Realia	Baskerville, Times, Van Dijck
Didonis	Didones	Didonia	Didot, Bodoni, Walbaum
Mecanos	Mecanos	Mecana	Clarendon, Beton, Rockwell
Lineais	Lineales	Linea	Gill, Futura, Univers, Folio
Incisos	Incisos	Incisa	Albertus, Pascal, Bavo, Optima
Escriturais	Escrituras	Scripta	Rondo, Mistral, Excelsior
Manuales	Manuales	Manuaria	Libra, Klang

Note: As originally conceived, the families were arranged in a ring, like a dial, so that numbers were unnecessary. We prefer to start with the manuals; *see*: 'Faisons le Point, cent caractères présentés par M. Vox, Union Bibliophile de France 1963.'

Typical as it is, it may be considered as a specimen of French methodology—and serve, therefore, as a conclusion.

Georg Kurt Schauer

THE ART OF THE BOOK
IN GERMANY
IN THE NINETEENTH AND
TWENTIETH CENTURIES

In the first decade of the nineteenth century Germany, as a state, was torn asunder and her economy in ruins. But she was rich in learning and creative ability. The Brothers Grimm had begun their Germanistic and folkloristic studies. Wilhelm von Humboldt founded the University of Berlin and revived the humanistic school curriculum. His brother Alexander had already achieved a world-wide reputation as a naturalist and geographer. Out of the 'Sturm und Drang' period arose Germany's romantic movement. This, among its most noble works, produced not only the paintings of Caspar David Friedrich and the famous anthology of folksongs, *Des Knaben Wunderhorn*, but also saw the beginnings of the modern scientific approach to history (Georg Heinrich Pertz and Leopold von Ranke); a new theory of art; and a great flowering of translations into German (August Wilhelm von Schlegel and Friedrich von Schlegel). Such German poets as Lessing and Wieland, Goethe and Schiller, Klopstock and Jean Paul, had already established European reputations before the turn of the century. But German type and book design lagged behind the best produced in England (Baskerville), France (Didot) and Italy (Bodoni). It was only after 1800 that Germany made a contribution of international significance to these arts.

In 1803 Justus Erich Walbaum (1768–1837) moved his small typefoundry from Goslar, where he had started it, to Weimar. It is likely that soon afterwards he produced his roman, which has become one of the most important vehicles of typographic expression in the German language. Even today Walbaum roman, available on all composing machines and for hand-composition, is one of the most popular German type faces for the arts and poetry. Walbaum-Fraktur is unmistakably its sister-face. Together these two type faces mirror the dual tendencies of classicism and romanticism which at that time gave German thought its peculiar character. But this pair is also the most impressive example of the duality in German typography, which has been more strongly in evidence than elsewhere ever since the early days of printing. By 'classical' we mean the organically consistent, largely static and rational, language and graphic form, based on ideals akin to those of antiquity. The 'romantic' trend is dynamic and flexible, seeks for simplicity and naturalness. The romantic man tries to achieve fulfilment by devoting himself to the elemental, which he hopes to find in the customs and practices of peoples close to nature. The two type faces correspond with these two approaches to design: the rounded roman faces derived from antiquity, and the broken faces influenced by transcendental Gothic form.

A number of attempts were made shortly before 1800 to merge roman and fraktur. The latter was to become simpler, the former, more lively. J. G. I. Breitkopf produced the Jean-Paul-Fraktur in 1794. It did not survive for long. Even Johann Friedrich Unger's attempts had no great influence on the nineteenth century, though the final version of Unger-Fraktur, 1794, was at first one of the more widely used romantic type faces. Both faces were rediscovered shortly after 1900 and the Unger-Fraktur in particular enjoyed great popularity for decades as a book face for belles lettres. When E. R. Weiss, in the years preceding 1909, searched for a type face that was to embody both traditions of German design, he based himself on the classico-romantic experiments of Unger and Breitkopf.

Walbaum designed his roman in the style of Didot and Bodoni. Like the copper-engravers he sharply differentiated thin and thick strokes; the curves are fairly wide, tending somewhat towards rectangularity; serifs are set at right angles to the letters. The letters are in repose. The type face is dignified, thoughtful and lucid, but it lacks all brilliance. Walbaum roman is reserved, totally *bürgerlich* (*Translator's note*: the nearest equivalent term is *bourgeois*—without its derogatory implications.), and very much a German way of homage to the Greeks and the dignity of antiquity. This German variant of classicism is known as the neo-humanistic version of the Biedermeier era. (Similar to, but slightly preceding the early Victorian style.) The romantic tendencies of that epoch, which covers the first four decades of the nineteenth century, are embodied in Walbaum-Fraktur, which cannot have been produced later than 1828. Its lower-case letters show all the typical lattice-work of fraktur stems, and all the corners of this broken face are there. The capitals, however, are rotund, portly, and thick-set. Angularity plays a subsidiary role—it is the broad, friendly curves that dominate.

Industrialisation and world economic trends created prosperity in Germany in the latter half of the nineteenth century, but this had only a quantitative effect on bookwork. Design was as sterile as technology was efficient. The cathedrals of Ulm, Regensburg, and Cologne were completed in high-Gothic. A mixture of Renaissance and baroque was the idiom for government buildings. Similarly, nothing new emerged in book typography. Title pages were only moderately affected by the historicising decorative craze of the times: the typographical ideal for the title-page was to have a different type face or at least a different size in every line. In this way a number of type faces originally intended for display work found their way into books. The virtuoso punchcutter came to the fore in competition with lithography. Small foundries, mainly supplying display demands, shot up overnight. The greater the caseroom's preoccupation with borders, vignettes, and decorative types, the greater their neglect of book typography and book faces. Not until the end of the century did people remember that a type face is not just a signal or vehicle of communication but also the expression and image of a language. The printers of the early nineteenth century, who were also publishers, had fully understood this. Today, 150 years later, we can see that Walbaum roman and fraktur were the most important German type faces of the nineteenth century. They were fully attuned to the needs of the humanistically educated and romantically inclined middle classes that gave the age its character. Even today Walbaum roman is regarded as a face suitable for works that have their roots in this tradition.

ILLUSTRATION DURING THE NINETEENTH CENTURY

The novels of Gustav Freytag and Theodor Fontane, or Jacob Burckhardt's *Civilization of the Renaissance in Italy* and Victor Hehn's *Kulturpflanzen und Haustiere*, reveal far more of nineteenth-century culture than the type specimen sheets or de luxe bindings in the style of the German Renaissance. The illustrator's art of the mid and late nineteenth century tells more about the time than its types and typography. It reflects the thoughts and feelings of important groups in that society. It is rarely of much significance artistically, but it is factual, full of pointed anecdote, and tirelessly narrative.

Johann Nepomuk Mayrhoffer (1764–1832) is one of the greatest botanical painters of his time, as well as an excellent lithographer, whose picture series (e.g. his *Vorlagenwerke* and his *Flora Monacensis* of 1811–18)—are among the most sought-after incunabula of lithography. The warm-hearted fairy-tale illustrations of Ludwig Richter (1803–84) put into pictorial form the idyllic aspects of the romantic *Bürgerlichkeit*. Alfred Rethel (1816–59), who witnessed the May Revolution at Dresden in 1849, was the only German artist to convey, in his series *Auch ein Totentantz* the tragedy of the most important political event in Germany in the nineteenth century. Adolf Menzel (1815–1905) invented the style of historical and military reportage that became characteristic in the Prussian parts of Germany. His manner of depicting the country and the people living at the time of Frederick the Great—particularly in Kugler's *Geschichte Friedrichs des Grossen* (1840)—has created the image most Germans have of that epoch. Wilhelm Busch (1832–1908), humorist and satirist, wrote veritable novels in the form of pen illustrations, and enriched the art of story-telling in pictures—a characteristic nineteenth-century phenomenon—in his own German way. His *Max und Moritz* (1865) is as well known as Heinrich Hoffmann's *Struwwelpeter* (1847). His trilogy about Tobias Knopp (1875–7) is an endearing satire of the German petit-bourgeoisie.

THE MUNICH RENAISSANCE

Among the historicising movements in later nineteenth-century Germany the most vigorous and lasting was the 'Renaissance of the Renaissance' 1876–88, which began in Munich. In the field of typography this specifically south-German phenomenon culminated in the desire to renew the type face most expressive of the German language, namely the round gothic alphabet, which is older than fraktur and closer to roman. It was hoped that this would end the split in German type design. In 1800 unity had been sought in fraktur; a hundred years later, fortified by the arguments of the Mainz printer Heinrich Wallau (1852–1925), 'Rotunda' was the great hope. In 1900 no fewer than three such faces appeared. They did not establish themselves. Once again it was impossible to remove the dichotomy in Germany's book printing. The type faces of Eckmann and Behrens (1900–02) had more success. They too were based on Rotunda, but now it was the younger, though short-lived, influence of the Jugendstil (Art Nouveau), and the drive of a youthful manufacturer, the typefounder Karl Klingspor, that carried them. In the last decade of the nineteenth century the typographical offshoots of the Munich Renaissance and its gothic type faces ran side by side with those of the Jugendstil, a movement that had the support of Germany's western neighbours and was very much in the ascendant at the time. There were many points of contact. The old verses of Josef Sattler's *Nibelunge* (1898–1904) were set in a gothic type face, but the new dynamic style could be felt in the swinging lines of the illustrations. The most talented man to link the Munich Renaissance with the new century was Otto Hupp (1859–1949). All connoisseurs of vigorous heraldry find the fifty annual issues of his *Munich Calendar* (1885–1935), with their magnificently coloured coats of arms and disciplined almanacs unforgettable. The revival of the round gothic around 1900 was not Hupp's only contribution: he also convincingly used the Textura, the sacral type face of Gutenberg's 42-line Bible. But apart from Hupp's free variations, Renaissance ornamentation did not survive the turn of the century, after which F. H. Ehmcke began to develop a new ornamentation, sometimes a little sombre, but free of all historicising elements and enriched by the folk art of Scandinavia. After the abrupt, but rapidly waning, break-through of the Jugendstil, historical influences returned on the crest of a new wave of romanticism.

II THE JUGENDSTIL

Shortly before 1900 creative artists in several parts of Europe were seized by a curious restlessness. They turned their backs on pure art, and began to devote themselves to the applied arts. There were a number of reasons for this change. The romantic ideal of inspired craftsmanship—as glorified by Ruskin and realised by William Morris—was perhaps the most important cause of this search for a new fulfilment. As the new movement got under way, the craft aspect was pushed more into the background, though never lost sight of, and in the twentieth century inspired the Arts and Crafts movement. But first it was to be overwhelmed by a new concept of form, which emphatically did not aim at utility. The new style was dynamic in the extreme—it was movement itself. It manifested itself in various ways—in sweeping lines and fluttering ribbons,

103

in tendrils and the tangled shapes of seaweed, in smoke and running water, in veils and wind-swept hair. Nowhere was Art Nouveau, this rebellion against the tradition-loving nineteenth century, more tellingly named than in Germany, where from the outset it was known as the Jugendstil.

FOUR PERIODICALS

Four periodicals turned against the dying century. *Pan* (1895–1900) tried to make tradition and its formative powers the pacemaker for the contemporary. The periodical failed because in the long run it was impossible—figuratively speaking—to put old wine into new skins. But without a doubt *Pan* was a valuable proving-ground; most of the important new departures of the next twenty years can be traced back to this periodical. The Munich periodical *Jugend* whose name may have given the style its name was founded in 1896 by Georg Hirth, a pioneer of the Munich Renaissance. It was by no means typical of what we mean by Jugendstil today. It was not committed to any theory and took part almost unconsciously in the dissolution of traditional forms. Symbolistic mysticism, the trend towards the abstract, the abandonment of everything firm and certain—all these were far from the mind of its editor. It was full of zest and talkative, but its cover illustrations at any rate are among the significant examples of Jugendstil. Everything in them was movement. The trends of the new style can be seen even in the changing title-line of every issue—as dozens of examples will prove. Together with *Jugend* appeared the periodical *Simplicissimus*, founded in 1896 by Albert Langen (1869–1909), a passionate lover of books and art. From the start the periodical had a culturally critical bent, and was given to satire. During its first six years its leading illustrator was Th. Th. Heine (1867–1948). He enlisted the sweeping lines of the Jugendstil in the service of biting satire. Later a young genius from Scandinavia, Olav Gulbransson (1873–1958), came to the fore. His work also developed in the fields of parody and caricature. But behind every graphic exaggeration could be sensed a sincere and sometimes profound humanity. His graphic mastery gave the art of satire and humorous book illustration a status seldom attained in Germany. *Die Insel* (1899–1902), also the result of dilettante publishing fervour, was, so to speak, the continuation of *Pan*. It was founded by Alfred Walter von Heymel (1878–1914) of Bremen, helped by his cousin Rudolf Alexander Schröder (1878–1962), and out of it later grew the famous publishing house, Insel-Verlag. The Insel-Bücherei (founded 1912), which belonged to this house, gained its editorial programme from the periodical, and its characteristic appearance, valid to this day: board bindings with decorative covers and pasted-on title labels. The third quarterly issue of *Die Insel* in 1900 was a milestone in the history of German book design—a turning-point in the work of E. R. Weiss, and at the same time one of the most important signals for the abandonment of the Jugendstil and the beginning of a new era in book design.

If everything inert is turned into movement, all mass into energy, then lettering too becomes painterly or a structure of rhythmically ordered lines. That is how Rudolf von Larisch's decorative letters began, related to the poster lettering of Toulouse-Lautrec and the gothicising alphabets of Melchior Lechter. The dissolution of traditional letterforms which took place in the Austrian version of the new style stimulated German type designers like Rudolf Koch and F. H. Ehmcke to experiment with decorative faces, particularly at the beginning of the twentieth century. These experiments, interrupted for several decades, were recently taken up again, for instance at Hamburg and Mainz.

OTTO ECKMANN

The master of Jugendstil decoration, the most important and versatile of those who practised this aesthetic movement, which rose so meteorically and exhausted itself within a decade, was Otto Eckmann (1865–1902). After early successes Eckmann had abruptly abandoned painting, and decided to make man's environment—his home and utensils, and thus books and type faces—his new sphere of activities. Eckmann's organically lively borders in *Pan* began to attract attention; at Munich's seventh Glaspalast exhibition visitors crowded his exhibits of metalwork, glassware, and graphic design. His early carpets have as their dominating motif swans and watercourses—which soon enjoyed widespread popularity—but later abstract patterns began to appear in carpets and on the many bindings he designed in a brief few years for the publishing house of S. Fischer. By putting plant patterns at the service of his dynamic style in a quite uninhibited and undoctrinaire way, he became the antithesis of Henry van de Velde, who considered everything concrete as the enemy of expressive decoration. Encouraged by the young Offenbach typefounder, Karl Klingspor, Eckmann also tried his hand at designing printing types. These he based on gothic forms, designing them with a brush and thus producing softly-contoured, expansive letters. None of this would ever have become an effective bookface if his typefounders and punch-cutters had not throughly adapted his designs. Fundamentally the discipline of the punch and the tightly regimented order of a line of type contradict Jugendstil letterforms. The same process was repeated with a face by Peter Behrens (1868-1940). In both cases the transformation into a usable printing type, though of highly individual design, is a symptom of the liquidation of the Jugendstil. Its dynamism slowed down, and by 1902, the year of Eckmann's death, all essential possibilities of the style had come to full flower. What followed was a mere echo and a dying chord. Henceforth industry exploited the store of new forms. As it became popular, Jugendstil descended to a lower level of taste. E. R. Weiss became the leader of a new style in type and book design. Peter Behrens devoted himself exclusively to architecture and industrial design.

MELCHIOR LECHTER

One man who remained rooted in the Jugendstil was Melchior Lechter (1865-1937), who created the graphic and typographic style for Stefan George's circle. Starting with the fundamental Jugendstil principle that environment and habits should be fitting for the soul of man, he adapted his ornamentation and lettering to the almost religious ideas of George and his disciples. His quasi-gothic titlings and book decorations always kept at a distance from their related historic forms. Maeterlinck's *Schatz der Armen* (1898), for Eugen Diederichs' publishing house, and *Das Jahr der Seele* (1897) and *Der Teppich des Lebens* (1900), by Stefan George, were early pinnacles of his great ability to convey a balance between the mysticism of the soul and the cult of beauty. In Lechter's life, just as in George's, there was no chopping and changing. While the George circle progressively lost its sectarian character, Lechter's style calcified. The five works from his Einhorn-Presse (Unicorn Press—1905-35) stuck to the symbolism of the turn of the century, towering magnificently, though oddly, into an era which was practical, romantic, and individualistic.

In the course of some ten years—between 1895 and 1905—the change of style in Europe penetrated into practically every field of design. The graphic arts—type, book, and binding design—were the least affected by this change. The new style was limited to the outside of the book and the decoration of a few of its inside pages, since both the printed page and the body of the book, as befits their conservative nature, could not be turned into illusions of movement. The destruction of the nineteenth-century's historicising habits was almost complete, and tradition was pushed into the background. Everything modern, everything that had never been seen before, was given higher status. Historical values have never quite recovered from this rout, and the label 'modern' is still a term of high praise. This is as true of popular taste as of the arts, but it does not apply to really discriminating bibliophiles, their publishers and designers. For the past ten years there has been no lack of attempts to make the aesthetic phenomenon of 1900 the sole basis of current artistic endeavour. Indeed, we encounter many works of a dynamic, irrational, and formalistic character, which steadily, or like a streak of lighting, remind us of the awakening of youth in those days. But only one part of current design falls into that category. Another—the greater, perhaps—originates in the rational and pragmatic decades that followed the turn of the century.

III CRAFTSMANSHIP/ROMANTICISM/INDIVIDUALISM

ARTS AND CRAFTS BOOK DESIGN

In 1901 the Steglitzer Werkstatt, a working group of young graphic artists, called for a stand against exaggerated decorative trends. In October 1907, the Deutsche Werkbund was founded in Munich. Among the founders were F. H. Ehmcke (1878–1965), the spokesman of the Steglitzer Werkstatt; the publisher Eugen Diederichs; the architect Hermann Muthesius; and the industrialists Wolf Dohrn and Peter Bruckmann. At first the new group took as lively an interest in publishing and typography as in industrial design and architecture. The Werkbund did not represent any particular style, but unanimously rejected decorative formalism and advocated functional working methods. For more than thirty years now, the Deutsche Werkbund has had next to nothing to do with the graphic arts, devoting nearly all its energies to industrial design and architecture. But in its first twenty years it exerted a most valuable influence on the art of the book. Its respect for materials affected paper and bindings. Design and materials had to be appropriate—the word 'decorative' was anathema. The job of applied art was to serve its purpose and to represent. But the style that superseded Jugendstil is more than merely practical and fit for its purpose. It also respects tradition, and tends towards individualism. The new style was pragmatic, personal, and true to tradition—one might

107

call it romantic-individualist pragmatism. A new wave of romanticism—represented in literature by Rilke, Stefan George, and Hofmannsthal—was carried by a feeling of spiritual kinship with the historical epochs in which Germany's culture is rooted. Karl Klingspor made the Jugendstil's attempts at type design right for the age. His designers, Otto Hupp, Walter Tiemann and Rudolf Koch, called on the traditional forms of 500 years to create their own forms. They did not imitate them, but produced something original. Before long Klingspor became the model for the small number of typefoundries still active in the twentieth century. Like Klingspor, they afforded their designers freedom to let their creative personalities develop; there was D. Stempel, who sponsored the work of F. W. Kleukens and F. H. Ehmcke; C. E. Weber (G. Trump); and the Bauersche Giesserei (E. R. Weiss and Paul Renner, later also Ernst F. H. Schneidler). During the period 1905 to 1945 the initiative for new type faces came chiefly from the designers, whereas earlier and subsequently it was usually the typefounder who commissioned them. The determining factor was the principle of personality. There was no such thing as division of labour. Every type designer wanted to modify all current and traditional type faces according to his own taste. Thus individual *œuvres* stand side by side like self-contained families. There are faces by Tiemann, Trump, and Schneidler based on seventeenth-century Dutch Gothic, old face romans by Tiemann, Weiss, Ehmcke, and Trump. This wealth of variations was not thought confusing: it met the great demand for a wide choice of individualistic type designs.

ROMANTIC INDIVIDUALISM

From the very first after founding his publishing house in Florence (1896) Eugen Diederichs (1867–1930) worked on the principle that the contents of every book must be given appropriate typographical expression. This became the guiding light of twentieth-century romantic individualism. This differentiation was achieved in three stages: there was typifying, characterising, and individualising book design, and these three stages were also reflected in production. By the choice of format and paper several distinct types of book were developed: this resulted in different groups. Page image and binding could be differentiated by sharper characterisation. Illustrations and dust jacket offered the maximum opportunity for individualism. The style of the great publisher, translator, and book designer Jakob Hegner (1882–1962) exemplified the tastes of a certain type of reader—the Christian intellectual. The Insel-Verlag, whose output had greater variety, made the design of its books characteristic of individual authors or series. The house of S. Fischer tried to solve its design problems by making its works as individual as possible. All this, aiming at appropriateness and the self-containment of individual or group, contrasted dramatically with the Jugendstil, which tried to merge everything into an all-embracing universe, or make it a small particle in a great flow. While Jugendstil, which would treat a songbook and a cookery book in the same way, tended towards formalism, its successor tried to be craftsmanlike and practical. The dynamic design dominant in 1900 wanted to be recognised above all by its total effect. Werkbund individualism, on the other hand, aimed at appropriateness and differentiation. For Eugen Diederichs book publishing was an extension of his personality. Similarly the publishing ventures of Albert Langen, Georg Müller, and Hans von Weber, so astonishingly versatile and wide-ranging, have their origin in the wish to unfold themselves rather than in any narrow programme.

One of the citadels of individualism was the Staatliche Akademie der graphischen Künste (State Academy for the Graphic Arts) at Leipzig, where Walter Tiemann (1876–1951) taught from 1903, for more than twenty years as its head. He enlisted the services of the outstanding calligrapher of the thirties, Rudo Spemann (1905–47), and the best bookbinder of that time, Ignatz Wiemeler (1895–1952). In contrast with other schools—Stuttgart, Offenbach, and Munich—no specific style developed at Leipzig. Tiemann provided every possible opportunity for the unfolding of individual talent, in keeping with his urbane and unrestricted outlook. Like most type and book designers of the first half of the twentieth century he was a painter and illustrator. Next to Rudolf Koch he was the most important and prolific type designer at the Klingspor typefoundry. Together with his friend C. E. Poeschel he created an image for the publishing house of Julius Zeitler, of Leipzig, which had an active and imaginative life between 1904 and 1912. Later, it was chiefly the Insel-Verlag whose style he influenced, unobtrusively but lastingly. Soon after 1905, when Anton Kippenberg (1874–1950) had taken over this publishing house (its name derives from the periodical), it became famous for its literary achievements and its book design. By enlisting the help of English talents (Eric Gill, Emery Walker) Kippenberg kept his classics free from all contact with the dying Jugendstil. He stimulated and sponsored the German private presses, from the Ernst-Ludwig-Presse (1907) to the Drugulin-Presse (1938). The Insel-Bücherei, founded by Kippenberg in 1912 as a continuation, so to speak, of the magazine that had closed down in 1902, produced some eight hundred titles in 50 million little volumes in the first fifty years of its life.

From 1900 to 1950 few book designers acted exclusively for one publishing house. They worked free-lance, and were retained by publishers for particular books or collections. They were chosen according to their suitability for a particular task. Thus a group of independent publishers confronted a group of independent designers. Curiously, and more by accident than design, certain affinities nevertheless developed. Thus Tiemann, in spite of his many other connections, basically belonged to the Insel-Verlag; Ehmcke collaborated with Eugen Diederichs for twenty-five years and gave his publications their particular character, though Diederichs also commissioned single and group designs from E. R. Weiss, and some important early work from Ernst Schneidler, who later founded the Stuttgart school. It may have been the mysterious attraction of opposites that led to Diederichs' and Ehmcke's long collaboration. Diederichs was a grave North German. For his epitaph he chose *In Willen und Sehnsucht* ('In will and longing'). Filled with a passionate desire to gather around him the intellect and spirit of the world and of his nation, he made his publishing ventures almost limitless. His gigantic work was backed by great forces of native vitality. To the observer his collections, e.g. Märchen der Weltliteratur, Atlantis, and Das Zeitalter der Renaissance, seem rich and complete. For Diederichs all this was a mere beginning, a transition, something growing. His work could not be completed. Completion would have been against his nature. In contrast, Ehmcke was the persevering type, who weighed up and secured. His life's work rests on circumspection, completeness, and self-discipline. Ehmcke never tried to reach the unattainable, and thus his work is rarely incomplete. He seldom experimented and always tried to make a complete statement in his work. Hence he became the master of the device: it was he who designed the best versions of the Diederichs lion and the Ullstein owl. While his client, Diederichs, never reached this destination, was always on the road to it, Ehmcke secured the fragments, the phases of this journey. It is a great pity that he was able to influence permanently, only the early days of the publishing house (from 1902). In the later years of his life Eugen Diederichs' elasticity seems to have flagged, and his horizon to have shrunk. The great contributions to Germany's book production at the turn of the century had been made: the festive title pages of the Renaissance documents, Ehmcke's *Faust* (1909), the *Upanishads des Veda*, with type by Behrens (1914), and the collection *Sammlung Thule* (1912), the last two designed by Schneidler.

In 1903, at Munich, the young publisher Georg Müller (1877–1917) founded a 'belle-lettres' publishing concern, which produced no fewer than 400 titles in the first five years. In 1913, as many as 287 first and new editions were published. Georg Müller's aim was to enable every cultured German home to possess virtually all the treasures of world literature in critically edited complete editions. In 1907 Müller engaged the painter and architect Paul Renner (1878–1956) to take charge of design and production. Renner collaborated in this enormous venture for ten years, when it was cut short by Müller's untimely death. Most of the material was a hundred years old or more. Fear of the historical was forgotten: Renner almost exclusively used historical types and ornaments. Publisher and designer totally rejected rationalisation. Design depended on mood and subject. To this day Georg Müller's library editions are appreciated for their convincingly apt typography and bindings. What was produced by the firm after the death of its founder in 1917 is of little importance from the point of view of book design; Renner's work between 1907 and 1917 substantially contributed to the abandonment of the Jugendstil and a new attitude towards the historical.

Of all the publishing houses, S. Fischer played the most effective part in practising individually tailored book design during the first four decades of this century. Previously Eckmann had been commissioned to do many books. Though during that time Jugendstil decorations predominated, there are the beginnings of more special characterisation. Series of illustrations and complete book designs of the works of Thomas Mann and Hermann Hesse were among the work done over some thirty years by the Swiss painter and designer, Karl Walser (b. 1877). The illustrator and book designer Hans Meid (1883–1957) frequently contributed visual accompaniment for all parts of the book —the actual designer for S. Fischer before 1942 was E. R. Weiss, the outstanding and consistently most individual among the book designers of his day.

He also decisively influenced the dust jacket. This outer cover, which protects, appeals, explains, and represents, was considered by E. R. Weiss and his contemporaries as part of the book—the most personal and expressive part, in fact. Here individualism could find its fullest expression. Its forerunner had been the sturdy paper cover of the early Werkbund days, whose printing was identical with that on the binding. Still earlier, before 1900, the Broschur-Schauseite had made its appearance as a modest sales-aid and informative broadsheet—the influence of Toulouse-Lautrec can be felt. The 1930's were the heyday of the detachable dust jacket—independent, yet part of the book. E. R. Weiss, who had made significant contributions to the dust jacket in all its earlier phases, was decidedly the leading designer of jackets, which stylistically

are also the most impressive symbol of romantic-individualistic functionalism.

From 1927 a competitor began to make his appearance: Georg Salter (b.
1897), originally a stage designer. He did not see the dust jacket as an integral
part of the book, but as an informative addition, and, above all, as an indispensable advertising medium. He did not subscribe to the rule that the jacket
had to express what was inside the book. He *staged* his work, i.e. he used any
means that helped to put the book across to the prospective buyer. Between
1927 and 1934, when he emigrated to the United States, Salter, by means of
his precise theatrical technique, perfected the individualisation of the book in
his own way. At the same time he pointed the way to a new phase in jacket
design which was to be characteristic of the style of the early fifties.

As a young poet, painter, and graphic designer, Emil Rudolf Weiss (1875–
1942) was one of the great hopes of the Jugendstil. Yet he proved himself a
master at Werkbund-inspired, imaginatively functional design in his work
for S. Fischer, Eugen Diederichs, and the Insel-Verlag. He gave the publications of the Marées-Gesellschaft and the Tempel-Klassiker (Temple Classics)
their distinguished form. His work brought out all the characteristics of the
Werkbund and of romantic individualism. He was the chief protagonist of a
style that lasted from the beginning to almost the middle of this century. The
quarterly issue of *Die Insel* (mentioned earlier), which was designed by Weiss
in 1900, is not merely an indication of the development of the young Weiss
but also signalled the turn from Jugendstil to the individualism of the Werkbund. All decoration exactly suited the text, and was not merely dynamic and
in keeping with the style fashionable in 1900. It may have been his contact
with Eugen Diederichs and later with Georg Müller that awakened a feeling
for historical values in the young Jugendstil artist. Though he worked with
deep enthusiasm his work soon became disciplined and thus he was the favourite designer for complete editions and collections. In the course of thirty
years he designed nearly all collected editions of Gerhard Hauptmann for S.
Fischer, apart from numerous complete editions for Diederichs and Insel. He
proved himself a remarkable illustrator in his own travel book, *Drei Monate in
Spanien* (1931). The tribute in honour of his fiftieth birthday (*Festschrift*, Bauer
Typefoundry, 1925) is both an interim statement of thirty years of active
work and one of the most important documents on design in the first quarter
of the twentieth century.

His biggest project was, undoubtedly, the Tempel-Klassiker, for which
he also designed the type. Here he attempted—as others had done before him

WALBAUM-ANTIQUA

—

A B C D E F G H I J
K L M N O P Q R S
T U V W X Y Z

a b c d e f g h i j k l
m n o p q r s t u v w
x y z

1 2 3 4 5 6 7 8 9 0
1 2 3 4 5 6 7 8 9 0

1. Specimen Type Sheet of Walbaum-Antiqua (c. 1803)

2. Stefan George: *Das Jahr der Seele*, Berlin (1897). Cover design by Melchior Lechter

3. Hermann Sudermann: *Johannes* (1898). Cover design by Otto Eckmann

**Ein Märchen vom Tod und eine fremde Nach=
schrift dazu.**

Jch schaute noch immer hinauf in den langsam ver=
löschenden Abendhimmel, als jemand sagte: ☞
„Sie scheinen sich ja für das Land da oben sehr
zu interessieren?“ ☞ Mein Blick fiel schnell,
wie heruntergeschossen, und ich erkannte: Jch war an die
niedere Mauer unseres kleinen Kirchhofs geraten und vor mir,

77

4. *Die Insel* (1900). Illustrated page designed by E. R. Weiss

Pinſel geſtaltet, ſondern geſchrieben und noch ſtark – wie faſt alle angewandte Kunſt jener Zeit und beſonders die von Behrens – unter dem Einfluß programmatiſcher Vorſtellungen ſtehend. Auch hier ergaben ſich ähnliche Schwierigkeiten wie bei Eck-mann. – Mit dieſen beiden Schriften von Eckmann und Behrens iſt die Sturm- und Drangzeit der damaligen Schriftbewegung mit ihrem ſtarken Wollen, ſich von über-

ABCDEFGHIKLMNOP
K Jı ORSTUDWXYZ
abcdefghiKlmnopqrsſltßtz
uvwxyz ß ſſ ſch ſK ü !,—-?
1234567890

Zeichnung von Peter Behrens zu ſeiner Schrift.

abcddefghijklmnopq
rſstuvwxyz chckſchß
ABCDEFGHIJKLMNO
PQRSTUDW3 124890

Druckſchrift von Peter Behrens, geſchnitten von Gebr. Klingſpor, Offenbach a. M. in den Jahren 1900 / 02. Die Abbildungen geben die Entwicklung der Behrens-Schrift von der Zeichnung bis zur Druckſchrift wieder.

5. Behrens-Schrift Type Specimen (1902). Designed by Peter Behrens

HYPERION
EINE ZWEIMONATSSCHRIFT
HERAUSGEGEBEN VON FRANZ
BLEI & CARL STERNHEIM

ERSTER
BAND

MÜNCHEN 1908
HANS VON WEBER / VERLAG

6. The Journal *Hyperion*, Munich (1908). Title-page designed by Walter
Tiemann

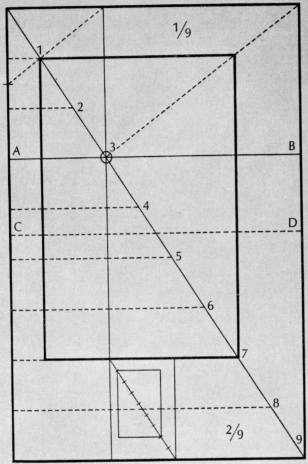

Raúl M. Rosarivo
DIVINA PROPORTIO TYPOGRAPHICA

$1/9$

1

2

A · B

3

4

C · D

5

6

7

8

$2/9$

9

Das Buch vom Goldenen typographischen Modul 1:1,5
in der Proportion 2:3, dem Modul
von Johannes Gutenberg und seiner Zeitgenossen

Scherpe Verlag in Krefeld

23. Rosarivo: *Divina Proportio Typographica* (1961). Designed by Hermann Zapf

Xanthias
Worüber?

Aiakos Es gilt in betreff der Künste hier ein Gesetz,
Daß, wer in einer von denen, die schön und edel sind,
Von seinen Kunstgenossen allen der Besten ist,
Die Ehrenspeisung, die in der Prytanei, dazu
Zunächst bei Pluton einen Sitz erhält —

Xanthias   Versteh!

Aiakos
Bis ein andrer herkommt, der in derselben Kunst noch mehr
Als jener kann, abtreten muß er dann den Thron.

Xanthias
Was hat denn aber jetzt den Aischylos aufgestört?

Aiakos
Er war es, der den tragischen Thron bisher besaß
Als unbestrittner Meister der Kunst.

Xanthias   Und wer denn jetzt?

Aiakos
Als drauf Euripides hergekommen, trat er gleich
Vor den Beutelschneidern, Taschendieben, Gaunervolk,
Den Vatermördern und anderm Lumpengesindel auf,
Die im Hades hier die Menge sind. Als diese nun
Sein mancherlei Einwurf, Wenn und Aber, Kniff und Pfiff
Gehört, da jauchzten sie, nannten den weisesten Dichter ihn,
So aufgeblasen nahm er den Thron, drauf Aischylos
Noch saß, in Anspruch.

Xanthias   Trieb man ihn nicht mit Steinen fort?

Aiakos
Bewahr, vielmehr schrie laut das Volk, ein Kunstgericht
Zu halten, wer von beiden der größere Meister sei.

Xanthias Das Schelmen-Volk?

24. Aristophanes: *Die Frösche*, Trajanus-Presse (1961). Illustration by
Imre Reiner

—to combine the rhythm and expressiveness of fraktur with the clarity and firmness of roman. Weiss-Fraktur, begun in 1908, is the most successful of all these experiments to date. Weiss used one of Unger's designs, made in the 1790's, as his starting point but he probably also had Breitkopf's Jean-Paul-Fraktur in mind. The Tempel-Klassiker covered the baroque, classicist, and romantic periods of literature. The type in which the books were set, and the very elastic binding decorations corresponded superbly with this literary background. The immense wealth of typographic ornament supplementing Weiss-Fraktur helped to create the appropriate mood, without being a mere imitation in period style. It was used for display and book typography as well as on the sides and spines of the bindings. Very soon, about 1913, the Tempel type began to be used outside the Klassiker group as well, and became a popular book face. In the bilingual Tempel editions it contrasted, yet harmonised successfully, with Tiemann old face, a roman popular at the time.

Next to these classics, Weiss's main task was Julius Meier-Graefe's 'Drucke der Marées-Gesellschaft', published by R. Piper between 1917 and 1929. The formats were as varied as the contents, ranging from octavo to imperial folio. Some were books, more often they were portfolios with loosely inserted texts. The literary programme of the Marées-Gesellschaft was a series of surprises, in which the Middle Ages, classical antiquity, the Far East, and the most recent artistic experiments were presented with great technical mastery. Gauguin, Cézanne and Renoir were vividly reproduced by facsimile collotype. In between there were texts by Goethe, Dostoyevsky or Novalis, usually illustrated. For the limited editions, totalling forty-seven titles, there were memorably designed prospectuses; and there was the annual *Ganymed*, of which five volumes appeared (1919–25). E. R. Weiss proved equal to the sometimes gigantic formats. The title-pages, full of deep pathos, are among the finest in German title design.

Some time after he had completed Weiss-Fraktur, E. R. Weiss once more turned to type design. Weiss roman, a type face which is used to this day in spite of its rather individual character, came out between 1925 and 1928; it was followed by Weiss-Gotisch (1936) and Weiss-Rundgotisch (1938)—late evidence of his unremitting care for the essence of German letterforms.

In spite of its variety, the book design of this great letterer and painter was, until 1920 characterising rather than individualising. In the thirties, the book of belles lettres underwent a change. Until then, the dust jacket had always been derived from the binding or paper cover. Everything was symmetrical, and borders were frequent. But a certain loosening-up began between 1912 and 1917. In the thirties and forties S. Fischer commissioned Weiss for the design of works by writers such as Jean Giono, Annette Kolb, Alexander Lernet-Holenia, and Oskar Loerke. Weiss separated the jacket from the book, not just physically, but also stylistically. The dust jacket afforded the greatest opportunity for giving the book individuality, though even in this late phase jacket and binding sometimes had the same drawing. They then served as joint vehicles of the individual character of the book. But on the whole Weiss strictly stuck to his three-fold task: the logical progression from the *typified* book itself, via the *characteristic* binding, to the *individualised* wrapper. All the best designs of his later years show this treble harmony.

What William Morris had accomplished for the arts and crafts in Britain, Rudolf Koch (1876–1934) did in Germany. They had in common a great veneration for the skills of the medieval craftsman and the early printer, and both mistrusted the rapid spread of industrial techniques. But while Morris took over many of the forms and typography of the early days of printing more or less unaltered, for Koch they were merely a stimulus and a means toward self-realisation as a craftsman. In his youth, under the influence of Rudolf von Larisch, he experimented with decorative alphabets. He came into his own when working at Offenbach for Klingspor (from 1906), and as a teacher (under Hugo Eberhardt) at the local Arts and Crafts School from 1908. The style of the Vienna Sezession and Jugendstil was alien to him. His talent for working in metals and woven fabrics, wood and stone, developed in the atmosphere of the young craft community around Hugo Eberhardt and Karl Klingspor. In everything, and above all, he was a penman and a designer of lettering. With F. H. Ehmcke and Ernst F. H. Schneidler he made the written word the basis of all work on printing type. For Koch the letter was the supreme expression of the human soul, the most important means of communication with the future and the past, with that which is closest and that which is highest— that is, with God. All materials, all utensils, attained a deeper meaning and greater significance as carriers of lettering. He put his calligraphic compositions, ornaments, and symbols not just on paper or parchment: the written word was also the origin of embroidered ceremonial robes and tapestries. The façade of Strassburg cathedral (1933) was not drawn but 'written' with a broad reed. In their manifold use of writing Koch and Larisch (1854–1934) were similar. But the work of the older man was part of the strangely dynamic movement of 1900, whereas the younger devoted his craft entirely to each individual task. Each thing he did, however, had its root in common ground. Rudolf Koch was the artisan of God, and the community of craftsmen around him were like a Christian order. His belief in the expressive power of writing bore the marks of a magical religious concept. Teaching and creating were for him tasks that carried great responsibility.

He was one of the strongest personalities of the romantic-individualistic phase and so gave new life to the entire range of type faces. His empathy for the old craft spirit was total, yet his way of re-interpreting traditional forms was free and even wilful. In fraktur he only saw delicacy (Frühling, 1913); his idea of roman tended towards extremes: the utmost severity of Marathon (1930) and elegant clarity of Koch-Antiqua (1918–22). His most mature narrow gothic face (Wilhelm-Klingspor-Schrift; 1920–26) was majestic and dignified. His round gothic designs (Wallau, 1925–30, and Peter Jessen, 1924–30) were a continuation of the attempts around 1900 to find a common German type face. The sans serifs of the age of technology he turned into the compass-constructed Kabel (1926–9). Some of his types, such as Neuland, consisting of heavy capitals (1922–3), or Claudius (1931–7), cannot easily be fitted into accepted categories.

Together with Rudolf Gerstung he produced the Rudolfinische Drucke (1911–24). These were occasional pieces of printing, done with great native strength; outstanding among them the block-books *Jesaia* and *Elia*. As early as 1914, and in more spacious conditions in 1921, young craftsmen began to collect around the master, who was always both teaching and learning. They wrote and spun, wove and dyed, cut in wood and metal, set type and embroidered. Here, too, the great map of Germany was created (1933). Everything was tried communally, but they managed only temporarily to overcome their natural individualism. Individual talents and accomplishments soon became apparent. Fritz Arnold, for instance, was first and foremost a printer, Fritz Kredel a wood-engraver (*Blumenbuch*, 1928), Berthold Wolpe a designer of devices. Herbert Post was among the scribes, and later a type designer (e.g. Post-Antiqua, 1937). Other scribes were Karl Vollmer, Hans Schreiber, and Friedrich Heinrichsen, all of whom continued in the spirit of the Offenbach workshop as teachers and designers. Rudolf Koch's son Paul carried on this workshop life at Haus Fürsteneck in Frankfurt-am-Main, specialising in the setting of folk and church music. Ignatz Wiemeler, the distinguished bookbinder taught side by side with Koch at the Offenbach School; so, from 1936, did Willy Harwerth, one of Tiemann's pupils, as head of the illustration class. Ernst Engel, who had brought Koch and the head of the school together, taught the young craftsmen to print on the hand-press.

Rudolf Koch and his workshop, together with Hugo Eberhardt, the distinguished Hessian architect, and Karl Klingspor, typefounder and patron, have made the name Offenbach a symbol of renewal in design through craftsmanship. Offenbach's influence did not depend on a large organisation or great capital resources, but on individual people. This gave it its remarkable and unique character, but also explains the transitory nature of this sort of creative life. The Klingspor Museum, endowed by the great typefounder, preserves not only the memory of those brilliant decades until Koch's death in 1934, but, using new means, also projects the spirit of its founding fathers into the future.

Ernst F. H. Schneidler (1882–1956), like his teacher Peter Behrens, began to study art as an architect at Düsseldorf. He owed a lot to F. H. Ehmcke (only slightly his senior), who brought him into contact with Eugen Diederichs, for whose publishing house he worked as an illustrator (*Hafis*, 1912) and book designer (*Thule*, 1912) particularly between 1910 and 1913. Together with Ehmcke and Poeschel he designed *Die Upanishads des Veda* (1914). From 1912 he began to apply himself to type design. Yet the only faces that ever achieved general recognition were issued in his later years, in 1937 and 1938—namely, his light Schneidler-Mediaeval, which shows to its best advantage in the *Römische Elegien*, with drawings by Yngve Berg (1938); his fascinating Zentenar-Fraktur, which has a magnificent alphabet of initials; and finally Legende, the starting point of all recent script faces, such as Roger Excoffon's Mistral (1953). For nearly thirty years Schneidler taught at the Stuttgarter Akademie from 1920 (when it was called the Württembergische Kunstgewerbeschule) until 1948. Here he laid the foundation of a style highly regarded today—that of the Stuttgart School. His Juniperus-Presse published fifteen titles between 1921 and 1925, some of them purely typographical, others printed on a handpress and illustrated by, for instance, Imre Reiner. The influence of the Stuttgart School is entirely the result of his teaching. He avoided publishing his own work, but from 1925 he began to collect the studies which had been produced under his influence. By 1933 the collection had grown to 700 sheets, which filled four large boxes. He only published the collection in 1945 in a small edition. Only about seventy complete sets may have come on to the market. They show in letterpress and lithography, in pictures and type, 'how to write or draw; how the basic, forms of a face are developed and modified'. They were 'studies for those who make books', but they also included abstract illustrations, trade marks and package designs. A particularly impressive item was the complete typographical design for an edition of Horace. The fragmentary character of the collections, which became famous as *Der Wasser-*

mann, was partly due to the adverse political climate at the time it was being formed; but the curiously unfinished quality of this admirable collection is just as much the result of Schneidler's aversion for everything finished and complete. He mistrusted all polishing and rounding-off. This was also evident in his later type faces. Handwriting for him was forever something growing, precious because incomplete, and yet full of hope. There is nothing more significant for Schneidler's dedication to *writing* than his exercises, which he continued until his last years, and in which he tried attain the ultimate in calligraphic expression. He would write a poem, a few lines, a name, a hundred times—as if transported—until he had turned language into image. During his Stuttgart years he became more and more a painter, not only in his subtle colour compositions, but also in his calligraphy. How a man like Schneidler, never satisfied, always searching, could have had such a lasting influence on generations of pupils remains one of the mysteries of teaching. Many of his students began to distinguish themselves even in their teacher's lifetime. Martin Kausche and H. H. Hagedorn became well-known lettering and book designers. Imre Reiner is one of the most brilliant wood-engravers of our time. Georg Trump has become famous chiefly for his type designs. Rudo Spemann became the leading calligrapher, Carl Keidel a fine typographer and printer. Eva Aschoff carried Schneidler's spirit into bookbinding and her decorated papers, which are among the best of our time. Walter Brudi, versatile like his master and, like him, concentrating on lettering, at present teaches at the Stuttgarter Akademie and upholds the great tradition which Schneidler established.

GERMAN PRIVATE PRESSES

A press, in German, denotes a printing implement as well as a printing workshop under intelligent and intellectual guidance. Here literary or graphic themes are weighed up, edited, and printed—occasionally also bound and sold. The private press is the home of the fine book. The difference between a private press and a publishing house with its own printing office is in the manner of working. The private-press printer is sure that his craftsmanship and the use of materials made by craftsmen are superior to industrial methods of manufacture.

It was the English private presses that inspired the Germans. Their actual origin was the glorification of the craftsman by William Morris and his Kelmscott Press (1891–8). Type and the book page were, however, more profoundly influenced by those who followed Morris, namely the Doves Press (1900–1916), whose character was determined by T. J. Cobden-Sanderson (1840–1922), and Emery Walker (1851–1933). Whereas the Kelmscott Press, to which Morris devoted the last six years of his life, laid great store by illustration and rich book decoration, the Doves Press concentrated on pure typography. This was the example followed by most German private presses, among them the first two, which started in 1907: the Janus-Presse, Leipzig, on which W. Tiemann and C. E. Poeschel produced a number of fine pieces; and the Ernst-Ludwig-Presse, founded by the brothers Friedrich Wilhelm and Christian Heinrich Kleukens at Darmstadt, under the patronage of the art enthusiast Grand-Duke Ernst Ludwig.

Together with F. H. Ehmcke and C. Belwe, F. W. Kleukens (1878–1956) ran the Steglitzer Werkstatt from 1900 to 1903—the first group enterprise for applied graphic art. He left the Ernst-Ludwig-Presse in 1914, and after the war, in 1919, founded the Ratio-Presse. It differed considerably in its choice of type, its typography, and its frequent use of illustration from the Ernst-Ludwig-Presse, where he had had to limit himself to initials and the decorating of title pages. Kleukens's early type faces differed from others current at the turn of the century and older ones in certain details, such as very short descenders. His later Ratio-Latein, however, was close to the Bodoni tradition.

C. H. Kleukens (1880–1955), whose policy at the Ernst-Ludwig-Presse had been to eschew all illustration, ran the press with an expanded programme from 1918 until 1937. It produced occasional work for the Grand-ducal house and other bibliophiles. Among these were ten 'books of hours' for Kurt Wolff (1920–22). Shortly after the First World War Kleukens, who now also began to design type faces, moved the press to Mainz, where he founded the Mainzer-Presse in 1927. Within ten years his press produced as many as fifty works. They were set in his own types, most of which were closely related with the early roman faces. Two projects were never completed: a monumental world edition of Goethe and a Shakespeare edition in many volumes. The press did not survive the Second World War.

F. H. Ehmcke's typography, which began to be widely known from 1909, was nowhere more impressive than in his work for the Rupprecht-Presse, which he ran in Munich between 1913 and 1934. The popular Crown Prince of Bavaria had acted as godfather at its christening. In the course of twenty years fifty-seven hand-printed works in small editions of 150 to 250 appeared with splendid regularity. They were all set in Ehmcke's own type faces, which form a conspectus of typographic tradition as interpreted by him: Fraktur, Schwabacher, Antiqua, Rustica, and their respective italics. No other private press has rendered Germany's national typography with greater variety and was less influenced by the rest of Europe than the Rupprecht-Presse, which ideally complemented Ehmcke's teaching at the Kunstgewerbeschule at Munich (today the Akademie). Ehmcke had fought the Jugendstil: a good many of the ideas of Germany's Werkbund movement derive from this designer and teacher, who succeeded in holding together generations of pupils in his circle. Indeed, Ehmcke can be called the founder of a distinct Munich school.

Apart from important works of world literature (Hölderlin, Dante, the Apocalypse) the Rupprecht-Presse produced lesser-known works from Germany's classic and romantic literature. Ehmcke confined himself to purely typographic expression, but within these limitations his work was amazingly varied and embraced every way of using and designing type. During most of his long life he worked not only as a designer, but also as a teacher, lecturer, and author. But none of the work of this true master and politician of typography was as important as his Rupprecht-Presse.

Of the German private presses that adhered to the strictest typographical forms none exerted a wider influence than the Bremer Presse (1911–39). It was born out of a happy combination of North- and South-German artists and enthusiasts. Among its founders were R. A. Schröder and L. Wolde, Hugo von Hofmannsthal and R. Borchardt. But the essential impetus came from Willy Wiegand (1886–1961). The press confined itself to a few sizes of a roman based on the earliest incunabula, a Greek fount, a liturgical face (for the great Missal), and a kind of round gothic for Martin Luther's New High German. Apart from the initials drawn by Edward Johnston's pupil, Anna Simons, the press, with one exception, did without any ornaments. It was deeply dedicated to the ideals of humanism and produced large-format works that are among the summits of book production in the first half of the twentieth century: Sophocles and Tacitus, Dante and Goethe, Homer and St Augustine, the five-volume Luther Bible and a psalter in Luther's translation. From 1922 the hand-set books were also printed on power-driven presses and distributed by the publishing branch of the Bremer Presse. Most of these works were of an educational nature: Hofmannthal's *Deutsches Lesebuch*, Borchardt's *Der Deutsche in der Landschaft*, and others. Two of the strangest publications were *Die Verfassung des Deutschen Reiches* (The Constitution of the German Reich) and Wiegand's *Vesalius*—the latter for a medical society in New York, incorporating woodcuts discovered by the editor and designer. Economic and political difficulties between 1930 and 1943 created increasing difficulties for the Bremer Presse, and ultimately killed it. It has had a greater and more lasting influence on the graphic arts than any other workshop.

Eduard Wilhelm Tieffenbach (1883–1948) and his Officina Serpentis (founded 1911) are closely related to the English private presses, both in origin and in working methods. However, its style differs from that of the Doves Press, for instance, in its use of an almost ornamental type face. This was a markedly rounded, sprightly gothic, frequently used in combination with illustrations, initials, and decorative borders. For Tieffenbach typography was the successor of and substitute for handwriting. Like Gutenberg he aimed at typography in the manner of the old scribes. After 1918 he began to specialise in large and small productions for bibliophile societies. He gradually introduced typefaces other than his own, among them Leibniz-Fraktur, Elzévir, Fleischmann- and Walbaum-Antiqua, Schwabacher, and Unger. For Tieffenbach the enthusiast, and his wife, who was his indispensable helper, there was no Past. The early days of printing were the Present for him—a romantic reality.

In its origin, the Italian Officina Bodoni is related to the German private presses. Hans Mardersteig (b. 1892), of Weimar, founded it in Rome in 1922, moved it to Montagnola in the Ticino in 1923, and finally to Verona in 1927— where it was able to develop fully. He had obtained permission to use Bodoni's matrices, which were kept at the Parma Museum. Between 1927 and 1936 the Italian Government commissioned him to set and print the collected works of Gabriele d'Annunzio—forty-nine volumes, some of them with up to 500 pages, 300 copies of which were printed by hand on vellum and imperial Japan and a further 2,500 on Fabriano paper, printed on cylinder presses. True to his principles not to cheapen Bodoni's memory by imitation, Mardersteig did not use only the Parma typographical archives. He developed some remarkable types for hand and Monotype setting from old Italian models. As printer for important clients in Italy, Britain, Germany and other countries, Mardersteig made hand-printing a direct model for high-speed presswork. The story of the early days of his press and a list of the first six years' production are contained in his *Werkbuch*, which Frans Masereel illustrated with twelve full-page woodcuts. The work of the Officina Bodoni is a happy combination of Italy's great tradition with the rebirth of craftsmanship in England and Germany.

The Cranach-Presse is the embodiment of everything European among German private presses. The creation of Count Harry Kessler (1868–1937), it was active, undergoing several changes, from 1913 until the beginning of the Hitler régime, which forced Kessler to emigrate and brought work to a standstill. Because of Europe's tragic disruption Count Kessler's work remained fragmentary. A few productions of the press at Weimar are among the immortal treasures of the art of the book in Germany, such as the German-English edition of Rilke's *Duineser Elegien* and the *Hohelied Salomonis* illustrated by Eric Gill. Even more is this true of Shakespeare's *Hamlet*, with woodcuts by Edward Gordon Craig, and Virgil's *Eclogen*, with woodcuts by Aristide Maillol. These are true examples of the European creative spirit—long dreamt of, realised over many years of endeavour, and soon after buried by an avalanche of barbaric nationalism.

Count Kessler, though German by origin, was equally at home in Paris, and London, in Bonn, Weimar, and Berlin. Eric Gill and Emery Walker were his English friends. He inspired Aristide Maillol (1861–1945) to try his hand at woodcuts. This is how the three editions of Virgil's *Eclogues* came to be produced—in Latin, with French, English, and German translations. They were begun as far back as 1913 and completed in 1927. The roman for this work was cut by Edward Prince from instructions by Emery Walker. The paper was hand-made by Maillol's nephew Gaspard, at Monval near Paris. His *Hamlet*, based on the text of the second quarto, and translated (1929) by Gerhart Hauptmann, was quite different. It represented the other side of Kessler's personality —the pull that the northern world exerted on him. Kessler used a gothic face with long ascenders for the German text of the play and a smaller round gothic for prose commentary in several languages. Both designs were by Edward Johnston, and again they were cut by Edward Prince. The dark page was made even more sombre by Craig's monumental woodcuts. Mediterranean clarity and the melancholy North: the two great pieces of printing symbolise these two poles that determined Kessler's life. His mission was to resolve the tensions between North and South, East and West, into a greater European harmony. The tragedy of his life was that he did not succeed.

Hans von Weber (1872–1924) was one of those to whom publishing gave a heightened sense of existence and for whom it was the true fulfilment of life. When he founded his publishing house at Munich in 1906 he was not concerned with the number of titles he could publish but with quality of design. In March 1908 he announced the appearance of his bi-monthly *Hyperion*, a successor of *Insel*, though significantly modified. Jugendstil was already a thing of the past, and history could once more exert its full magic. Weber welcomed the old original types of Drugulin in Leipzig, and Enschedé & Zonen in Haarlem. His publications are a museum of old type faces, from Schwabacher to Unger and Didot. Almost the only contemporary faces he used were those of Tiemann, Ehmcke, and Koch. Weber is best known for his Drucke für die Hundert (1909–23), 39 hand-printed works in all, in tiny editions, as the name implies. His speciality was the world of Germanic and Nordic sagas, and treasures of German literature from courtly poetry to Nietzsche. The collection opened with a re-creation of the oldest printed version of the Tristan legend of 1484. Many volumes were illustrated, by Max Unold, Emil Preetorius, and others. In his house journal, *Der Winkelhaken* (The Composing Stick, from 1913), the publisher explained his aims and work. Apart from this series he also published the Hyperion-Drucke (1912–14), with texts by Goethe, Byron, Dante, and others. These were masterpieces of printing by Poeschel and Enschedé & Zonen. Among them too, is Eichendorff's *Leben eines Taugenichts*, with lithographs by Preetorius. Together with S. Fischer and his authors, Weber began another library, the Reihe der Hundertfünfzig in 1914. Looking at some of these precious, beautifully printed books, one cannot help wondering if the choice of type faces was not determined by novelty and surprise rather than aptness. The name 'Hyperion' and a number of remaindered editions were sold to Ernst Rowohlt and Julius Schröder in 1913, and the Hyperion-Drucke continued under the name *Dreiangeldrucke* until 1923. Nearly all these books were illustrated—by Hans Meid, Waldo von May, Emil Preetorius, and other artists, of whom in those picture-loving days there were many. Economic troubles between 1914 and 1923 often brought Weber, who had been so successful a publisher and bibliophile in 1906–8, into difficult situations. The very small editions proved to be a dangerous risk. He had a great success at the 'Bugra' exhibition of 1914 and remained true to his ideals. In the course of the next decade, which was one of privation for him, the connoisseur of fine book design developed into a responsible pioneer of book collecting, a guardian and sponsor of books valuable both for their content and their artistic quality.

The house of W. E. Drugulin at Leipzig, throughout its long history, was a printing office as well as a printing workshop in the craft sense. The Drugulin-Drucke (from 1910–new series from 1919), first published by Rowohlt and later by Kurt Wolff, profited greatly from the fine range of old and new type faces owned by the press. The new series of Drugulin-Drucke had a strong penchant for contemporary literature. Kurt Wolff was the publisher of literary expressionism. After changing hands several times, the press enjoyed a new revival under Ernst Kellner (1899–1943). This book printer came from the printing department of the Klingspor foundry, and in 1936 he installed a hand-press, calling the new workshop Drugulin-Presse. He had found an able printer in Fritz Arnold, who had worked for Rudolf Koch's workshop and also for Victor Hammer, a printer and type designer whose work was highly esteemed in Vienna and New York. Apart from many nice ephemeral pieces for special occasions, the press produced only one major work: Plato's *Phaidros* (1939), set in Rudolf Koch's Marathon-Antiqua. It marked the end of an era, with its presswork in the grand manner, its marvellous colours, and its heavy handmade paper. Neither Ernst Kellner nor Fritz Arnold survived the Second World War, and the workshop was destroyed by bombs.

BINDING

The binding is a part of the design of the book, and is of course planned before the book is published. It plays a certain role even in small editions from private presses, and temporary binding—the Rupprecht-Presse did particularly fine ones—were usually in a uniform style. The creative bookbinder, however, who receives an individual book in sheets or with a temporary cover, makes something unique, which he does not normally repeat. The way it is bound makes a book into something personal. This is also true of the (now rare) occasions when the style and design of a binding are determined by the client. When this happens each book becomes part of a family, namely, that of a collector's library. A binding made with artistic intentions reflects not only the taste of the bookbinder, but also that of his client, and so is doubly revealing. Furthermore, such bindings show the taste and working methods of the country where and for which they are made. Nothing is more significant for the art of German bookbinding than the 380 or so leather bindings by Ignatz Wiemeler (1895–1952), bound for a few collectors, particularly Richard Doetsch-Benziger, Karl Klingspor, and Ernst Kyriss.

As a young man Wiemeler had been deeply impressed by Paul Kersten (1865–1943), who brilliantly expressed the spirit of the Jugendstil on his bindings. At Weimar Otto Dorfner (1885–1955), unperturbed by wars and revolutions, trained generations of technically most accomplished bookbinders. The working methods of the master binders, trained at numerous schools, vary greatly. It ranges from virtuoso performances to craftsmanship true to the materials used; it may be international in style, or it may have decorative, 'applied art' character. Particularly characteristic of the German style, which grew out of the Werkbund, is the work of Wiemeler, especially in his later years, and that of his last pupils.

As previously mentioned, Wiemeler worked in Rudolf Koch's community at Offenbach from 1921 to 1925. The twenty-six years he spent working with Walter Tiemann (1920–46) form the prolific middle period of his life. After the German defeat he worked for another six years in Hamburg, where he had originally learnt his trade with Franz Weisse (1878–1952), the distinguished craftsman, designer, and teacher.

Wiemeler had abandoned the decorative style early on. He chose the way of Cobden-Sanderson's Doves Bindery. This style, which eschews all, or nearly all, ornamentation, could be called the 'elemental' style. Wiemeler limited himself to simple but very lively stamped vignettes, lettering, and later more and more to fillets with or without gold. He rarely used inlays, and when he did, they were never elaborate. He enriched the book chiefly by the use of binding materials and colours, the sonorous tones of leather in contrast with the glowing doublures of silk or leather which meet the eye when the book is opened. Wiemeler was no theoretician, but he communicated some of his great knowledge in a few technical essays. Leather was his favourite material —but only when the methods of tanning and dyeing ensured its permanence. He did not use vellum. His leather bindings were models of craftsman-like precision. He improved the union of book and cover by adopting Cobden-Sanderson's zig-zag ends. His slip-cases, whose edges had the leather of the binding, were lined with silk. Outside, the slip-case was forthright, particularly in his early work. Choice of material and colours determines the general impression; the stamping does not obtrude: they are equal partners. He frequently used blind stamping. The dialogue between the two design components—between material and stamping—is the basic principle behind his designs. The volumes most typical of Wiemeler's work have simple lettering and geometrical divisions of the surface, or they are covered by fillets, usually blind-stamped: closely ruled areas of lines, zones of diagonals, nets of squares, side by side with, or superimposed on, the natural grain.

This sparseness, with a stamping technique so obviously perfect, is hard to understand. The surface of the leather is full of life. Its natural surface and grain are contrasted by stamping it diagonally, horizontally, and vertically. In other words, nature meets a strict order. What has grown and what has been stamped, these two together determine the appearance of cover and spine. The bookbinder's hand controls. It dominates the surface without suppressing its nature. The contrast between organic growth and the artist's will make for a profound tension which enhances the effect of both forces.

Kurt Londenberg (b. 1914) has been teaching in Franz Weisse's and Ignatz

Wiemeler's Hamburger Akademie since 1954, in the spirit of his predecessor and teacher. After Wiemeler's single-minded concentration on leather bindings, Londenberg tries to apply his predecessor's principles—honesty and simplicity—to wider fields of his craft, and to influence publishers' binding as well.

ILLUSTRATION

The printed or painted picture has always been able to become the actual object of a book, for instance as landscape or as visual material in scholarly texts. In such books the text took second place, while in most others, particularly in literary works, it dominated. With the latter a picture might be added as an illustration, helping to enhance and throw light on the text. Not every combination of image and text results in an illustrated book, even though outwardly all the qualities of the book are discernible. What is needed is an inner link between word and image. These partners in the book must be in the same relationship to one another as people in conversation, or musicians in a duet. The image, however wide in concept, must stand in a singular relation to the people, things, or ideas in the text. Decoration and ornament do not count as illustration.

Much of what was published after the First World War and in recent times in the form of a sequence of prints with text added, in books and portfolios, can hardly count as true illustration: the balance or inner link needed for a true dialogue is often missing. Among earlier examples of such work are Lovis Corinth's lithographs for the *Hohelied* (1911), which burst all limits of the book, and Max Liebermann's (1847–1935) series for Goethe texts (1921). The imaginative art of making pictures for children's books is proper illustration only when the pictures are in true dialogue with the text.

The romantic wave that followed the Jugendstil greatly stimulated illustration, while the Jugendstil itself had been alien to it. It had tried to transform everything static into movement; the frame always tried to devour the picture. The new romantics liked story-telling; occasionally, with a touch of irony, they donned the raiments of the Biedermeier era. Emil Preetorius (b. 1883) was a master at combining typography and picture. He approached a book as a painter and graphic artist. By 1907 his drawings and silhouettes for *Peter Schlemihl* by Chamisso had placed him in the forefront as a book illustrator. Uninfluenced by the offshoots of the Jugendstil, he also became an expert designer of bindings and dust jackets who knew how to combine firm composition with grace and inventiveness. He was a master at joining festive lettering with symbolic vignettes: with great wit he brought lettering and image together not only physically but also in the manner of his draughtsmanship. The cover of Jean Paul's *Luftschiffer Gianozzo* (1912) and several Insel almanacs are charming examples of this treatment. His most prolific years as an illustrator were 1912–17, during which, among others, he produced the lithographs for Eichendorff's *Taugenichts* (1914) and Gerstäcker's *Reiseabenteuer des Herrn Mahlhuber* (1917), unforgettable for their irony. Though in his later years Preetorius—highly esteemed as a stage designer and a collector of far-Eastern art—found less and less time for the book as a result of his public duties, he never entirely gave it up.

The art of the German book, during its romantic phase, owes a great deal to the illustrations and book designs of the Swiss, Karl Walser (b. 1877). We have already mentioned his work for the publisher S. Fischer, who was by no means his only client. His exquisite coloured lithographs for Gautier's *Mademoiselle de Maupin* (1913) were done in the great days of Georg Müller.

Max Slevogt (1868–1932) wanted to become an opera singer in his youth; hence his work is a mixture of the pictorial and the dramatic. His scenic sense and great vitality evoked such a deluge of images that his hand could hardly keep up with them. *Sindbad* (1908), *Lederstrumpf* (1909), *Benvenuto Cellini* (1913) and many other books are festooned with his stage-like scenes. *Faust*, Part II (1926–7) alone had 510 lithographs! Slevogt was not so much an illustrator as a painter who needed the literary happening as a stimulus.

The early work of Hans Meid (1883–1957)—also mentioned earlier in connection with S. Fischer—had certain characteristics in common with Max Slevogt, the impressionist of the stage (*Othello*, 1911; *Don Juan*, 1912). But soon he began to integrate his story-telling pictures with the text until they became a true component of the book, in keeping with its typography, binding, and dust jacket. Zuckmayer's *Liebesgeschichte* (1934) and Billinger's *Schutzengelhaus* (1934) are models of the richly illustrated, individualistic, book while *Carlos und Nicolas* (1930) by R. J. Schmied is a prototype of copious children's book illustration.

Expressionism, which lacked a typographical style of its own, was rarely able to find anything to balance the illustrator's work, and as a result the relationship between text and truly illustrative graphic sequences was uncertain. A fortunate exception was Georg Heim's *Umbra vitae* (1924), with woodcuts by E. L. Kirchner (1880–1938), which achieved complete harmony between typography and pictures. Ernst Barlach (1870–1938) was less lucky: his lithographs and woodcuts for *Der tote Tag* (1912) and *Der Kopf* (1919), are out of tune with the typography. Paul Klee (1879–1940), Richard Janthur (b. 1883), Oskar Kokoschka (b. 1886), and Alfred Kubin (1877–1959) did much graphic work for books, but harmony with the texts is often lacking. Frans Masereel (b. 1889), highly thought of in Germany as a master of graphic narration, probably came closest to achieving true book illustration, using woodcuts in juxtaposition with heavy text setting in Kurt Wolff's small octavo volumes. But text and picture are also well balanced in two large volumes of Coster's *Ulenspiegel*, translated by Wolfskehl (1926) and set in a large size of Luther-Fraktur.

In the decade preceding 1945 Josef Hegenbarth of Dresden (1884–1962) developed a curious realism by violently alternating between solid areas and lines. In the last prolific years of his long life he almost completely abandoned this manner in favour of a sweeping line with an almost obstinate stress on contour. Gerhard Oberländer (b. 1907) used luminous patches of colour behind a lively line for his children's books. Outstanding among his excellent illustrations for textbooks and novels are those for Grimmelshausen's *Simplicissimus* (1961). It is hard to say whether Gunter Böhmer (b. 1911) is more of a painter or an illustrator. He sculpts, does watercolours, and uses a brush and reed for his drawings. His illustrations for Thomas Mann's *Thamar* (1956) are just one example of his immense output; his work has ravishing verve; his many book jackets are brushwork stories in words and pictures. Fritz Busse (b. 1903) is very much the painter; he uses restrained, quiet colours. The most versatile illustrator of recent times is Werner Klemke (b. 1917); he commands a whole range of techniques, which he applies with some irony, as suggested by the subject. The drawings of Hannes Gaab (b. 1908) of Mainz have a curiously weightless quality. He will not so much outline an object as transmute it into delicate lines or scintillating strokes.

German book illustration has been virtually boundless since the beginning of the century, so that one cannot do more than touch upon it. But it is important to point to a sort of split that divides the whole field. All the work so far described, and the artists that produced it, are of a dynamic character, while those on the other side of the dividing line are static. This applies to the relationship between the picture and its typographic setting, as well as to the relationship of people and objects in a picture with one another. In the work of the artists already discussed the scene is usually full of movement, and people and things in the picture are directed towards the text. In the work about to be described the picture tends to be self-contained, and the figures in it stand next to each other like statues. But their brittle, sometimes rigid, bearing does not interfere with the 'dialogue'. The obvious and the direct do not always make for a genuine relationship. A taciturn conversation can be more intimate and instructive than a lively one.

The thoughtfully outlined figures and animals of Renée Sintenis (1888–1965) for *Daphnis und Cloe* or Sappho's verse are slow in their movement and reserved in expression. In the work of Richard Seewald (b. 1888), too, action is less important than bearing. In Robert Pudlich's (1905–62) softly and delicately built-up pictures, things, animals, and people act only through their 'being', their juxtaposition. The technique of the woodcut is by no means ideal for static illustration. The wood-engravings and woodcuts of Eugen Sporer (b. 1920) and Alfred Sacharias (b. 1901) are firm, yet very articulate. Nor are the wood-engravings of Hans Alexander Müller (b. 1888), resident in the United States for the last thirty years, exactly taciturn. The large panels of Hans Orlowski (b. 1894), the master of pathos in the woodcut, are of a totally different structure. His pictures tremble with passion, yet every thing, every face, is alone. Karl Rössing (b. 1897), starting with graphic stories, came to illustration as a storyteller and social critic. The mute juxtaposition of his figures is eloquent: he speaks in symbols. Thus, while appearing to be silent, he tells of the Peasants' War and the Fall of Jerusalem, or takes part in the Odyssey or Benvenuto Cellini's memoirs. This symbolic language is even richer in combination with lyrical poetry (Günter Eich: *Abgelegene Gehöfte*, 1948). For Otto Rohse (b. 1925), youngest of the masters of wood-engraving, the inner life of surfaces and materials is more important than the outward-directed outlines. When occasionally a single object—a burnt-out tower, a regal, crowing cock—is made to stand out, it appears to grow into unforgettable greatness.

IV FUNCTIONALISM

FUNCTIONALISM AND FORMALISM

When the typography and book design of the thirties are compared with those of the fifties, changes become apparent which make it likely that between 1940 and 1950 an altered style came in which went unnoticed during the war and its aftermath. The ideal is no longer the personality which imposes itself on the work. The *type* has become all-important—that which is *typical* in the design of books and typography. Readers become groups—*types* of reader. Types of reader adapt themselves to corresponding types of book. The personal and the unusual play a subsidiary role in design. The new type faces are directed towards specific functions and behave accordingly. Today's type faces have to be legible, technically fit for their purpose, and functional. Individuality and what is known as 'beauty' are no longer the chief criteria in bookwork. The 'typical' is identical with the functional, which is, however, more than just the practical. The artifice of giving typographic expression by size has not been forgotten, but more often effects are obtained by contrast. Functional and typical type faces and some very individual and personal display faces are used side by side: the contrast between them enhances their effect. Individuality, the foremost aim in the pre-forties, has become the component of polarity. It is difficult to describe a stylistic phase that has not yet come to an end—we cannot see it in perspective, but we can try to identify some of its characteristics. It may even be possible to pinpoint these by comparing today's style with yesterday's. At the outset of this chapter we sketched the results of such an attempt. Now let us try to fill in these outlines with some details. But it must be made clear that we are discussing only work in West Germany, and neighbouring territories can only briefly be hinted at. (To establish supra-national characteristics of style is the task of a more comprehensive survey, though the concepts 'type', 'polarity', and 'function' are also important in countries outside Germany but within the same cultural orbit).

From the outset the Bauhaus, founded by Walter Gropius at Weimar in 1919 and continued at Dessau as Hochschule für Bau und Gestaltung (High School for Building and Design), was no uniform phenomenon. It mirrors two tendencies in design that are once again—and emphatically with us today. For Walter Gropius, man was the measure of all work and planning. Gropius must not be accused of having aimed at an apotheosis of rationalism. He felt that all design should be informed by a *living sense of purpose*. In this way the concept of 'function' is put above all other values. It denotes practicality tempered by a regard for the meaning and essence of a thing, and controlled by the extent and limits of human nature. Such a concept was not alien to the Werkbund spirit and the romantic-individualistic notions of the epoch which preceded it. The difference lies in the emphasis the older theory put on the 'personal' which the Bauhaus followers, in particular, virtually replaced by the 'typical'. Side by side with the static and organic trends postulated by

Gropius, there was another, dynamic, approach in Weimar and Dessau. As far as the graphic arts were concerned, this was antagonistic to type and favoured the image. This school regarded the 'elementary' as the most important quality: form mattered more than matter. Though the attempts of the Bauhaus to break free from the historical nature of our type faces failed, its publication, the *Bauhausbuch* of 1923, pointed the way and had important repercussions. It is the clearest indication of the break-away of the book of pictures from the traditional arrangement, which above all serves the text. Freely composed pages of text and pictures have become ever more frequent since the twenties, and ultimately became almost the norm. The dynamic tendency of the Bauhaus and its present-day successors, with its stress on the formal and the elementary, is opposed by the followers of functional design. Briefly, one speaks of the contrast Formalism *v*. Functionalism. In a direct line of descent from the Werkbund, functionalism is obviously the stronger, and possibly for this reason today's stylistic trend is called 'functionalism'.

Independently of the Bauhaus, and in the spirit of the Werkbund, Paul Renner after working for Georg Müller (1907–17) found himself confronted by the problems of industrial techniques. He turned against traditional type design. In his view printing type should be a reading-symbol free from any connection with handwriting. His very successful type face Futura (1925–7) was an avowal of the need to 'typify' letter shapes; an acknowledgement of the age of technology, of the need to separate writing from printing types. As head of the Meisterschule für Deutschlands Buchdrucker at Munich (1926–33) he campaigned for a 'mechanised graphic art' (1930). His manual *Typographie als Kunst* (1922) is based on the wide experience gained while working for Georg Müller. Since 1932 it has reappeared several times under the new title *Die Kunst der Typographie*, with completely new specimens. *Ordnung und Harmonie der Farben* (1947) crowned the life work of this painter, teacher, systematiser, and prophet. In it he attacks Oswald's theory of colours—and thus all attempts at mechanisation of colour. His articles on typography in the *Gutenberg-Jahrbücher* 1944–9 and 1951 confirm that his views are rooted in the Werkbund and not the Bauhaus. His later theories attacked formalism and became an essential basis of functionalism. Of the new typography he said that it would *primarily be completely fit for its purpose*, so that one could call it *functional typography*.

THE TYPICAL

The idea of a type of book designed for a clearly defined type of reader was created by Jakob Hegner (1882–1962), who interpreted in his own way the Werkbund principle that content and form must be in full harmony. His reader is the Christian intellectual, for whom he created an appropriate book—not merely as a publisher and translator, but also as a printer and book designer. This type of book did not come into existence overnight; it underwent several changes. But he always stuck to certain principles: functional simplicity of jacket and binding, restriction to original type faces, no ornaments or illustrations. Originally Hegner had been a follower of the German dual tradition in the use of type—fraktur and roman—and at his publishing house and press at Hellerau he used faces ranging from Luther-Fraktur and Dutch gothic to Walbaum-Fraktur. He also had a wide range of roman faces. He liked Fleischmann, Janson, and Walbaum, but finally his favourite became Bembo, and only roman was used for his books. A Christian and a humanist, he paid homage to the Graeco-Roman foundations of our culture, not only in words, but also in his choice of type faces.

Hermann Zapf (b. 1918), who in his youth was greatly influenced by Edward Johnston, has designed a number of book faces of a 'typical' rather than 'personal' character. The Palatino group (1950), with its expanded and condensed variants, extended into Greek and monumental roman capitals, has its roots in the strongest cultural heritage of all: the Renaissance. The Melior family (1952), designed for technical work, is cool and eminently practical. Optima is a group of sans-serif faces with moderately differentiated thicks and thins, classical in character. It is friendly and sensible, easy to read, and free of the technical emphasis of so many sans serifs. All three of these have found wide use. Palatino (and Aldus, which belongs to it) is the most widely used German book face designed since 1945. By revising Janson for Linotype, Zapf increased the range of baroque faces available today; he did the same for the classicist period by his work on Walbaum. The design of a 'typical' book succeeds most when all details of the design are based on a unifying plan. Zapf is one of the most successful book designers of our day. He has developed a new formula for the design of complete works, attractively varied, and different from the Insel tradition. He is one of those who put their faith in the expressiveness of a well-chosen book face, and his effects are achieved by purely typographical means. This is the more surprising since he is also an accomplished calligrapher and designer of ornaments. He sees printing type as more than a mere reading-symbol. In his view calligraphy is the 'fleet in being' of printing-type. It is significant that after his album *Feder und Stichel* (1952) a calligraphic compendium of western scripts, he produced, in the same format, his *Manuale typographicum* (1955), which contains variations of sixty-four type faces. He has published numerous studies on type classification, history, and technology. His Bible designs formed part of the international symposium *Liber librorum* (1955) and were greatly admired. Zapf is one of the most successful experts of his day as a book designer, a teacher of international renown, a calligrapher, typographer, and publicist.

Jan Tschichold (b. 1902), typographer and book designer, now in Basel, after the Second World War became the leading pioneer of typography that is finely tuned for its purpose, rational, and psychologically sound. He was trained at the Leipzig Academy and by Walter Tiemann; in 1926 he became an advocate in word and deed of Paul Renner's Elementare Typographie at Munich. But his involvement with the Bauhaus was short-lived. Experience in Britain and Switzerland may have helped to shift his interest towards traditional typography. He published a number of books showing and analysing historical type faces and written alphabets, and has entirely overhauled our tenets of book and display typography. He opposed formalistic typographic trends in several critical treatises. His typographical doctrine, perfected more painstakingly year after year, has been put into practice in his extensive international work, as his book *Im Dienste der Schrift* eloquently proves. However much he stresses that common sense and respect for purpose are the mainsprings of good book design, his work shows clearly that imagination, even a sense of play, are also a part of it. *Grace comes about almost by itself when the compositor loves his work*—this statement proves that his work is not determined by cold reasoning but by a very lively intelligence. Whether as teacher or designer, historian or theorist—Tschichold always brings tension into his activities, of which he, the advocate of rational harmony, is probably only half-conscious. He shows the present and the past in constant dialogue. Printing type depends on handwriting. Tschichold loves the refreshing contrast of roman text and fraktur display and is an advocate of Germany's dual tradition in type design. Without the deliberate use of contrast, without the playful urge of the compositor, which he calls 'grace', Tschichold's rational and 'typified' typography would never have achieved the extraordinary admiration which it commands among experts.

POLARITY

Imre Reiner (b. 1900 in Hungary) has lived in Switzerland for many years and has made the polarity which is, so to speak, concealed in Tschichold's work into a means of achieving almost violent effects. His work, chiefly book typography, titles, and jobbing work, and, like Tschichold's, collected in manuals and compendia, alternates surprisingly between a highly dynamic and totally static style of composition. He is one of the élite among Schneidler's pupils, and his work embraces not only all fields of typography with its graphic and calligraphic accessories, but also the fine arts (he is a master of wood-engraving) and type design. His printing types are somewhat bizarre designs based on calligraphic experiments and are useful chiefly in contrasts with severe roman book faces. His classicist Corvinus and his elaborate script Symphonie make an attractive pair; in spite of their contrasting appearance, several definite though inconspicuous family traits make them related to each other.

Georg Trump (b. 1896), like most of the better-known members of the Stuttgart School, draws, illustrates, and is a typographer and type designer. Since the thirties type design has been his chief concern. Apart from his almost classicist Schadow roman (1935-45) with its accentuated serifs, and his old-face Trump Mediaeval (1954), he designed a number of contrasting freely written scripts. Delphin (1951), reminiscent of the earliest italics *ca.* 1500, was followed by Time Script (1956) and Codex (1953), the latter half-way between a book- and a display-face. All of Trump's work delights by the change between gay, unobtrusive typography and the free play of drawn and written lettering.

Walter Brudi (b. 1907), as we mentioned earlier, succeeded Schneidler as a teacher of book design and typography at the Stuttgart Academy in 1949. Like his predecessor he is versatile but regards the book as his main task—the design of lettering and calligraphy, typography and illustration, binding and dust jacket. A portfolio of his pupils' work shows that merging of picture and ornament, type and device which is so characteristic of Schneidler's followers. In a folio volume illustrated with lino-cuts by his pupils he glorifies the importance of the written letter. His approach to design is clearly dynamic in character. This is obvious in his book-face Brudi-Mediaeval (1958), and even more so in Pan (1954), an abstruse, gnarled display-type, which has ornaments as extraordinary as those of the Eckmann-Schrift in its time. Polarity as a characteristic of our time manifests itself uniquely in his work for the Rainer Wunderlich Verlag Hermann Leins, a publishing house whose book design was entirely in Brudi's charge for a time. The titles, often elaborate and long, invite calligraphic treatment. They alternate with inscriptional groups of capital letters and groups in light roman. Text pages, titles, bindings, and dust jacket harmonise and contrast in enchanting variations. Yet, with all their variety, these books have a remarkable unity.

RECENT ACHIEVEMENTS IN THE SERVICE OF THE BOOK

The last of the German presses to be run on the model of the English private presses was the Drugulin-Presse, which came to an end during the Second World War. Hand and machine composition, high-speed printing and paper-making are the pupils of the age of private presses. The works of the latter are venerated and studied. But that is not enough. Our studies must continue. As the speed of printing-presses and the cómpetition between various composing and printing techniques increases, constant reference to good examples and assessment of the most recent work become ever more important. This cannot be done by technical experiments, but only by looking at and analysing models which can stimulate industrial manufacture throughout the trade. This was the function of the earlier private presses, and it is the task of present-day printing workshops too.

Hand-printing has become rare; only a few hand-presses survived the Second World War, and they are used only occasionally. The Grillen-Presse at Hamburg has produced a sequence of books in the old style, most of them illustrated with woodcuts by the sculptor Gerhard Marcks (b. 1889): *Das Buch Jona* (1950), *Äsop* (1950), *Von dem Fischer un syner Fru* (1955). The press has also done a lot of work for the Maximilian Gesellschaft. Its founder and head is Richard von Sichowsky (b. 1911), who teaches at the Hamburg Academy. He is also the typographer for this Society, which is not only dedicated to the study of books as books, but also stimulates and promotes good design. Sichowsky's spacious and well-reasoned typography has influenced book design in Hamburg and further afield.

After the political division of Germany, the great Leipzig traditions of Poeschel and Kellner have been carried on by Horst Erich Wolter at the Offizin Haag Drugulin (now Offizin Andersen Nexö). Walter Schiller and Oskar Zech have produced important pieces in small editions at the Institut für Buchgestaltung: Hölderlin's poems (1959); Kalidasa's *Kreis der Jahreszeiten* (1956–7) and *Der Wolkenbote* (1959); Reymont's *Der Kampf im Wald* (1956). Part of these special editions was printed on a hand-press, and the type hand-set from famous faces by Fleischmann, Tiemann, and Hammer. Until the death of its founder in 1946 the Eggebrecht-Presse (founded 1936) at Mainz produced and distributed exemplary small pieces. Various techniques are used now for books large and small. Among the works the press has been commissioned to do are some remarkable items for Armin Renker, the Zerkall papermaker, among them *Die Reise nach Filigranistan* (1957). Many items were done jointly with Helmut Presser of the Gutenberg-Museum, and with the illustrator Hannes Gaab. Notable among these are the *Sappho-Fragmente* (1952) and a new printing of Goethe's *Bericht über die Belagerung von Mainz* (1961).

Among the printing school presses the Höhere Fachschule für das graphische Gewerbe in Stuttgart under Gustav Barthel has distinguished itself with its annual pieces of book production (*Schwäbische Dichter*, 1958, and Hermann Hesse's *Magie des Buches*, 1956). The Akademie für das graphische Gewerbe at Munich, under Herbert Post, produces slight and sometimes serious pieces of work, which for some time showed the influence of Georg Trump, Post's predecessor. Post's earlier work from the time he spent in Rudolf Koch's circle, from his second period at Offenbach, and at Giebichenstein near Halle, can also be sensed.

The Trajanus-Presse has close ties with the Stempel foundry at Frankfurt-am-Main. Its founder and head, Gotthard de Beauclair (b. 1907), was concerned with production and design at the Insel-Verlag under Anton Kippenberg from 1928. He had sole charge of design from 1950 until 1962, and made the books of the Insel-Bücherei collectors' items of good typography. During that time he was the most frequent prize-winner in 'Die schönsten deutschen Bücher'—the annual Finest German Books contests. The Trajanus-Presse (1951) had produced only twelve pieces of work by 1962, but some of them rank among the best done in Germany in the last thirty years. The house press of Stempel has produced masterpieces of composition and presswork under Beauclair's direction, hand-set and machine-printed. Apart from the first small pieces, editions are no larger than those of the early private presses. The papers used are mould-mades and Japanese papers of the highest quality. Thus the older custom of the private presses—hand-press printing and handmade papers—has come to an end. These are workshop products whose perfection must have a direct and immediate effect on others. Three of the works (Bergengruen's *Drei Falken*, Hofmannsthal's *Lucidor*, and Boccaccio's *Die Nymphe von Fiesole*) are illustrated by the Swiss artist, Felix Hoffmann, using various woodcut techniques. Aristophanes' *Frösche* (1961) had numerous wood-engravings by Imre Reiner. No less important is the purely typographical work, such as Gertrud von Le Fort's *Plus ultra* (1953), and *Das Johannes-Evangelium* in Greek and German (1960). Since 1962 Gotthard de Beauclair has published in his own Press Ars Librorum notable works, for instance: *Der Gast* by Albert Camus (1965, illustrated by Eduard Borgheer) and *Das Gastmahl* by Platon (1965, illustrated by Heinz Battke). As Hans von Weber used to do with his Hundertdrucke the two private presses commission the binding of books from the best hand-binders, such as Willy Pingel of Heidelberg.

The workshop of the Trajanus-Presse also produces the prestige publications and type specimens for the Stempel foundry, which were suggested and designed in the fifties by Gotthard de Beauclair and Hermann Zapf. Here Stempel's new type faces have been predominantly used. Such work is intended to show the trade what can be achieved with types, old and new. Only a few foundries continue to produce type for hand composition today, and even design for machine composition is concentrated almost exclusively on three large firms. In their annual keepsakes and other publications they all set a high standard of excellence. Beside the Stempel foundry, the Bauersche Giesserei (Bauer Type Foundry) of Frankfurt-am-Main deserves special mention. Under the artistic direction of Heinrich Jost and Konrad F. Bauer it has done great things not only for the study of books and printing, but also aesthetically and technically. Memorable among its output are *Die Vögel des Aristophanes*, with watercolours by Karel Svohlinsky (1940)—a brilliant combination with offset printing; and Goethe's *Römische Elegien* (mentioned earlier) with illustrations by Yngve Berg. Konrad F. Bauer's majestic *Aventur und Kunst* (1940) is a famous chronology of printing during the past five centuries and a museum of its history and technology. The tradition established by these works has been continued. Beside many attractive trifles, Alexander Orlowski's large series of woodcuts on the tragic theme of *Orpheus und Euridice* will be remembered.

The thoughtfully planned, meticulously produced piece of workman-like printing is the measure we must use in judging present-day achievements. If we let the average and the mediocre become our criterion, the art of the book will disappear. If we make no high demands, good book design will die. Not only an individualistic epoch is judged by a small number of outstanding personalities. Any epoch, including the present, can only be understood by seeking out its best work. This is not easy when we have to deal with our own time. We must ask precise questions. But in the end, perhaps, we have to use our intuition after all.

P. M. Handover

BRITISH BOOK TYPOGRAPHY

Between 1794 and 1796 William Bulmer printed *The History of the River Thames*, two volumes folio with a folding map and seventy-six aquatint plates in sepia and colour, one of the finest pieces of native printing that this country had then seen. In 1916 Thomas Cobden-Sanderson cast into the river Thames the punches, matrices and type that had been used for the Doves Bible, the finest five-volume folio that had been printed in this country since Bulmer's day. By this action it now seems that Bulmer's ghost was laid. The two printers, otherwise disparate, had shared a conviction that when the speed of composition rose above a thousand ens an hour and the speed of printing above three hundred impressions a typographical Eden was lost: between 1917 and 1960 this theory could effectively receive disproof.

Before 1800 the history of book printing in England is the history of an undistinguished craft that except for brief periods was content with the mean typography appropriate to an activity that seldom aspired to be an art. Until 1800 this country borrowed and imitated and depended on Continental models as well as upon Continental materials. The native product was—with a few notable exceptions—inferior to the European. After 1800 the position was reversed: Britain led the world in steadying the ancient trade under the impact of mass demands and mass production, and in reconciling the differences between art, craft and industry. The adjustment was slow, and even a hundred years after the invention of the powered press few men believed that it would prove possible.

By the end of the eighteenth century books had reached a comparatively small section of the community. Many people knew only the advertising leaflets of the quack doctor and the ballad sheets of the travelling pedlar. The cripplingly high proportion of those unable to read the simplest piece of print was offset only by the habit of public reading-aloud in places such as the local inn. By this means the contents of newspapers and other periodicals, usually political or religious, were communicated to those who otherwise knew only of the Bible.

Yet in the eighteenth century all letterpress typography was based on that of books. The single exception was the relatively small amount of jobbing that used script types and in England this work had increasingly become the responsibility of the engraver on copper. The distinctive columnar arrangement of the newspaper was developing slowly, but so long as book types and a book size of sheet were used for newspapers, and they were used so long as the newspaper was printed on the hand-press, the layout of the newspaper remained unspecialised. Even John Bell's *The World* (1787), which was the first newspaper to be typographically planned, was closer to Bulmer's editions than to the newspapers of the late-nineteenth century.

The typography or arrangement on a page of the printing materials, the types, ornaments, illustrations, is inseparable from the nature of those materials. Bulmer's pages would have had a different visual effect had his types been Caslon's old face. His heavy leading depended for success upon the contrast of thick and thin in the design of modern-face type, for the vertical weight accumulated in the mainstrokes balanced the horizontal lightness of the page.

In his achievement he carried book typography to a point at which it could no longer serve as a model for newspaper and job printing. This was approved by the classes that could afford his sumptuous editions. A Bulmer book had the exclusiveness that Chippendale gave to chairs and cabinets: possession made the owner one of a charmed circle. His *Thames* stated more emphatically than, say, the Mazarin Bible that it was a book. Indeed, he perhaps carried the typography of the book as far as it could be taken without destroying the rationale of a book's existence as reading matter. His typography was not, however, entirely original: the Italian Bodoni was his master.

After 1800 the Industrial Revolution affected the printing trade in three ways. First, there was an abnormal increase in overall population and particularly in the mentally more alert urban districts; this provided a potential new market for printed material. Secondly, the mechanisation of methods of production meant an increased number of manufactured goods of all kinds for which markets had to be found; as competitive selling developed printed advertising was needed in quantity. Lastly, the increased output of manufactured goods that was made possible by powered machinery affected printing itself; not only could more material be printed on a powered press but the shorter time needed for the run freed a press for a variety of work.

The application of power to the printing-press was not of first importance to inventors concerned with turbines and transport. No more than slight changes had been made to the instrument with which Gutenberg began until about 1800 Lord Stanhope, scholar, scientist and eccentric, constructed an all-metal press incorporating a longer platen and a system of compound levers to exert greater pressure. The reduction of the pressman's labour in swinging the bar to move the platen and the ability to print a sheet 32 × 22 in. in a single operation increased the speed of printing by perhaps fifty impressions an hour and were therefore the most progressive modifications yet made to the hand-press. Quality, the sharpness of impression and accuracy of register, was improved and not merely preserved. Although Stanhope's press was welcomed and its manufacture established on a commercial basis, the increased output was far from so radical an improvement as that of, for example, the power over the hand loom. In printing as in weaving the fundamental and dramatic change came with steam.

The first steam-powered press capable of a thousand impressions an hour of a large sheet was shown in 1812 by the inventor Friedrich Koenig and his engineer Andreas Bauer to John Walter, then the managing conductor of *The Times* newspaper. The circumstances of news publishing, the necessity to print the latest reports, of which at that period Walter's energy and foresight were securing the monopoly, together with the popularity of *The Times* as an advertising medium, enabled him at once to perceive the importance of the invention and to purchase the rights to its use. Having ordered the first two powered presses he was able on the early morning of 29 November 1814 to astonish his staff with the announcement: 'Gentlemen, *The Times* is already printed—by steam.' No like enfranchisement of man as a reader had been proclaimed since Gutenberg perfected his mould.

The speed was 1100 impressions an hour of a sheet 32 × 22 in. and *The Times* was the first printed matter ever to be run so swiftly from the press. The Koenig and Bauer invention made several basic changes in the instrument of printing. The sheet of paper was no longer run in under the platen but carried over the inked type by a cylinder, the impression cylinder which is still a feature of the modern flat-bed press. The rate of feeding sheets into the press was thus increased but more important was the removal of the restriction on sheet size imposed by the heavy, rectangular platen. The Koenig and Bauer press was mechanically inked by a system of rollers supplied from a reservoir on the principle familiar today, and the laborious operation of hand-inking was entirely superseded. The impression cylinder, the inking system and the type bed were all moved automatically and no longer depended on tiring human muscle. The press first used by *The Times* brought the printing trade within the ambit of the Industrial Revolution.

Thomas Bensley, Bulmer's contemporary and rival, recognised that improved machinery was indispensable if book printers were to take up the nineteenth century's opportunities. Since 1804 he had been interested in Koenig's experiments and after the success of 1814 he continued himself to experiment with a version of the power press that could be capable of perfecting, i.e. of printing both sides of the paper in one run through the machine. His lordly clientele echoed the disgust Cardinal Bessarion had bestowed on the first Italian printers.

Hitherto, except for the typefoundries, the equipment needed by the printing trade had been bespoken from individual craftsmen and the Stanhope was the first press that needed to be built by a specialised manufacturer. The problem of the supply of printing machinery was intensified by Koenig's invention and as the two Germans returned to their own country in 1817, there to set up near Würzburg a factory that still thrives, their place was taken by two British engineers, Augustus Applegath and Edward Cowper. The former began his career as a letterpress-printer but soon after 1812 was joined by his brother-in-law Cowper and thereafter they not only manufactured for the trade but worked on various patents connected with the powered press. It was they who revised Bensley's model into the practical bookprinting press on the drum-cylinder principle. The problem on the steam press was to secure the return of the type-bed without marking the sheet for a second time. In drum-cylinder machines the impression cylinder was enlarged in order to give the type-bed time to return while a full revolution was completed.

The 'fine' printers had shown that Britain could match the Continent for quality of typecasting, paper, ink and presswork and for elegance of layout. Theirs was however an achievement of prestige and not to be equated with the economic value of mechanising the press. Baskerville and Bell, Bulmer and Bensley, are welcome in the history of British taste and design since they warrant a claim to typographical distinction, but this claim is not of material consequence to the history of the trade, whereas the powered press marked the beginning of a new epoch of progress and profit.

In 1827 John McCreery, disciple of Bulmer, lamented in his poem *The Press*:

Where'er we cast our eye,
For steam and cheapness there is one dull cry.

The printing trade was not however transformed overnight. Houses remained small with perhaps no more than one press and two or three compositors. Those that could not afford a steam press, and they were the majority, had to be content with the all-metal hand presses, the Stanhope, the Columbian, an American invention patented in Britain in 1817, or the native Albion of 1824. The last two were manufactured in a range of platen sizes that satisfied the printers of trade cards as well as of poster sheets and were equally practical for short-run bookwork.

Bulmer's work for the Roxburghe Club, founded in 1812, reached in the large format so splendid and inimitable a standard that he was allowed to reign undisputed in the king-size book. The Lee Priory Press, privately founded in 1813, issued limited editions of minor Elizabethan poets that were attractive octavos although at the time overshadowed by Bulmer's folios and quartos. The influence of Thomas Dibdin, the bibliophile, in maintaining standards was not insignificant. With such books as the *Bibliographical Decameron* (1817) and the *Library Companion* (1824), with such cries as 'The printing is delicious!', he transmitted an enthusiasm for fine books to a circle that gradually extended beyond his titled patrons.

Lesser people had to be content with lesser printers and lesser formats, but besides the Lee Priory books others spaciously planned and neatly laid-out were executed for publishers such as young William Pickering, whose 'Wreath' series in the 1820's was, for instance, intended for the middle-class reader. The first machine-made papers were coming on the market after the Fourdrinier machine of 1798 was in this country perfected by Bryan Donkin in 1806, and since the early reams had to compete with the hand-made article their quality was high. Book-lovers of the twentieth century were to recall the pre-Whittingham era with nostalgia as one in which good paper and good ink had been generally available. The fast running printing machine was to make both uneconomic.

Apart from the Office of *The Times* the King's Printers was probably the first works to be organised on an industrial scale. Before 1814 George Eyre and Andrew Strahan, the latter being the active printer, made so considerable a profit by wartime Government printing that they were content to leave Bible production, of which by patent they had the monopoly, to the University Presses of Oxford and Cambridge, which were licensed to share the patent. When peace was signed, however, and the many recently founded Bible and missionary societies were free to dispense the Word of God, the King's Printers turned to the lucrative production of small Bibles for Sunday schools and missions, and their house was, because of their large markets, among the first to follow *The Times* and to install powered presses. In 1820 Strahan was already nicknamed 'many-engin'd'.

The enlargement of the sheet was scarcely less important to the King's Printers than to *The Times* since it reduced the number of workings in the Bible. By the 1830's they were machining duodecimo testaments of no more than seven and one-sixth sheets with forty-eight pages to a sheet. The progress of punchcutting and improved casting methods enabled the modern-face type to be reduced to the minimum size and set solid with the smallest possible margin. Thus the pocket Bible represented a conspicuous gain in value for money.

A similar economic typography was adopted by other houses which found that a steam press could be profitably employed in printing fiction in weekly parts of eight pages to be sold at a penny. By 1827 McCreery was lamenting that 'large pennyworths supply the greedy town'. The page size of such a number being larger than that of the pocket Bible, the small type (about 7 point) needed to be set in two columns to make it readable. The rule which separated these columns and was continued round the page always suffered under the pressure of stereotyping. Each weekly number contained a line block on the first page and the wrapped parts were followed by a bound volume printed from the stereotype plates.

The fiction of the penny numbers was often of the style that won for them the nickname of 'the penny dreadful'. It represented the crudest expansion of the market for 'horror' that the ballad-mongers or broadsheet-printers of 'last confessions' had exploited since the sixteenth century; but never on such a scale. As the work of the printer came into the hands of more people of small means and little education, illustration became a necessity not a luxury. The ancient fanes and ivied castles, the ghosts, vampires and highwaymen, the wooing of ladies by lords and their betrayal by rakes, had to be depicted in line as well as in word. The standard method of cutting, rather than engraving, blocks could not be supplanted for the cheap publications.

Cheap publishing and mass advertising created an unprecedented demand for type at a period when the printer could not cast for himself. The prosperity of the typefounders rested on the solid and unceasing demand for modern-face text types in 7 or 8 point and of economic set width. As the quantity of job printing increased, however, so did their ingenuity in devising appropriate faces. Some pretty titlings, such as Fry's Open and Union Pearl, had been cut by the end of the eighteenth century, but the first visually striking letterform was Robert Thorne's fattening-up of large sizes of modern face. The French had since the mid-eighteenth century created a poster-style letter by adding weight to the mainstrokes and curves while retaining the contrast of the hairline serif: Thorne doubled this contrast.

No longer, however, did competitive advertisers hold that a single style of letter was enough to catch the public's eye. As the result of the pressure for novelty in display advertising Britain made her most important contribution to type design: the new 'black' letters. There were two versions, both monoline and they were distinguished by the serif form: in one dominant and slablike, in the other altogether absent. The first version was shown in 1815 by the typefounder Vincent Figgins, who named it Antique because the rectangular emphasis was thought to recall ancient Greek and Egyptian architecture. The second, actually named Egyptian, was shown in 1816 by William Caslon IV. The Caslon innovation, which today pervades so much advertising and even bookwork, was neglected until the 1830's, by which time the name Egyptian had been appropriated for the slab-serifs and their unseriffed counterparts became commonly known as sans serif or grotesque. Both letterforms were regarded as display designs but the smaller sizes were used on title pages when variety was desired.

Book typography, like that of jobbing, must be governed by the type designs available to the printers. All the ingenuity of Victorian invention was poured into designs for display and jobbing. Apart from the moderns the only new design in text sizes at the mid-century was Clarendon, a black face with a bracketed serif intended as a companion to roman in catalogue or time-table setting. The book publisher or printer who wanted to break away from conventional typography was obliged to ransack disused stock. When this was done Caslon was re-discovered.

At the end of the 1830's William Pickering the publisher was discussing with the printer Charles Whittingham junior of the Chiswick Press a collaboration on volumes intended to be examples of sound rather than fine printing and undertaken for the general market in which Pickering had always been interested. Among the books projected for 1840 were works by sixteenth- and seventeenth-century authors, such as the *Holy War* of Fuller and the *Holy Living* of Jeremy Taylor. In the title pages and preliminaries the pre-vailing taste for modern with a line or two of blackletter was shunned. In-stead, small quantities of the original Caslon old face were introduced and the type on the title page of, for instance, *The Rules and Exercise of Holy Dying* (1840), was enclosed in an architectural frame in late sixteenth-century style.

The type was by then not easily found: Caslons had laid away the original matrices of William Caslon I long before the end of the eighteenth century in the belief that they were obsolete, and not until 1844 did Whittingham use the face for the text of Herbert's *The Temple*. In 1844, when he printed for Long-man the *Diary of Lady Willoughby*, he not only used Caslon for the text but adopted a period arrangement of rules to accommodate marginal notes. Al-though the popularity of the volume warranted *Further Portions* in 1848 the style was not continued without self-consciousness: an apologetic prefatory note explained that it was used because the author 'personates a lady of the seventeenth century'.

The success of the revival owed much to the excellence of the presswork for eyes used to the absolute regularity of modern face were distressed by the re-lative irregularity of Caslon, especially in the italic. Admirers appear to have included that patron of the arts, the Prince Consort, who no doubt saw the folio Book of Common Prayer set in Caslon great primer by the Chiswick Press (1844), and who is alleged to have suggested that the catalogue of the 1851 Exhibition be set in old face. He encountered the insurmountable objec-tion of the Victorians to this design: that it was uneconomic.

The revival of Caslon old face, whether associated with a 'period' style of typography or not, was in general limited to devotional books, and particu-larly those of the Tractarians or the Oxford Movement, to which Pickering himself adhered. As the note in the *Further Portions* of the Willoughby diary had implied, there was a consciousness that the typographical novelty ought to be appropriate to the subject matter. No doubt Victorians by then baulked at the long ſ and even at tied ﬅ and ﬆ, except in short volumes of prayer, meditation or poetry. Caslon was not the face chosen for reading matter in-tended for mass circulation or for the bulky productions of the three-decker novelists. Nor was it chosen for the various series of cheap reprints that be-came a strong feature of Victorian publishing.

In 1821 Pickering, whose motto was 'Aldi discipulus', had experimented with the first cloth edition binding, which he proceeded to apply to his series of reprints of the classics issued at 6s., followed in the 1830's by the Aldine Poets at 5s. a volume. There were other publishers' series, such as Bentley's

146

Standard Novels (1831-), judged by Michael Sadleir to be 'the most famous series of cheap novels ever published', the Parlour Library (1s. in boards, 1s. 6d. in cloth, 1847-), Routledge's Railway Library (1s. in 'fancy' boards, 1849-) and their Standard Novels (1851-). These series were stimulated by the opening of the first railway bookstall in 1848. As in the penny weekly numbers, typographic style was governed by the overriding pressure for economy, and the moderns, in the equivalent of 8 or 7½ point and usually set unleaded, were admirable for the publisher's pocket if not for the reader's eye.

As a result of the success of the Willoughby *Diary* and other books Whittingham was encouraged to revive a face of greater antiquity, the so-called Basle roman, which he commissioned William Howard to cut for him early in the 1850's and first used in 1854 for a volume of religious verse, *The Wife's Manual*. The design was basically that used in Basle or Lyons in the first decades of the sixteenth century before the influence of Garamond became supreme. Whittingham laid out his pages with Aldine leaves and woodcut frames and initials engraved by Mary Byfield and devised in collaboration with his daughters, and as before he accurately perceived the elements that distinguished the typography of his chosen period.

The Caslon revival was not the only reversion to the past in the 1840's. The mock Gothic, which rested on the use of blackletter, was the style Pickering developed in his reprints of the Prayer Book (1844), splendid folios in red and black on handmade paper and the outstanding achievement of Pickering's partnership with Whittingham. Another Gothic revivalist was the publisher James Burns, who ministered to worshippers stimulated by Keble and Newman in the High Church movement. In 1844 he issued an Order of Daily Service printed in red and black, with blackletter text and staves of plainsong enclosed in ornamental woodcut borders. These were octavo size pretentiously printed on a quarto page. The Gothic style became popular for ecclesiastical printing but for jobs rather than bookwork since those prepared to read more than a sentence or two of blackletter were not numerous.

Neither revival deflected the general trend, the universal admiration of modern, nor was either so fresh and inspired an interpretation that it had the force of originality. Neither took account of the circumstances of Victorian printing, the rapid advances in mechanisation. They looked backward to the hand-press at a time when even the Albion and Columbian were becoming obsolete.

The founders did however begin to consider recutting old face in terms of modern. The result was old style, of which two sizes were tentatively cut by Miller & Richard in 1858, with a reception so heartening that they completed a range of founts by 1860. Old Style is the nineteenth century's one contribution to the permanent repertoire of text-type design. The sharp contrast of thick and thin was retained; the serifs were bracketed but the delicacy of modern cutting was imposed upon them; economy in set-width was a little sacrificed to preserve a vestige of old face roundness; and the italic was perfectly regular and somewhat insipid. Although the design could not oust modern face it was paid the compliment of wholesale imitation and was not incapable of typographic distinction.

In the hands of the publisher Alexander Macmillan old style was the foundation of an individual typography that achieved dignity without the aid of ornament. The edition of *Hymni Ecclesiae* selected by Newman, a small octavo that Macmillan prepared in 1865, has a plain title page set in various sizes, all small, of old style capitals, the only departure being 'Londini' in blackletter. Facing this page is a small circular device, a cross on the 'popular' stippled ground, which is placed to the right of centre so that it is linked to the adjacent lines of type. The preliminaries are in a brilliantly cut 6 point generously leaded and 8 point set more closely is used for the hymns.

The basic simplicity and neatness of this style was retained in the *Book of Praise* (1866), a selection by Roundell Palmer of popular hymns in English. Here, the lines in general being longer than those in Latin hymns, the verses are in 7 point old style and the preliminaries in a small-bodied 9 point. The title page is dominated by a copper engraving of David and his harp, a typographic element that Macmillan continued throughout his Golden Treasury series of poets. Apart from the typographical attention, these books were distinguished by good quality paper and fine-mesh cloth for the binding. Clay, who printed most of the Macmillan books in the early period, bestowed care on the presswork although in the current fashion the pages are lightly inked.

This restrained typography still looked well at the end of the century when Macmillan's were publishing the Cranford Series of illustrated reprints elaborately bound in green blocked with gold, and the Illustrated Standard Novels, five in a cloth cabinet for 25s. These were printed by R. & R. Clark of Edinburgh, Scottish rates being by the end of the century lower than those of the London and even of the English provincial printers.

The typography of Alexander Macmillan, in its simplicity so alien to the Gothic revival, is the equivalent of a nineteenth-century revival of the Renaissance or humanist ideal. Yet it remains nineteenth century and this is not entirely due to the use of old style type. If a twentieth-century face of the same set were used to copy a Macmillan layout of the 1860's the modern typographer would insert space between some lines and reduce it elsewhere: spacing and the positioning of typographic elements within the page area, no less than type design, are components of a period style.

Approval of old style was hastened by its use in the *Pall Mall Gazette* founded in 1865, 'the paper written by gentlemen for gentlemen', but the bulk of Victorian fiction was unaffected by innovation or revival. The part-issue was throughout its heyday, 1840–1855, always set in moderns and usually subjected to stereotyping. After 1855 it yielded to magazine serialisation which offered the purchaser better value for money. The three-decker, the part-issue and the serial all encouraged the author to write at length and all were therefore best set in modern face. All were to be published as cheaply as possible and therefore best printed by the house that had adapted its equipment to the long run at high speed. The mechanical inventions in which the century was so rich were all the result of the demands of printers who specialised in periodical work or in bookwork which had similar requirements.

After the invention of steam printing the movements of the hand compositor appeared painfully slow and as early as 1822 Dr William Church patented a keyboard type-composer with a clockwork mechanism. This was never manufactured and in 1840 the more practical Young-Delcambre machine was adopted by the *Family Herald*, a periodical which by 1851 had a circulation of 200,000. Though an unreliable machine it demonstrated the benefit of mechanical composition, and in 1857 the energetic Robert Hattersley patented the first of several versions of a keyboard composer that by 1866 could set 3000–4000 ens an hour. In 1867 Dr Alexander Mackie patented his machine incorporating perforated tape for which a speed of 12,000 ens an hour was soon claimed. In 1869 Karl Kastenbein completed his keyboard machine and by 1872 had built five for use in the Office of *The Times*. Their installation in so powerful and progressive a house was a sign that mechanical composition was becoming an established aid. That adoption of the process by the other metropolitan newspapers was slow was due to the trade unions, who since 1841 had steadfastly—and mistakenly—resisted their introduction. The climax of the process was the Linotype, patented in 1884, which not only set the convenient slug but could recast afresh for each operation and so avoid the burden of distribution.

The advance of casting machines was until the advent of the Linotype equally irresistible. The first successful French machine, the Polytype of H. F. Didot, brought to London by J. L. Pouchée, was destroyed before 1851, allegedly by the hostility of the founders, but by that time Miller & Richard were using an American caster patented by David Bruce in 1838. In 1872 a speed of 4,800 perfect, i.e. dressed, types an hour was claimed for a British invention, the fixed-mould machine of J. R. Johnson. The most important typecaster was however the rotary machine of F. Wicks, invented partly at the instigation of *The Times*. It was patented in 1881 and was capable of producing from 35,000 to 70,000 types an hour according to size.

The making of printing plates was assisted by the invention of electrotyping, patented by Thomas Spencer of Liverpool in 1839. In 1855 the Swiss-born Dellagana brothers patented the type-high stereotype made from the papier-maché mould which was successfully developed at the Office of *The Times*. Stereotyping by this method rather than by the plaster-of-paris mould was important not only for flat-bed printing but for the development of the rotary reel-fed press.

To print off the enormous output of composing room and foundry, and of illustrations reproduced by photographic means, the press room had been enlarged and transformed. The Albions and Columbians were outdated after the mid-century when the jobbing Croppers, some worked by treadle, some by power, came to this country from America. The four-feeder of Applegath and Cowper was superseded at *The Times* in 1848 by the vertical eight-feeder, the largest piece of printing machinery that had then been seen, and in 1857 by the Hoe ten-feeder, the largest single unit that has yet been seen, the 'Lightning' press, employing twenty-four men and producing 20,000 impressions an hour. It was followed within a decade by the outstanding achievement of newspaper printing, the reel-fed rotary. The Walter Press, the first in this country and designed and built in the Office of *The Times*, was a relatively compact machine run by a man and two boys; but the output was 12,000 eight-page copies an hour.

Flat-bed printers were not so spectacularly served. Their mainstays were either the two-revolution press, such as that constructed by David Napier in 1827 or the later stop- or fixed-cylinder press devised about 1858 of which the most celebrated example is the Wharfedale, both being improvements on the drum-cylinder. By the 1870's two- and four-feeders were common, the two-colour press had been introduced and a press that combined letterpress and lithography was popular. The demand for these machines came however not so often from book houses as from those printing a periodical with a circulation of about 20,000, one that did not warrant a machine such as the rotaries at *The Times* Office.

Thus every year and almost every month the Victorian printer heard of new inventions, from eight-feeders down to the humble metallic quoin or rule-and-lead cutter. It was a time of vigorous competition, of exciting experiment, and of domination by periodical publishers. The spread of the new machinery was of course slow and the majority of houses remained small and served by a single large powered press. Yet the acreage of printed matter that could be produced when speeds of 4,000 impressions an hour were commonplace was breathtaking to many who as apprentices had used the hand-press, the hand-cast type, the wooden furniture and the wooden block.

The typographical problems that faced the Victorian printer can be paralleled by those in a modern newspaper office. When an unceasing flow of copy must be set and printed at the highest possible speed all casual experiment and even the mildest variation must be eschewed; the more rigid the standardisation of typography, so that every piece of copy is interchangeable, the higher the efficiency of composing and press rooms. The efficiency becomes mechanical, that of the ball bearing and the well-greased cog; and as soulless. It was the failure to stimulate the experience of the craftsman that William Morris was so passionately to attack.

Technical efficiency pervaded the biggest book and newspaper houses and received its most perfect expression perhaps in the huge and crowded pages of *The Times* during the 1880's. The feat of producing nightly such a quantity of printed matter could most easily be accomplished by packing each column to the quoins with text type. Items, whatever their length or importance, were separated only by the most unobtrusive of headlines. No typographical aid, except that of a legible text design and reasonable presswork, was given to the reader. Insistence on a standardised layout even laid a heavy hand on the enterprising George Newnes and Alfred Harmsworth when they brought out magazines intended for the new reading public enfranchised by the Elementary Education Act of 1870. Both *Tit-Bits* (1881) and *Answers* (1888) were made typographically attractive on broad principles. The type size was large for easy reading, the short paragraphs were leaded, and so forth; but within the page there was almost no variation. Nothing impelled the publishers of the yellow-back, the railway novel and the three-decker of the 'eighties and 'nineties to change a typography satisfactorily standardised in the 'thirties and 'forties.

There was no time to ponder on principles of typography. Indeed, masters and men were equally ill-equipped to design their printing and what initiative existed in bookwork came from the publisher. In general his instructions referred only to the wrapper or boards, and the burden of the text pages fell on the compositor, who followed the style of preceding publications. Thirteen words to a line, 6 point set solid in the novels of G. W. M. Reynolds when they were reprinted in the 1880's by John 'value-for-money' Dicks, 8 point set solid in Ward Lock's 2s. 6d. series for the bookstalls, were accepted without protest. If chapter initials were needed to raise the standard of a publication, then it was easy to raid the well-stocked jobbing cases for a rustic alphabet already cast.

The mechanical progress of the trade dominated the exhibitions after 1851 with the exception of the Caxton Celebration of 1877. This was inspired by the growing interest in antiquarianism, itself an offshoot of the Gothic revival, which was for instance leading Edward Arber to transcribe the registers of the Stationers' Company for the sixteenth and seventeenth centuries, and of which an exponent was William Blades, himself the head of one of the most prosperous and active London houses.

Pride of place in the exhibition went to the assembly of Caxtons and Wynkyn de Wordes but whether the massive bombardment of blackletter did much except stun the trade visitors may be doubted. They liked the spindly blackletters of their own era, a thick that looked as if it were linked by wire rather than a penstroke, and the exhibition did not change their views. The antiquarian section was flanked by others that in less detail brought the trade's history down to the 1870's and the section devoted to Bibles was sufficiently large to merit its own catalogue. Thus the visitor was able to see the roman and italic faces of other periods. He was also able to see the work of the University Presses of Oxford and Cambridge.

It was apparently by chance that Blades was able to include an exhibit of twenty-three, mostly multiple, items of ancient typographical material preserved at the University Press, Oxford. Early in the previous year Dr C. H. O. Daniel, Provost of Worcester College, whose hobby was his private press, had in searching for a text type rummaged among the stocks of the Press. According to the notes of the Oxford librarian Falconer Madan, 'his artistic eye hit on a broken and imperfect fount, a dusty, disused legacy left by "the unreasonably hated" Dr Fell...he divined its possibilities.' Daniel may have known what he was looking for: type used at least once in the 1860's. Daniel's first book after his search in which the types, usually known after their collector as the Fell types, were used was *A New Sermon, Of the Newest Fashion*, printed at the Daniel Press in 1877. The news reached Blades and thus, neglected for more than a century and a half, the sixteenth- and seventeenth-century types collected by Bishop Fell were shown to the public at the Caxton Celebration.

Like Whittingham, Daniel combined his type with seventeenth-century contents but there resemblance ended and the typography made no attempt to recapture the past. This book was without decoration and even on the title-page only a solitary rule was employed. The Daniel Press continued however to function until 1903 and the later books, of which the best known is *The Garland of Rachel* (1881), contained headpieces, tailpieces, flowers and borders and devices, conservative in style, all commissioned by Daniel or obtained from the University Press. Madan considered that 'the use of Fell type in 1877 and the production of *The Garland of Rachel* in 1881 may fairly be regarded as the first genuine signs of the Revival of Printing in this country'.

The influence of individual volumes of the Daniel Press was not great for they were undistinguished typographically, the presswork was poor and the editions, often of less than fifty copies, were restricted to circulation in Oxford or among his academic friends elsewhere. The effect of the revival of the Fell types was however considerable. Hitherto the only material of the past that had been available in quantity had been Caslon's types. Those working to raise standards in typography and in the printing trade had now an alternative.

The University Press could not immediately take advantage of Daniel's dusty find. Following the death in 1872 of the senior member of the partnership responsible for printing, the Delegates decided to appoint their own representative, but not until 1883 did they secure in Horace Hart a man suitably qualified to be the Printer to the University. His first task was the modernisation of a house already one of the largest in the country. He bought a new hot-rolling press, new printing machines and a gas engine, and he renovated the typefoundry. This department was essential since Oxford type height differed from that in general use (and still does) which obliged the Press to cast from matrices. Since neither the London nor the Scottish founders would sell other than type Hart turned to foreign sources, and the designs he found being no more attractive than those of his own country, his admiration of the Fell founts was increased. Thus Hart was familiar with the latest mechanical inventions and prepared to participate in a highly competitive trade at the same time that he began seriously to investigate the Fell types. In this remarkable man two disparate worlds, one professional, commercialised, committed to mass production and driven to keep down costs, the other meditative, often scholarly and sometimes amateur, were united. He was not however able to use the Fell types until 1896, an interval which covered the entire typographical adventure of Morris's Kelmscott Press.

In 1888, the same year that Robert Miehle perfected the modern two-revolution press, Morris was stirred to enthusiasm by a lecture that the printer Emery Walker gave at the Arts and Crafts Exhibition of that year. Walker had a thorough knowledge of printing technique and strong views on typographical detail, and the illustrations that he had chosen for his lecture were then a novelty to all except the few like William Blades of the London trade or Henry Bradshaw of the Cambridge Library who had begun to interest themselves in the physique of books of the past. Morris, who had always been a student of manuscripts, resolved to emulate the artists of the printed letter. Since 1858 he had been writing poetry based on medieval legend and its publication in old style or modern had always discontented him. In Walker he found the adviser who responded to his cry, 'Let's make a new type!', the expert who could help to create a private press that would be no mere hobby but a passion.

Morris could come to no terms at all with the nineteenth century. For him printing was still the craft evolved by medieval workmen and the skills of the punchcutter and compositor were those of the goldsmith or cabinet-maker. He loathed the routine movements of mass production, he rebelled against the products of Victorian technical progress. Although to him the thin grey modern and old style were 'hideous', he was not enamoured of the Fell types. Historically they were too young for him: for the saga or the minstrel's tale he rightly considered inappropriate the type designs of the sixteenth and seventeenth centuries. 'Sudden', for instance, could not without absurdity be spelt 'sodaine' in modern and even in Fell type there was an effect of fancy dress. Archaic spelling demanded an archaic type.

He experimented first with Howard's Basle roman for *The Roots of the Mountains* (1889) but a type which Whittingham had intended heavily to lead and lightly to ink had too much of the nineteenth century for Morris. A copy of one of Caxton's types that had also been cut at Whittingham's direction was no more suitable. The Golden, and later the Troy and Chaucer types, had to be 'made' because no other satisfactory founts were available and they were made to suit his special needs.

What Morris recognised was the fundamental relationship between type design and typography, or the disposition of the typographical elements within the page; although to Morris the unit of typography was not the page but the opening. The Golden type was planned in conjunction with the decorative blocks, and the visual aspect of his medieval romances supports and is supported by the verbal. The perfect relationship that he secured between his typography and his text was never intended by him to have a general application and he never sought to impose his deliberate archaism upon current printed matter.

The inadequacy of the range of contemporary founders' type was more serious for men who lacked the resources of Morris. Bernard Newdigate, who in 1890 joined his father in a small press, found to his dismay that 'the only founts in general use were just the "old style" and the "modern"'. He had to turn to Caslon in his effort to follow the example Walker had shown. In 1894, C. H. St John Hornby, also influenced by Walker, asked Oxford for Fell type and began to set the second Ashendene Press book, Dante's *Vita Nuova* (1895), having used Caslon for the first. Both men were to produce books grounded on the Morris-Oxford principle that the design of the type, and its compatibility with woodcut illustration, were fundamental to the unity of the page.

There were others, such as those who admired Oscar Wilde, of whom Aubrey Beardsley and Charles Ricketts are for students of the graphic arts now the best remembered, to whom decoration and layout were more estimable than type. Their ideas were promoted in their literary journal, *The Century Guild Hobby Horse* (1887), printed by the Chiswick Press in old style, its pages laid out with the fanatical severity of the reformer. The only decorations were initials and tailpieces by the architect Herbert Horne and a bold line block for the cover by Selwyn Image, the editor. Here was no love of the medieval; or even of the Gothic. Both used the motifs of Art Nouveau, the romantic stylisation of natural forms stirred by an invisible wind, for which the freer line drawing was fitter than the meticulous line engraving.

Old style or Caslon satisfied these young men. They were not interested in type design although mildly attracted to brush-drawn lettering, and they were chiefly occupied with layout. They were not disturbed by the irregularity of Caslon italic capitals but on the contrary found it appropriate to a typography that was increasingly asymmetrical. They set text in upper-case or italics, they broke up the tradition of a centred title page—their most extreme experiment being perhaps that for Wilde's poem, *The Sphinx*, published in 1894 by Elkin Mathews and John Lane—and they were constantly drawing decoration.

This highly sophisticated coterie was as absorbed in the appearance of books as Morris and Walker; but they did not exclaim, 'Let's make a new type!', as the prelude to their experiments.

The failure of a typography that ignored type design was exposed in the *Morte d'Arthur* (1893) that Beardsley was commissioned by the publisher J. M. Dent to prepare in emulation of the Kelmscott Press. Dent had been struck by the 'wonderful balance in black and white' of Beardsley's work which gave, he recalled in his memoirs, 'force and concentration as well as a sense of colour'. Unhappily old style had neither force nor colour and in old style the book was set. Beardsley contributed a wealth of drawings that in richness of invention surpassed Burne-Jones and he fluently interpreted what is eerie and unearthly in Malory's world. Yet instead of the harmony between decoration and text, the cohesion of a Morris page, Dent's is dominated by Beardsley's magnificent black-and-white and the text fails to command attention.

The asymmetricists suffered from the discrediting of Wilde in 1895 and the early death of Beardsley in 1898. Ricketts abandoned the most extreme typographical *jeux d'esprit* and joined the ranks of the orthodox in designing three text founts for his own imprint of the Vale Press, his books being printed by the Ballantyne Press. All the founts were disfigured by over-emphasis of the calligraphic origin of letterform which he misunderstood.

The most penetrating effect of the ideas of these young men was on their chief publishers, Elkin Mathews and John Lane of the Bodley Head, but Dent showed his receptiveness in, for instance, *The Book of Job* (1896), with its full-page line illustrations drawn by Herbert Granville Fell in the Beardsley style and captioned in handdrawn lettering. In this book old style is combined with a highly calligraphic blackletter that contrasts with it both in weight and letterform. Handmade paper uncut and a binding of glossy linen with an intricate design stamped in gold completed a stylised and ambitious publication in which good materials were competently employed in the most advanced taste of the period.

At the same time Dent was preparing for the general market low-priced series such as the Temple Shakespeare (1894) and the Temple Classics (1896), 'choice literature', he explained in his memoirs, 'for the real book-lover, produced on good paper, thin, opaque and strong, so that a volume like Bacon's *Essays* could be carried lightly in the pocket without disturbing the symmetry of the most fashionably cut coat and might be a constant companion'. A greater restraint makes the second series typographically preferable to the first. Dent's aesthete friends were recalled in the decorated title-pages and such typographical embellishments as shoulder-notes set in a type heavier in weight and design than the text fount. Thus he brought into commercial book production the treatment of printing as an art rather than a craft that was a characteristic of the 1890's.

The successes of nineteenth-century book typography were in the small format. Failure with the larger sizes marked the long period between Bulmer and Morris, and the latter learnt painfully that a large-paper edition of an octavo did not make a fine book and extra margins effected no magical transformation. The collection of Bibles in the Caxton Celebration of 1877 pitilessly underlined the inability of the privileged printers to produce a book that compared well even with the folio of 1611, let alone with Baskerville. The Revised Version, of which the Old Testament appeared in 1881 as a joint enterprise of Oxford and Cambridge, took no typographical chances and was content with the most conventional and staid dress. At Oxford it was the rehabilitation of the Fell material that was to stimulate the Printer to venture on larger formats.

In 1899 Hart completed the printing of a quarto, *The Yattendon Hymnal* edited by Robert Bridges and H. Ellis Wooldridge, which was set in Fell types with the music types of Peter Walpergen that had lain unused since the end of the seventeenth century. A novel and attractive feature of the typography was the setting of the Fell ornaments, most of them arabesques, in single rows or columns to divide or border the text. Thus apart from the music the decoration was the metal fleuron, the flower of lead, antimony and tin, assorting by nature and this case by design with the type. Hart's own mastery of technical as distinct from artistic typography was shown in the appendix, where the long measure that had been required by the lines of music was skilfully interwoven by notes, staves, biographical paragraphs and references to sources.

In the following year he collected his research on the old material into a quarto, *Notes on a Century of Typography at the University Press, Oxford, 1693–1794*, 1693 being the year in which the first printed specimen sheet was issued by the Press. The Printer's prefatory remarks, admirably leaded, were set within fleuron borders reinforced with rows to separate the running heads and footnotes and with clumps of flowers at the beginning and the end of the text, giving an effect of Moorish magnificence. A simpler, workmanlike layout was used for the analysis of the material, in which his notes were enclosed by plain rules. Thus the two parts of the book form a striking contrast, the mosque and the office.

The Fell italic appeased a hundred-year-old longing for a strong calligraphic face. In the interests of efficiency italic had gone to the wall during the nineteenth century. The compositor worked faster if he did not have to change his cases and in composing machines a switch to italic impeded the purpose of mechanisation; for the same reason a modern daily newspaper avoids italic. Part of the interest of the Caslon revival was the resurgence of italic as a companion to roman and even as an independent fount. The title-pages of Oxford books, for instance the Tudor and Stuart Library, were increasingly strengthened by the use of Fell. Among the most luxurious productions at this period were the Common Prayer books of 1911 and 1913 in red and black with the Fell ornaments woven into frames or piled in intricate patterns.

That the Fell types had to be cast by hand limited their use. By 1900 the biggest book houses were already welcoming the hot-metal composing machine. The slug-casting Linotype was installed in a number of London newspaper offices and the Monotype, the single-type composing machine invented by Tolbert Lanston, was available in this country after 1897 and was used for a book published by Heinemann in 1899 and for Oxford books after 1902. The Monotype was the more complicated machine and since it consisted of two units, a keybord and a caster, required two fully-trained men. As the first book faces cut were old style and moderns there was still no type available for the aspiring printer.

Two of the most famous of the private-press founts were now created, both revivals of the fifteenth-century Italian letterform which had inspired Morris. In 1900 Walker joined T. J. Cobden-Sanderson in founding the Doves Press, equipped with a fount based on a Jenson roman used in 1470, and in 1901 St John Hornby had Subiaco, based on the Sweynheym and Pannartz face of 1465. Both designs had that blackness that Morris had taught was a virtue and neither had, or was intended to have, the economy of set that was demanded by the scale of contemporary book publishing. Subiaco was first used in Dante's *Inferno* (1902) with woodcut illustration, printed in red and black with initials in gold and colours, and when the *Purgatorio* (1904) and *Paradiso* (1905) had been added St John Hornby completed for Dante a presentation comparable in typographical splendour to that which Morris had bestowed on Chaucer.

Cobden-Sanderson and Walker courageously undertook the book by which Morris had never been attracted, the book which seems beyond the capacity of a small press, the book which throughout the centuries has suffered more than any other from the standardisation of typography: the Bible. The five small folio volumes of the Doves Bible (1903–05) had only one English precedent: that of Baskerville in 1763. In its pages Cobden-Sanderson proved the truth of Morris's dictum, that a book without decoration could be positively 'un-ugly'. This Bible is the triumph of perfect austerity. Cobden-Sanderson put nothing upon the page except the essential typographical sorts, using his single fount, which then had no italic, and the initials to the book openings that were drawn by Edward Johnston are the bare structure of the letter represented. The text is run on without paragraphing and the only relief is an occasional paragraph mark and the setting of certain books, such as Isaiah and the Psalms, in a verse form which Cobden-Sanderson himself arranged.

In the spacing of type and the planning of the page, in choice of ink and paper and in quality of presswork both the Doves and Ashendene Presses set standards that may be equalled but cannot be surpassed. The Doves Bible was the last monumental edition of Holy Writ to be composed by hand.

The fashion for private faces continued. Philip Lee Warner, of Chatto & Windus and of the Medici Society, commissioned Horne to design for each a private type, Florence and Riccardi, both completed in 1909. The Medici Society's Riccardi was successfully used for the Bibliotheca Classica Riccardiana. Shortly afterwards Dent made typographical history by asking the Lanston Monotype Corporation, which till then had exclusively served the commercial trade, to cut for him a design, Veronese, completed in 1911. Like the private-press faces it was based on the fifteenth-century Italian letter that Walker and Morris had canonised, and Veronese proved impractical for general bookwork although it conferred distinction on Dent's catalogues.

Morris and Cobden-Sanderson wrote on their principles in bookmaking and were attentively read by the cognoscenti. The ordinary educated man and woman learnt next to nothing of a trade as industrialised as iron-founding and supposed to be a *métier* of as little general interest. On 10 September 1912 *The Times* celebrated the publication of the 40,000th number with a Supplement that disclosed the glorious achievements of the nineteenth century and demonstrated that the ancient craft yielded in interest to none.

The idea of the Supplement was Lord Northcliffe's. He had bought the newspaper in 1908 and had at once replaced the Walter presses by new rotaries and the Kastenbeins by Monotypes and later by Intertypes, a slug-composing machine. It was natural for the newspaper's Supplement to concentrate on aspects of production and appropriate when that newspaper had been responsible for every technical advance in this country until the reel-fed rotary. The Supplement was the first justification to appear outside the trade papers of the vast changes which had transformed the craft into an industry. Almost exactly a century after the introduction of the powered press the first unalloyed welcome was given to the principle of mechanisation. 'The design and efficiency of present-day machines are apt to induce the idea that finality is being approached,' observed a contributor, 'but there is every reason to suppose that the future has even greater developments to unfold.'

The Supplement gave considerable space to new methods of illustration and to colour printing, techniques which at this time concerned the periodical publishers more than the book houses. The latter had received the half-tone process with even greater caution than hot-metal composition. The private-press printers had remained faithful to woodcut illustration but Beardsley had made the zinco respectable. Half-tones however required their own paper and in 1912 the problem of incorporating a coated paper satisfactorily in a book had not been solved; nor was the process itself perfect. Thus publishers of travel books, such as Macmillan with the Highways and Byways series, preferred to use artists' drawings rather than photographic originals.

Normally the half-tone degraded rather than improved: reprints of such steady-sellers as the school stories of Talbot Baines Reed, fully illustrated in line when first published in the 1880's and 1890's, were being granted a single half-tone that lacked depth of contrast or detail. Even at The Times Office the half-tone was a poor relation of the zinco.

In recounting the history of printing, of which Morris was the terminus ad quem, the Supplement recognised the work of the private presses but ignored commercial book production. To the problems of the latter only one contributor (A. W. Pollard) made a passing reference: 'The fifteenth-century men were fine fellows and good to follow, but not to follow slavishly. Very real improvements have been made; but there are still problems to be solved in book-building, and they cannot all be surmounted by an appeal to the practice of Jenson.' This was a heretical doctrine in 1912 when the worship of the Italian printer and his letter was at its height.

Even as the Supplement went to press a printer, Gerald Meynell of the Westminster Press, was preparing to remedy the lack of practical founts. He planned a new trade paper printed in a new type face, Imprint, cut for him by the Monotype Corporation. Imprint was a reformed Caslon, regularised on the principles that had inspired old style which now resulted in another and

THE PASTIME AND RECREATION
OF
THE QUEEN OF FAIRIES IN FAIRY-LAND,
THE CENTRE OF THE EARTH.[a]

QUEEN MAB, and all her company
Dance on a pleasant mole-hill high,
To small straw-pipes, wherein great pleasure
They take, and keep just time and measure;
All hand in hand, around, around,
They dance upon this fairy-ground;
And when she leaves her dancing ball,
She doth for her attendants call,
To wait upon her to a bower,
Where she doth sit under a flower,
To shade her from the moon-shine bright,
Where gnats do sing for her delight,
Some high, some low, some middle strain,
Making a concert very plain;
The whilst the bat doth fly about,
To keep in order all the rout,
And with her wings doth soundly pay
Those, that make noise, and not obey.
A dewy waving leaf's made fit[b]
For the Queen's bath, where she doth sit,

[a] This is a beautiful little poem; and, indeed, has been more than once cited for its merit. It contains in general a playful and happy selection, both of imagery and language. A few flat or coarse circumstances occur (as in all her Grace's compositions) to deform this piece, in common with those of the same age.

[b] *A dewy waving leaf's made fit*, &c. down to, *That from sweet flowers, &c.*---are exquisite; and worthy of "*The Midsummer Night's Dream*."

1. Duchess of Newcastle: *Select Poems*, Lee Priory Press (1813).
Text page set in 'modern' face

THE

HOLY BIBLE,

CONTAINING

THE OLD TESTAMENT,

AND

THE NEW;

TRANSLATED OUT OF

The Original Tongues;

AND WITH

**THE FORMER TRANSLATIONS DILIGENTLY
COMPARED AND REVISED,**

BY HIS MAJESTY'S SPECIAL COMMAND.

Appointed to be read in Churches.

LONDON:
Printed for GEORGE EYRE and ANDREW STRAHAN,
Printers to the King's Most Excellent Majesty.
Sold by LONGMAN, HURST, REES, ORME, and BROWN,
Paternoster Row. 1814.

2. *The Holy Bible*, The King's Printers (1814). Title-page set in 'modern' face

VIRGIDEMIARUM:

SATIRES,

BY

JOSEPH HALL,

BISHOP OF EXETER AND OF NORWICH.

IN SIX BOOKS.

LONDON:

WILLIAM PICKERING, CHANCERY LANE.

M.DCCC.XXV.

3. Joseph Hall: *Virgidemiarum*, William Pickering (1825). Title-page with wreath device, set in 'modern' face

PREFACE *to the Second Part of the Diary of* Lady Willoughby.

THE ſtyle of Printing and general appearance of this Volume have been adopted, as they were in the firſt Part of the *Diary*, merely to be in accordance with the Deſign of the Author, who in this Work perſonates a Lady of the Seventeenth Century.

4. *Some Further Portions of the Diary of Lady Willoughby* (1848). Designed by Charles Whittingham the Younger, set in Caslon

EDITH HERON;

OR,

THE EARL AND THE COUNTESS.

CHAPTER I.

THE VAULT IN WESTMINSTER ABBEY AND ITS OCCUPANTS.

It was just as the midnight hour was solemnly given forth by the various church clocks of London on the night of that eventful day which had hailed Captain Felix Heron, of Epping Forest, and his fair and gentle Edith as the veritable Earl and Countess of Whitcombe, that a fearful storm

No. 1.—EDITH HERON.

that had raged for more than two hours over the metropolis reached its height.

The incessant flashing of the blue lightning was confounding and terrible.

The roar of the loud-mouthed thunder seemed as if it were splitting to fragments the vault of heaven, and as it died away in prolonged echoes it appeared seeking for some crevice in the solid earth through which the continents and oceans could be ripped up and dashed together in chaotic confusion.

The few pedestrians whom chance or necessity

5. *Edith Heron; etc.*, John Dicks (c. 1862). Opening page from an 'octavo'

THE

BOOK OF PRAISE

FROM THE BEST ENGLISH HYMN WRITERS

SELECTED AND ARRANGED BY

ROUNDELL PALMER

MACMILLAN AND CO.

London and Cambridge.

1866

6. Roundell Palmer (*ed.*): *The Book of Praise*, Macmillan and Co (1866).
Title-page designed for Alexander Macmillan, set in Old Style

The Book of Praise.

PART THE FIRST.

I.

THE HOLY TRINITY.

" The Catholic Faith is this: that we worship one God in Trinity, and Trinity in Unity."

I.

Holy, holy, holy, Lord God Almighty !
  Early in the morning our song shall rise to Thee;
Holy, holy, holy ! Merciful and Mighty !
  God in Three Persons, blessed Trinity !

Holy, holy, holy ! all the saints adore Thee,
  Casting down their golden crowns around the
    glassy sea,
Cherubim and seraphim falling down before Thee,
  Which wert, and art, and evermore shalt be.

Holy, holy, holy ! though the darkness hide Thee,
  Though the eye of sinful man Thy glory may
    not see,
Only Thou art holy, there is none beside Thee,
  Perfect in power, in love and purity.

Holy, holy, holy, Lord God Almighty !
  All Thy works shall praise Thy Name in earth
    and sky and sea ;
Holy, holy, holy ! Merciful and Mighty !
  God in Three Persons, blessed Trinity !

               Bishop Reginald Heber. 1827.

B

7. Roundell Palmer (*ed.*) : *The Book of Praise*, Macmillan and Co (1866). Text
page designed for Alexander Macmillan, set in Old Style

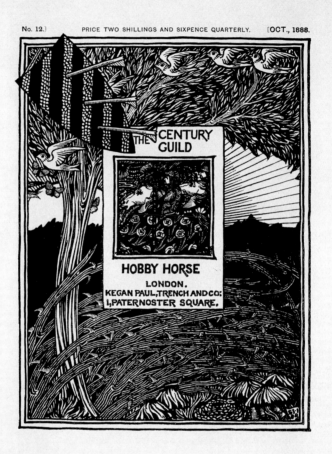

8. *The Century Guild Hobby Horse*, Kegan Paul, Trench & Co (1884). Cover design by Selwyn Image

Book iij   Chapter j

HOW KING ARTHUR TOOK A WIFE, AND
WEDDED GUENEVER, DAUGHTER TO LEODE-
GRANCE, KING OF THE LAND OF CAMELIARD,
WITH WHOM HE HAD THE ROUND TABLE

IN the beginning of Arthur, after he was chosen king by adventure and by grace; for the most part of the barons knew not that he was Uther Pendragon's son, but as Merlin made it openly known. But yet many kings and lords held great war against him for that cause, but well Arthur overcame them all, for the most part the days of his life he was ruled much by the counsel of Merlin. So it fell on a time King Arthur said unto Merlin, My barons will let me have no rest, but needs I must take a wife, and I will none take but by thy counsel and by thine advice. It is well done, said Merlin, that ye take a wife, for a man of your bounty and noblesse should not be without a

9. *Morte d'Arthur* (1893). Text page set in Old Style, with initial and border by Aubrey Beardsley

2
Welcome and dear unto my soul
Are these sweet feasts of Love :
But what a sabbath shall I keep
When I shall rest above !
I bless . . .

3
I come, I wait, I hear, I pray,
Thy footsteps, Lord, I trace :
I sing to think this is the way
Unto my Saviour's face.

AT END OF ODD SECTIONS THE CROWNED MINIM AND DOUBLE BAR
ARE SUBSTITUTED FOR SEMIBREVE AND MINIM REST OF UNBAR'D ORIGINAL.

10. *The Yattendon Hymnal* (1899). Page set in Fell types and music by Peter Walpergen

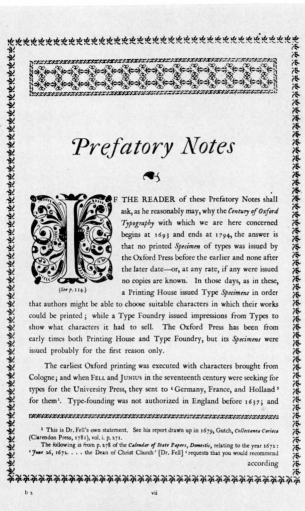

Prefatory Notes

❧

(See p. 114.)

I F THE READER of these Prefatory Notes shall ask, as he reasonably may, why the *Century of Oxford Typography* with which we are here concerned begins at 1693 and ends at 1794, the answer is that no printed *Specimen* of types was issued by the Oxford Press before the earlier and none after the later date—or, at any rate, if any were issued no copies are known. In those days, as in these, a Printing House issued Type *Specimens* in order that authors might be able to choose suitable characters in which their works could be printed; while a Type Foundry issued impressions from Types to show what characters it had to sell. The Oxford Press has been from early times both Printing House and Type Foundry, but its *Specimens* were issued probably for the first reason only.

The earliest Oxford printing was executed with characters brought from Cologne; and when FELL and JUNIUS in the seventeenth century were seeking for types for the University Press, they sent to 'Germany, France, and Holland' for them[1]. Type-founding was not authorized in England before 1637; and

[1] This is Dr. Fell's own statement. See his report drawn up in 1679, Gutch, *Collectanea Curiosa* (Clarendon Press, 1781), vol. i. p. 271.

The following is from p. 278 of the *Calendar of State Papers, Domestic*, relating to the year 1672: '*June 26*, 1672. . . . the Dean of Christ Church' [Dr. Fell] 'requests that you would recommend according

11. Horace Hart: *Notes on a Century of Typography, etc.*, Oxford (1900). Text page set in Fell types and ornaments

Browne's
Religio Medici

And Digby's Observations

At the Clarendon Press
MCMIX

12. Tudor and Stuart Library, Oxford at the Clarendon Press (1909). Title-page set in Fell

13. *The Times Printing Number*, London (1912). Title-page of the issue in
book form

translation of the "Odyssey," by Rudolf Alexander Schroeder. The interest in this revival of handwriting induced the German Government, immediately after the great Arts and Crafts Exhibition at Dresden in 1906, to invite Miss Simons over to Germany in order that she might give lessons to the pupils of the Royal Art School at Düsseldorf. Soon she was also commissioned for courses to the writing masters of the Prussian Volksschulen (elementary schools). Since then Miss Simons herself and her German pupils have been strenuously teaching the new art all over Germany ; and their influence has already been considerable. German masters of the craft, such as Weiss, Walter Tiemann, Ehmke, Kleukens, have begun to produce work which is altogether creditable. Up to now, however, they have been successful principally with roman lettering. But the art of writing

beautifully in roman characters may eventually bring forth a purer form of gothic ; and hereon hangs the main hope for the ultimate survival of a separate German script.

It has been impossible to give more than a very brief retrospect of the movement which has replaced so suddenly the dismal German books of our childhood by an immense crop of attractive and often very handsome work, giving promise, at the same time, of perhaps still more interesting developments. But the British public will soon have an opportunity of judging for itself what Germany has done latterly in the way of good printing. In 1914 an International Exhibition of all that is related to the production of books will be held in Leipzig. It is to be hoped that a great many of those interested in fine printing in England will not only come over, but will exhibit there themselves.

14. *The Times Printing Number*, London (1912). Text page from the issue in book form

The Imprint

ART AND WORKMANSHIP : By Professor W. R. LETHABY

WE have been in the habit of writing so lyrically of art and of the temperament of the artist that the average man who lives in the street, sometimes a very mean street, is likely to think of it as remote and luxurious, not " for the likes of him." There is the danger in habitual excess of language that the plain man is likely to be frightened by it. It may be feared that much current exposition of the place and purpose of art only widens the gap between it and common lives.

A proper function of criticism should be to foster our national arts and not to frighten timid people off with high-pitched definitions and far-fetched metaphors mixed with a flood of (as Morris said) " sham technical twaddle." It is a pity to make a mystery of what should most easily be understood. There is nothing occult about the thought that all things may be made well or made ill. A work of art is a well-made thing, that is all. It may be a well-made statue or a well-made chair, or a well-made book. Art is not a special sauce applied to ordinary cooking ; it is the cooking itself if it is good. Most simply and generally art may be thought of as THE WELL-DOING OF WHAT NEEDS DOING. If the thing is not worth doing it can hardly be a work of art, however well it may be done. A thing worth doing which is ill done is hardly a thing at all.

Fortunately people are artists who know it not—bootmakers (the few left), gardeners and basketmakers, and all players of games. We do not allow shoddy in cricket or football, but reserve it for serious things like houses and books, furniture and funerals.

If it is necessary that everything must be translated into words, our art critics might occupy quite a useful place if they would be good enough to realise that behind the picture shows of the moment is the vast and important art of the country, the arts of the builder, furniture maker, printer and the rest, which are matters of national well-being.

It is doubtful if we have it in us to form a leading school of painting at

I   B

15. *The Imprint* (1913). Opening page from the first number, set in Imprint, with titling and initial by Edward Johnston

Fifteenth Sunday after Trinity

THE GOSPEL.
St. Matthew vi. 24.

NO man can serve two masters: for either he will hate the one, and love the other; or else he will hold to the one, and despise the other. Ye cannot serve God and Mammon. Therefore I say unto you, Take no thought for your life, what ye shall eat, or what ye shall drink; nor yet for your body, what ye shall put on: Is not the life more than meat, and the body than raiment? Behold the fowls of the air; for they sow not, neither do they reap, nor gather into barns; yet your heavenly Father feedeth them. Are ye not much better than they? Which of you by taking thought can add one cubit unto his stature? And why take ye thought for raiment? Consider the lilies of the field how they grow: they toil not, neither do they spin: and yet I say unto you, That even Solomon in all his glory was not arrayed like one of these. Wherefore, if God so clothe the grass of the field, which to-day is, and to-morrow is cast into the oven; shall he not much more clothe you, O ye of little faith? Therefore take no thought, saying, What shall we eat? or what shall we drink? or wherewithal shall we be clothed? (for after all these things do the Gentiles seek:) for your heavenly Father knoweth that ye have need of all these things. But seek ye first the kingdom of God, and his righteousness, and all these things shall be added unto you. Take therefore no thought for the morrow; for the morrow shall take thought for the things of itself: sufficient unto the day is the evil thereof.

THE.

16. *The Book of Common Prayer*, University Press, Oxford (1913). Text page set in Fell types and ornaments

§ 106. Perilla Oil.

Character.

Resembles Linseed oil in odour and flavour.

Physical and Chemical Data.

(1)	Specific gravity 15·5° C.		·9305 [1]
(8)	Solidifying point fatty acids ° C.		
(4)	Refractive index 40° C.		1·4753 [1]
(6)	Valenta		49·5 [2]
(8)	Iodine value		206 [3]
	(a) Bromine thermal test		
	(b) Maumené		124 [1]
	(c) Livache		
(11)	Insoluble bromide value fatty acids		64 [4]
(18)	Acid value		

Remarks.

It is characterised by its very high **Iodine value** which is the greatest of all known oils.

Technical.

Source.

The nuts of the Perilla Ocimoides, an annual plant, occurring in China, Japan and E. Indies.

Content of oil.

About 36 per cent.

General.

The oil is obtained by crude native methods and is used in Manchuria largely for edible purposes. In Japan it is employed as an adulterant of **lacquer.** Curiously enough, in view of its larger content of unsaturated glycerides, the oil is inferior as a drier to Linseed.

§ 107. Typical Oil. **LINSEED OIL.**

I. General and Analytical.

Character.

COLOUR. Pale yellow to brown.

ODOUR. Faint, but distinctive. Easily recognised on boiling with water.

STEARINE. None separates at ordinary temperatures.

Remarks.

The Iodine Value is the highest in the case of the **Baltic Oil,** which is from the purest seed. Other grades of oil containing

---

[1] Rosenthal.   [2] Fryer and Weston.   [3] Wijs.
[4] Eibner and Muggenthaler.

17. Cambridge University Press (1917). Text page from a technical handbook

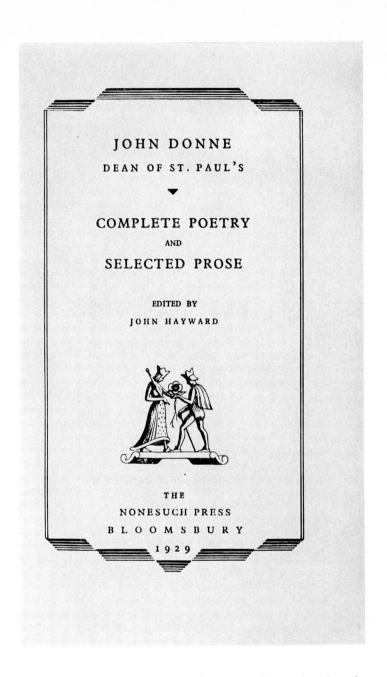

JOHN DONNE

DEAN OF ST. PAUL'S

▼

COMPLETE POETRY

AND

SELECTED PROSE

EDITED BY

JOHN HAYWARD

THE
NONESUCH PRESS
BLOOMSBURY
1929

18. John Donne: *Complete Poetry, etc.*, The Nonesuch Press (1929). Title-page
set in Plantin with ornaments by Beatrice Warde

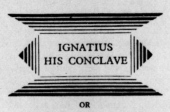

**IGNATIUS
HIS CONCLAVE**

OR
HIS INTHRONISATION IN A LATE ELECTION
IN HELL :
WHEREIN MANY THINGS ARE MINGLED BY
WAY OF SATYR ;
Concerning
The Disposition of Jesuits,
The Creation of a new Hell,
The establishing of a Church in the Moone.
There is also added an Apology
for Jesuites.
All dedicated to the two Adversary
Angels, which are protectors of
the Papall Consistory, and of
the Colledge of Sorbon.
Translated out of Latine.

THE PRINTER TO THE READER

D O E S T thou seeke after the Author ? It is in vaine ;
for hee is harder to be found than the parents of Popes
were in the old times : yet if thou have an itch of gessing,
receive from me so much, as a friend of his, to whom he
sent his booke to bee read, writ to me. " The Author was
" unwilling to have this booke published, thinking it unfit
" both for the matter which in it selfe is weighty and
" serious, and for that gravity which himselfe had pro-
" posed and observed in an other booke formerly pub-
" lished, to descend to this kinde of writing. But I on
" the other side, mustered my forces against him, and

19. John Donne: *Complete Poetry, etc.*, The Nonesuch Press (1929). Opening
page set in Plantin with ornaments by Beatrice Warde

DE CONSOLATIONE PHILOSOPHIAE

LIBER PRIMVS

[I. AEGRITVDO BOETHI]

METRVM I

Boethius dolet fortunam aduersam

CARMINA qui quondam studio florente peregi,
flebilis heu maestos cogor inire modos.
Ecce mihi lacerae dictant scribenda camenae
et ueris elegi fletibus ora rigant.
5 Has saltem nullus potuit peruincere terror,
ne nostrum comites prosequerentur iter.
Gloria felicis olim uiridisque iuuentae
solantur maesti nunc mea fata senis.
Venit enim properata malis inopina senectus
10 et dolor aetatem iussit inesse suam.
Intempestiui funduntur uertice cani

M. I, 7 *olim* Vall. Ob. Eng. (p. 53); Pp. *quondam.* 8 *solantur*
Vall. Pp. Ob.; alii *solatur.*

Metrum I elegiacum.
1   *Carmina peregi.* Anecd. Holderi: "condidit et carmen bucoli-
     cum." Robertus Cessi in *Rerum Ital. Script.* nouae ser. xxiv,
     parte 4 (p. cxxxvii) suspicatur nonnulla horum metrorum
     iam antea scripta et collecta a Boethio, haec ergo esse carmen
     bucolicum de quo Anecdoton.
2   *flebilis.* Ouidi *Trist.* v, 1, 5: "flebilis ut noster status est, ita
     flebile carmen."
1-4 citat Waldrammus Eppus Argentinensis (†c. 905) in poemate
     elegiaco ad Salomonem Constantiensem (P.L. cxxxii, 572 b).
     Cfr. Chaucer, *Troilus and Criseyde,* v, 1373–1379 (ed. W.
     Skeat, Oxon. p. 318).
3-4 Cfr. *Aen.* vi, 699; ix, 251; *Octauiam* (inter tragoedias Senecae)
     339–340: "(Augusta) laceratque comas rigat et moestis fle-
     tibus ora."
6   Ouidi *Trist.* iv, 1, 20.
7   *felicis olim.* Vltima syll. 'felicis' prolongata ante caesuram.
     Sic Boethius qui saepius admittit anomalum metrum. 'Quon-
     dam' emendatum ab editoribus (cfr. Eng. l.c. p. 53).
8   Ouidi *Pont.* i, 4, 19–20.
9   *properata malis senectus.* Diog. Laert. iv, c. 7, *Bion:* τὸ γῆρας
     ἔλεγεν ὅρμον εἶναι τῶν κακῶν· εἰς αὐτὸ γοῦν πάντα κατα-
     φεύγειν (ed. Cobet, ap. Didot, p. 105, 32–33).

I

20. *De Consolatione Philosophiae* (1929). Opening page set in Imprint designed
by Stanley Morison

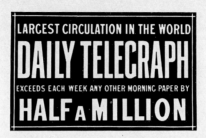

LARGEST CIRCULATION IN THE WORLD

DAILY TELEGRAPH

EXCEEDS EACH WEEK ANY OTHER MORNING PAPER BY

HALF A MILLION

XIV THE NEW JOURNALISM

WHEN the law imposing the penny fiscal stamp ceased to operate on 30 June, 1855, there occurred two revolutionary changes in the news trade. First of all, new dailies were established where they had never been published before. Provincial daily papers made their first regular[1] appearance in the same June, 1855, at Manchester (the *Guardian*, hitherto a weekly, founded 5 May, 1821), Liverpool (*Post*), Sheffield (*Telegraph*), Birmingham (*Mercury*), and Edinburgh (*Scotsman*), to mention only a few centres. Forthwith the London dailies found themselves in competition with new journals which, if they were inferior in talent, were supported by a very vigorous local patriotism and, as a previous chapter has shown, helped against *The Times* by the high postage rate. For the new country journals to compete successfully with the powerful metropolitan Press unquestionably demanded great resources. At first it was natural for them to follow the style of the journal with the largest circulation in town and country—namely, *The Times*—but the attempt ran them into difficulty. Mowbray Morris, writing to his agent in Manchester, put his finger on the source of the trouble. 'There is no reason why a daily newspaper should not be published for one penny with a moderate profit,'[2] but, he wrote, 'it is impossible to produce a first-class paper at that price.' The country at length saw the wisdom of abstaining from such an attempt. Nor in 1855 was there any effort made by the sponsors of the penny Press in London to produce a first-class paper in Morris's sense of the word. London's effort was to produce a cheap paper at a cheap price; and it was a rapid success.

This, the second revolutionary change which followed the repeal of 1855, *i.e.* the establishment of the metropolitan cheap Press, originated in the enterprise of

---

[1] There had been penny provincial papers of irregular appearance during the Crimean War—*e.g.* the *Manchester Examiner Extraordinary* (four days a week from October, 1854). This paper was renamed the *Manchester Daily Times* on and from 12 December, 1854.
[2] Morris to W. P. Stokes, 4 January, 1858.

21. *The History of the Times* (1935). Page from the de-luxe edition set in Times New Roman

THE

NEW TESTAMENT

OF OUR LORD AND SAVIOUR

JESUS CHRIST

Translated out of the Original Greek
and with the former Translations
diligently compared and revised
by His Majesty's special
Command

Appointed to be read in Churches

22. *Oxford Lectern Bible* (1935). Title-page set in Centaur designed by Bruce
Rogers

and magnetic fields are merely useful mathematical vector-concepts, and that the question of their physical reality has no meaning since it cannot be decided by experiment, we now see that by regarding the vector potential in exactly the same light, we have three field concepts which have specific functions:

(A) The electro-static field, $\mathscr{E}_s$, deals with the effects of the *positions* of charges.

(B) The magnetic field, B, is particularly fitted to deal with the effects of the *velocities* of charges.

(C) The vector potential, A, is particularly fitted to deal with the effects of the *accelerations* of charges.

Combining all three effects into one resultant force on a unit charge, we obtain the total electric field (due to all causes) at a point

$$\mathscr{E} = \mathscr{E}_s + (\mathbf{B} \times \mathbf{v}) - \frac{\partial \mathbf{A}}{\partial t}, \qquad (33)*\dagger$$

where, of course, the separate components are to be combined vectorially. If a charge q is moving with velocity v' relative to the point, the force on this charge is then

$$\mathbf{F} = q\{\mathscr{E} + (\mathbf{v}' \times \mathbf{B})\}. \qquad 2(10a)$$

Equation 5(33) gives the general expression for the resultant electric-field intensity at a point, as measured by an observer at that point, due to all electro-magnetic causes. The different quantities are to be calculated thus:

(A) $\mathscr{E}_s$, the electro-static field, is to be calculated from the positions of charges on bodies, on the assumption that the uniform motion of an isolated magnet does not result in any shifting of its constituent charges. The restricted-relativity correction, p. 135, is negligible for all practical velocities, but may be used if necessary.

---

* To this expression should be added the "force per unit charge" due to thermal, chemical, or contact e.m.f.'s. The laws governing these effects, however, give only the line-integral of this force over a finite length of path, or in a complete circuit. Such e.m.f.'s are not included in the term "electro-magnetic".

† In expressions using vector notation **clarendon** type denotes quantities which are vectors. It has been considered unnecessary to carry out this convention through the body of the text.

23. Cambridge University Press (1939). Text page from a science textbook

The corresponding integrals for $W_{k,m}(x)$ are

$$\Gamma(\tfrac{1}{2}+m-k)\,W_{k,m}(x) = x^{\frac{1}{2}-m}\,e^{-\frac{1}{2}x}\int_0^\infty e^{-u}u^{m-\frac{1}{2}-k}(x+u)^{m-\frac{1}{2}+k}\,du, \tag{3.5.9}$$

$$= x^{\frac{1}{2}+m}\,e^{-\frac{1}{2}x}\int_0^\infty e^{-xt}t^{m-k-\frac{1}{2}}(1+t)^{m+k-\frac{1}{2}}\,dt, \tag{3.5.10}$$

$$= x^{\frac{1}{2}+m}\,e^{\frac{1}{2}x}\int_1^\infty e^{-xw}(w-1)^{m-k-\frac{1}{2}}w^{m+k-\frac{1}{2}}\,dw, \tag{3.5.11}$$

$$= x^{\frac{1}{2}+m}2^{-2m}\int_1^\infty e^{-\frac{1}{2}xs}(s-1)^{m-k-\frac{1}{2}}(s+1)^{m+k-\frac{1}{2}}\,ds, \tag{3.5.12}$$

$$= x^{\frac{1}{2}+m}2^{-2m}\int_\pi^\infty e^{-\frac{1}{2}x\cosh\theta}\sinh^{2m}\theta\,\coth^{2k}(\tfrac{1}{2}\theta)\,d\theta, \tag{3.5.13}$$

$$= x^{\frac{1}{2}+m}\,e^{\frac{1}{2}x}(d-c)^{\frac{1}{2}+m+k}\int_c^d \exp\left\{\frac{x(d-c)}{d-u}\right\}(u-c)^{m-k-\frac{1}{2}}(d-u)^{-1-\frac{1}{2}-2m}\,du, \tag{3.5.14}$$

all under the conditions $\mathrm{Rl}\,(\tfrac{1}{2}+m\pm k) > 0$, $|\arg x| < \pi$.

3.5.1 Barnes type integrals for the Whittaker functions

The Barnes integral for $M_{k,m}(x)$ is

$$M_{k,m}(x) = \frac{x^{m+\frac{1}{2}}e^{-\frac{1}{2}x}\,\Gamma(1+2m)}{\Gamma(\tfrac{1}{2}+m-k)\,2\pi i}\int_{c-i\infty}^{c+i\infty}\frac{\Gamma(-s)\,\Gamma(\tfrac{1}{2}+m-k+s)}{\Gamma(1+2m+s)}(-x)^s\,ds, \tag{3.5.15}$$

for $|\arg x| < \tfrac{1}{2}\pi$, and $1 + 2m \neq 0, -1, -2, \ldots$. This follows from the definition of $M_{k,m}(x)$ in terms of $_1F_1[a;b;x]$ and the corresponding integral (3.1.15) for $_1F_1[a;b;x]$, or it can be proved directly by considering the integral round a rectangular contour as for Kummer's function.

The Barnes integral for $W_{k,m}(x)$ is

$$\Gamma(\tfrac{1}{2}-m-k)\,\Gamma(\tfrac{1}{2}+m-k)\,W_{k,m}(x) = \frac{x^k e^{-\frac{1}{2}x}}{2\pi i}\int_{c-i\infty}^{c+i\infty}\Gamma(-s)\,\Gamma(\tfrac{1}{2}+s-m-k)\,\Gamma(\tfrac{1}{2}+s+m-k)\,x^{-s}\,ds, \tag{3.5.16}$$

for $|\arg x| < \tfrac{3}{2}\pi$, and $\tfrac{1}{2}+k\pm m \neq 0, 1, 2, \ldots$. This also follows from the expression of $W_{k,m}(x)$ in terms of $U(a;b;x)$ and the corresponding integral for $U(a;b;x)$ (3.1.18), or directly, as for $M_{k,m}(x)$, by contour integration.

3.5.2 Pochhammer contour integrals for the Whittaker functions

Again we can relax the conditions of validity by extending the elementary integrals for Whittaker's functions to contour integrals of Pochhammer's type. Thus for $M_{k,m}(x)$ we have

$$M_{k,m}(x) = \Gamma(\tfrac{1}{2}-m+k)\,\Gamma(\tfrac{1}{2}-m-k)\,\Gamma(1+2m)\,x^{\frac{1}{2}+m}2^{-2m}\exp\{-\pi i(m-\tfrac{1}{2}\pm k)\}$$

$$\times \frac{1}{4\pi^2}\int_{\pm 1}^{(+1+,-1+,+1-,-1-)}e^{\mp\frac{1}{2}xs}(s^2-1)^{m-\frac{1}{2}}\left(\frac{s+1}{s-1}\right)^{\pm k}\,ds, \tag{3.5.17}$$

for $\arg(s+1) = 0$, $\arg(s-1) = -\pi$ initially, where the integration is round a contour similar to Fig. 3.4, about the points -1 and $+1$, and the upper or lower signs should be taken throughout the equation.

more distinguished face. Meynell's intention was to combine the dignity and pedigree of a private press style of letter with the economy demanded by the trade printer, and he had also considered the application of the type to the coated paper needed for half-tones. Weight had been subtly added so that Imprint was not a grey letter, and the graduation of stroke was firm rather than sharp. The 'dazzle' beloved by the Victorians and abhorred by the private presses was rejected.

The type had been named after the new paper, *The Imprint*, of which no. 1 appeared in January 1913. The typography was not dissimilar to that of Horne's *Hobby Horse*, shorn of the Art Nouveau motifs, and Meynell relieved the simplicity with illustration by trade processes or with calligraphic elements prepared by one of his collaborators, Edward Johnston. Unlike the *Hobby Horse*, *The Imprint* was a trade paper, predominantly written by and for those connected with printing, in which Meynell hoped to present the gospel of the private presses in practical terms. The provision of Imprint, a face created for mechanical composition, was his first step. He held his convictions as determinedly as Morris and among those impressed by them was a recruit to his staff, Stanley Morison.

Financially *The Imprint* proved so insecure that Meynell was forced to discontinue it in 1914 and Morison joined Wilfred Meynell, Gerard Meynell's uncle, and his son Francis at Burns, Oates. This publishing house had maintained the standard of liturgical typography set by James Burns in the 1840's, and early in the twentieth century Wilfrid Meynell had employed Newdigate to design and print several books, including the folio *Of God and his Creatures. An Annotated Translation (with some Abridgement) of the Summa Contra Gentiles of Saint Thomas Aquinas* (1905). The complications of the title page were displayed in Fell, the text of the book being handset in Caslon.

The popularity of Caslon was unabated and soon after the Monotype Corporation had cut Plantin (1913), based on the types preserved at the Plantin Museum at Antwerp, William Maxwell of R. & R. Clark asked that Caslon should be cut for the Monotype. Maxwell was one of the Corporation's first and biggest customers and with his printing orders from London publishers, including Macmillan, and his work for George Bernard Shaw, who was a nothing-but-Caslon man, it was imperative for him to be able to set Caslon mechanically. In carrying out his request in 1916 the Corporation mastered the technique of reproducing for the machine a heavily kerned type.

In 1916 Bruce Rogers, the American typographer, sailed to join Emery Walker in what has been described as 'a Caslon-ridden country'. Throughout this period Walker, although taking a less active part in printing—he left the Doves Press in 1909—was always at the service of those who sought advice and to his unobtrusive activity, manifest only in discourse and example for he wrote nothing, British book typography is deeply in debt. He and Rogers had planned to set up a press but instead Rogers became one of the instruments of the reconciliation between the trade and the fine printers.

The enhanced prestige that the Fell types had given to Oxford had not gone unobserved at the other University and the Syndics listened with disquiet when the publications of the Press were criticised by the then Director of the Fitzwilliam Museum at Cambridge, Sydney Cockerell, the associate of Morris and Walker and Rogers. It was apparent that Hart's use of the Fell material had given Oxford books a distinction befitting a University Press, whereas contemporary Cambridge books were little different from those of any competent London publisher. Pressed by Cockerell, the Syndics invited Rogers in 1917 to become their typographical adviser. Methodically he set himself to examine the available material and the publications, ranging from single books in exotic types to the many volumes of the *Cambridge Modern History*, that the Press was required to print.

His report, presented to the Syndics within a few months, was a detailed appraisal of type, its design and its use. His critical eye noted not only stylistic differences but variations between founts of the same face, and marked arbitrary departures from original body size, the lack of certain sorts in a fount, the letters that had been spoilt by rubbing down as initials. Interspersed with the detail were general reflections, such as, 'the proportions of the average small letter of the fount should be approximately those of the page itself, a broad round letter for a square page and a narrower letter for a long and narrow page'. Except for Newdigate and Walker no one in this country had discussed typography in such terms.

Although Rogers reverenced Morris he himself had in America been associated with presses that were not private in the British sense and he was no fanatic for handsetting. He recognised that a University Press must be highly mechanised—although his report did not touch on the Bible production to which much of the plant was perpetually committed—and a separate section of the report was given to Monotype faces.

At a time when many publishers were loath to admit that their books were machine-set and believed themselves obliged to apologise for the regularity of single-type composition, he had not a word to say in criticism. Perhaps because he came from a country where craft traditions were not strong and where mass production was approved, it was not for him in dispute that the Press must to an increasing degree rely upon the Monotype. It was undesirable that, for instance, the *Cambridge History of English Literature* should be handset. The question for him was which faces should be bought, and hence he discussed the designs available from the Corporation as dispassionately as those of the founders. Some were poor; others, like Imprint and Plantin, good.

'Commonplace materials of book-making may be arranged in the most faultless manner—yet the result will always be commonplace,' he warned the Syndics. In respect of paper and ink he considered that Morris was an unsuitable model for modern plant, although he admitted that contemporary paper and ink had deserved Morris's contempt. Rogers suggested that there was much to be said for the machine-made papers of the early nineteenth century and he recommended that the Syndics should have certain papers made to order. As to ink, the Press was, to his mind, guilty of pursuing the fashionable effect: 'sharpness and cleanness are most desirable qualities,' he wrote, 'but they can be obtained sometimes at too great a sacrifice of strength and blackness.' He advocated a black base with a warm or brownish tint and a varnish that did not dry to a high gloss, the speed of machine printing being borne in mind. Hart, he reminded the Syndics, had already found such a formula for the Tudor and Stuart Library.

Thus in paragraph after paragraph Rogers censured the currently approved principles of book-making. Nor did type design escape. Like every other printing house in the country, the Press was well stocked with Caslon and old style: the first was in Rogers' judgement 'much overrated' and the second 'has less to recommend it; nothing, in fact, except the negative quality of inoffensiveness'. In 1917 a typography that had been avant-garde in 1844, hallowed in 1884 and respectable in 1914 felt the edge of the headsman's axe.

Rogers' method was as unfamiliar to the Syndics as to most other printers and publishers: as Walker realised, the American did not have his equal in the methodical appraisal of a typographical situation. Having called in the doctor they accepted his prescription although they were obliged to wait until the Monotype Corporation, which during the war worked on armament contracts, was ready to assist the Press to change over 'as much as possible of the old type into additional facilities for Monotype composition'.

At this period the financiers and engineers who controlled the Corporation had not envisaged the potential association of their machine with fine printing.

They acquiesced in the general view, that machine composition was a degradation in which only publishing houses committed to large-scale low-cost projects, such as Cassell's Popular Educator, were constrained to indulge.

Owing to the disruption of war neither Imprint nor Plantin had made headway. On the other hand, these were the years when the Cheltenham of American Type Founders, cut at the turn of the century, was flooding into the cases of British general printers and establishing a position from which it has been dislodged only in recent years. Young designers like Francis Meynell and Morison watched with alarm as the hot-metal composing-machine companies hurried to cut their versions of Cheltenham so that not a newspaper or jobbing office in the country was condemned to lack the face. In 1916 Meynell persuaded the Victoria House Publishing Company, which supported the Labour Party's then weekly newspaper, to allot a separate imprint, the Pelican Press, for his own job and newspaper advertisement setting. He imported the more desirable American faces, such as Frederic Goudy's Kennerly and Cloister, and added Monotype faces including Imprint and Plantin. In collaboration with Morison he now revealed in a multiplicity of jobbing and manifestos that the French Renaissance and the printing of sixteenth-century Lyons or Paris offered richer typographical inspiration than fifteenth-century Venice.

Although the resources of the Pelican Press for bookwork were limited, Meynell induced the Corporation to improve various sorts in Plantin and to add others, such as tied ƌt and ſt, and then produced the booklets such as The Best of Both Worlds, a selection of poems by Henry Vaughan and Andrew Marvell (1918), which were forerunners of his Nonesuch Press. In the nineteenth century jobbing and bookwork had followed separate paths, the first giving no assistance to the second. Meynell was to prove that both could be produced from a common stock of types and upon the same machines.

Caslon began to lose ground. Among the advertising agents who employed the Pelican Press for setting was C. W. Hobson who in 1920 decided to set up his own Cloister Press at Heaton Mersey near Manchester, placing it in the charge of a printer, Walter Lewis. The equipment included not only Goudy's Cloister but the Garamond cut in 1916 by American Type Founders. Urged by Lewis and by Morison, who had become first the typographer and then the London representative of the Cloister Press, the publishers Sidgwick & Jackson adopted Garamond for Catherine: A Romantic Poem by R. C. K. Ensor (1921). Heinemann used Imprint for The Beggar's Opera and Plantin for An Anthology of Italian Poems (both 1922), the latter printed at the Cloister Press.

Meanwhile, Cambridge had begun to use Imprint for books ranging from A. N. Whitehead's *An Enquiry concerning the Principles of Natural Knowledge* (1919) and an edition of the Book of Common Prayer prepared by J. N. Dalton (1920) to the *History of British Foreign Policy 1783–1919* (1923). Such books were the spearhead of a typographical reformation of the general trade.

The extent to which between 1910 and 1922 this country was 'Caslon-ridden' was amply demonstrated in an exhibition of Twentieth-Century Printed Books, British and foreign, at the Medici Society's galleries in June 1923. A few private press books were selected but the bulk of the exhibition was, as the catalogue noted with pride, 'of workaday books whose soundness of construction is due more to thoughtful arrangement than to expensive manufacture'.

Oliver Simon, of the Curwen Press, and Morison, who had instigated the exhibition and did most of the selection and cataloguing, stressed the interest of type design by specifically noting the face in which each book was set. Of twenty books shown by Macmillan ten were set in Caslon, Oxford with their twenty books admitted five in Caslon among all those in Fell, Chatto & Windus out of nineteen had thirteen in Caslon, Cambridge out of seventeen had nine, Burns & Oates out of fourteen eight, Heinemann out of thirteen seven, and even the Medici Society itself, with its own Riccardi face, had eight books in Caslon in an exhibit of twenty-one. The catalogue did not distinguish between founders' Caslon and the 1916 Monotype version; but whatever the origin the face was dominant, giving the exhibition the appearance of being, unintentionally, almost a bicentenary celebration.

Old Style accounted for a number of books with pre-war dates but its presence later was due almost solely to Macmillan, a house which had many of its books printed by R. & R. Clark. Scotch Roman, the only orthodox modern, appeared occasionally and besides the books in the new or relatively new Monotype faces there were one or two in the important Kennerly.

The support given by certain publishers to the new faces marked the extent to which an interest in fine printing was dispersing from the Mall at Hammersmith into the hinterland of publishing beyond the Charing Cross Road. By 1922 the doctrine that no book not produced on an Albion was fit for a connoisseur had been called in doubt. Young men like Meynell and Morison and Simon were as eager for reform as Horne and Ricketts of the earlier generation but to them the Monotype and the Miehle were to be challenged and mastered. They approved the inevitability of industrialisation and confronted the problem of using machines for ends that they considered to be civilised.

One of their ideas in 1922 was to form the Fleuron Society, dedicated to the production of one fine book a year to be composed and printed by machine. The project collapsed when at the Society's second meeting Newdigate, then in charge of the Shakespeare Head Press of Basil Blackwell, proclaimed so firmly the superiority of handsetting that the group could no longer proceed in unanimity. Instead, Meynell, whose office after 1918 was in Carmelite Street, where he had in his ears the thunder of the newspaper rotaries to remind him of mass production, and whose political creed carried Morris's to the logical conclusion that all men should have equal opportunity to buy as well as to print fine books, now resolved to found his own publishing imprint, the Nonesuch Press. His object was to maintain a private press typography without restriction on the means of production. 'Our stock-in-trade,' he recalled in 1936, 'has been the theory that mechanical means could be made to serve fine ends; that the machine in printing was a controllable tool.'

The appointment in 1922 of Morison as typographical adviser to the Monotype Corporation promised control of that particular machine by easing the problem of equipping it with desirable type faces, since the Corporation had agreed to a programme of cutting and opened it at once with the italic of Monotype Garamond, followed by the roman in 1923. The italic was the most calligraphic face to be cut in this country or in America, and was a technical triumph for the punch-cutting machine invented by Lynn Boyd Benton of Milwaukee in 1885, the crucial invention which had enabled the hot-metal composing machines to be supplied with matrices for mass production.

The Garamond fount included some forty terminal sorts as well as the long ſ combinations, a rich provision that received the instant accolade of Meynell who used it for his second Nonesuch book—the first was in Fell—*The Letters of George Meredith to Alice Meynell*, published in May 1923. The later discovery that the roman of Monotype Garamond was based on a seventeenth-century copy of an original Garamond did not affect the popularity of the face which in its crisp and vivacious letterforms and in the fireworks of the italic out-old-faced Caslon, and rivalled Fell.

In 1923, when no one could visualise the success of the Nonesuch Press, a substantial prop to the Corporation's programme was the appointment of Lewis to be University Printer at Cambridge. Here was a large printing house, already equipped with Monotype plant and likely to extend the installation. Lewis had the support of the Syndics in committing the Press to this form of composition and he was prepared to hearten the Corporation by making known his willingness to consider the purchase of new text faces at an early stage of cutting.

Interest in type design was accelerated by the publication in 1922 of Daniel Berkeley Updike's *Printing Types: Their History, Forms and Use*. Although Updike was opposed to composing machines, the lightly-borne scholarship of his book set in perspective the types that the Corporation was to revive. Baskerville, also cut in 1923, was the next on the programme, the Corporation's model being the great primer of the 1763 Bible. Although not so picturesque as Caslon or Garamond, Monotype Baskerville proved more efficient and economic as a book face without sacrifice of proportions and elegance.

Other faces followed: Poliphilus roman with Blado italic (also 1923), Fournier (1925), a consequence of the esteem in which French typography was held at this period, Centaur (1929), the most successful of the many revivals modelled on Jenson and originally designed by Rogers in 1913 for handsetting, and Bembo (also 1929), cut after Morison had traced the lineal descent of old face and proved that the model used by Claude Garamond that descended to Caslon was derived from Aldus and not from Jenson. Thus the twentieth-century printing house with Monotype plant could possess a stock of type faces derived from the finest designs of the unmechanised past.

Concurrently, there was campaigning for the proper employment of the new faces. 'There is nothing more irritating to the reader,' Morison wrote in 1925, 'than to be made conscious at every other page of some attempted typographical dexterity which consequently renders him incapable of considering the sense of the words apart from their forced arrangement into some triangular or other unnatural shape. Even the simple square is often only attained by stretching words until their sense loses itself in the vast spaces left between the letters in the supposed interest of distinctive setting.' The kind of distinctive setting advocated by the reformers was codified in Morison's *First Principles of Typography* (first prepared in 1929), expounded in *The Fleuron* (1923–30), the journal founded by Simon, recorded in Morison's folios, *Four Centuries of Fine Printing* (1924) and *Modern Fine Printing* (1925), and exemplified by Meynell in successive Nonesuch books.

Paradoxically, the Nonesuch books were in theory easily imitable for the materials of the typography were those in common supply. In practice the versatility of Meynell's talent enabled him effortlessly to hold his own and to daunt the plagiarists because he did not even imitate himself: 'I have tried,' he said when opening an exhibition of contemporary book typography in 1933, 'not to design any book which would, by the repetition of some fortunate effect, become no more than the echo of the one before it.'

Although the Press was based on the availability of machine-cut type, he did not accept the Monotype faces uncritically so that for the five-volume Bible (1925–27) light-face Plantin was equipped with special long descenders, and for the seven-volume Shakespeare (1923–33) Monotype Fournier was given special capitals. The standards of setting and presswork he maintained are remarkable when the number of printing houses engaged are considered, from the largest such as R. & R. Clark or the University Presses to the relatively small such as the Kynoch Press of Birmingham. He was no less exacting in his choice of paper and binding for it was his tenet that a book should be agreeable to handle as well as to read. Because costs had to be kept down he was unable extensively to illustrate and it was in the decoration of his books by the fleuron or the rule-combination that he showed his resourcefulness.

An example of the ultimate value of the Nonesuch Press was the attention later to be given to the book the requirements of which are closer to the newspaper than the novel: the commercially produced Bible. Collins in Scotland, the King's Printers and the two University Presses in England, relied upon the machine for their Bibles. From the Nonesuch they learned that reliance need not mean domination and that type design could be adapted for their specialised needs. In 1929 Collins commissioned from the Corporation a brevier fount with drastically abbreviated descenders, and during the 1930's all the English houses changed their setting, Eyre & Spottiswoode to a specially cut Royal Minion, Oxford to a Bible-face version of The Times New Roman, and Cambridge to The Times New Roman semi-bold for the Pitt Octavo which sold at 2s. 6d.

Less specialised publishers were meanwhile giving ear to the reaction against Morris that was forcibly expressed by A. J. A. Symons, the founder of the First Edition Club, when he wrote: 'William Morris set the trade printer a standard which he could never hope to reach, and...widened rather than diminished the gap between the ideal book...and the book of every day.' To prove that Dives could reach Abraham's bosom Symons instituted in 1928 the Fifty Books exhibition, based on the American model flourishing since 1923. That of Symons was governed by a complicated system of marking that put the cheap, commercially produced book on equal terms with the luxury edition. The chance of selection soon became prized and had a marked effect on publishers' standards of production.

Successive exhibitions revealed that the long reign of Caslon and old style was at an end. Monotype Baskerville was for some years the most popular face, to be overtaken in the mid-thirties by Bembo. This was the face that Morison had predicted would close the gap between the commercial edition and the fine book, for it had qualities to appeal to all printers. 'It possesses,' he wrote in 1930, 'all the virtues in an eminent degree: a first-class legibility..., an englishness conferred by our use of Caslon for two centuries, economy in A-Z space, adequate but not extravagant ascenders and descenders and...a due capacity for enlargement.'

After the first world war only two substantial private presses were founded. In 1922 the Misses G. E. and M. S. Davies set up a private press named after their village of Gregynog in Montgomeryshire with the intention of reviving Welsh craftsmanship by printing Welsh and English literature. Many of the handset books were illustrated with wood-engravings but a deliberate exclusion of zinco and half-tone did not entail a total exclusion of the machine: the founts were Monotype faces, such as Poliphilus and Baskerville, cast by the Monotype method, and most of the books were printed on an ordinary platen.

The Golden Cockerel Press was truer to the exclusive spirit of the pre-war period. Originally founded to publish books by unknown authors, it was taken over by Robert Gibbings in 1924 to produce by craft methods books illustrated with wood-engravings. Many of these were executed by Eric Gill, whose work had graced the output of one of the smallest private presses, St Dominic's, founded by Hilary Pepler in 1916, and notable for *Horae Beatae Virginis Mariae* (1923) which Gill illustrated. For the Golden Cockerel his most memorable work was the *Four Gospels* (1931) in which the architectural letterforms of the headings blend inextricably with figures and foliage and in harmony with the text type of his design to give one of the two or three finest decorated Gospels ever to be printed.

At Cambridge Lewis had the hardest task. A University Press is required to print only a limited amount of poetry and literature: an equal if not greater regard must be paid to treatises on religion and philosophy, science and mathematics, and to reprints of textbooks and schoolbooks. In these a Golden Cockerel artistry or a Nonesuch liveliness was out of place: yet Lewis understood it to be his duty to impose on Cambridge typography a consistent standard. He therefore proposed to the Syndics that Morison should become typographical adviser, an appointment confirmed in 1925. In this year R. B. McKerrow noted that Cambridge was competently attempting 'to produce, let us say, a mathematical treatise bristling with formulae and odd-shaped figures in such a way that it brings equal satisfaction to the mathematician who desires to read it and the lover of well-ordered printing.' The quality of ink and paper, composition and presswork, exacted by Lewis was the highest attainable in a house committed to mass production.

The association of Lewis and Morison was not confined to chores for the post-war slump obliged the Press to take in outside printing. To advertise the capabilities of Cambridge Morison asked the Printer to undertake several books that more approached the fine edition. In 1929, when Morison was experimenting with illustration by copper-engraving, the Press was responsible for the sheets, though not the engravings, of Farquhar's *The Beaux' Stratagem*, illustrated by J. E. Laboureur and issued with all the paraphernalia of the limited edition, including extra sets of engravings in the first state.

There were a number of small volumes written and designed by Morison for the Printer to circulate at Christmas, and Lewis also printed Morison's own *John Bell* (1930), which perhaps equals any private press book of the twenties or thirties. It was set not in Monotype Bell, cut that year, but in types from the original matrices. This book, with its full yet well-ordered title page and decorative headpieces and thick-and-thin rules, as well as the abundantly varied illustrative matter, displayed Morison's skill as an inventive typographer, whereas the *Consolations* of Boethius (1929), which he prepared for Burns, Oates & Washbourne (as the house had become), is remarkable for the sober ingenuity with which a complicated text, annotated with comments upon comments, was presented for easy reading. Different talents were shown in his standardisation in Baskerville of the novels (Scotch Roman for the demy octavos) of the house of Gollancz, of which he became a director in 1928, and his introduction of eye-catching yellow jackets set with new-fangled types from abroad.

In 1929 the Corporation cut Perpetua, designed by Gill. It was the first distinctively twentieth-century face and came from the hand of a practising artist. In 1932 *The Times* was re-dressed in its own type, designed on principles of legibility and capable of withstanding the pressure of stereotyping. A year later The Times New Roman was made available to the trade, and in 1935 it was successfully used for the first volume of the *History of 'The Times'*, which appeared in both a trade and a de-luxe edition. The latter was a folio, separately set and spectacularly extra-illustrated not only with zincos but with wood-engravings, gravure and collotype.

This typographical apogee of any newspaper office at any period was partnered in 1935 by the most monumental piece of fine printing to appear in the twentieth century: the Oxford Lectern Bible designed by Rogers. After discarding experiments with Goudy Modern and Bembo, Rogers returned to what had been his first choice, his own Centaur, but in order that the page should not be cramped and the letter should fit satisfactorily the 22 point was recut on an 18-point body and the 1238 pages of the two volumes, full lectern size, were mechanically set. The Oxford Bible can be compared with only two other folios of the Word of God: that by Estienne in 1532 and that by Baskerville in 1763.

The problems of the 'thirties in this country were of the small format and not of the large. The growth of the twopenny lending libraries was a serious threat to publishers already menaced by the economic depression, and their reaction was to institute series of pocket-size volumes, Monotype set and costing 3s. 6d. or less. Oxford had the World's Classics, Cape the Traveller's Library, Cassell the Pocket Library, Methuen the Gateway Library and Chatto & Windus the Phoenix Library. All were in hard covers.

Early in 1932 copies of the paper-back Albatross library of English-language fiction reprints, set abroad in such Monotype faces as Baskerville and Garamond, were being brought back by travellers and at the same time Benn's Ninepenny Novels came on the market here. These were new fiction, set in Garamond and wrappered in grey paper printed in blue with a decorative border taken from sixteenth-century Lyons. Whereas the Everyman Library of 1906 had been priced at 1s. on a sale of 10,000 copies, the Benn series was priced in expectation of a sale of 100,000; this was not achieved. But in 1935 Allen Lane introduced the sixpenny Penguins gaily wrappered in orange on white with a modern design. The typography, perforce condensed, was at first over-dependent on the printer and often on a printer equipped for slug-setting, but after an experiment with standardisation in Monotype Imprint, The Times New Roman was adopted in 1937, being a face not only available on both kinds of hot-metal composing machine but offering the economy in setting which the low price made obligatory.

The Penguins were intended for all classes of the community and Lane believed it imperative that his books should be cheap only in price and not in appearance. As success brought a wider dispersion of printing orders he employed a typographer, first Jan Tschichold and then Hans Schmoller, to prepare and enforce house rules that covered every contingency of setting. The emphasis was on detail: spacing of letters, leading, margins and so forth. Thus the mechanised printers of the sixpenny Penguins were instructed as precisely as the craftsmen of the Kelmscott Press.

By 1939 it would seem that British book typography had completed a full revolution of the cylinder: Bulmer-Morris had been followed by Pickering-Nonesuch, and the market for *l'homme moyen sensuel* by the mass market of Bentley-Lane. The last group was one which depended entirely upon standardisation and mechanisation. But in Bentley's day the machines were novelties. The pressman on the new Napier or Wharfedale was more concerned with obtaining any impression at all from the unfamiliar machinery than with 'kissing' the sheet, and the elastic band which was an essential component of the Hattersley machine figured more largely in its owner's mind than the type face in the magazines. In the course of the century the machines had become commonplace as well as perfected and the Linotype and Monotype, the Miehle and Heidelberg of the later day presented no such problems. If the operator desired satisfaction from his work it must lie in quality and not in victory over a recalcitrant cog.

Another difference between Bentley and Lane was that whereas the 'million' in the nineteenth century had rarely seen a book except the lectern Bible in the parish church, the enormous production for which machines had over a century been responsible had made the book a familiar article in the home, the school and the public library. The later generations were no longer grateful for any book however shoddy, and they had accumulated experience on which to base a choice between the typography of competing editions of a cheap reprint.

The Monotype faces were designed for different purposes and not for different publishers—the number cut for private use has been small. At the present time, although the variety of faces to be seen in British books is far richer than in the nineteenth century, it is with few exceptions not easy to identify the individual publisher given any page except the title. The means of distinction commonly lie in the device, the binding, in some cases the treatment of the preliminaries, and, though not always intentionally, in the treatment of illustrations if these are present.

For the general run of unillustrated books a lack of individual traits may be inevitable, and even desirable since the effort of forming a house style can lead to vagaries that reduce legibility and eventually repel the reader. The typographical problems that were confronted in Boethius' *Consolations* of 1929 occur more frequently in academic, liturgical or scientific books and the employment elsewhere than at a University Press of a typographer sufficiently skilled to encounter exceptional problems of setting would usually be a waste of his talents.

On the other hand, the striking maintenance of individuality by Penguin Books in that apparently most limited of typographical fields, the popular paperback, testifies to the value of minute attention, the attention advocated by Walker and Newdigate, in the preservation of identity by a publishing house.

The relative ease with which, owing to electronics, colour can now be used, led in the fifties to an increase in the number of books on art or travel illustrated from photographic orginals. The intention of many of these books, in which the value of the picture was assumed to be superior to that of the text, was akin to that of the Victorian keepsake album, which in its day could not hold its own against the book that expected to be read. Typographers, influenced by the fashions abroad which hitherto had not affected British book typography, were able to exercise a talent for layout and to assuage a craving to use the 'progressive' unseriffed types. The arranging of the blocks to form attractive or abstract patterns integrated with paragraphs of text is a game that is likely to pall for typographer and reader. The function of the true typographer is to assist the reader, not to entertain him: he is an almoner and not an actor.

Scientific books however are increasingly appearing under imprints not hitherto considered academic and in such books, where the typographer is obliged to exert his skill on the analysis and presentation of the material, his new opportunity may be found to lie. Already founts are being designed for computer printing. The typographer of the 'sixties is likely to be better equipped with a facility for four-line mathematical setting than for bled-off halftones.

Within the last few years the typographer has faced the eventual replacement of all his leaden apparatus—and that had been consistent through the centuries—by strips of transparent film. Those responsible for the appearance of British books find they have triumphed over the Monotype and the Miehle only to be confronted by the film composer and the wrap-round plate. So far the reaction has been fainthearted and the incunabula of English filmsetting include no Schoeffer Psalter (1457), Pannartz *Livy* (1469) or Johann Zainer *De Claris Mulieribus* (1473), to name a few of the books the pages of which ravished the heart of Morris at the lecture in 1888.

At least, however, we ought not now to fall into the trap that Bulmer laid for the nineteenth century when he refused to place his undoubted talents at the service of the steam press; or, if we do, then extrication should not require a hundred years. The lesson of the types successfully revived in the 1920's is that typography does not change because the method of production changes.

The letter or the symbol and the space around them stand in a relationship obedient only to the rules imposed by the human eye, which are as constant as the capacity of that organ and unaffected by an increase in the speed of composition from 1,000 ens an hour to 10,000 or an increase in the speed of printing from 200 to 5,000 impressions an hour. The degree of relationship between type and space may vary by a pica or a point at different periods according to taste, as may the strengthening or refining of a serif. These details are the true mutants. The machine is still required to conform to absolute standards, whether of presswork or of punch-cutting, and the typographer has all his ancient rights since he judges the efficiency with which the standards are maintained. The inventions of Koenig, Hattersley, Walter, Lanston and Miehle may have battered at his peace but they have not eroded his authority. McCreery, writing in 1827, still speaks for the modern book typographer:

Ours is no counter-service, no dull trade...
The form indelible our art bestows
Will last unchanged till time itself shall close.

Franco Riva

BOOK PRINTING IN ITALY
FROM 1800 TO THE PRESENT DAY

I

1. End of the Neoclassical phase | Decline of means and of men. 2. The Memoirs *of Gaspero Barbera/Three stages in Italian book printing. 3. Census of printers and publishers between 1800 and 1900. 4. 'National' printing | Between the First and Second World Wars.*

1. The nineteenth century found printing in Italy in a definite state of decline, although it was the splendid moment when G. B. Bodoni was acclaimed, as never before, by Italy and Europe. But the cultural decadence of Venice, which was revealed by the collapse of the Republic beneath the attacks of Napoleon's armies, the crisis prevailing in every province of Italy and the rise of a new society which was taking root beneath the ruins of the old one, these are the general elements which explain—apart from the phenomenon of Bodoni— the decline of the particular traditions of Italian printing.

It was this period that produced the noble but abortive experiment of a Veronese aristocrat, Count Bartolomeo Giuliari, who, in order to react, as he said, against the decline of printing in the country, set up a printing works in his palace, and, becoming a printer himself, fought idealistically but in vain, with a full printing programme, against the decadence of the art, at least in Verona. The letter in which he communicated his magnanimous proposition to Bodoni illustrates very clearly this dramatic situation (F. Riva, *La dimèstica Stamperia del veronese conte Giuliari (1794–1827)*. Florence, 1956); but for us the incident tells its own story: the nobleman who made himself a printer and tried, with his well-prepared and well-printed books, to halt the collapse.

A situation which was not unique to Italy but which found in Italy the most favourable conditions. It was not precisely that the new century had brought about a crisis in an aristocratic and private culture (a contemporary phenomenon affecting almost the whole of Europe), but in Italy the dissolution of a certain political situation that was fragmented and incommunicable could only accentuate and dramatise the characteristics of an emancipatory and bourgeois phenomenon (others might call it simply industrial) which, to repeat, was European in character. The idea of unification, which at the beginning of the century had begun to make some headway in people's minds, with the more or less enlightened experiments, by the Napoleonic administrations, had demanded an unusual amount of sacrifice, of mediocrity and renunciation. (P. Barbera, *Editori e Autori*. Florence 1904, the chapter: 'Printing and the Italian Risorgimento'.)

'Once the Master had disappeared', wrote Bertieri, 'before mid-century had been reached, a new decadence afflicted the art of printing in Italy, which had returned once more to forms and expressions which were not its own, with a particular predilection for heavy French forms.' (*Il Libro Italiano nel Novecento*. Milan 1928.) We should have joined in the disapproval of Bodoni and of his art, not because it was not art, but only because it was dedicated to a few and because it was aristocratic—it did not belong to the people. And we should add that the progressive restrictions of censorship, exercised either by the Papacy or the Bourbon rulers, although they had spread the lofty ideal, had, on the other hand, gradually weakened the opportunities for furthering an art whose development it has intimidated and restricted at all times. These limitations have been of all kinds, not only in the choice of works to be printed, but particularly in the organisation of technique itself: the number of printing-shops closed and the consequent reduction of the hand-presses functioning, the decline of the foundries and, no less inevitable, the dispersal of qualified workers.

It was in 1829 that the first cylinder-press was brought to the Tipografia Pomba in Turin, but Tito Ricordi had to go abroad to learn the art of lithography ('Officine Grafiche Ricordi' in: *Libri e Riviste d'Italia* XIV, 1962) and Barbera had also to go for machines and types. It was abroad that the more serious printing-works acquired type while the old Italian foundries and the new ones did not obtain satisfactory results, and the characters they produced were badly cast, with obvious deficiences in alignment and cutting. So many books of this period appear ugly to us solely because they were printed with old and worn types.

2. The *Memoirs* of Gaspero Barbera is a very useful book, on account of the detailed information it contains and for the fervour that buoys it up. He was a printer and publisher of Piedmontese origin who had grown up in Florence, living and developing right in the heart of this century of expectation and hope: between the first Risorgimento and the unification of the country, from which developed finally the unfolding of an art that became less subject and began to occupy a less secondary position. (*Memorie di un editore*. Florence 1883.)

Barbera, like all other shrewd printers, hastened to go abroad for all his needs, and made regular journeys in order to learn more and carry out research. 'I saw Paris with astonishment,' he wrote in 1856, 'and when I saw the leading printing-works I was bewildered by their size, by the number of machines, by the unusual number of operatives and the order and discipline which reigned in their midst.' It was abroad, in Leipzig to be precise, that he had discovered the drying-room for sheets that had come off the press, a room adjacent to the works in which the sheets were hung up to dry, whereas in his own country, until then, they had been placed to dry over the heads of the workers, causing serious damage to health. (*Memorie, idem.*)

As far as type faces were concerned, this is what he wrote: 'In all principal Italian cities there was one foundry and sometimes more. No printers had their own. In this way the types they produced could not compete with those from abroad. Before 1840 there existed in Milan, Claudio Wilmant, a German... This first Wilmant achieved a certain perfection in typecasting as far as the alignment was concerned, but he did not succeed in correcting the defect of an overweak metal, with the result that if one of his types or letters was pulled between two fingers of each hand, instead of cracking right across like glass, it finally bent and broke. In addition to the aforementioned Wilmant, Ponthenier at Geneva and Alessandri in Florence had a certain reputation as typefounders... I was compelled to give up the Italian typefounders from the beginning of 1860, since I was attracted by the design of type faces from abroad, which were sometimes so elegant and classical. I sent my orders to the Flinsch foundry at Frankfurt-am-Main.' (*Memorie, idem.*)

And Barbera returned to Paris in 1856 in order to acquire 'a mechanically-operated press'; also for paper; and for ink: 'I have always bought printers' ink abroad, first in London, then in Paris and for a long time in Hanover.' (*Memorie, idem.*)

Finally the unification was achieved, and after so much struggle and hope came peace and greater security. Then: 'the book trade also', said Barbera, 'expanded and became more rapid-moving. If the classics did not sell, newspapers were started, political works were published, everyone wanted to say what he felt...' Orders of a cultural nature increased, books and newspapers were published. The attack on illiteracy in the name of popular and democratic culture was begun. Barbera in fact did not feel it necessary to expend himself too much in commemorating Bodoni. ('I never had excessive admiration for Bodoni, because he printed only princely editions; so much so that at a banquet in honour of G. B. Bodoni, presided over by him, after beginning with praise for the great printer from Saluzzo, he passed on to speak of Giuseppe Pomba, who was amongst the first to make printing serviceable in the spread of education among the people.' *Memorie, idem,* note by his son.)

At this period popular editions were published in vast numbers, also collections of pocket classics, romances and classics in serial form; this age saw the triumph of illustrated editions with ornaments inserted, in obvious contract to the Bodonian canons of pure typography. 'New workshops were opened and a national body of operatives came forward to acquire qualifications, while for a long time printers remained dependent on foreign technical production for their tools.' Barbera states about 1850: 'All this important and continual work on journals caused a real change in the art of printing... And then it was natural that a large supply of operatives, compositors and machinists became available, they did not emerge from the art itself, but came as best they could, without knowing the principles of perfection.' (*Memorie, idem.*)

But by mid-century the way had not been prepared: on one side was the splendour of Bodoni's great 'folio' limited edition of Fénelon, on the other Ferrario's pocket editions of Sir Walter Scott's romances, the serialised edition of the *Amori* of Dante distributed with filibustering enthusiasm by the popular publisher Perino. If printing in Italy needed an idol at this point it would certainly not have been supplied by Bodoni but by a philanthropist and idealist like Benjamin Franklin. 'I believe,' wrote Barbera, 'that by dint of reading and thinking about Franklin I have gradually become a hundredth part of him.' (*Memorie, idem.*) This was the climate; and the lack of means, the difficulty caused by imitations and the poverty of invention, the mass of improvisations and mistakes, were overcome by an enthusiasm and a desire for achievement which were moving. The value of the works published by the Tipografia Elvetica at Capolago for example, which penetrated into Italy and nourished this high ideal of liberty and unity, is clearly of a moral order, and is among the more lofty examples in the long phase of our new hopes for civil life. (R. Caddeo, *La Tipografia Elvetica di Capolago.* Milan 1931.)

The real and proper technico-philological analysis that we made earlier in this historical introduction is in fact limited to three phases: the first, which we will call the Bodonian phase, was prolonged and extended until 1830–1840; the second lasted until the unification of the country, that is to 1870–1880, characterised by production that was inferior and often improvised, although it was rich and interesting and during which there were many experiments, while the modernity of the new techniques and the suggestions from abroad were still in a disorganised state; the third, which lasted to the outbreak of the Second World War, during which the experiments and suggestions of the previous period assisted in the revaluation and in a form of return to the work of Bodoni, re-acquired finally by this technical and artistic mastery which remains his undeniable and supreme privilege: the perfection of tools and execution, the irresistible enchantment of one of his pages. Finally, and it was natural, the prospect of a national printing-works, Italian in its tools and its conception of work. And our first theorists emerged: Pozzoli, Landi, Arneudo, Gianolio Dalmazzo, Bertieri; our schools of graphic art; Italian founding came to life again, discussions opened and experiments followed, with successes and bitterness as was inevitable.

3. It is indispensable at this point to take a rapid glance at the situation of printers and publishers who followed each other between 1800 and 1900, a kind of rapid census which we will carry out from a regional point of view for the evident convenience of ourselves and of our readers.

In Lombardy the Napoleonic administration, among its worthwhile undertakings, had organised a Stamperia Reale (which had printed works by Foscolo and Monti), with the aim of taking Bodoni directly to Milan. (G. Vittani, 'G. B. Bodoni e la Stamperia Reale di Milano' in: *Il Libro e la Stampa* VII, 1913.) But in Milan right at the beginning of the century there had appeared the 'Società de' Classici Italiani' which printed in clear editions, in a format which if not popular was economical, the works of our major writers; and in Milan there worked at the beginning of the century, with varying success: Giacomo Pirotta, R. Fanfani, A. Bonfanti, P. E. Giusti, G. De Stefanis, L. Mussi, O. Manini, F. Rusconi, Redaelli, Truffi, Gnocchi, and among others, F. Stella, (in 1817 he printed Leopardi's first translation from Greek), V. Ferrario, G. Bernardoni, G. Silvestri with his 'Selected Library of Ancient and Modern Italian Works' (a collection which reached the surprising number of 736 volumes). (Information concerning nineteenth-century Italian printers in: M. Parenti, *Ottocento questo sconosciuto*. Florence 1954.)

The press of Edoardo Sonzogno and Brothers, printing first musical works and then popular editions, continued until the last war and was destroyed by air-raids; and in Milan too, about the mid-century, works were set up by Emilio Treves, whose fortune and successors (he was the publisher of Verga, Gozzano, D'Annunzio, Deledda and Negri) have only recently declined (Garzanti succeeded him).

We have already mentioned Ricordi, who later specialised in music publishing; at the beginning of the century also there appeared in Milan Francesco and Antonio Vallardi, who were dedicated to the printing of scientific and educational works and also Hoepli, a firm which is now thriving. (*See* M. Bonetti, *Storia dell'Editoria Italiana*. Rome 1960.) In Brescia finally, there was Nicolo Bettoni, the first printer of Foscolo's *I Sepolcri* (1807) who worked first in Brescia and later in Milan, without great success. (A. Lodolini, 'Il centenario dell'attività di un tipografo editore patriota' in: *Il Risorgimento Grafico* XXVIII, 1931.)

In Turin the Stamperia Reale dated from 1740 and its activity continued until 1873 (its works were taken over by Paravia, an educational publisher whose firm still functions) until with the unification of Italy the capital of the kingdom was moved from Turin to Florence and finally to Rome. In Turin were Galletti, Favale, Fontana, Dumolard (M. Parenti, *Ottocento questo scon*, *idem*.) Fodratti, the Brothers Bocca, the Tipografia Letteraria, Marietti and Perino, with democratic direction, while among them the Tipografia Pomba excelled and became justifiably famous for its clear printing and the validity of its literary collections. (M. Bonetti, *Storia dell'Editoria Ital.*, *idem*; G. Barbera, *Memorie*, *idem*; P. Barbera, *Editori e Autori*, *idem*; M. Parenti, *Ottocento*, *idem*.)

In Venice, however, in contrast to Lombardy and Piedmont which had been favoured by the new course of history, decadence was acute and continued for a long time with no further chance of recovery. It is enough to say that Venice alone in 1735 had ninety-four printing works which had been reduced to fifty-seven in 1793 and right down to twelve in 1812. Worse still: in Verona, Padua and Vicenze, through the Viceregal decree of 1812, the number of printing works were reduced to six, four and two respectively, while right until the end of the century they were counted in tens.

In Venice then were Zatta, Andreola, Andruzzi, Picotti, Palese, Valle, Orlandelli, the Tipografia del Gondoliere, Antonelli and later Naratovich and the Tipografia del Commercio. In Vicenza were Paroni and Parise; in Verona were Ramanzini, the Merlo family, Giuliari and later Libanti, Mainardi, Gamberetti, Civelli, Vicentini and Franchini; in Padua were Conzatti, the Tipografia del Seminario, the Tipografia alla Minerva, Crescini and Penada. And meanwhile at Bassano the famous Stamperia dei Remondini (G. Barioli, *Mostra dei Remondini calcografi stampatori bassanesi*. Bassano, 1958.) continued to decline, while at Portogruaro progress was made by the Tipografia di Alvisopoli, which was an indirect offshoot of Remondini.

The famous foundries and printing-works of Amoretti and Paganino in Parma passed into melancholy decline (E. Morpurgo, 'Don Andrea Amoretti,' in: *Amor librorum*, Zurich 1958.); but in 1831 the Amorettis moved to Bologna, in partnership with F. Negroni, and the activity of the new press continued until it was absorbed by part of Nebiolo, the new star in the firmament of Italian printing.

In Bologna the Regia Tipografia rose to fame, succeeding Della Volpe, and among the others were Lucchesini, Nobili, Masi, Ramponi and Marsigli; in the meantime Imola earned a place in history with the Tipografia di Ignazio Galeati and Sons, printers in 1873 of Carducci's *Nuove Poesie*. In Genoa Dagnino was the first publisher of Mazzini.

In Tuscany Nicolò Capurro printed in Pisa during the early years of the century some very beautiful 'folio' editions displaying the characters designed by the Amorettis; in Pisa with Capurro there also appeared the 'Tipografia della Società Letteraria' and later Nistri; in Florence, in addition to Pazzini, Molini, Magheri and Pagani, outstanding names included Passigli, Piatti, who was the publisher of the first *Canti* by Leopardi (1831) and Batelli, whose works was staffed by 150 operatives. (M. Bonetti, *Storia*, *idem*; M. Parenti, *Ottocento*, *idem*.)

Barbera's printing works in Florence began its activity in 1854, having grown from Le Monnier, another Florentine printer, whose name is well-known for historical and literary studies. ('Le Monnier printed almost everything to order and worked mainly for the Società Editrice Fiorentina, which published in separate numbers somewhat voluminous works in large octavo printed in two columns, for example the Greek poets and prose-writers, translations of the Latin poets...' *Memorie*, *idem*.) A publication by Barbera which will remain very famous is the 'Diamante' collection (the first one was printed in 1856) with its two valuable volumes of small pocket size, composed in the smallest possible type which was extremely clear and correct (later Carducci took over the organisation, bringing it new success). Barbera tells himself that he had seen in Paris a small edition of Machiavelli's *Prince:* 'ten and a half centimetres high and six and a half centimetres wide... The really attractive format of the volume gave me the idea for the collection many years later.' (*Memorie, idem.*)

In the second half of the century, still in Florence, Salvatore Landi had begun his activity, a cardinal point in the rebirth of Italian printing (not forgetting his *Manual*) not only for his printing but for his noteworthy theoretical contribution, with the discussions and proposals in his journal *L'Arte della Stampa*, an early example, if I am not mistaken, of its kind.

In Rome there were at first the printing works of Ludovico Cecchini, C. Mardacchini, Pietro Aureli, De Romanis and Salviucci (both publishers of Belli); then later the 'Civiltà Cattolica' press and after the unification of the country, the presses of Colombo, Forzani, the Chamber of Deputies, Bardi, and the Senate, but without very notable results, At the end of the century there appeared in Rome that remarkable printer Angelo Sommaruga, a man as fertile in ideas as he was lacking in scruples (but he was the publisher of Carducci, D'Annunzio, Scarfoglio, Serao, Capuana, Panzacchi and De Amicis). (G. Squarciapino: *Roma bizantina*. Turin 1950.)

At Naples, by 1860, there were few printers and not very much money (although in 1835 Saverio Starita had published Leopardi's *Canti e Operette morali*); but after the annexation to the Kingdom of Italy the cultural life of the country recovered, and printing works and publishers finally arose at speed. Mention should be made of Antonio and Domenico Morano (who printed books by De Sanctis, Settembrini, Imbriani and Bonghi); afterwards came Gaetano Nobile, A. Trani's printing works, Fernando Bideri and Luigi Pierro.

This brings us to the end of the century. Printing became industrialised, imposing organisations or reorganised concerns arose from the ashes of the past and as in every other country the difference between publisher and printer became more marked: publishers with their own printing presses rarer; later the typographer appeared (preferably imported from Germany or German Switzerland), and the printer was asked only to execute as well as he could the plans drawn up in the publisher's office.

Italian culture during the early nineteenth century looked to Bologna and then to Naples where the outstanding figures were Benedetto Croce, Salvatore Di Giacomo and Ferdinando Russo. The romantic era came to an end: Carducci died, Fogazzaro, Bracco and Pascoli also disappeared, while D'Annunzio lost his reason. In the meantime Carducci and Deledda won for Italy her first Nobel prizes for literature.

However, Art Nouveau spread from England; from this point of view also the influence was great and far-reaching and appeared phenomenal for a very long time. However, new experiments took place (the violent wave of futurism, for example), new leaders and new theories, more or less national in character; book fairs were organised; schools of printing and design were raised to high standards (at Milan, Bologna and Urbino) after founding at the end of the century. Italian foundries created some of their own types and Italian books began to appear with success at international sales and exhibitions.

4. The most interesting figure of this period is certainly Raffaello Bertieri (1875–1945), a Florentine who had been a pupil of Landi; 'a cultured idealist', as *The Times* defined him, 'whose knowledge of the art of the book was profound enough for him to realise that the punch-cutting for the type face is the artistic essential as far as book-printing is concerned.' (T. Grandi, 'Libri belli d'Italia' in: *Il Risorgimento Grafico* XXXII, 1935.)

At the Congress of the Italian Society for the Progress of Science, in 1917, in the midst of the fashion for flowery printing, Bertieri attacked the possibility of finally creating a national printing concern as opposed to the long period of apprenticeship and foreign influence. The country was unified: so let there be mechanically operated Italian printing-works, Italian foundries, Italian type faces, Italian schools of graphic art. He even allowed Fascism to take advantage of his absurd nationalistic fervour, his State books, etc; and the first to suffer the consequences was Bertieri himself, who was led astray, given a high position and in the end merely tolerated.

But his fame spread so widely that Italian printing at last began to earn consideration and success abroad. In 1925 Bertieri was invited to show his books at the famous Plantin-Moretus Museum in Antwerp, while in 1925 also prizes were given to Bertieri, Ricordi, Alinari, Mondadori, Zanichelli, Formìggini and others. And at the Exhibition 'Italian Books from 1400 to 1900' in Buenos Aires the new type faces cast in Italy were shown.

The first part of this century was certainly characterised by immense enthusiasm and inevitably by a moderate amount of confusion. On one side was the profession of a kind of classical recovery, on the other was opposition to classicism, while in reality the Art Nouveau and its derivatives—thanks principally to the influence of the school of wood-engraving led by De Karolis—still emerged from beneath them.

But the important thing was that ideas circulated, leading to discussions and interminable polemics, often not very constructive. The classical appeal was all the same evident and Bertieri wisely sought at length to modify it with the new ideas that were coming from Germany and England. This modification was sought with intelligence and also with low resources. But on the other hand in 1931 the Fonderia Reggiani in Milan transformed its commercial information bulletin into a genuine militant periodical *(Tipografia 1931)* whose declared anti-classicism was soon taken up (in 1933) by another Milan review, *Campo Grafico*, which laid out each number in a different style, anti-classical and asymmetrical, in praise of the 'aerodynamic line, abstraction, the civilisation of the machine'. An advantage gained from futurism, obviously. At the same time many of these attractive novelties found their expression in the development of commercial and magazine art, and the compromise between classicism and avant-garde feeling in book-printing, with the inevitable drawbacks of an industry that was continually further overwhelmed with orders and with its own demands, appeared fundamentally appropriate. The regular use of classical type faces, pages laid out in the traditional proportions, the placing of the illustrations, the accuracy of execution, these are all elements underlining this newly-acquired truth; and the cautious margins for the page numbering, the asymmetrical layout of some title-pages, the extremely derivative quality shown in the type faces, the suggestive design of the showy covers, do not get to the root of the matter. They reinforce more strongly our conviction that innovations are merely liberties in the deep-set courses of tradition.

As I have said therefore the identification that was almost complete until the beginning of the century between printer and publisher gradually slackened, but the phenomenon is well-known, it did not occur only in Italy and there are clear economic reasons which forced the separation in many cases.

The printing and publishing concerns which have developed since the Second World War are impressive, and among the printing presses in the Italian provinces a prize, if it were available, should be awarded to Verona, which now has the Officine Grafiche Mondadori, the most modern in Europe, with 2000 workers, and the Officina Bodoni (with the Stamperia Valdonega attached) run by Giovanni Mardersteig, the press which prints with the most refined and rare beauty and justifiably excels in the world of art. (A. Ramelli, 'L'Officina Bodoni di G.M.', in: *Gutenberg Jahrbuch* 1955; F. Riva 'Una mostra dell'Officina Bodoni,' in: *Comunità* IX 1955; F. Riva, 'Il Principe degli stampatori: G. M.,' in: *Vita* 1960; H. Schmoller, 'A Gentleman of Verona,' in: *The Penrose Annual 52,* 1958.)

This introduction could certainly not close without a rapid glance at the major contemporary concerns, in the same order as we have described the preceding situation; and it is better if we indicate each time whether the publisher has his own printing press.

In Milan are the editorial offices of Mondadori, and in addition: Rizzoli and Garzanti (with printing works), Bompiani, Hoepli, Feltrinelli (all without); next, Longanesi, Parenti, Martello, Giuffré, Schwarz, Comunità, Vallardi, Ricciardi, Nuova Accademia, Baldini & Castoldi, Ceschina, Lerici, Sugar, Scheiwiller, the Italian Touring Club, all without; Fabbri, Vita & Pensiero, Istituto Editoriale Italiano (with printing works), La Conchiglia di Giani. Barion, Bocca, Gentile, Rosa & Ballo disappeared recently. In Brescia are La Morcelliana and La Scuola; in Bergamo, Istituto Italiano d'Arti Grafiche.

In Turin we make special mention of Einaudi (without printing works), the Unione Tipografico Editoriale Torinese (with printing works, succeeding Pomba) and the great combine of the I.L.T.E.; then come Boringhieri, Loescher, Lattes, Paravia, Taylor and the S.E.I. (without printing works), and the Edizioni Radio Italiana. In Novara is the Istituto Geografico De Agostini (with printing works) and at Alpignano the unusual works of Alberto Tallone. In Bologna is Zanichelli (without) and Capelli (with printing works), both of which started at the end of last century; Il Mulino and the Poligrafici of the *Resto del Carlino* (but the Tipografia Azzoguidi, starting in 1875 and active until recently, should not be forgotten).

In Florence are Le Monnier, Sansoni, La Nuova Italia, Alinari (without printing works but equipped with first-class gravure machinery), Vallecchi (with printing works), D'Anna (without), Salani, Marzocco which succeeded Bemporad as publisher of juvenile and school books; the famous imprint of 'La Voce' (without printing works) came to an end only recently, the firm whose best years closed with the First World War; the same is true of 'Il Leonardo' and of Quattrini, the likeable publisher of works in serial form. The large printing works of the Brothers Stianti at San Casciano Val di Pesa is worth noting.

In Rome, Formìggini worked between the two wars; mention should be made of the good publishing and printing concerns of Tumminelli, Staderini, Editori Riuniti, De Luca, Palombi and the Tipografia Poliglotta Vaticana.

In Bari, from the beginning of the century (but Cressanti and the Società Editoriale Barese should be mentioned) the outstanding firm is Laterza (with works) to which the Leonardo da Vinci has now been joined (without). At Palermo there is Sandron, at Catania Giannotta and at Messina Principato.

II

1. *Bodoni's books.* 2. *Echoes of Bodoni.* 3. *Architecture and technique after Bodoni |*
The imprint | The date | the numbering of pages. 4. *The type faces |* The Manuale
Tipografico *| Developments and contradictions | Lithographed title-pages.*

1. When Bodoni began work—at the end of the eighteenth century—books
were dominated by decoration and illustrations. 'Engraving occupies the major part of the title-pages, the pages facing the half-title, tables of contents,
headings, tail-pieces, initial letters with historical figures, and there were no
limitations in anything: a Metastasio by Zatta, for example, was illustrated
with 250 vignettes; a Goldoni with about 400 and an Ariosto with 1900' (P.
Trevisani, *Bodoni.* Milan 1940), and certainly the results were superior, as far
as the finish of the design and the reproduction (by copperplates) were concerned, in relation to the preceding century when decoration was entirely
ruled by the woodcut that was continually more flat and mannered. (A. Ber-
tarelli, 'L'ornamentazione del libro in Italia nel sec. XVIII' in: *Il libro e la*
Stampa II, 1908.)

This was the major objective of Bodoni's renovation. It is obvious moreover that at first Bodoni himself was not free from the defect of the age; in the
first books he printed in fact his title-pages are filled to the same extent and his
pages are covered with rules, borders and ornaments. It is extremely useful to
make a comparison between the decorated title-page of his first Specimen
Fregi e Maiuscole of 1771 (influenced by Fournier and his *Manuel Typographique*
of 1766) with the unadorned and pure title-page in his famous *Manuale* of
forty years later.

Writers about Bodoni usually distinguish three periods in the Master's
work: the first, spent partly in Rome, was imitative (until 1780); the second,
consisting of research, lasting until the turn of the century, included the two
masterpieces: *Gli Amori Pastorali di Dafni e Cloe* and Tasso's *Aminta;* the third
was the classical period of maturity when the triumph of printing produced
countless masterpieces. Between the point of departure and the final success
there can be seen in the unending series of books printed in his workshops,
that ideal way of printing that I believe with reason to be the highest achievement of his mastery.

In the preface to his *Manuale,* Bodoni mentions Baskerville being praised
precisely because he banished from books the ornamental rules, scrolls or

brackets and large flowers (*Manuale* I, xvii), and not so much true illustration, which he justly recognises as unseemly only if it is ugly or badly executed (*Manuale* I, xix). 'When a book is classical, I say, it is all the better that the beauty of the characters should appear on their own: in fact it is in this that the sovereign glory of the art consists and becomes obvious' (*Manuale* I, xxi).

But in Bodoni's work the title-page, in contrast to what is found in the work of Baskerville and Didot, who usually tend to 'cover' the entire surface of the pages, tends to become progressively simpler, and striking only through the magnificent spacing of the capitals (the fundamental thing is the almost constant use of capitals alone and of the roman face, a touchstone in the appraisal of the decadence which followed); in the harmony of the blanks and the spaces between the lines: a reduction to essentials therefore (author-title of the work-printing details), a clear symbol on a page that became progressively emptier.

There was a time however when this refinement of the title-page was attacked as 'monotonous', and Bodoni was reproved for lack of variety in his type faces, just when, during the decadence which followed his disappearance, the less educated printers rivalled each other in an uncontrolled variety of type faces, juxtaposing with impunity not only italics and roman faces, but Grotesque, Egyptian and even Gothic letters with capitals. But the cause of this ugliness was due not only to the ignorance of the printers, but to the fact that books were beginning to be merchandise for sale, so that we could, without exaggeration, consider this as the first part of a commercial operation, which developed further in the design of the covers and the impact of publicity.

Bodoni aimed to remove everything from books that was not printing, and this remains his great merit: maximum elegance and purity of page design, as well as of characters adorned sometimes with their natural graces. Bodoni's so-called 'display pieces' count for us today inasmuch as they represent an astonishing series of typographical monotypes, to which he always had recourse because of their harmony and well-chosen proportions, and also for the perfect execution as regards register, inking and the calendering of their pages; all important aspects of that technical execution which we look for in vain among his successors.

His *Oratio Dominica in CLV. Linguas* belongs to 1806; *Les Aventures de Télémaque*, in two folio volumes, belongs to 1812: his two finest works. Bodoni died in 1813 and his work was carried on by his widow who supervised the production of works which had remained incomplete, for example: Boileau's *Œuvres Poétiques* (1814), and the *Manuale Tipografico* (1818).

2. Bodoni's printing house therefore, directed by his widow, continued for a few further decades, printing books which were accurately carried out but showing a decline in inventiveness. The number of operatives was increased through schools and the press could continue to live on its large technical output, which it did. There are some books dating from these years which would have made the Master turn in his grave: *Favole Letterarie* by Tommaso de Yriarte, for example, which came out in 1834, with a title-page in which can be seen together, italics, lower case, capitals and small capitals. But on the whole the impression was good and the characters well delineated. Perhaps the contrast between the size of the characters (16 point in the introduction and 12 point in the text proper) is too obvious; note finally that on the preface pages the roman number is placed at the top in the centre of the measure while throughout the text the page numbers, in Arabic, appear at the top over the outside margin. (As is known, the size of the characters was not indicated according to the point-size, and until the nineteenth century the so-called *testo* corresponded to 16 point; *silvio* to 14 point; *lettura* to 12 point; *filosofia* to 11 point; *garamone* to 10 point; *testino* to 8 point; *mignona* to 6 point, etc. (*See* on this subject G. I. Arneudo, *Dizionario esegetico tecnico storico per le Arti Grafiche*. Turin 1917–1925; Gianolio Dalmazzo, *Il libro e l'Arte della Stampa*. Turin 1926).

On the other hand let us look at an average book printed by Bodoni himself (1802), *Amori* by Savioli, in which the title-page is entirely set in capitals, decorated with a bracket and a cast ornament, and in a circle a portrait of the author reproduced by copper-plate engraving and placed between the title and the imprint (a form approved by Bodoni and other contemporary typographers). The dedication and the text are set in type of the same size, but the former is in italics and the latter in roman; the page numbers are all at the top over the centre of the measure and framed. Initial letters are set larger, and in the text a simple cast ornament ends the short pages instead of the tail-pieces and vignettes used previously. But let us take a couple of books printed for special occasions, in which the printer's own convictions could have been influenced by obligations towards commitments. On one side: *Orazione Funebre in morte di Ferdinando I di Borbone* of 1803. A portrait facing the half-title (by Rosaspina), a title-page that is crowded but entirely in capitals, initial letters and some ornamentation; the page-numbers also—at the top and in the centre—are framed and decorated. On the other side: *Sul Sepolcro di sua Al-*

tezza Reale la Principessa Carlotta Augusta di Galles of 1818, when Bodoni had already died. In comparing them, treating them as two 'occasional' pieces of printing and therefore restricted to the occasion itself, the second results in a major defect: its title-page is badly proportioned and smaller letters appear between the small capitals.

Better certainly is the *Lettera ad un Amico intorno al Regolamento degli Studi di un Giovanetto*, dating from 1817: the title-page is entirely in capitals, delightfully designed, the dedication in italics and the text in roman, and there is a harmony between the various point sizes used. Also there is the *Saggio sull' Uomo-Epistole di Alessandro Pope* dating from 1819: the half-title is entirely in capitals but is marred by the abundant use of punctuation and partly by over-regular spacing between the lines.

Bertieri has stated that 'Bodoni is not the legislator and creator of the printed book in Italy,' that Bodoni was not a theoretician, that in fact he did not start a school, that 'Bodoni was an artist too unusual to have an effective influence on the work of printers who were forced to struggle with practical necessities,' etc. (*L'Arte di G. B. Bodoni.* Milan 1913) And he goes on: 'Bodoni treated the book as printed by Bodoni and that is all.' But perhaps it is not all? The fact that Italian printers, for reasons of economy and singular lack of knowledge criticised his beauty as against theirs, which could only with difficulty be called beauty, is another matter. Just as it is another matter that the printers of the political Risorgimento of the country criticised Bodoni's mastery as against the popular and humanitarian ideals of the new century.

At the same time there was no lack of printers who were won over by the fascination exercised from near and from afar by Bodoni's books: these part-imitations were sometimes very beautiful and sometimes unusual. They included work by Carmignani, Paganino, the Amorettis of Parma; Masi of Leghorn, Vincenzi of Modena, Bettoni of Brescia, the Tipografia della Società Letteraria, Capurro of Pisa and from certain points of view, Giuliari of Verona. Finally, and certainly the most insipid, Galeati of Imola.

Giuseppe Paganino owned the oldest printing works in Parma (dating from 1709) and worked with three hand-presses. He printed ably on coloured paper (azure, green) with care and precision: the title-pages were entirely in capitals and for decoration he used a few rules or cast ornaments, according to the Bodoni style. His defects were the spacing of the letters and the proportion of the point sizes, as well as the inking.

Bettoni worked between Padua, Brescia and Milan with varying success, as has been said. He preferred the illustration on the blank page before the half-title, the system which had been adopted and become habitual at this period. His formats of between 7⅜ and 9⅜ ins. in height are graceful; the size of the page is in proportion, the impression good, apart from the use of badly cast characters. But his small formats and the printing of small point sizes are beautiful and harmonious while the graphic effect on the white paper (used however at times with little glue and against the grain) resemble strongly the printing of the master of Parma.

Next we turn to the monumental 'in folio' editions of the Italian Classics by the Tipografia della Società Letteraria of Pisa. The format is increased in length (the proportion being 9⅜ by 18⅜ ins.); each volume carries on the page facing the half-title the etched portrait of the author; the blackness of the inking is handsome, although the paper has lost some of its whiteness due to the passing of time. Amoretti's types displayed by the Tipografia, at least in the higher point sizes (from 14 to 20) are well-cut: headings, ample spacing between the lines of the text; numbering of the pages at the top, at the outside; exclusion of any but the smallest ornaments; title-page entirely in capitals but with disproportionate differences in height. If we take: *Rime di Francesco Petrarca* of 1805, the line FRANCESCO is in larger type than PETRARCA, with a fundamental lack of equilibrium that immediately leaps to the eye. This must have been a habit, if we can call it that, dear to the good printers of Pisa, for we find it in many of their books.

Another famous printer of Pisa who took his inspiration from Bodoni is Nicolò Capurro, whose folio editions had competed against the already famous imprints of Parma, revealing on the title-page itself of their editions the use of Didot characters, although they also used those of Amoretti. Not only this, but he imitated and tried to perfect the editions of the 'Società de'Classici di Milano' with a literary collection which was called 'Collezione di ottimi scrittori Italiani in supplemento ai Classici Milanesi' (Collection of the Best Italian Writers, as a Supplement to the Classics of Milan). Title-page completely in capitals, illustration facing half-title, wide margins, good inking, accurate register, decorated by 'scrolls' and cast ornaments, page numbers at the top, but sometimes in the centre and sometimes placed on the right. A few flaws in the spacing of the titles.

3. But outside this province of noble experiments, which attempted, in vain, to preserve within the art fitting qualities of inspiration and execution, a decline was certainly setting in. Perhaps the publication of 'Latin Classics' by Pomba of Turin, not only through the austerity and simplicity of the title-

pages, but also in the layout of the text itself, even with the notes closely printed in small type, preserve the sign of the Bodonian canons: in the layout of
their pages and margins, I repeat, in the use of capitals only on the title-pages
and in their spacing, for this forms a principal argument, an invariable touchstone. At this juncture there begins 'piecework composition', with the operatives paid 'by the page'. Whereby capital letters are simply juxtaposed and
completely lack the spacing indispensable for occupying the reader's eye pleasantly. Certain good and estimable books printed by Libanti of Verona, or by
Silvestri or Ferrario of Milan, offend the eyes when they are opened, entirely
because of this elementary mistake.

But even here we find an earnest attempt to renew ideas and to adapt the
more attractive models which with the new century appear on the horizon in
large numbers, and certainly in a state of disorder. The tendency to 'cover' the
entire title-page and consequently to replace the exceptional simplicity acquired by Bodoni, gradually begins again, even if the motives which now lie
behind it are completely different from those that applied earlier and obligations of a strictly commercial kind (which can be seen from some of Pomba's
educational books), have replaced the pompous obligations of the eighteenth
century. In the best printing-houses the typographer used medium-sized characters arranged in the various point sizes, alternating tastefully italics with
roman and entrusting to the various sizes of type the task of signifying with a
certain amount of harmony the greater or lesser importance of what has been
ordered: in the worst cases this makes it necessary to indicate that what is
suggested by an order will be entrusted to a corrupt juxtaposition, often para-
doxical, of diverse type faces which do not go together. As a rule the paragraphing was always, with minor or major adjustments, stabilised on the central axis of the page, symmetrically, and followed the 'urn' or 'chalice' system,
as it used to be called. The printer's degree of sensitivity controlled the layout
and spacing of the lines among themselves, as with the choice of the point size,
and these questions give rise to major discord and naturally to comparison.

The title page for example, of the *Memorie della Reale Accademia delle Scienze
di Torino* (Stamperia Reale, Turin), however praiseworthy as far as the sobriety and symmetrical layout of the lines is concerned, reveals considerable
disorder in the choice of the sizes: between the printing details and the title
itself of the work the relationship is at least from three to one. And this is true
of Salviucci of Rome, Remondini of Bassano and Libanti of Verona.

And the practice continued—at least in popular editions—of inserting on
the page before the half-title either an illustration from the text or the portrait

of the author, and often the proportions of one formed a contrast with the proportions of the title-page itself. The custom was brought to perfection of re-inserting the printer's device between the title of the work and the imprint and there was a contrast between a simplified and unadorned device in contrast to the seventeenth-century practice, when it was enlarged, and adorned with frames and decorative wood-engravings. Remondini used the initials G.R.F. lightly intertwined (a model which found favour again at the end of the century and was used by Sommaruga, Bocca, Treves, Zanichelli, Hoepli, U.T.E.T., Formìggini, down to Feltrinelli today); the device for the Tipografia del Gondoliere was a gondola on the waters of the Venetian lagoon, for Marietti of Turin it was Holy Sacrament, for Giuliari of Verona it was the aristocratic family tree. A practice which was still unpredictable but which gradually acquired strength until it reached our times: with the Mondadori rose, the Einaudi ostrich, the white circles used by Laterza and the campanile of San Marco used by Pozza.

There was one practice which was already usual and gradually became more obvious: in the past recourse was had to decoration that was ornamental in a simple way and showing a certain relationship with the themes of the text: a funeral urn for *Il Campo Santo di Brescia* by Bettoni, flowers for books of poems, but also the cast ornament and the scroll and the large flower that had been used by Bodoni.

There was a tendency to cover the available space, and if the technique and art of Bodoni was worth anything this consisted, in the most attentive printing-houses, of a kind of compromise between too much pre-Bodoni and too little of Bodoni himself: a medley full of defects and lack of balance, which moreover represents in embryo the model for the title-page of today, at least until the outbreak of the last war: when, that is, asymmetry is added to traditional symmetry and the experiments and innovations attempted at the beginning of the twentieth century were revalued with a recognition of the major causes behind them.

From about 1830 and the following years, the dating of a book, which until then had almost always been shown in roman numerals, appeared in arabic numerals, sometimes in varying sizes or in bold type, and this often increased the lack of balance in the layout of the title-page. Nowadays the tendency to omit the date has become more established, although it is usual to use arabic numerals.

As far as the position of the page number is concerned we can discern a single-minded attitude, with the obvious backing of so many modern experiments, more or less plausible and more or less new. It was normal and regular during the immediate post-Bodoni years for this number to be high up outside the type area, but there are cases in which it was placed at the top to the left and right breaking up a square of white (as done by La Società Letteraria in Pisa, Mussi in Milan, for example). It became less frequent to place the page number at the top but over the centre of the type area. In the following century controversy about the position of the page number was opened again and that poor number is still forced to jump about from one place to another in order to make it easier—it is thought—for the reader to read the book (or to make it more complicated).

In 1925 Bertieri put forward explicit theories about it, and did not conceal the difficulty that this number had always represented. ('Il numero di pagina nel libro moderno' in: *Il Risorgimento Grafico* XXII, 1925.) He made the outright suggestion that it should be omitted and that the pages should not be numbered, so that the compact block of the type area should not be broken up. Or at the most it should be 'made a little more interesting and decorative'. He explained that this should be done by adding to it a few ornaments, a grace, a leaf, or a star. (Or by printing it in a second colour, as he himself printed in fact in 1933 his *20 Alfabeti brevemente illustrati*.) But he had difficulty in understanding to what extent he had helped to solve the problem through his extreme innovation of preceding the number with the word *page* (i.e. *page* 22, *page* 23), usually placed at the foot, outside to left and right.

It is true that the placing of the number at the top and on the outside (more or less adopted by the printing industry between 1870 and the end of the century) performed a strictly utilitarian function in the rapid perusal of the book; and on the other hand I do not see why, with direct participation in the text, that is with spacing equal to that of the text and not twice as wide as happens today, one should not obtain good results with this isolated number lost in the margin; proportion and the architectonic harmony suffer from it.

It is clear that for reasons of time and space we are obliged to limit the analysis of the development of the printed book in Italy to various points and yet we are bound to neglect others which are no less important: such as the treatment of textual notes, previously collected in an appendix and later almost always at the foot of the page, for obvious practical reasons (and practicality upsets beauty) at some distance from the text, in the best printing houses separated by a space or by a rule (and where the claims of the book were greater, this rule would be printed in colour. For example *La Vita Nuova* of Dante published in Pisa by Nistri in 1872).

And the treatment of punctuation, until when for example it became a habit to give space both to the comma and the full stop (and I would say it was about 1840: in the books printed by Fontana in Turin, also in those by Libanti in Verona, the space is omitted, being an obvious improvement: but in the accurate and contemporary books printed by Pomba, the old rule is sometimes in force).

These are all points which as I said I can only mention and restrict myself to examples, but which are of an exceptional interest and deserve fuller treatment. (The trouble is, and I might as well say so once and for all, studies on Italian printing undertaken from a less romantic point of view hardly exist and there is a great need for them.)

4. The decline in Italian founding certainly did not follow the death of Bodoni and dates from somewhat further back. 'Bodoni found characters as originally cut, evidently out of alignment, clumsy in appearance, without artistic appeal, devoid of grace; italics designed on a slope, with the same defects, ornaments carelessly cast. He improved them every day... He gave an elegant clear-cut edge to the punches, balancing the contrast between light and shade. He made alphabets with extremely subtle strokes which gradually enclosed the counters in an admirable fashion, while today we have the help of precision machines. He constructed many, some with strong contrasts, others lighter; but everything at once reveals his hand, which achieved a great effect of elegance.' (P. Trevisani, *Bodoni* op. cit.) For example 'shapes that were slightly solid and full of French characteristics were used for Bodoni's work and became continually more refined; at the printing works of the Tipografia Ducale in Parma the rather squat and graceless Fournier capital letters were gradually replaced by highly expressive characters of a colour wonderfully well suited to their art.' (R. Bertieri, *L'arte di G. B. Bodoni, idem.*)

The fact is that the one swallow of Parma did not make a spring and that the Italian foundries which were producing badly cut and badly cast types faces were certainly not suffering from this fervent pursuit of beauty and perfection. Zatta of Venice, for example, who supplied the whole of the Veneto province (the clumsy printing of his collection 'Il Parnaso di ogni Nazione' is evidence enough) continued to produce type faces which were badly cut and with bad alignment as well as monotony of outline.

Reasons of economy had certainly prevented the foundries from refurbishing themselves and the printing houses from changing their suppliers: it is a fact that the Parma foundry did not work for one third of the number of Italians as they worked for printers abroad (Spain and even Russia) and naturally the prices were higher when attention was given to care and precision rather than to the mere awareness of keeping up prestige.

In the meantime in 1818 the two volumes of the *Manuale Tipografico* were published, a vast documentation of Bodoni's creative genius and a perpetual source of inspiration and information. In it are represented 142 roman faces with the corresponding italics and capitals in a great variety of sizes, from the 'Parmigianina' to the 'Papal', seventeen scripts of which thirteen have the decorative swash capitals. Seven English series and various roman and italic capitals: the romans and scripts are in the first volume, and in the second the Greek and exotic series together with some ornaments, borders, frames and musical signs. But it would be out of place to repeat the praise of this work (elegant and deep-cut characters, strong contrast between the black and the extremely subtle strokes; clarity and elegance of the italics) or to pick out once again the abnormal quality (censure is always questionable) of certain capitals, of the numerals or the useless splendour of the exotic alphabets, which were apt to arouse in particular the admiration of the princely patrons, because apart from supplying material for comment they are not very much use to us.

In the meantime printing in two or more colours continued to be almost excluded and this, too, was to be an affirmation of Bodoni's mastery; he was anxious to better the examples from the preceding centuries and to emerge from the solitary splendour of black. (But in two masterpieces of the second period: *Aminta* and *Gli Amori Pastorali di Dafni e Cloe* the portraits of the authors are encircled with red and the ornament in the imprint is also in red.) Only when the mid-century had been reached, when printing houses had benefited from the improvement in technique and from expanding business did title-pages in two colours again become more popular; red and black had been usual and traditional, but now blue and black could be seen, also gold and silver, grey and so on, and the decoration of the page went beyond the limits of elegance and good taste: printers rivalled each other in supplying their clients with products that were in many colours and above all suggestive in style.

Initial letters in colour became more popular, and this was worse later when during the period of Art Nouveau these initials were enveloped in festoons and foliage of luxuriant vegetation (the books of Sommaruga are full of it).

The juxtaposition of type faces was no doubt a sign of this future decadence which at the mid-century, as the abandonment of Bodoni's high standards

197

progressed further, came to be average in Italian book production; it was certainly favoured by the variety of the series that the foundries, especially those abroad, placed on the market. To faces which were considered as classic different variations were added, the so-called Elzévir faces, and then the Egyptian and Etruscan faces, in fact all the type faces that were produced to meet the demands of a sector that was just coming into being, the printing of newspapers and commercial work, which left the printer more and more to his own devices and suggested to him unimaginable experiments. This phenomenon, which was caused by ignorance, inevitably had a bad effect.

But at least after 1830–1835, although title-pages were still artificially filled, there was all the same a limit to this process of invasion; the better-informed printers restricted themselves completely to the juxtaposition of type faces belonging to the same series or those that were closely related, between the roman and italics of various sizes, adopting sometimes, but with extreme caution, a few characters in 'bold'. From this point of view the outstanding printing houses were the Tipografia del Gondoliere in Venice, Libanti and the Società Tipografica Editrice in Verona, the Tipografia di Alvisopoli, the Società de'Classici, Silvestri, Ferrario, and also Sonzogno in Milan (but in 1880 Sonzogno was already a publisher of 'serials').

A *Compendio di Geografia* by Adriano Balbi published by Pomba in 1840 has a title-page which, apart from the way the information is wedged in, is a pure sample book of type faces: from lower case to capitals and small capitals, from roman to Egyptian. A *Prose e Rime* by Angeli Gaetano which was printed by Libanti of Verona in 1846, although it is not badly printed, is another typical example of the linguistic decadence into which book printing was declining. The ten lines of the title page contain at least six alphabets, from bold roman to English italics. It was even worse later when lithographed title-pages came in (during the seventeenth and eighteenth centuries the copperplate engravings were not rare and the early Bodoni books contain some which are really splendid) and the same can be said of books which belonged entirely to the illustrator or typographer. A few examples will suffice: a *Storia della Guerra dell' Independenza degli Stati Uniti d'America* by Carlo Botta (with allegorical illustrations), Milan, Schiepatti (printer Truffi, 1829); and even here the typographer has used a different alphabet for every line, Egyptian, Gothic, English italics. And then *Marino Faliero* by Giulio Pullè illustrated with stage directions, Verona, 1840 Libanti, where Gothic characters appear with flourishes.

The printing industry was no longer sufficient unto itself and sought renewed vigour by going abroad, searching vaguely, rejecting the possibilities to be found within itself, to which seemed to be added better resources and the new technical processes of printing and illustration. The revolution in technique could not fail to upset fixed paradigms, while it took advantage all the more of the singular lack of professional artistry which distinguished printing establishments.

III

1. *Illustrated books / Popular publishing / Gift books.* 2. *Coming of Art Nouveau.* 3. *The Art Nouveau and futurism.* 4. *Wood-engraving and book production.*

1. In Rome the lithographic process (in Italian it was sometimes called 'poli-autografia') made its first appearance in 1805; in 1807 it reached Milan, and in 1816 it reached Naples and Turin; in 1828 the first manual of lithography came out from F. Rusconi. All the same the lithographic process, at least at first, was not of great use to the book trade because the lithographic ink was not easily adaptable to the limited forms of illustrations in the text, but on the other hand it rendered immediate and excellent service in the printing of newspapers. It is true that small plates and wood-engravings suitable for use in the text were often made from large lithographs. (A. Calabi, *Saggio sulla Litografia; la prima produzione italiana in rapporto a quella degli altri paesi sino al 1840.* Milan 1958.) When during 1825–26 Ferrario published Manzoni's *I Promessi Sposi* he adorned the book with anonymous lithographs which did not meet with the author's approval, while in the following edition (Milan 1840), which was tidied up and 'Tuscanised' the lithographs disappeared and in place of them Redaelli printed the beautiful wood-engravings (400 of them) by Francesco Gonin. (For 'The Limited Editions Club' the Officina Bodoni in Verona reprinted in 1951 the English translation of *I Promessi Sposi* decorating it with Gonin's wood-engravings recut by Bruno Bramanti.)

It was natural, in view of the bourgeois and humanitarian nature of the century which had become romantic, that book illustration assumed great importance. (Although educational books, which in fact had a greater right to be illustrated, continued to be presented in ways which were not only slovenly but completely unattractive.) A demand which was a consequence of the triumph of romanticism and also of the competitive situation of publishing which was going through a stage of rapid development. Illustrations were inserted *in the text*, with a lack of proportion that was sometimes disastrous, capital letters were given figurative illustrations (but this was very usual in seventeenth and eighteenth century printing), headings were framed, sometimes with simple rules, sometimes with double rules printed in black, later with floral motifs that were stylised or as a rule ornamental.

The success of *I Promessi Sposi* by Manzoni already mentioned, which came out in serial form from the presses of Redaelli in Milan, in 1840, with the pages of the text framed by two rules, title-page baroque illustration including the characters of the story all round it, and with the wood-engravings by Gonin, offered an exceptional incentive to many series of romantic books. In the same year Fontana in Turin brought out, also in serial form, *Il Diavolo Zoppo* by Lesage, illustrated by Tony Johannot, with equally attractive frames and woodcuts; in 1843 he brought out *Margherita Pusterla* by C. Cantù, and in this book also the pages are framed by double rules, but in the former the chapter headings consist of vignettes showing landscapes, while in the latter the headings are composed of ugly geometrical motives.

In 1843 also Fontana and Pomba published jointly *Ettore Fieramosca o la Disfida di Barletta* by Massimo D'Azeglio, an edition said to be a companion volume to the earlier book by Cantù. In the text, illustrated by I. De Moraine, appear 200 engravings (but the title page is inferior because of the variety of type faces used). The edition is important however on account of the way in which the two printers clarified the situation of the illustrated book, the relationship with Redaelli's edition of Manzoni and above all the necessity for so much 'printing for entertainment', together with uneasiness at being still forced to go to foreign artists. (As a footnote to the decadent mixture of type faces, the signatures of the two printers are in Gothic characters.)

'So-called illustrated editions', they wrote, 'have been appearing recently and have found so much favour with everyone that there is hardly a city, nor a country nor a province, where some have not appeared, with as great a display of engravings and type faces as conditions would permit. The rapid and pleasing success of illustrated volumes is to be admired impartially, for the supreme delight they give to the eye and the great help they provide towards the understanding of the text, and lastly through the very fine link they provide between the arts and literature.' Finally, in justification of the designs by foreign artists: 'if, in spite of our more ardent hopes, we sought the engravings from famous foreign engravers, as well as those by artists born in the same country as we were, the only reason for this, to be just, is the novelty of the *genre*, in which as yet no one amongst us has shown more than mediocrity'. These expedients of book-illustration and decoration were typical of the beginning of the century. Among the illustrated travel books which came out from Treves at the end of the century (I quote Treves because during those years he had established himself as the most enterprising Italian publisher) and those seen now on a grand scale, the differences are not great: the model is the same, sanctified by an ever-increasing success with the reading public, and inferior, it must be said, from the printing point of view, through inaccurate and slovenly workmanship.

The first popular editions produced by Silvestri, Ferrario, Sonzogno and Barbera were small in format, with a portrait facing the title-page, clear layout, neat printing, pages with wide margins, and still remained within certain limits of linguistic severity; but between these and the publications of Perino, the new Sonzogno, Bemporad, there is already a wide gulf. 'The principal characteristic was the deplorable slovenliness: paper of the lowest quality, unplanned pages totally unrelated to the format of the book and set in type faces devoid of significance, without margins and with very little space between the lines, the printing was extremely careless, carried out with ink that was more grey than black, and with ornaments in poor taste.' (R. Bertieri, *Il Libro Italiano, idem.*)

And the so-called 'Gift-books', the 'Almanacks' which, stuffed with verse and prose, periodically flooded the market during the second half of the century, are the extreme testimony of a habit which had now been acquired. Just as in bourgeois households of the post-Risorgimento period, with its framed flowers and stuffed birds, along with velvet, beads and imitation gold, during the long period of peace which followed up to the First World War, our gift-books were adorned with ribbons, printed in several colours, enriched with the latest successes of photo-engraving, as in the melancholy and loving definition of Gozzano these were still 'good things in the worst possible taste'. A wood-engraver with fervid (and unbounded) imagination like Gustave Doré was still successful in Italy and meanwhile his illustrated classics appeared to satisfy the deep greed of the first middle-class collectors: *The Bible, The Divine Comedy, Don Quixote,* and so on, but in quarto and octavo for the 'cheap editions' in Italy, naturally in serial form, laid out in a tasteless way, badly printed by Sonzogno or Treves, editions which, printed in vast numbers with many reprints, on bad paper, destroyed the value of the great 'in folio' originals in French and English.

2. In Rome there was already a triumphal reception for the graceful publications of Angelo Sommaruga, which were sometimes printed in huge numbers (*Alle Porte d'Italia* by E. De Amicis had already reached 42,000 in 1884.) Even today the books issued by this adventurous publisher, whose endeavours in the field of decoration struck the popular imagination, occupy our attention as historical curiosities, and we only mention them here in order to put forward a 'Fantasy' contrast with the first Art Nouveau with geometrical decorative motives seen in 1840 and the years that followed.

If novelties can be mentioned, reference should be made to book covers, which Sommaruga published in two or more colours; the cover for G. Carducci's *Confessioni e Battaglie* (Rome 1884) is in three colours, yellow, dark green and red; the title-page is in two colours only, black and red; and as ornamentation there are, in addition to purely geometrical decoration, Renaissance motives, cherubs and large flowers, advance arguments for the development of all the ornamentation that followed, more or less determined by the Morris-Ruskin code.

In *Alle Porte D'Italia*, for example, the title-page overflows with it: the name of the author and the title of the work are inscribed in two panels and there are stylised flowers in profusion, while the publisher's initial is framed with a shield of leaves, in two colours, the headings are framed with flowers and there are initial letters on an ornamental background with a cover also in three colours (Sommaruga did not dislike pink).

Title pages in two colours were becoming usual: black and red; and in general the name of the author and the year of printing appeared in black, with the title of the work in red, often also the place of printing and the name of the publisher. With the spread of photogravure processes critical books and histories of art were beginning to come out, whose expressive forms and almost exemplary austerity in the flood of decoration can be reasonably described as enterprising even now. They were profusely illustrated both in the text and outside it, printed on coated paper, in formats from between 9¼ and 13¾ ins. in height, with many pages and solid binding in discreet taste, which all made these suitable for bringing Italian printing its first successes in international markets and at exhibitions.

I said that the title pages were extremely sober (as an example: *Raffello* of Marco Minghetti, Bologna, Nicola Zanichelli, 1885, all in black capitals) and even if they were over-decorated it would have been very difficult to criticise the title-page, limiting oneself to a few initial letters and some head-pieces. Bernardoni of Milan was one of the first to deserve mention as far as books on the history of art are concerned; for example: Le mie Memorie dettate by Francesco Hayez, 1890; better still: E. Müntz, L'Arte Italiana nel Quattrocento, 1894 (title-page in black and red). The flowery style intrudes into the text and the headings, tail-pieces and initial letters. Müntz' cover has the fine novelty of having been designed (by V. Turati) and of having been printed in colour (by the Cromotipografia Mora). It is true that the design of the cover and the title of the work (ornamented to excess) can only testify to the weaknesses of the period in which the book appeared. It is obvious however that certain linguistic limits had been overcome and there was already a tendency to restore a slightly more reserved expressiveness to the page, leaving to the covers however that freedom of invention and suggestion that good taste had excluded from the book itself.

Between 1901 and 1935 Hoepli published in Milan the Storia dell'Arte Italiana by Adolfo Venturi, a true monument to publishing as well as to the history of art. It is unnecessary to say that the title-page is in two colours in the version finally seen in Italy (the title and the publisher's name in red); I will limit myself to indicating the difference between the cover of the first volume of 1901 and that of the last one published in 1935, which provide clear evidence of developing taste. The first has a wood-engraving: a border of vine-tendrils and bunches of grapes with the title of the work in script, while in the latter, although it is also the work of a wood-engraver (Cisari), the decorative border has been abandoned and only one figure appears on the monochrome cover.

3. Even among the advanced shapes put forward by Morris himself near the end of the century and those which were adopted in Italy, as amongst the most ardent supporters of stylisation and fantasy in printing there was already a kind of compromise, in the sense that acceptance, as I see it, was never complete, at least in the normal field of work. Decorative motifs and suggestions were accepted; typefounders placed on the market type faces and ornaments that appeared on covers and title-pages, but architectonic freedom, as far as relationships and spaces were concerned, the fantasy proposed by Morris, was applied in Italy up to a certain point and in accordance with a traditional sense of proportion that was never forgotten.

'Forty years ago our printers,' wrote Paolo Galeati in 1899, 'went straight to Derriey (Ch. Derriey: Spécimen Album. Paris 1862). I do not know how many mishaps overtook my colleagues when they went to France; it is a fact that all at once they abandoned Paris and looked to Frankfurt, Berlin, Leipzig. And here I want to be fair: from France our printers learnt little: decorative type faces, the ornaments designed by Laurent and De Berny and those of Derriey did not appear to good account in the hands of our colleagues; on the contrary they later imitated the German models very well. At present I do not know if they have been to America or England or China to find Pre-Raphaelitism, Symbolism, Botticelli and the Art Nouveau. My friend Sala and the the good Nebiolos, who in any case are the leading typefounders in Italy, are enthusiastic about them, even fanatic in fact.' (P. Galeati, *L'Arte e il Bello nel Libro. Imola* 1899; and again P. Barbera, *Editori, idem.*) On the other hand Ratta, who had moreover praised this symbolism and stylisation, noted in 1925: 'women's profiles that were rather thin and pronounced; slender little bodies with hair that was linear or twisted over the shoulders or given exaggerated volume, forming a disproportionate mass on top of the head...' (C. Ratta, *L'arte del libro e della Rivista nei paesi d'Europa e d'America.* Bologna 1927.)

Galeati was certainly the fiercest opponent of the Art Nouveau style during those years, and even if he raised his voice in the provinces we cannot say that the clear-cut precision of his objections counted during that period on the Italian scene, when that particular kind of restricted Art Nouveau reached Italy. 'These type faces', as Galeati observed, 'even if they were free from ornamentation, could not stand up to Didot or Bodoni. And if we have to use ornaments why must we have recourse to this style, imposed on us by foreign typefounders, to whom we are still forced to go owing to the decline of our own?'

The controversy over Art Nouveau, with its presumptions of originality and luxurious simplicity drawn from Renaissance sources, is one which lasted longer than is generally believed and to which many have been found to pay their own tribute, even our good Bertieri. And the entire artistic side of Italian book production, at least until shortly before the Second World War, was affected by it, naturally with ups and downs, even if in the meantime printers abandoned decorated initial letters, headings with spirals, lotuses, chrysanthemums, and sunflowers. One aspect of this uninterrupted presence has been the widespread use of wood-engraving, the predominance of which can be widely seen in the monumental work of Cesare Ratta about the decoration in Italian books.

Perhaps the most representative publisher during these years was A. F. Formìggini, who began work in Genoa in 1908 and stopped before the Second World War, in Rome. Formìggini was a man of taste and culture; his title-pages and pseudo-Renaissance book covers had richness and it is always useful to compare the historical and cultural approach of Sommaruga with that of

Formìggini, on the basis of this choice. Owing to the number of wood-engravers who illustrated his books, Bernardini, Capelli, Cisari, De Karolis, Gustavino, Mariani, Mazzoni, Artioli, Oppo, Salvadori, Servolini, Vellani-Marchi (A. F. Formìggini, *Venticinque anni dopo.* Rome 1933), he is certainly the most interesting exponent of this tendency which lasted, although it became progressively restricted, until the Second World War.

As a rule the titles of his books (in red) are set out between Renaissance pillars, with cherubs, angels, young girls, flowers and leaves in abundance, and without doubt they owed their existence to the books of the sixteenth century, even if there is a vast difference between these spectral-constructions and the graceful finesse of the earlier period.

The two collections 'I Profili' and 'Classici del Ridere' with title-pages designed by Artioli and De Karolis, have remained continually famous and successful. Garlands of leaves, drawn with pleasing stylisation, are placed round panels and pillars; 'all the rich flowering of vegetable life' as Ratta wrote (*Il libro e la rivista, idem.*) were the motifs that became appropriate to book illustration during these years; the style overcame the break caused by the First World War, and continued to repeat itself for a long period of time. Treves did not remain immune from it, although through the direction taken by some of his cheap editions, he brought about some deterioration in the forms (his pocket 'Collezione di Teatro', for example). Later Treves again, with his collection 'Le Più Belle Pagine' (edited by Ugo Ojetti) although he tolerated decoration on the title-page, reduced it in the prelims, and still used leaves and open flowers designed by Parmeggiani.

The out-of-date and insipid type of decorative title-page is still repeated today by the Istituto Editoriale Italiano with their 'Classici' directed by Ferdinando Martini, by Zanichelli in his *Poesie* by Giovanni Pascoli (we are already in 1920) down to the Società Tipografica Modenese who use it on the covers of their best collection 'Testi e Manuali dell'Istituto di Filologia Romanza dell'Università di Roma.' (The last to give up the attractions of pseudo-classical ornamentation was Laterza in Bari, who has only recently dropped the white spirals on the cover of the immensely successful 'Biblioteca di Cultura Moderna'.)

But even Formìggini himself, after having printed the same design on the title-page and on the cover, adapted things within a few years and left his Renaissance constructions on the cover only, while the title-page returned to the traditional orderly layout. About 1930 he improved further and began to abandon wood-engravings on the covers, experimenting with designs that

205

were truly admirable in their simplicity and balance (I remember among the most beautiful books of those years, *Canto Fermo* by Giorgio Vigolo).

This is to say that although this was the dominant style in book production there was no lack of opposition to the classical extremists from the early years of the century to the First World War; at its best it stood for moderation in the triumphal course of this invasion by the commonplace.

In 1914 F. T. Marinetti, with the publication in Milan of his *Zang Tumb Tumb*, backed by French experiments (from Apollinaire to Mallarmé), proclaimed in Italy the futurist revolution in printing. 'I am starting a revolution in printing... Books must be the means of futurist expression... Not only this. My revolution is directed against the so-called typographical harmony of the page, which is contrary to the ebb and flow, the jolts and explosions of the style which moves over the page itself.' And the technical resources of the innovation were terribly old. 'We shall use for this purpose three or four different coloured inks on one page (he had probably never seen any illuminated manuscripts) and also twenty different type faces, if necessary...'

A revolution which took place more or less without any blows being struck, but for a short time its repercussions were felt all over Italy. Carlo Frassinelli for example, one of the most sensitive theorists among our printers, was temporarily affected by it, so much so that his *Il Risorgimento Grafico* published between 1921 and 1922 'A graphic revolution', concerned with establishing the theoretical basis of a *vibrant* and *psychological* style of printing with type faces that were expressive, with the sound, the colour and even the smell of the ink.

But Frassinelli himself soon narrowed these limits and fixed the more restrictive ones that a conscientious printer like himself could not fail to do, and these were: a revolution there should be, but not such as to upset the classical principles of printing. Later in fact he wrote that these attempts at innovation were no more than 'poor attempts, absurd, schemes made up of confused words...' (*Trattato di Architettura Tipografica*. Turin 1940). In spite of all this the echo of Galeati's wise advice could still be heard: 'I do not tell you to be *Bodoni* nor to imitate Bodoni in a servile fashion, no... I will say that you should receive your baptism from Bodoni then accumulate all the improvements that famous printers have been able to achieve since his day.' (*Lo Stile Floreale e la Tipografia*. Imola 1900.)

I have quoted Galeati's declaration here not because this is not self-evident, but because others quoted it at the time, and it was *Il Risorgimento Grafico* team for example who opposed Bertieri and took up this theme again (although in ambiguous terms), making it their battle-cry. If it were true that

Bodoni did not create book-printing in Italy, that Bodoni did not start a school of thought, it is more true than all this to say that his lesson has always been the most disturbing and the most influential in the history of our printing. That rejecting him has always meant turning more consciously towards him and his mastery. 'The Italians do not copy Bodoni, but they take their inspiration from Bodoni...', wrote Bertieri (*Il Libro Italiano, idem.*); but Bertieri, caught in the thick of his campaign for a national printing works, and because of his unconcealed regret both at the temporary assignment of the Bodoni registers at the Officina Bodoni to Montagnola and the triumphal entry into Italy of Giovanni Mardersteig (1928) for the publishing of the 'Collected Works' of D'Annunzio, had protracted this kind of argument, exchanging too often arguments purporting to be based on Bodoni which were in effect only obvious manipulations of the Art Nouveau paradigm.

4. After the title-pages with copperplate engravings of the seventeenth and eighteenth centuries, came the lithographs of the nineteenth century and then those that were entirely carried out in wood-engraving: the engravers, who naturally furthered their own cause, willingly placed on a Renaissance-type layout the title of the work, and all round added trees and flowers and fruit and birds. The design was clean and clear, the lettering of the titles—which was drawn—belonged to the same family, using naturally the inevitable licence of the calligrapher.

D. Tofani for example designed title-pages for Bemporad and Barbera; see *I Toscani dell'Ottocento* by Pietro Pancrazi in Bemporad's collection 'Libri Necessari'; or *Novelle di Giovanni Boccaccio* from Barbera (1924). The architectonic layout of the design is almost identical: in both of them there occurs the ornament of a fountain which occupies the centre of the design; the three figures which animate the scene in the *Novelle*, drawn in the Art Nouveau idiom, are inspired by the well-known representation of Spring by Botticelli.

Purely ornamental motives, geometrical leaves, construct a frame round the square of the title, for example in the work *La Decorazione del Libro* by Cesare Ratta published in Alessandria by Ariel during these years. F. Gamba signed the cover for Luigi Fallacara, *Illuminazioni*, vignette: a heart with three candles, the whole framed by a double black rule; B. Disertori, the cover for G. A. Borgese *L'Arciduca* Mondadori, Milan and Rome. Bruno Da Osimo designed the frame for Mondadori's educational collection, among panels and symbols more or less classical in character (the frame lasted a long time). The same policy was followed by Zanichelli, Alpes, L'Eroica and Alinari. It was better finally when wood-engraving was limited to decorating the title-pages themselves with a vignette, allowing type faces proper to be used for the titles (see the 'Collezione Romana' edited by Ettore Romagnoli; some were printed by La Voce in Florence, while others came from Alinari, Mondadori and Bertieri).

In any case, about 1930 wood-engraving, which until then had predominated in book-printing, entered a state of crisis. A rapid and inevitable decadence came with the developments and new prospects in the graphic arts and was caused finally by the drying-up of the pseudo-Renaissance theme.

Warnings of this decline were already in the air. Gianolio Dalmazzo spoke of them in 1926 when he suggested avoiding 'ornaments and specially modelled type faces', to 'substitute stylisation for exact reproduction of natural forms', to 'give special care to the layout of the text', for the latter constitutes 'an element of beauty apart from any contribution by ornamentation.' Meaning that there should be less of all 'the cumbrous baggage of decoration and polychrome drawings which disfigure printed books.' (*Il libro e l'Arte*, *idem*.)

There was praise and rejection; Bertieri for example said that wood-engraving 'is the most aristocratic and artistic method of illustration and decoration and is truly original inasmuch as the printing is carried out directly from the wood which has been engraved by the artist', but later, 'decorative shapes are seen which weigh the book down instead of beautifying it, either by their mass or by the type of design which is not suited to the text'. (*Come nasce un Libro*. Milan 1931.) 'The new Italian book is essentially typographical, that is determined by the architecture of the page and by the choice and use of type faces rather than by any element of decoration and illustration.' (A. Calabi, *L'Arte Tipografica in Italia al 1928*. Milan 1928.)

The reality concealed behind this triumph was somewhat mediocre. In spite of the great number of wood-engraver artists (I have already noted some and will add: Wildt, de Witt, Carnevali, Marussig, Veneziani, Sergi, Betti, Sartorio, Ricci, Conti, Bramanti, Zetti, Marangoni) their contribution as a rule was limited to the covers and the title-pages, almost completely failing to produce an illustrated book; failing in fact to please not only the publisher who projected illustrated books with artistic aims, but the artists themselves who knew how to interpret an author; a lack which still occurs today (and anyone who writes knows very well the fatigue caused by certain very poorly illustrated editions of poetry). Ferrigni himself admitted it ('Il disegno e la stampa' in: *Il Risorgimento Grafico* XXIII, 1926), Calabi emphasised it: 'the

208

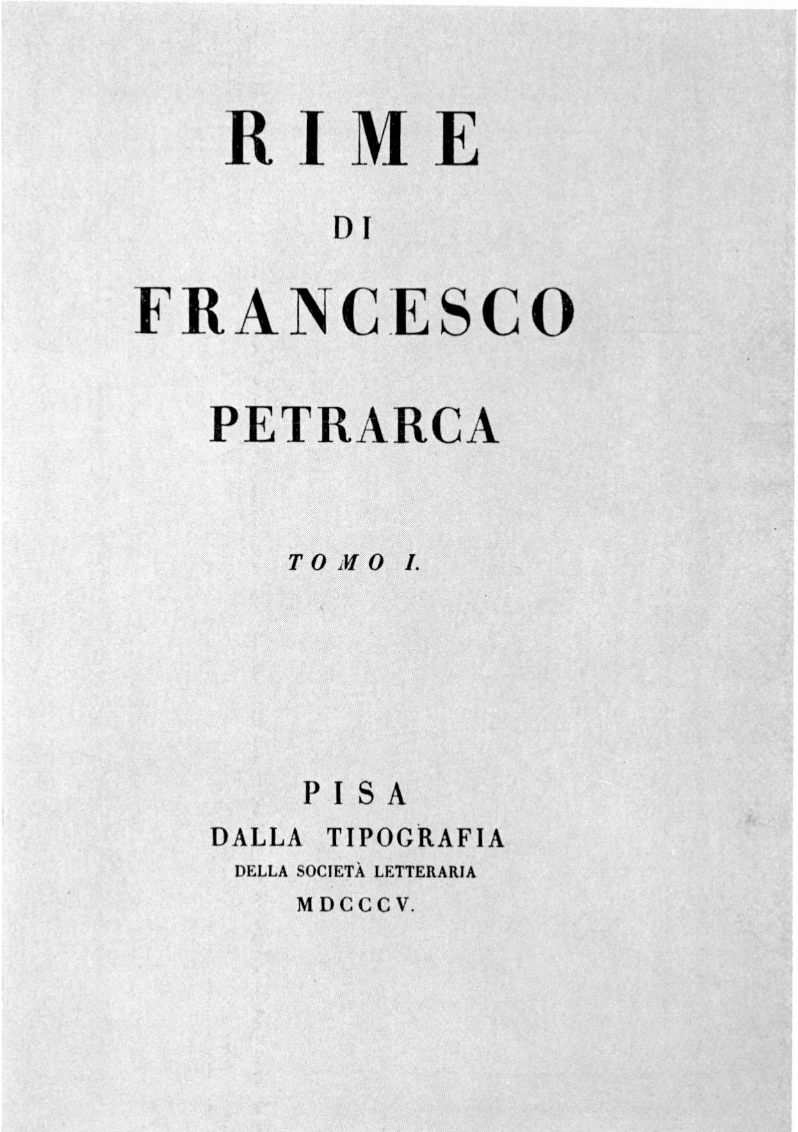

R I M E

DI

FRANCESCO

PETRARCA

T O M O I.

P I S A

DALLA TIPOGRAFIA

DELLA SOCIETÀ LETTERARIA

M D C C C V.

1. Petrarca: *Rime*, Dalla Tipografia della Società Letteraria,
Pisa (1805). Title-page

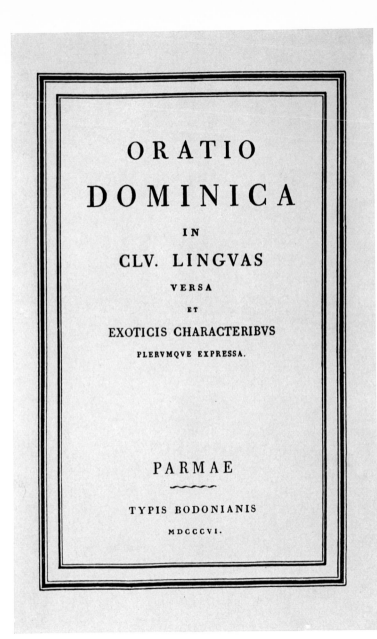

ORATIO
DOMINICA

IN

CLV. LINGVAS

VERSA

ET

EXOTICIS CHARACTERIBVS

PLERVMQVE EXPRESSA.

PARMAE

TYPIS BODONIANIS

MDCCCVI.

2. *Oratio Dominica in CLV Linguas*, Bodoni, Parma (1806). Title-page

3. Type Specimen Book of Amoretti (1811). Page of ornaments

4. G. B. Bodoni: *Manuale Tipografico*, Vedora Bodoni, Parma (1818).
Specimen page

LA COMMEDIA

DI

DANTE ALLIGHIERI

COL COMENTO

DI N. TOMMASEO.

VOLUME PRIMO.

VENEZIA,

CO' TIPI DEL GONDOLIERE.

M DCCC XXXVII.

5. Dante: *La Commedia*, Tipografia del Gondoliere, Venice (1837).
Title-page with allusive 'house mark'

6 G. Pullè: *Marino Faliero*, Libanti, Verona (1840). Lithographed title-page

CAPITOLO XX

UN FRATE E UN PRINCIPE

Fra Buonvicino, come l'altra notte, aveva serenato, aspettando coi cavalli al noce di Quadronno: perocchè le regole del suo ordine erano scevre di ogni severità; e per poco che l'abuso le avesse rilassate, non si faceva caso che alcuno stesse anche tutta la notte fuori di convento. Aveva, dissi, vegliato in aspetto, pregando il Signore, e talvolta abbandonandosi ad una gioconda speranza che questi darebbe favore all'innocenza, tanto da operar un miracolo per trarla in libertà: immaginava la gioja di sapere salve persone tanto care, il contento di rivederle una volta ancora, e poi mandarle dove fossero sicure dalla tirannia. Ma queste lusinghe davano tosto luogo ad un arcano spavento, ai calcoli desolati della ragione; e figurandosi tutti i pericoli possibili, gelava, sudava e buttavasi colla faccia sulla terra, pregando Iddio che li salvasse, egli che solo il poteva.

7. C. Cantù: *Margherita Pusterla*, Fontana, Milan (1843). Text opening page

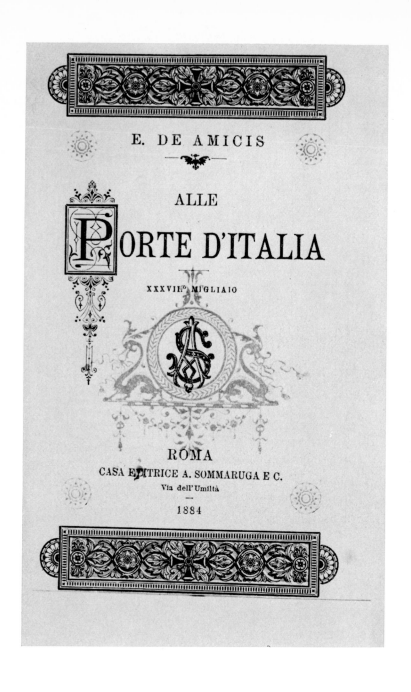

8. E. De Amicis: *Alle Porte D'Italia*, A. Sommaruga, Rome (1884). Title-page

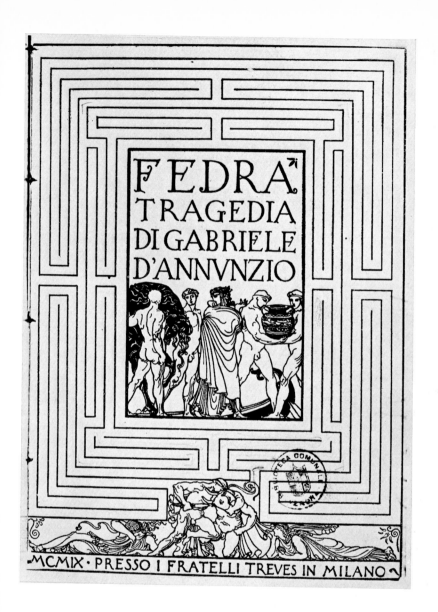

9. Gabriele D'Annunzio: *Fedra*, Fratelli Treves, Milan (1909). Title-page

115-50-6 - Corpo 6   Kg. 1,75 (A-100)

NESSUN MAGGIOR DOLORE CHE RICORDARSI DEL TEMPO GIOIOSO
QUANDO SI È IN MISERIA. L'ECONOMO HA VECCHIAIA ASSICURATA

115-50-8 - Corpo 8   Kg. 2,- (A-80)

ALESSANDRO DUMAS FECONDISSIMO DRAMMATURGO
E ROMANZIERE FRANCESE, SCRISSE REGINA MARGOT

115-50-10 - Corpo 10   Kg. 2,50 (A-72)

L'INVIDIA FA LA FOSSA E POI CASCA DENTRO

115-50-12 - Corpo 12   Kg. 3,- (A-60)

USO CI CONDANNA A MOLTE FOLLIE

115-50-16 - Corpo 16   Kg. 3,25 (A-34)

IMPARA LEGGERE E SCRIVERE

115-50-20 - Corpo 20   Kg. 4,25 (A-26)

MASSIMO D'AZEGLIO

115-50-28 - Corpo 28   Kg. 5,25 (A-16)

BOURBONNAIS

115-50-36 - Corpo 36   Kg 5,75 (A-10)

DECURIONI

115-50-48 - Corpo 48   Kg. 8,- (A-8)

MONACI

10. Type Specimen Sheet of Inkunabula (1911)

11. Gabriele D'Annunzio: *Alcione*, Fratelli Treves, Milan (1914). Title-page
engraved on wood by A. De Karolis

12. F. T. Marinetti: *Zang Tumb Tumb*, Edizioni Futuriste, Milan (1914).
Title-page

13. Gabriele D'Annunzio: *La Riscossa*, Bestelli & Tumminelli, Milan (1918).
Title-page engraved on wood by G. A. Sartorio

14. Boccaccio: *Novelle*, G. Barbera, Florence (1924). Series title-page engraved on wood by D. Tofani

15. Type Specimen Sheet of Paganini, designed by Raffaello Bertieri (1926)

LUIGI ZANONI

ORDINARIO DI LETTERE ITALIANE E LATINE
NEL R. LICEO "TORQUATO TASSO" DI ROMA

IL
SECONDO LIBRO
DI LATINO

*LETTURE, CONVERSAZIONI, REGOLE
ED ESERCIZI*

AD USO DEI GINNASI

*

A. MONDADORI - MILANO

BRVNO·DA·OSIMO

16. L. Zanoni: *Il Secondo libro di Latino*, A. Mondadori, Milan (1930). Series
cover with wood-engraved border by Bruno Da Osimo

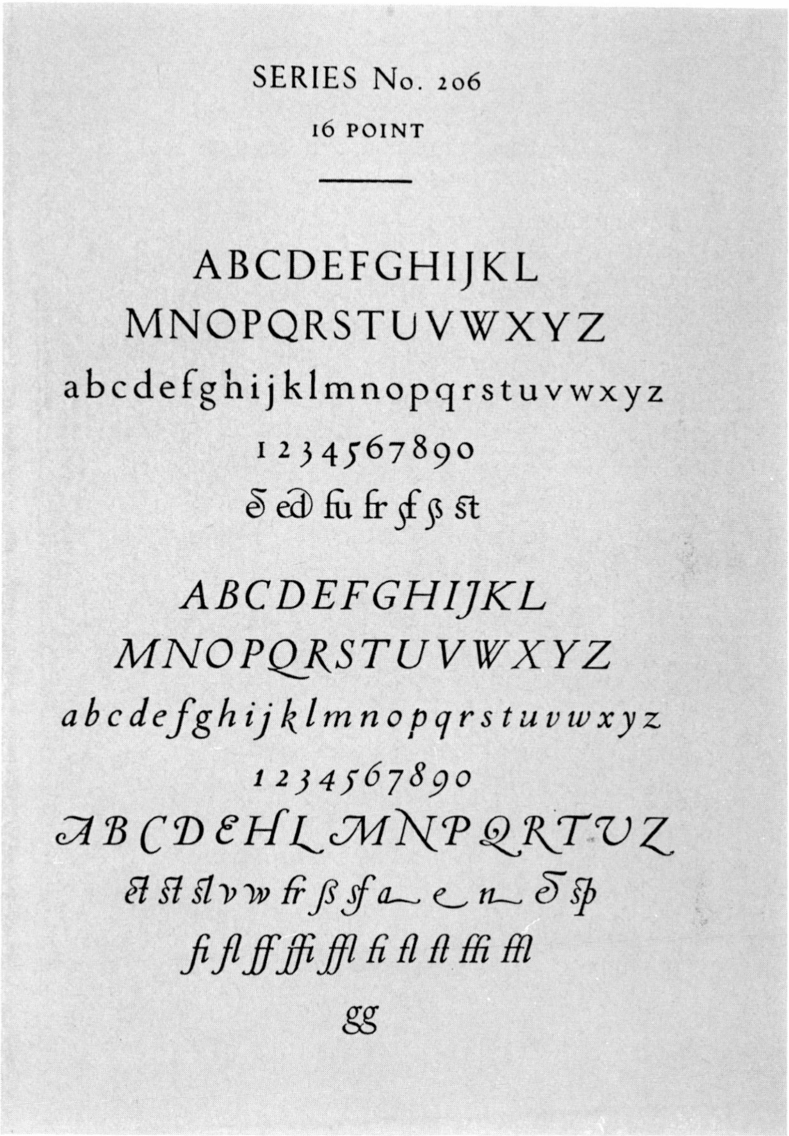

SERIES No. 206

16 POINT

———

ABCDEFGHIJKL
MNOPQRSTUVWXYZ
abcdefghijklmnopqrstuvwxyz
1234567890
ẟ ꝏ ſu ſr ſf ß st

ABCDEFGHIJKL
MNOPQRSTUVWXYZ
abcdefghijklmnopqrstuvwxyz
1234567890
ABCDEHL MNPQRTVZ
et st slvw fr ß sf a e n ẟ sp
fi fl ff ffi ffl ſi ſl ſt ſſi ſſl
gg

17. Type Specimen Sheet of Pastonchi, designed by Francesco Pastonchi and
Eduardo Cotti (c. 1930)

Voilà la montagne· dépouillée des chœurs qui parcouraient ses sommets; les prêtresses, les flambeaux, les clameurs divines sont retombés dans les vallées; la fête se dissipe, les mystères sont rentrés dans le sein des dieux. Je suis la plus jeune des bacchantes qui se sont élevées sur le mont Cithéron. Les chœurs ne m'avaient pas encore transportée sur les cimes, car les rites sacrés écartaient ma jeunesse et m'ordonnaient de combler la mesure des temps qu'il faut offrir pour entrer dans l'action des solennités. Enfin, les HEURES, ces secrètes nourrices, mais qui emploient tant de durée à nous rendre propres pour les dieux, m'ont placée parmi les bacchantes, et je sors aujourd'hui des premiers mystères qui m'aient enveloppée.

Tandis que je recueillais les années réclamées pour les rites, j'étais semblable aux jeunes pêcheurs qui vivent sur le bord des mers. A la cime d'un rocher, ils paraissent quelque temps, les bras tendus vers les eaux et le corps incliné, comme un dieu prêt à se replonger; mais leur âme balance dans leur

31

18. Text page set in Griffo, designed by Giovanni Mardersteig (1930)

CLASSICI DEL RIDERE

TRILUSSA

CAMPIONARIO

Con prefazione di FERDINANDO MARTINI
e con illustrazioni di GUGLIELMO WOHLGEMUTH.

AMOR ET LABOR

A.F.FORMÌGGINI EDITORE IN ROMA

19. Trilussa: *Campionario*, A. F. Formìggini, Rome (1931). Series title-page
with engraved border by A. De Karolis

20

ALFABETI
BREVEMENTE
ILLUSTRATI
DA
RAFFAELLO
BERTIERI

IMPRESSO IN MILANO
COI TIPI DEL BERTIERI NEL 1933
ANNO UNDECIMO

20. *20 Alfabeti*, *etc.*, Bertieri, Milan (1933). Title-page designed by Raffaello
Bertieri

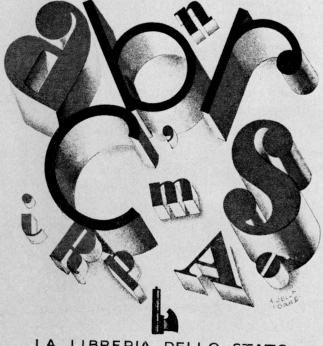

21. *Sillabario e piccole letture*, La Libreria dello Stato (1935). Title-page

constantly on the watch for the Evil One.
Thus, one day, seeing a yoke of oxen dash-
ing wildly towards the river, with a terri-
fied peasant in the cart behind them, the
Saint realized at once that this behaviour in
such placid animals could only be of dia-
bolical origin and, by promptly making the
sign of the Cross, he caused a howling devil
to issue from the animals' bodies. ✠ This
was the first of his three most celebrated
miracles. With one mighty leap the evicted
devil reached the court of the Emperor Gallienus in Rome (learned scholars object to
this on chronological grounds and insist
that it must have been another Gallienus),

9

22. Text page set in Zeno, designed by Giovanni Mardersteig (1936)

IL NINFALE FIESOLANO

DI GIOVANNI BOCCACCIO CON LE FIGURE
DI UNA PERDUTA EDIZIONE FIORENTINA
DEL QUATTROCENTO ORA RIUNITE
DA VARI LIBRI DEL CINQUE-
CENTO E REINCISE
IN LEGNO

EDITIONES OFFICINAE BODONI
VERONA

23. Boccaccio: *Il Ninfale Fiesolano*, Officinae Bodoni, Verona (1940).
Title-page

BIBLIOTECA DI CULTURA
MODERNA

FRANCESCO POLITI

LA LIRICA
DEL MINNESANG

TESTI - PROFILI - VERSIONI

BARI
GIUS. LATERZA & FIGLI
TIPOGRAFI-EDITORI-LIBRAI
1948

24. F. Politi: *La Lirica, etc.*, Laterza & Figli, Bari (1948). Series cover design

lack of special editions, the poor and brief preparation with which publishers attempt to bring out fine illustrated editions, the habit on the contrary of illustrating lavishly with designs *for their own sake*'. (*Il Risorgimento Grafico* XXIII, 1926.) And the unfortunate thing was this ignorance on the part of publishers and artists in dealing with the texts to be illustrated (it could have been also the gigantic ghost of someone like Doré, but I hardly believe this); for this purpose I recommend again the Pomba-Fontana declaration which was inadequately applied to Italy. It was also the predominance of a kind of illustration as limited and monotonous as wood-engraving which Art Nouveau had brought back to life, but one which was inevitably driven into a state of crisis by the decadence of that style itself. As for lithography and photogravure, both processes were affected by costs in a business with limited prospects as it was in Italy, in spite of the grand statements issued by the Fascist dictatorship which was in power at the time.

Experiments and concealed confusion occurred, even among so many trials, and although from a distance and in isolation, the influence of the Dutch 'De Stijl' and the German 'Bauhaus' were taken up again: the size of the page and the margins, the proportions between margins and the layout of the type, the very choice of the type faces with the design of some alphabets directly based on Renaissance manuscripts, although their practicality was to reveal itself in time as imaginary only. But as far as execution was concerned, attention to register, the choice of inks and papers, if one merit is ascribed to our Bertieri, in the heat of his discussions about the possibilities of nationalisation, it is fitting to mention this progressive and difficult recovery of conscientiousness in printing, the demand for perfection in execution, the permanent stimulus to consider book production with more clarity of ideas, without relying on circumstances and above all having confidence (here at least the influence of Bodoni had its value) in the expressive capacity of printing.

IV

1 *'National style' | Evolution of a particular taste.* 2 *The new type faces: Inkunabula, Sinibaldi, Ruano and Paganini.* 3 *New Bodoni series and Garaldus | Mardersteig's three type faces: Griffo, Zeno and Dante | Pastonchi.*

1. 'During the last years of the nineteenth century and the first years of the twentieth there was a fairly strong wave of admiration for English and then for American printing. This admiration gave rise to a desire for imitation which found an insurmountable obstacle in the insufficient and inadequate national production of type faces, inks and machinery. During these twenty years the Italians created for themselves, through their graphic arts, foundries and factories for producing inks and machinery. At the same time the more detailed study of the artistic forms of American printing made it evident to the Italian printers that these forms were derived directly, although refurbished and cut from original type faces, from Italian artistic expressions of the Renaissance. This discovery led to the movement for renewal in Italian printing which sought in the classical forms of early printing and fifteenth-century script inspiration, guidance and direction for the creation of a *national style*'. (R. Bertieri in: *Il Risorgimento Grafico* XXIII, 1926.)

The belief that afterwards the national style (at this point Fascist attempts, as well as the Fascist 'state book', took advantage of a situation that was already most confused in itself),—more or less exchanged for Art Nouveau—remained at the stage of intentions is a known fact. But I believe that the best fact is the one that sprang from these nationalistic presumptions, and that is that the theorists concerned with Italian book-production and printing, had finally put the question as one that was predominantly technical, discussing the use of the means available, the elements that determine the beauty of a book. Through the cautious advice that appeared in Bertieri's *Risorgimento Grafico*, the books by Gianolio Dalmazzo and Ratta to the aegis of *Campo Grafico* down to the *Trattato* by Carlo Frassinelli, between 1925 and 1940 there was a development of that professional conscientiousness which I believe constitutes the most advanced point of our progress in the art of printing since the Bodoni period.

A fine documentation through which to follow the evolution of taste and the Italian conception of graphic art is provided by a few publications, spaced out over the years, by an author who at that time was as famous and as widely published as D'Annunzio. I have beside me a book by Sommaruga, *Terra Vergine*, of 1884, small in format, unpretentious and with a slight lack of harmony in the layout of the title, in which the initial letters T and V have been brought out in a larger point size; but the publisher's address in italics is ugly and the date is out of place in the margin below.

There is a title-page carried out entirely in wood-engraving (by G. A. Sartorio) with similar illustration on the page facing the half-title in another book: Gabriele D'Annunzio's *La Riscossa* (Bestetti and Tumminelli, Milan, 1918) in pocket-size format. Everything has been framed in a stylised surround of large flowers, leaves, tendrils and fruit; but it is evident that the design and the engraving are in harmony, not so much with the decoration as with the nature of the text.

Next comes: *Le Elegie Romane* of Gabriele D'Annunzio (Milano, Editrice Lombarda, 1905), in medium format. The title-page is entirely designed and perhaps also engraved (but the name of the artist does not appear): a large frame of stylised leaves and flowers (there are also two birds below) entwined with open spirals. The date is drawn out: the initial L is two lines high, the U is represented by V; the turned point is used before the date. In the centre, in order to give a stronger suggestion of manuscript writing, a D'Annunzio motto is engraved, with the letters joined together or concealed, all this in a medallion surrounded with laurel leaves and swathed in bows. Gabriele D'Annunzio, *Laudi del Cielo, del Mare, della Terra e degli Eroi; libro III: Alcione* (Treves, Milan 1914). Illustrations by A. De Karolis. Medium format, title-page drawn out and engraved with type faces which imitate in a clumsy way alphabets and ornamentation of the Renaissance type (naturally U is rendered by V); in the large illustration, placed between the four lines of the title and the publishing data (slight faults in layout), over the heads of the two human figures flies a banner with the title of the third book of the *Laudi:* ALCIONE.

Again from Treves: *Fedra-Tragedia* by Gabriele D'Annunzio (Milan 1909). Of medium format, and here also the type face imitates a Renaissance alphabet. The layout is noteworthy all the same: a Greek cornice frames the title and the illustration (but the Greek-style cornice, more or less rigidly geometric, is obviously the extreme reduction of a floral-type stylisation that does in fact predominate). On the other hand there is no decoration in the splendid edition of the *Opera Omnia* printed by the Officina Bodoni and Mondadori between 1928 and 1936 in Verona, for which various Bodoni series of type faces were purposely re-cast from the matrices preserved at the Biblioteca Palatina in Parma. The title-page has a high-quality, formal purity and the architectonic layout is strict. Black is the only colour used and there is no decoration except for a few cast ornaments. (Later the Officina Bodoni printed: *L'Oleandro* by G. D'Annunzio, folio, in 20 point Bodoni characters, with lithographs printed in pink by G. G. Boehmer.)

But in the meantime another edition of *L'Oleandro* in Rome (1933) can be considered, and at the same time the new sobriety of the layout and the severe beauty of a smooth cornice, designed by G. Mardersteig.

2. As I said, since the dependence on foreign countries for the supply of type faces had now been reduced, Nebiolo of Turin, out of the few Italian foundries, was now in a leading position, and although it still lacked an adequate drawing office it looked after the creation and design of a few alphabets that attained a certain level. At the beginning of the century Art Nouveau was triumphant (Nestore Leoni was the most reliable representative) and as a result the market was flooded with type faces and ornaments with 'contorted lines' wrote Trevisani, 'which made it look as though a co-operative of snakes was having a disagreement.' (*Storia della Stampa*. Rome 1953.) But as it has also been said, between contrasts and experiments, a less conventional tendency was gaining strength, one that was clearer and freer: a return to classicism which sooner or later was bound to produce results.

'A printer's first responsibility,' Bertieri explicitly remembered, 'is the choice of a type face which in size and type is in keeping with the book he has to print, and consequently an interpretation of the text which must be made in order to decide on the type face, while it is necessary to have a special knowledge of the expressive value of individual alphabets in order to choose the most suitable one. Because every type face has its own expressiveness and a different use: from the smallest type, but *clearly legible*, which can be used for a dictionary to the large, open type face necessary for a spelling-book; from ordinary type, without any particular expressiveness, but *easy to read* [our italics] which can be used for study books, to the classical character, which is the most suitable for attractive literary books, to the narrow one (but still *legible*) which can be highly suitable for a book of the Marinetti type. For this reason there are type faces which are robust, sound, strong and agile, mellow and so on.' (*Come nasce un Libro, idem.*) Our italics and Bertieri's own terminology point to a classical approach, not very severe but clear enough to establish on what lines he was working. (But Bodoni writes: 'The more a type face possesses regularity, clearcut outlines, good taste and grace, the more beautiful it will be... but in order for it to display itself well and stand out well on the pages, the type must be carefully drawn up in clear and extremely even lines, not crowded and not out of proportion with their height.')

A classical claim that *Il Risorgimento Grafico*, in spite of inevitable contradictions, had constantly made their own, now adopting the type face Inkunabula (it was also called Venezia) copied from an alphabet used in Venice in 1476 by Erhard Ratdolt and cast in 1911 by Nebiolo 'while agreeable to the eye', wrote Updike, 'there is too much space between individual letters to make it wholly successful'. (D. B. Updike, *Printing Types: Their History, Forms and Use*. Cambridge, Mass. 1922.) C. Ratta, *Il libro e la rivista, idem*: 'In spite of the many attempts our few foundries made in order to create a national type face, they never succeeded in their aim... Only the Nebiolo Foundry in Turin turned their hand to it for several years and finally cast the type face Inkunabula, copied from a book published at the very dawn of printing. It was an exhumation and not a creation.' Finally, R. Bertieri, *20 alfabeti brevemente illustrati*. (Milan 1933): 'It is interesting through its expression which derives for the most part from the variety of the strokes which brings it fairly close to the Sinibaldi alphabet'); now ascribing to their own exclusive merit the casting of two alphabets of classical type, one being Umanistico (or Sinibaldi) suggested and illustrated by a library director (Guido Biagi), taken from the manuscripts of Antonio Sinibaldi in the Medicea-Laurenziana Library in Florence, and cast by an American foundry (but later entered in the Nebiolo catalogue), and the other Ruano, reconstructed by Bertieri (the capitals were missing) from the calligraphic examples of Ferdinando Ruano from the Biblioteca Vaticana, and again cast by Nebiolo in Turin.

These alphabets had more curiosity value than beauty; about Sinibaldi, Bertieri wrote: 'It has the true and proper Roman character, most gracious and harmonious in the expression it preserves in the flow of the letters and the endings of the stroke, or else it is graceful, with all the mellowness and all the close spacing, often irregular, of the original manuscript, with the result that the letters appear vibrant or sharp as though they had been traced now with the broad-tipped quill pen used by the copyist.' (*20 alfabeti, idem*.)

However, this proposition leads to a serious question. New and classical alphabets were being sought (it had become a mania) and what was perhaps the finest 'old style' type face created at the end of the century by Italian typefounders was being dropped. I refer to Blado. A harmonious type face with outstanding grace and an extremely open counter; it had a rectangular body, had been produced by Nebiolo and remained in their catalogue until about twenty years ago. Its precise date of origin has remained obscure to me and when I questioned the Foundry itself they could not tell me anything that was not already known. Aldo Novarese wrote to me, in fact, saying that he had not succeeded in finding anything in the archives, neither the year of production nor the name of the designer. 'I can assure you', he went on, 'that it was cut at the end of the nineteenth century or at the beginning of the twentieth; the designer probably took his inspiration from the capitals of the face from Perrin of Lyons, that is from the faces that came out about mid-way through the last century in France and signified a return to the classical forms of the

213

Renaissance.' I, for example, found it already used in 1885 by Zanichelli in Bologna; better, I find that in 1926 a theorist like Gianolio Dalmazzo did not in fact call this face Blado but by the more generic name Romano Antico or Elzévir. These are mysteries still to be cleared up.

Paganini (1926) was entirely created by Bertieri, a harmonious alphabet, in which the full strokes were always vertical, the only one out of the others which is still alive and fairly often in demand (this too is entered in the Nebiolo catalogue, since Bertieri was their artistic adviser).

'In constructing this alphabet', wrote Bertieri, 'I wanted to create a face which had no close relationship to any other... without adopting an over-rigid expression I took care to limit the flow of the lines to the minimum, leading to an alphabet which would be smooth but not excessively so... I was concerned also with avoiding those differences in width which are shown by the letters of many alphabets. In Paganini (it was named after the famous sixteenth-century printers) the reader will in fact find that no letter is excessively narrow in contrast to the others.' (*20 alfabeti, idem.*) Paganini was used for the first time in the little book by A. Calabi already mentioned (*L'Arte Tipografica in Italia al 1928*). This is an example, given the fact that it was laid out and printed by Bertieri, rich in many eccentricities through which Bertieri hoped to find new directions in Italian printing. (Example: the name of the author is entirely in small letters as compared to the title of the work which is entirely in capitals. Worse—and I think that it is the only example of its kind, the short lines on the pages with even numbers start normally on the left, with the white space on the right, but those on the pages with uneven numbers, incredible though it is, are definitely placed on the right with the space preceding them.)

But Inkunabula, it is fairly clear (the placing of the dot over the *i* to one side is incomprehensible) and without strong contrasts of weight (its geometrical base is the square) resulted in a limited use; Sinibaldi (on a rectangular body), with the serifs and strokes very much prolonged in the small point sizes, loses elegance and becomes difficult to read.

Ruano finally is a type of Italian Gothic (on a rectangular body) which is used less often and less successfully than the others, used in fact somewhat rarely (the only ones, I believe, who still use it in Italy are the noble students of the Scuola di Urbino).

These were type faces which with the best will in the world could not be used very much in book-production, for the latter cannot manage without clarity, legibility and elegance; with the result that after the first wave of enthusiasm had passed they went out of circulation. Another face put on the market by Nebiolo in about 1930 is questionable, being heavy and of uncertain size: Iliade, classified precisely as 'the free union of classical elements'. (*20 alfabeti, idem.*)

3. Paganini on the other hand, remained in circulation, although to a reduced extent; whilst various Bodoni series came into circulation with ever-increasing success and have lasted more or less until the present. These series have been strengthened or lightened and have shown themselves all the same to be more suitable for use in periodicals than in books. And no typefounders' catalogue today is without its Bodoni series, original or re-modelled to a greater or lesser extent. (The series Normanna is interesting, derived from a Bodoni face but on a square body and very black: R. Bertieri, *20 alfabeti; idem.*)

About 1925 C. Ratta wrote: 'The textual type faces, with strokes sufficiently wide apart and in proportion to the shape of the letters, have great clarity... The Didot type faces, the so-called Garamond and the Bodoni style faces are the ones mostly used at the moment, because they are light, graceful and legible... Narrow type faces are not much used; on the contrary the Elzévir faces seem to be coming back into fashion. Titles and sub-titles are set in the same types as the text... Only the covers, a kind of literary disposition in the work, have assumed since this time a bolder appearance which is in contrast to the Bodoni title-page.' (*Il libro e la rivista, idem.*)

It is true that the creation of four or five alphabets, three of which were hardly ever used, was not a big thing for a state foundry. Bertieri himself recognised this with a certain bitterness: 'The Italian typefounding industry', he wrote, 'during this quarter of a century has only created a very small number of original type faces, that is Italian ones. And they are almost all (four or five) through the work of one single foundry, out of the ten or twelve operating in Italy.' (*Il Risorgimento Grafico XXXII*, 1935.)

But at the present time it cannot be said that the situation, at least from Bertieri's point of view, is much better. If I am not mistaken, since the last war only one alphabet of a certain classical nature has emerged, Garaldus, designed by Aldo Novarese (so far roman and bold italics), an unexpected influence in which the characteristics of Garamond, also in the narrower and elongated counters, appear to predominate. The capitals are really beautiful.

The predominance of Monotype in book-printing and hence in the choice of type faces for the text, I would say, leads at the moment to a lack of contrast. From the books of Mondadori to those of Einaudi, Feltrinelli, Comunità, Garzanti, Ricciardi, the faces used for the text are only Baskerville, Bembo and Garamond, to which is now added Dante, a fine creation by Giovanni Mardersteig issued in 1958 and now in circulation in Italy.

Then on a small scale (but his small scale is fairly big) came the three alphabets designed by Mardersteig: Griffo (1929–1930): based on the alphabet of Francesco Griffo in the Aldine edition of Bembo's *De Aetna*, the same used and designed by Monotype, in the mechanical reproduction called Bembo; Zeno, in 1936, on a square body, outstandingly graceful and dark, devised above all for works of a religious character (his finest printed book is coming out now, dealing with the Four Gospels decorated with 114 wood-engravings); and Dante, issued in 1954, has certainly played its part in Italian book printing.

It is true that about 1930 a man of letters like Francesco Pastonchi devised and prepared a type face of clearly classical affinity, to which he afterwards gave his name the design however was by Eduardo Cotti (*Il Risorgimento Grafico* XXXII, 1935), a face which had a modest success and was much appreciated. *The Times* wrote:'The result is of great interest because this is a new design which is firmly attached to tradition: it is almost the only contribution made by modern Italy to English commercial printing, compensating in this way for the ever-increasing use made of English designs and type faces in the best Italian books'. (*The Pastonchi face: A specimen of a new Letter for use on the Monotype.* Verona 1928.)

Only as things are today even Mondadori, who was its most reliable patron, no longer uses it. Pastonchi was used with the others in his fine collection 'Lo Specchio' (contemporary poetry and prose) at least until immediately after the war; a Bodoni face replaced it, and now the collection has finally been redesigned (in controversial taste) and the publisher has adopted Dante.

It is true that many groups of type faces are produced from Semplicità (some of these are truly beautiful) to Fantasia (but of sober invention), decorations and ornaments which serve printing generally, and often with results which are also helpful in book-printing (limited to books of art and science), while the catalogues of our major typefounders certainly include a wide variety.

216

V

1. *The post-war period | Popular editions | Typographical experts. 2. Books by offset | Difficulties concerning illustrated books | Books for collectors. 3. The three contemporary categories, traditional, modern and the two combined.*

1. Just before the outbreak of the Second World War the so-called 'black period' came to an end; there had been a preference for Bastone and Grotesque faces, an exaggerated use of rules and vast areas of black. The Mefistofele face from Fonderia Reggiani of Milan is memorable at least for its curiosity. This 'black period' had preoccupied most of all the interested parties in our country, behind the obvious influence of German printing. In this postwar period, there was a prodigious development in industry and book-publishing, which was immensely favoured by the return of liberty as well as by the new marvels in the technical field. The enthusiasm which broke out in the editorial world after the war was moving: new imprints, publishers working in improvised style but taking a bold approach and pledged to make up for lost time with books printed at the worst on the poorest possible paper, but of great cultural value. Things were partly clarified and the more sane and practical part of earlier passions and experiments was accepted with praise. The vast development of periodical publishing absorbed it with results that were really appreciable, although, in the total collapse of the most distant provincial barriers, influences, exchanges, derivative practices and imitations were, from then on, uncontrollable.

I believe we can now say this about book-production. It is true that those of us here concern ourselves with classifying the results in the least categoric way possible, remembering also how difficult and almost impossible it is from now on to define the directions in which it is moving and the choices that are made. The whole world is becoming a single country, exchanges have become extremely rapid, production is uncontrollable and publishers themselves redesign their books from one year to another. But it was important for us to say that the best from the 'black period' has been salvaged and used by periodical publishing and sometimes by book-publishing: the best example is Giampiero Giani with some of the art books published by 'La Conchiglia'.

The question of education for everyone, the near-complete solution of the illiteracy problem on one side and the demands of editorial development which from now on is, in fact, on an industrial and competitive plane, have obviously expanded and consolidated the tendency towards 'popular' publishing which had illuminated the century from which it took its incentives. Great successes have, however, roused popular publishing which during the post-war period have appeared in the bookshops. The 'Biblioteca Universale Rizzoli' (B.U.R.) with their extremely cheap pocket editions, printed carefully in traditional fashion, with classical literary texts, satisfied the demands of the market for several years (this could be considered as a more or less direct take-over from the 'Biblioteca Universale Sonzogno' which dominated the field for many years): then Mondadori introduced several others on his part: the 'Biblioteca Moderna Mondadori' (B.M.M.: letters, science and art). The 'Biblioteca Contemporanea Mondadori' (B.C.M.: literary), the 'Pavone', the 'Girasole', the 'Bosco' and so on: books of medium format with coloured covers, but with low quality paper and printing. Einaudi did the same thing with his 'Piccola Biblioteca Einaudi' (P.B.E.: science and arts); Feltrinelli with the 'Universale Economica' (U.E.) to quote those with the largest readership.

Reduced costs and increased distribution: as a result the necessity for large printings and the best sales organisations; these aspects concern us indirectly, in the sense of their effects within the graphic arts pure and simple. But it is clear that in the light of a similar situation books have remained a means of expressing culture and yet they have become, today as never before, saleable merchandise. There is no other explanation for the way in which commercial and advertising art has become incorporated and used in the art of book-production, and for the creation of advertising offices which take the public by storm; better still is the creation of editorial offices in which the experts operate, whose attention is too often restricted to the presentation of the book and the splendour of all that accompanies it. This profession is crowded with dilettantes of the printing world, who to be truthful satisfy their employers to the extent that attractive appearances do so: daring book jackets, which are highly-coloured and 'jazzed-up' like film posters. An old trouble, I repeat, which was noticed forty years ago. 'Turning over the pages of most books with beautiful jackets', wrote C. Ratta, 'brings bitter disillusionment, since the text is decorated in a negligent fashion, if not actually unbecoming'. And later: 'the decoration and illustration of the cover have a purely suggestive value for authors and publishers who intend to sell their product and for this reason only perhaps it is the aspect of the graphic arts which receives most attention.' Better still: 'For some time the book jacket has triumphed; it is this which attracts the eye of the passer-by and draws the attention of the studious and the admiring.' (*Il libro e la rivista, idem.*)

2. Most noteworthy and almost revolutionary is the triumph of *offset*, with all the dazzling production of 'books for children' (Mondadori is the accepted king in this field) which are almost entirely imported from America, profusely illustrated and charming to look at. But it is clear that printing by offset is not limited to children's books: it is useful for popular science books, for example, printed in large numbers, and also for the mass of splendid encyclopaedias which come out in serial form *(Il Milione, Universo, Atlante)*.

It is true that the difficulty of finding illustrators of quality has not yet been solved (as we have seen, there is a lack of tradition in Italy) and the merely splendid 'Gift books' which each year seasonally crowd the bookshops: Einaudi with literary gift books, Feltrinelli with art gift books, Mondadori, Sansoni, Martello, Rizzoli, from the smallest to the largest (from the great, alarming folio editions by Einaudi, *Opera Grafica* by Morandi and Manzù, to the extremely attractive little pocket-books issued by Scheiwiller) have benefitted greatly from them.

A good publisher like Laterza has now even courageously started the collection of the 'Classici Illustrati' and there is already a remarkable edition of Machiavelli with drawings by Fabrizio Clerici. Canesi has put out a *Bertoldo* illustrated by Tono Zancanaro; earlier, Einaudi published Neruda's *Poesie* with drawings by Renato Guttuso.

Outstanding examples are rare, however, since Italian artists seem to consider the genre as a minor one. The recent exhibition in Boston: 'The Artist and the Book' (1961) indicated clearly, from the astonishing volumes shown there, the small quantity of work that we have available. Out of three hundred works exhibited only six were Italian and four were from Verona!

An important symptom of the postwar period is the fact that alongside the excellent 'Book Clubs' (large printings and low prices) books 'for collectors' have flourished, with valuable editions (sometimes very well printed, sometimes less so) and illustrated with lithographs, etchings, to a lesser extent with woodcuts, in which from time to time the leading Italian artists were employed: from Manzù to Campigli, from Guttuso to Clerici, Vespignani, Maccari, Gentilini, Zancanaro, Messina, Cantatore. Hoepli in Milan, 'Il Cavallino' in Venice, 'La Conchiglia' in Milan, the Officina Bodoni in Verona, Tallone in Alpignano are certainly the most representative names in this very new category.

The Officina Bodoni in Verona is the most outstanding of all: the limited editions of Hoepli, such as the *Il Milione* editions of Marco Polo (1942) with lithographs by Campigli, *I Carmi* of Catullus (1945) with lithographs by De

Pisis, *Le Georgiche* of Virgil (1948) with etchings by Manzù, were all published by this press. Also *Le Liriche* of Sappho (1944), an astonishing folio edition with lithographs by Campigli for 'Il Cavallino' and *Viaggio d'Europa* by Massimo Bontempelli (1942) with lithographs by Martini for 'Le Edizioni della Chimera'. (F. Riva, *L'Officina Bodoni di Verona: catalogo*. Verona 1962.)

But the irreplaceable value of these Verona publications lies not so much in the admirable choice of type faces (Bodoni, Garamond, Griffo, Zeno, Dante, Vicentino, Centaur, Paganini, Baskerville) or in the high-quality paper, the harmony between the composition and the illustrations, but in the actual printing itself executed on a hand-press, an instrument which was rediscovered and certainly valued in England at the beginning of the century, but now I believe, used with such skill only in Verona.

The experiments carried out in Verona on the hand-press began about 1930, that is with the copies on parchment and papier de Japon of the works of D'Annunzio. No machine, however well-directed, will ever succeed in giving the softness and perfection of printing on a hand-press; no machine will print on paper as hard as that which a hand-press, thanks to the dampening procedures, can utilise with so much finesse. (F. Riva, *Il mio dimèstico Torchio*. Trieste 1958).

Of the books produced until today by the Officina Bodoni after their removal to Verona the following remain memorable: *Ovidii Amores* (1932), *Il Ninfale Fiesolano* by Boccaccio (1940), *Trattatello in Laude di Dante* by Boccaccio (1954), *De Divina Proportione* by Luca Pacioli (1956), *Alphabetum* by Felice Feliciano (1960). The beautiful books of Alberto Tallone (worthy of mention are *I Canti* of Leopardi, *Le Poesie* of Foscolo, *La Divina Commedia* of Dante, and it should be remembered that Tallone designed for himself a type face with a classical look and good proportions) although they lack that rare quality produced by an instrument as refined as a hand-press, reveal all the same the substantial difference existing between this and a mechanical press, in inking and register, fundamental elements which combine with the true architectonic conception of the book to achieve discernment.

3. As I said earlier it is not easy to establish a classification for the period closer to our own time which is plausible from a technical point of view. Type faces have already been discussed, and it remains necessary to take a closer view of the architecture of the book as far as the arrangement of the material, the size of the title-page, are concerned, something which is difficult to analyse because it can be said that every publisher, while using the traditional models, now

enjoys offering models which break with tradition and with his own custom. Mondadori himself, who until recently was the most conservative of the traditional Italian printers (also because Mondadori, before being a publisher, was first a printer) has for some time been showing examples with innovations, reducing the margins, displacing the equilibrium of the page, re-designing some of his collections which were already established. Laterza also has re-designed not only the cover but the title-page of his 'Biblioteca di Cultura Moderna' in accordance with a model adopted years ago for example by Einaudi and on the question of its historical record we could invoke the shade of P. Galeati: 'Take capital letters all of the same size, make the lines long or short, it does not matter which, and align them all on the left. The title-page is finished…' (*L'Arte e il Bello nel Libro, idem.*)

And the fact that this so-called 'dynamic asymmetry' represents the basic approach of many contemporary experts on layout is something that we shall soon see. The 'audacity' of someone like Frassinelli between 1940 and 1945 is reduced to nothing in comparison with the bizarre effects of today. I think that it would be useful to limit these experiments to three categories: the first of a conservative nature, concerned with the harmony of a page which observes the traditional difference between the margins, with the page number as high as possible and beneath the outside edge of the page, with the type area centralised on the title-page, set in the same type face as the text, also in two colours, with the facts restricted to the author, title of the work and publication details. It is really touching to see how a publisher like Le Monnier has preserved his own traditional models (see the literary and philological collections, the national edition of Foscolo's works) and how nineteenth-century cornices and ornaments are now re-appearing on his book-covers.

For their 'Classici Italiani' directed by F. Neri the u.t.e.t. use a cornice with oak leaves in two colours, reproduced by wood-engraving; Zanichelli also does not like to abandon this kind of traditional frugality. And it is only recently that Mondadori, Laterza and Rizzoli have begun to revolutionise some title-pages and renounce certain traditions. But traditions remain: the Mondadori collection 'Le Scie' with title-page in two colours; also Rizzoli's 'Classici'; Ricciardi's 'Letteratura Italiana—Storia e testi'. In the small-format books published by Longanesi there are ostentatious ornaments and nineteenth-century preciousness in strange taste; his books, considering the publisher does not have his own printing-works, are always beautifully produced.

The second category is definitely one of innovation and includes many experiments: from the renunciation of the title-page to the most unexpected and provocative arrangement of the type area on the page: sometimes in the very centre of the area leading to a widening of the lower and upper margins which are almost equal while the back and fore margins are very much reduced. For example the collection 'Pittori e Scultori italiani contemporanei' published by La Conchiglia: and here the margins measure ⅞ ins on the inside and outside of the text while the upper margin measures 4 and the lower 3 ins. (It can be understood that on opening the book one tends to turn it upside down!) At present in fact this skirmish by Giani seems to be taken to extremes here and there and it is not rare to find books with half-pages—the top half is blank. But this is only new up to a certain point: it is a question of having extended to the whole book the extremely usual technique used for the 'dedication' of the work which until not long ago used to begin half-way down the page.

And along with the extremely narrow margins on all four sides the page-number continually roams about from the bottom to the side, at the top, in the centre, on the outside, and a little further inside. (Obviously the formats of books are affected by this, tending fairly often to be square, in order to carry so much 'movement'.)

In the most recent Mondadori collection 'I Mondi dell'Uomo' the title-page is aligned towards the left (but, I add, this layout is adapted to periodical publishing, which detaches the captions from the illustrations, lining up the text, which may be set in long or short lines, to one side). The page has three margins of equal width and the lower one is at least twice as wide: the page number (in bold) has fallen to the extreme edge; the illustrations take up the whole page, without mentioning the mixture of type faces. The title in capitals is in one of the Semplicità faces, very black, the sub-title in lower case is in a Garamont fount and the publishing details are in Garaldus, lower case. It could be thought that in establishing the structural conception of an imported book in its Italian translation ideas would have been based on the foreign original (although I do not know it) but it again adopts the layout based on lining up the text outside the central axis of the page at least as far as the title-page is concerned, sometimes all to the left and sometimes all to the right, and it is now so common that we can consider it as having become part of the less attractive customs of today.

In Einaudi's eighth 'Saggi' collection the title-page is lined up to the left (the type face used is a narrow Bodoni, with a large and small roman); in Schwarz's 'Collana di Storia e Cultura' everything is lined up to the left and the face used is a normal Bodoni, with large and small roman (bold italics for the publishing notes). In Einaudi's 'I Coralli' and in 'La Nuova Società' collection the text is lined up on the right. On the other hand it is lined up to the left for the P.B.E. (on the title-page a Bastone is used for the title of the work, while the name of the author and the publication details are set in roman). An ugly combination of the two uses is found in a big work published by Sansoni, Gustavo Reese: *La Musica nel Medioevo*, (1960): the names of the author and publisher are lined up to the right, while the title of the work is lined up to the left. Type face used: Garamont roman upper and lower case.

This could be our third category then, remaining always within the orbit of an ideal distinction through which we have suggested systematising the new trends in typography, but it is clear that the variations within our ideal categories are infinite and we can only mention the most obvious.

This third category could only be a combination of the first and second as we have seen them so far, which consist of traditional elements combined with elements of innovation: the page cut to the traditional size, set in classical type faces and the title-page laid out in an anti-traditional way, that is outside the central axis of the page and often set in non-classical type faces, belonging to the Semplicità or Bastone families.

Mondadori's literary collection 'I grandi narratori d'ogni paese' otherwise called 'Medusa', for example, is conceived entirely from a traditional point of view, but on the cover, in contrast to the classical type faces of the text and the title-page, there is a Semplicità face. Everyone knows now that book-jackets, once the book has been bought, are destined to vanish quickly. It is true that as a rule the jackets of our books are beautiful and attractive: the inspiration and inventiveness of our designers are being cured of their own whims and express fantasy in a pleasing way supported by a lively palette of colours which the new techniques involving the use of plastics render even more luminous. Without doubt a book-jacket is not a book, but a very small part of it and the most ephemeral; and at this point it only remains to tell oneself again and wish that beyond all these experiments and curiosities, between sudden changes and combinations the wonderful hope expressed by Bodoni can be achieved in a deeper awareness: 'Oh, would that this art, so ingenious, useful and beautiful, were practised more generally with dexterity and love, and favoured with taste and good judgement!'

G. W. Ovink

150 YEARS OF BOOK TYPOGRAPHY
IN THE NETHERLANDS

It is a precarious task to sketch in a few pages the development through the ages of an object such as the book, in which so many cultural, technical, economic and social factors are combined into an almost inextricable tangle. If anywhere, it is here that the danger of such historiography occurs, namely that the reader is insufficiently protected against his natural inclination to project his own time back along that unbroken line of development, and in doing so to falsify the standard with which he could value the past in a reasonable way—that is to get a really correct insight into it. We still consider the eighteenth century as completely different from our time; we see the nineteenth as a beginning of ours, but smaller in everything than we think we are now. To this the historian Pieter Geyl's warning pre-eminently applies: 'Nothing is easier than to work with models or simplifications of the past in which reality experienced by former generations with no less effort than we have, is hardly present any more, but which give the contrast desirable for effect.' For example we do not blame the eighteenth-century printer for the fact that he still plodded with a wooden hand-press, but we think the Dutch book-printers stupid that they introduced the cylinder presses only after 1850, when after all, they had existed for about forty years. An unfair difference in standard of evaluation.

Therefore, in the following survey an attempt is made to evaluate the achievements in proportion to the possibilities which, in our opinion, were to a reasonable extent available to capable book-printers.

It is striking then that in the first part of those 150 years typography offers a relatively favourable picture, not in comparison with England and France, but with the low standard of prosperity and lack of enterprise in Holland. This could perhaps be attributed to the fact that the structure of publishing firms and printing plants was often such that one person could manage the whole, but could also supervise the parts, and in spite of that reach a production which was of importance for cultural and social prosperity. Furthermore in our country the book is an article which stands in high esteem—the continuous complaints about its under-valuation prove that—which implies that from national capacity it attracts a relatively high proportion of talent and money. In the period of apathy and poverty of the nineteenth century a number of extremely experienced individuals brought, also as a result of the readers' interest, our typography to a level which one would not expect judging from the signs of prosperity and of vision in other fields of cultural, political and economic activity.

In general those first seventy-five years offered the able person more opportunity to distinguish himself than the time following. It may be asked why today works of outstanding originality and volume, which can be found in quantities in the previous century, seem to be available only rarely. The answer has to be found in the variety of circumstances which, together, put less obstacles in the way of the capable individual than nowadays, and which also allowed him to maintain a simplicity of aims which would now be called narrow-minded and inhuman. Everyone knew his place in society and the rights and duties attached to it. With that formula the whole line of conduct was settled. It was not necessary to waste energy on unrealisable aspirations or blind revolts. People in higher positions did not have to bother about the interests of the lower classes. When grumbling arose about wages, the Leiden publisher A. W. Sijthoff dismissed his whole staff in one letter; he who wanted to was allowed to return, provided the subject was not mentioned again! In making such short shrift Sijthoff and his like found time for a number of activities which are still of great value today. Until well into our century assistants in scientific libraries earned as little as stokers; they published all the more.

Darwin's theory, in which he relates his biological doctrine to social organisations—'There should be free competition between all human beings; and the most able man should not be prevented by laws or customs from succeeding best'—could on the one hand stimulate the class-war, but gave on the other hand a charter to those who thought they were more capable once they had obtained a higher position.

The final goal of all our present education and development work, viz. the complete development of everybody's individual possibilities, was considered senseless—if not immediately objectionable—in the nineteenth century. The clever brains from the lower classes would come to the fore anyhow and the rest simply had nothing which could be developed, so it was thought. Therefore, the able man had a number of people under him whom he could model as he liked and whom he let work for him; people who from sheer necessity, but also from a sense of duty and loyalty, did their work in such a way that the proprietor had time left either for a gradual expansion of his business or for other activities. In so far as our literary men were not clergymen they had their business activities; the same holds good for many writers of bibliographical and historical works. Besides their actual occupation, they had more time left for their artistic and scientific activities than their colleagues of today. Their way of life was simpler, their patience, willingness and ability for long, detailed work much greater. As a result of the fact that the different tasks were less in number and less advanced than now—how much more literature an investigator now has to work through than in those days—each task could find a much bigger field. Even though the individualistic working method resulted in many amateurish, incomplete and unnecessary products, where somebody could rely on his ability and the correctness of his method, enormous achievements were attained.

We had in the nineteenth century people in typography and printing who nationally were just as great as its greatest pioneers in banking, commerce and industry; even some of international calibre who, if they had been able to work from a linguistic region bigger than the Dutch one, would have exercised an even greater influence on the general history of the book than they did already. But the merits of their achievements concerned the contents; the appearance of their works was of no more than an honest but also fusty solidity. The limited sales possibilities were not only to blame for this.

The Dutchman loves his home and because of his calvinistic nature—whether protestant or catholic—he is averse to idle diversion. In the previous century this nature resulted in a veritable hunger to read, mainly devotional and educational works. At all times the greater part of the readers, predominantly belonging to the well-to-do middle-classes, were prepared to buy expensive books. Between 1830 and 1839, still a period of poverty, thirty historical publications appeared which cost more than twenty guilders and sometimes a lot more, a high amount for that time. The big botanical, zoological and geographical pictorial works involved several hundreds of guilders.

The eagerness to read in the nineteenth century guaranteed a sale for all those books which were in conformity with just the interest and taste of that special readers' public. What was lacking in this country of self-confident theologisers was some extravagance, some sense of relativity and humour, some sense of magnificence, gruesomeness, atrocity; some courage to envisage the demoniac otherwise than in moralising sermons. There was here no Blake, Cruikshank, Doyle, Leech, Keene, Lear, Tenniel, Du Maurier, Caldecott; no Delacroix, Daumier, Grandville, Johannot, Gavarni, Doré; no Menzel, no Wilhelm Busch. Of the few illustrators we had, Charles Rochussen was *facile princeps;* in his many routine works he will neither ever descend to the depths of a hack, nor come above the European average. There was in general little illustration and the good woodcuts had to come from elsewhere.

Although the publishing trade was commercially active, in scientific work sometimes great, in execution correct, so in the whole of national industry certainly not the least energetic group, the guaranteed sale of the 'calm, self-earning publications' (as a contemporary publisher called them) and the solid and constructive contents of the more speculative books made superfluous a more than correct, an animating, an exciting appearance. The fixed pattern of conduct and the fixed place of the individual in society find their pendants in fixed book forms, set up according to fixed form rules.

The reason why nineteenth-century typography is considered a bad period in the history of the book (although the achievements in illustration techniques now undergo a revaluation) is, however, more to be found in the loss of a pure sense of form, material and colour which then characterised all visual arts. Rationalism applied to art led to the conviction that beauty could be commanded by expressing eternally moving themes according to eternal laws of harmony with diligence and perfect technique. That the art of earlier centuries, of the classics, Gothic, Renaissance or Baroque had to serve as examples, was generally accepted, but the all-penetrating evolution idea convinced people that they could do better themselves with the knowledge and capability since acquired.

All historical styles were copied, according to their most flamboyant monuments, 'in the way the artists from the past would have wanted it if only they had had the modern means and skill'; in other words the exterior characteristics were copied with an icy consistency and mortal precision; everything finished off regularly and smoothly in today's materials; without a real idea of the relation between form, material and technique. If no historical example was available, the existing was perfected. This means that of each component the specific quality was carried to extremes. For instance the paper was made as smooth and even as possible, the engraving as fine as possible; the ornament luxurious; the elegant, loose; the severe, immovable.

Moderation was rejected as a proof of a poor insight into the essential nature of the adapted principles of form, materials and techniques: all that, in the technical field, looked like an irregularity, was considered primitive, but if on the other hand a work was destined 'to show an artistic touch', then it had to ooze curlicues like anything.

A contemporary reports about the period after 1850: 'The smooth machine-made paper looked so much better than the hand-made paper' it was so much more perfect! And when a reaction came to the eighty years of supremacy of the classicist Didot-types in the fashion of the Elzévir-types (*see* John C. Tarr, 'The romantic revival in mid-nineteenth century French typography', *British Printer*, April 1960)—for the rest they (the Elzévirs) were typical nineteenth-century products with their poor precision—this reaction was exposed by the German *Journal für Buchdruckerkunst* as another expression of French decadence which 'like all varieties and eccentricities of fashion apparently wants to make its way in our country, too. As a great number of newer productions show, the French are in all seriousness trying to reintroduce sixteenth-century characters instead of their beautiful modern faces, and in doing so to return by the way that typography has gone since Elzévir, and other typographical celebrities of that period. What gives today's modern faces their unfortunately indisputable advantage over blackletter is the perfect parallelism of down stroke or stress, and particularly of the hair lines, which mark the limits under and above the various characters; furthermore the beautiful, symmetrical division of light and shade, the uniform distribution of space in the characters separately and between all characters mutually. Several centuries had to elapse before these laws could become prevailing, and now that we have enjoyed our splendid acquisitions for a few years only, the seducer comes to us with a total subversion of what has been achieved in age-long progress.' (*Journal für Buchdruckerkunst, Schriftgiesserei und die verwandten Fächer*, XIX, 21, 1862.)

From this criticism emerges the opinion of those times: admiration for the artistic skill, the ingenuity and the power by means of which one had succeeded in mastering materials and human weaknesses, tried by the old, but at long last achieved in their own times as a result of progress. The nineteenth-century academic and commercial art was produced with intellect and perseverance, not with senses and emotion. The artists did not look; they made their paintings 'by heart' in the workshop. Their beauty was known, not seen. The plein-airism of the Barbizon school and of the Impressionists, and painting from living models, did not become the rule until the seventies, but it was just in the period 1870–1890 that the official free and applied arts, continuing their fatal course to the far extreme, also reached the lowest point of hollow splendour.

In typographic design this mental attitude expresses itself in the conviction that a thing of beauty was automatically obtained by using expensive ingredients and much display of effort. Big formats, big margins, big, very cleverly cut types, characterised the luxury book, but the mutual relations of these values were not taken into consideration. Design was dictated by adding up the separate components, of which the separate nature was not felt, nor their mutual contradictions. The line-ductus and tone-value of type, composition and illustration, the volume of a blank space, the surface-structure, the weight and tone of a paper, the dynamics of a colour or page-size—all these expressive values were not recognised and could thus not be co-ordinated.

This disintegration of the original unity between the human function within the individual and within society, which allowed their individual development, and with this both the gigantic progress in everything that can be obtained by analysis and the atrocious regression in everything that needs synthesis—this disintegration, which exploded socially in the French Revolution, develops first slowly after the Napoleonic epoch, reaches its turning-point in the nineties and comes to an end in our times, if signs do not mislead. In this context I will now try to sketch the further development of book typography.

In order to gain an insight into the multitude of phenomena, some lines of development have been drawn, partly implicit, partly explicit, from the viewpoint that in art (so also in the art of the book), in conformity with the different kinds of temperament among artists, there are always two wings to distinguish, with a middle course between. That is, on the one hand a more static, traditional, intellectual, sober classicist trend, and on the other hand a more dynamic, emotional, revolutionary, romantic one, with pathos and splendour. From the beginning of the nineteenth century these trends stand opposed to each other clearly and with equal power for the first time, and according to their aspects in those times they also got their names. The ordinary book, by its nature bound to tradition and appealing to the intellect, mostly falls rather to the share of the classicist trend, to the extent that Stanley Morison and his colleagues wish to let the book (and even the newspaper and periodical) be governed exclusively by the principles of that trend, and this with wilful neglect of other, equally legitimate book functions. These, with which the book does not appeal to the reader's intellect but to his organs of sense and his emotion, receive attention rather from the romantic trend; therefore, this kind of book, which does not want so much to be read as to be seen, flourishes in proportion as this trend in art possesses power and esteem.

1800–1850: TRANSITION TO INDUSTRIAL REVOLUTION;
GRADUAL RECOVERY AND WIDENING OF HORIZON

The style with which the Dutch book printers entered the nineteenth century
was of a meagre but kind rationalism, dull and anaemic in comparison with
the vital Baroque of our Golden Age, but mild and well-balanced in proportion to the further development of classicism, to which it formed, itself, the
introduction. This style is that of 1760, gradually becoming less grand in manner towards 1800: types of Fleischman and nothing but these, printed with
wooden hand-presses in greyish ink on laid paper in rather square sizes. (The
two largest Dutch typefoundries at the end of the eighteenth century were
those of Joh. Enschedé in Haarlem and of the brothers Ploos van Amstel in
Amsterdam. Both sold book types, cut by J. M. Fleischman (who died in
1768), but did not produce new types during the rest of the century. In 1799
the Amsterdam firm merged with the one in Haarlem after which—apart
from the still existing old foundries of Hendrik Bruyn & Co. (C. Woudman)
and of Harmsen—Enschedé remained the only national supplier until 1838.
The imports came from France; after 1815, probably from Belgium (then the
'southern provinces') and for the display faces, where the difference in system
of size and height was less inconvenient than in respect of the text letter, also
from England. (*See* J. W. Enschedé, *Gedenkboek, C. A. Spin & Zn*, Amsterdam
1919; Ch. Enschedé, *Fonderies de caractères dans les Pays-Bas et leur matériel du
quinzième au dix-neuvième siècle*, Haarlem 1908; G. W. Ovink, *Honderd jaren
lettergieterij in Amsterdam*, Amsterdam 1951). The style predominated till 1820,
albeit with sometimes Didot-like admixtures, after that as a powerful under-
stream, and only disappearing in about 1850; souvenirs for some of a lost *douceur de vivre*, for others of a powerless and short-sighted *ancien régime*. (The old
and the new type were used promiscuously for a long time, in spite of their
stylistic difference. Considerations of economy led to this and no refined form
feeling opposed it, anyway not in the normal enterprises. Volume 4 of Sepp
(*see* below), which appeared from 1810 till 1821, is still completely in eighteenth-century type; in volume 5 (1821–1836) didones appear in the titles; in
volume 6 (1836–1840) they become larger and a shaded Egyptienne is added;
in volume 7 (1843–1855) they both become much coarser, and from the ninth
chapter of this volume Fleischman's text letter is gradually replaced by a didone. In the forty-third (1850?) hand-coloured engravings are replaced by
hand-coloured lithographs. This situation remains unchanged in the eighth
and last volume (1855–1860). Just because the existing model was maintained

as long as possible, these dates indicate when the printing firm could not, or did not want to, maintain any longer the old kinds of type, or replace them by new identical founts, and the copper-plates had become unbearably more expensive than lithography.—The word 'didone' has been adopted from Maximilien Vox's letter classification and indicates the classicist kinds, mainly developed by the Didot family and by Bodoni. *See* page 94.)

The rich eighteenth-century style is confirmed in coloured pictorial works of grand manner, such as the illustrated book on insects (referred to above) by J. Chr. Sepp, *Beschouwing der wonderen Gods in de minst geachtte schepzelen, of Nederlandse insecten*, which appeared from 1762 till 1860 in eight folio volumes, or in the repertory of costumes of E. Maaskamp, *Afbeeldingen van de kleeding, zeden en gewoonten in de Bataafsche republiek*, 1803–1807, also with hand-coloured engravings (plate 1). Both are specimens of the kind of sumptuous pictorial biological and topographical works which also in bad times continued to appear for an international circle of customers—scientific libraries and wealthy (often snobbish) collectors; indeed, in our country, by no means in the quantity, but still in the quality, of what was done in England and France.

A curious sample of a very classic simplicity—clearly directed against both *Schöngeisterei* and the sweet boudoir sphere which characterises the literary almanacs still fifty years later—is an edition of 1800 of Hieronymus van Alphen, a popular moralising poet, whose nature could very well have given rise to another treatment (plate 2). This line is continued in a more suitable and generous way (albeit with a mild didone, and unfortunately also printed greyishly on the poor paper of its time) in one of the first works of the Algemeene Landsdrukkerij (Government Printing Office), founded by King William I, viz. Krayenhoff's report of the first national triangulation, projected and executed by him, a monument in the history of our science and public works (plate 3).

(For the whole Dutch nineteenth-century paper situation see B. W. de Vries' detailed study *De Nederlandse papiernijverheid in de negentiende eeuw*, The Hague 1957, which contains much detailed information. The Napoleonic epoch was fatal for our paper producers, a serious shortage of rags appeared, if only because the better kind was used for wound bandages during the wars; exports fell off. Moreover, three important technical improvements were not applied here, or too late, because of self-sufficiency and short-sightedness: rosin-sizing in the tub instead of gelatine-sizing per sheet afterwards; bleaching of the rags with chlorine instead of sunlight, which would have made it possible to use bad and coloured rags for white paper; machine production with the Robert-Gamble-Fourdrinier-Donkin and the Dickinson machines. De Vries calls the period 1815–1835 a 'black page in the history of the Dutch paper industry' because of technical arrears and economic depression.)

The establishment of the kingdom puts an end to the eighteenth-century spirit; the very first evidence of the nineteenth century becomes apparent. William I, assisted by a group of hand-picked civil servants and merchants of his own frame of mind, tried to stimulate among the Dutch citizens the spirit of enterprise; comprehension of, faith in, modern forms of industry, trade, agriculture and finance. Many active Englishmen settled down here and brought with them something of the energetic, progressive spirit of their own country, where the 'industrial revolution' was already fully advanced. (J. W. Enschedé, *Gedenkboek Spin*). Contact between the cities in the West with the rural areas in the North, East and South was improved. The four big, recent technical improvements in the printing industry were going to exercise their influence here, too, after the isolation during the French occupation.

In the first place, lithography as illustration and printing process, could partly replace the laborious engraving (in wood for book printing, in metal for intaglio printing); also the lithographic press yielded a higher output than the intaglio press. Moreover, lithography could directly reproduce the spontaneous drawing; if desired the illustrator worked himself on the stone, without the intervention of a reproducing craftsman. After a hesitant start, at Rotterdam in 1809, lithographic printing plants followed in Amsterdam and in The Hague in 1816, but the process got a firm footing only ten years later. (*See* J. W. Enschedé, *Gedenkboek Spin*; S. Moulijn, *De eerste jaren der lithografische prentkunst in Nederland*. The Hague 1927.)

Secondly, stereotyping, which, after the Rev. Joh. Müller's start in 1701, had to be re-invented several times. In 1816 Joh. Enschedé & Zonen again bought the secret from Richard Watts in London. Stereotyping made it possible to produce much more cheaply reprints of unchanged or hardly changed texts and also long runs of multiple formes; in the beginning this was only of importance for the big book printers.

Thirdly, the invention of the iron hand-press, which could handle bigger printing formes than the wooden one, and this with a much higher pressure and production. C. A. Spin in Amsterdam had the first one in 1819, probably one of the Columbian type, the Stanhope construction improved by Clymer. Both Stanhopes and Columbians were demonstrated here to printers and sold by Belgian manufacturers; for Belgium had a fast developing iron industry and apparently devoted her attention early to the production of printing presses which, in the growing reprint industry (described in the chapter about Belgian book typography, *see* p. 12.) could expect good sales possibilities.

The invention of the cylinder high-speed press became important for the Netherlands only after 1850. Until the middle of the century it was considered suitable and profitable only for newspapers; in 1828 Joh. Enschedé had a Koenig & Bauer for their newspaper the *Oprechte Haarlemmer*, and about 1840 Spin obtained one for the *Algemeen Handelsblad*. Until well into the century the wooden hand-press continued to work beside the iron one for light and small work. The latter had a production of 100–150 sheets per hour, as against 1000–1200 for the cylinder press.

Fourthly, the improvement of paper production, mentioned above. It was carried through late in the Netherlands; its earlier application in other countries was one of the reasons for the decline of our paper industry. As, however, the cylinder press because of its existence, destined the iron hand-press to be a temporary solution, even before it was introduced, so the paper machine made the hand-mould obsolete. From now on the printers would know that in their trade, which for centuries had hardly undergone any technical changes, there could be no pause in the improvements. Here, too, the industrial revolution had begun, very slowly, but with a clear implication of the survival of the fittest in evolution: he wins who can first predict the development correctly, and who knows how to operate energetically afterwards.

The new spirit of the most active printers after 1815 expresses itself in a reaction against the modest Fleischman-typography by a further development of the severe, crisp Didot-style, with a stronger contrast between black and white, both in the type—Enschedé was quickly obliged to get the original, correct didones from France and Belgium—and in print: more forceful, on smoother and whiter paper. It is the firm, resolute side of the Empire which appeals and which under the Restauration gains emphasis.

No doubt this new spirit animated the twenty-seven-year-old Christiaan Andersen Spin, who settled down at Amsterdam in 1819 with the most modern materials. His office was a leader in our country during the next thirty years because of his printing quality and tasteful application of a severe, classicist style, which his biographer J. W. Enschedé called 'Franco-Belgian'. Only Wahlen in Brussels was his equal—and until the Separation of Holland and Belgium also his rival—in this style. His title-pages avoid decorated frames and an excess of ornamental letters or big type sizes; they are based on the effect of spaced small capitals, displayed in well-defined groups, and if need be, tightened-up by a simple thick-thin frame (plate 4).

How strict Spin was in the 'French style' is shown by the title of the first specimen of the twenty-three-year-old printer J. F. Thieme, in Nijmegen. However, French too, and good in its kind, the title with its heavy decorative frame remains more on the pompous side of the Restauration style (plate 5).

If the readers should have a strong impression of refinement, festivity or sumptuousness, the typographical means on the normal laid paper did not suffice and an engraved or drawn title was inserted on thick wove paper, which then fulfilled the function of the coloured cover today. (Titles illustrated with vignettes were usually by copper-engraving, the more luxurious kind of travel books also with foreign steel-engravings; the cheaper novels after 1835 with drawings in crayon lithography. Titles with decorative letters were often done in litho engraving. The latter is not always easily distinguishable from copper-engraving, because the characteristic plate edge of the intaglio could be flattened out or, with the use of a bigger plate, cut off. A good stone-engraving is as sharp, black and 'dry' as a moderate, rough copper-engraving. For both processes thick wove paper was used. The advantage of the stone engraving was the higher production of the litho press. *See* in this connection J. W. Enschedé, *idem*.) It was possible to give them graceful and fine lines and tones—with many flourishes, open types and elegant curved lines—which look completely different from what book-printing could offer then. Only after 1850 improved printing techniques, heavily calendered paper and typographic ornaments such as Charles Derriey's, the 'Raphael of the engravers', could begin to imitate these specific effects of metal engraving and lithography in letterpress printing.

Thus the title engraving was obligatory in the many literary almanacs which were, for long, a favourite medium for the publication of all sorts of literary products. Because of their cultural pretensions they required a refined typography; Spin printed many of them. The numerous provincial, urban, professional and juvenile almanacs for a simpler public had typographic titles; the literary ones, however, were marked as such by vignettes with goddesses, lyres, temples and altars of beauty, as desperately monotonous and silly as the contents. The authors had really no reason to rely only on the standard of their writings as self-confidently as Schiller, who charged his editor Cotta with the following: 'We want to avoid everything which is flourish and pomp, and in a book flourish is to me anything not being letter or punctuation.'

A noble standpoint, that from 1900 onwards would come into vogue again, but which can only satisfy the reader if he is eager to read the text before seeing it, and his only object is to grasp its explicit meaning. How important the right atmosphere is as well—which need not go hand-in-hand with objectively determinable legibility—proves the well-known fact that the 'church goods' were acceptable for many orthodox protestants only if they were composed in blackletter, until well into the twentieth century.

One of the positive effects of the Napoleonic government in Holland was the regulation of primary school teaching in 1806, which immediately resulted in a stream of school-books by hundreds of thousands. For typography they were primarily of indirect importance as educators of a larger number of readers in the next decades, but their typographic design shows a kind of innate decency, which, as commercialisation went on during the century, got lost and which so far has not been sufficiently cultivated again in this sector.

The first encyclopaedia for the rising new circle of readers appeared in the years 1820–1829 through H. C. A. Thieme in Zutfen in eight volumes (based on the German work of Thieme's friend F. A. Brockhaus who started his career in Amsterdam. Brockhaus did not object to this apparently unauthorised copy, because it was taken from an already out-dated edition.) It was a poor edition on grey paper without illustrations, obviously destined for the middle-class. Of course, the publication would have gained in usefulness with illustrations; however, there were not yet cheap enough illustration processes to provide them. The woodcut was in deep decline; wood-engraving (which, for that matter required also wove paper and strong iron-presses) was yet to develop. An international trade in printing plates for illustration, started in the thirties as a basis for many pictorial works which as entire original productions would have been uneconomic, did not yet exist. Copper- and steel-engravings were not qualified for this kind of book because of the price. Lithography only started its development with difficulty; if there were printers, there were no skilled lithographers. They came when King William I energetically stimulated a better artists' training.

The first collective achievement of the young royal scholars was a monumental work which appeared from 1828: *Le Musée Royal de la Haye*, by Desguerrois & Co. in Amsterdam—a folio work that clearly showed a Belgian signature. The lithographer-editor Desguerrois came from the workshop which the Belgian court lithographer A. Jobard brought to prosperity and fame between 1824 and 1830, and he showed his good training in a printing quality which had not yet been seen in north-Netherlands. The sheets of the

Museum book had been smoothed over a surface of the size of the stone before printing, and covered with smooth grey tissue paper, in order to obtain a faultless impression and, in spite of poor inking, a full-toned solid print. The stones were rather roughly-grained and practically exclusively drawn in crayon; only here and there touched up with the needle. The drawings were decent as impersonal interpretations. The explanatory texts were at first printed in Brussels by Louis Tencée, but from the eighth volume on, after 1830, by Spin in a strangely primitive, poorly-fitting large didone. As the first good lithographic illustrations in our country it is certainly of importance, but the grand manner of this book is of Belgian provenance rather than Dutch (plate 6).

In general the spiritual outlook of the Dutch at that time was narrow; it was directed towards finding comfortable rules of life with a christian-national foundation; opposed to any activity or experience which could disturb mental and physical peace, thus opposed to heroic idealism, to critical scientific research, to enjoyment of beauty if not immediately leading to moral improvement; to phantasy, thrill or passion or any supernatural experience which could have disturbed the certitude of the divine institutions. In the visual arts this mentality corresponds with an anaemic but firm classicism, in which the superhuman law has become an easily applicable rule, and the severe and grandiose a dreary simplicity, if not a mustiness.

A romantic veneration for the middle-ages, in other countries so characteristic of this period, never found any real acceptance here. It started in England from the mid-eighteenth century in a sort of rococo play of ruins, through the Ossianic poems, the preservation of monuments spreading from about 1800, and the church-building after the Church Building Act of 1818, and came there to its first flowering in the Oxford Movement and Cambridge Camden Society of the thirties and forties, with the 'Christian architecture' of Pugin in his Houses of Parliament as the apogee; in Germany with the action of romantic poets and painters and the Brothers Boisserée in the completion of the Cologne Cathedral. In the Netherlands something of it appeared under William II only, in whom some neo-gothic romanticism was left from his students' years in England, and who had for example a court minstrel in mediaeval costume. It is only in 1850 that an author claims: 'Narrow-minded contempt for the middle-ages is slowly passing'.

There was no principle either which could have offered a higher inspiration for our visual arts. Although the strict character of the calvinistic spirit fits in with classicism, this character—being contemplative and averse to sensual pleasure—could not bring this style to success in artistic application. The baroque exuberance and splendour of the Golden Age (the seventeenth century), serving as an example to the later epoch because of its orthodoxy and material successes, was not appreciated and could in fact not be followed in view of the general poverty. A return to Gothic did not appeal either, for it was popish, and the reigns of the Holy Roman, Bavarian and Hainault monarchs in the Low Countries could hardly serve as a glorious national past of the middle ages. In short, of that mighty neo-gothic movement, which so strongly affected England and Germany (but much less France, which, however, had the greatest authority in the Netherlands as foreign cultural power) no more than a trace of watered-down 'troubadour-gothic' remained besides the powerless post-classicism. Only many decades later neo-gothic and neo-renaissance were propagated and practised as examples of style, and public opinion—in two opposing camps—became interested.

Therefore, typography hardly shows any neo-gothic influences: if so, at the most in some *reliures à la cathédrale* and in some blackletter, but this last could just as well be considered as 'Old-Dutch', consequently of unsuspect Protestant origin.

The history of our bookbinding has largely yet to be written. It follows that of the greater foreign countries, at a distance, and simplified according to our national customs. The cloth binding seems to have been introduced here soon after the English initiation (and indeed by an Englishman, Nayler) in 1827, without becoming popular straightaway. Of the Victorian products of art, with their multicoloured interlays or *à jour papier maché* in relief with vividly coloured backgrounds, I have not seen any Dutch imitations earlier than the 'sixties. (*See* F. L. van der Bom in *Vijf Eeuwen Boek*. Haarlem 1940. I have not had an opportunity to confirm this information. See about the colourful figure of Benjamin Suggitt Nayler—publisher, charlatan and elocutionist, but also author, praised by no less than that worthy man of letters, Professor Jacob Geel, who translated for Nayler, Sterne's *Sentimental Journey*-: A. C. Kruseman, *Bouwstoffen voor een geschiedenis van den Nederlandschen boekhandel 1830–1880*, 1886; H. Frijlink, *Nieuwsblad voor den Boekhandel*, 1883; J. H. Scheltema de Heere, *Jaarboek Amstelodamum* VIII, 1910; J. W. Enschedé, *idem.*)

With the accession of William II to the throne in 1840 the picture of life in the Netherlands undergoes an important change. Twenty-five years of William I's activating policy began to fructify. The steam-engine took its place in inland navigation and railways (slowly until the Expropriation Act of 1851) but also in paper production, though not yet in printing-offices. A post-war generation became active, looked beyond the frontiers, travelled and did not regard active sales methods as beneath the dignity of a decent businessman. (Businessmen had their regular customers, and articles which did not need recommendation in the manner of the market square. It was Joseph Meyer, founder of the 'Bibliographisches Institut' in Leipzig and publisher of *inter alia* the well-known encyclopaedia—Kruseman, calls him a 'merchant in folio, impertinent without example and of rapacious nature'—who introduced here in 1836 the premium plate as an enticement for subscribers on the occasion of the publication of a Bible; and that in a period when 'selling books outside the walls of their own locality was equal to an act of robbery.') They were more skilled and had as customers equally capable men. In the preceding twenty-five years many English antiquarians came here every year to buy old books cheaply (particularly publications of the classics) in which the Dutch people themselves were not interested. However, with the establishment of Frederik Muller (from 1834 with his uncle Joh. Muller, from 1843 independent) and other active Dutch antiquarians this business came back, on a new basis with thorough bibliographic description and clear, fixed price quotations. (R. van der Meulen, *Over de liefhebberij van oude boeken*. Leiden 1896. About Frederik Muller: M. Nijhoff, 'F.M.', in *Bijdragen Gesch. Ned. Boekhandel* I, and A. C. Kruseman, *F. M. In Memoriam*, in *Jaarboek van de Maatschappij der Nederlandsche Letterkunde*, Leiden, and separately in Haarlem, 1881.)

Although the number of printing plants in the Netherlands had remained about 147 since 1850, their production had certainly increased and their quality improved, as a result of better equipment. The wood-engraving was really acquiring importance as a means of illustration. The need for it was acute. In the first place for reasons of business economics: all illustrations with fine lines or half-tones had to be done separately (and therefore at great expense) in lithography or plate printing, because the woodcut—the only medium of letterpress—did not lend itself to that. Secondly, because the readers could simply no longer do without the illustrations, even less after the invention of daguerrotype, when they had become accustomed to having elaborate and life-like pictures. However, the Netherlands did not have skilled wood-engravers, for there were neither schools nor books; in England and France also they were trained only just prior to Bewick's death in 1828: at first the blocks of the *Magasin Pittoresque* (1833) were still engraved in London and we know of the struggle which Menzel had to carry on in Germany in the years from 1839 onwards to get capable engravers. (*See* Mason Jackson, *The pictorial press, its origin and progress*, London, 1885; John Jackson, *Treatise on Wood-engraving*,

London, 1839, reprinted and extended by W. A. Chatto and Henry G. Bohn in 1866; G. W. Ovink, *Het aanzien van een eeuw*, Haarlem, 1958; *Adolph von Menzels Briefe*, ed. Hans Wolff, Berlin, 1914.) The first good text-book was that of John Jackson, 1839. In 1834 the Brothers Diederichs (publishers of the *Algemeen Handelsblad*) set up the *Nederlands Magazijn*, in imitation of Charles Knight's *Penny Magazine* of 1832, which, in fact, created in England the reproductive wood-engraving. This *Nederlands Magazijn* made possible here, too, the education of facsimile wood-engravers. Besides English stereotypes, also original blocks of W. Bal, A. Cranendoncq and R. J. van Arum were used, who in the next decades would carry out most of the simplest work in book illustration. Good printing of the engravings had to be learned also; the pressmen of Spin, who was also the printer of this magazine, had to acquire a knowledge of the make-ready of illustration formes, but on the uncalendered paper the result was never very satisfactory. (*See* J. W. Enschedé, *idem.*)

The foundation of the Maatschappij van Schoone Kunsten (Society of Arts) in The Hague was important. It was the north-Netherlands counterpart of the society of the same name, created by Dewasme in Brussels in 1836 (*see* page 14) assisted by a Royal Engraving School. Under the active patronage of William I, and particularly of the crown-prince (in due course William II), who entrusted a number of members of the royal household with it, the publishing house of the Hague Society was founded, also linked with an engraving school, which started with as many as fifty pupils under the leadership of the twenty-four-year-old Englishman Henry Brown. He had been engaged from Paris for Brussels in 1837, married Dewasme's sister, worked in The Hague for two years, but returned to Belgium in 1842, where he became a professor at the Antwerp Academy. It is likely that after the definite break between Holland and Belgium his wife, born in Brussels, was not very happy in The Hague; moreover Belgium offered more opportunities. However, the set-up of the Society proved to be too extensive for the Dutch needs and it made the mistake of by-passing the booksellers; it perished in 1844, but its principal assets, the magazine *De Kunstkronijk* and the engraving school went over to the capable but ill-fated Koenraad Fuhri and from him to his pupil A. W. Sijthoff in 1855.

Apart from *De Kunstkronijk* during its short existence the Society succeeded in publishing some remarkable books, amongst others *De Nederlanden, karakterschetsen, kleederdrachten, houding en voorkomen van verschillende standen*, with forty-two plates and 126 vignettes, 1841 (plate 7). This book, excellently printed in the Franco-Belgian style on smooth paper, is also curious because it does not mention the names of the illustrators, though giving the name of

242

the engraver Brown in large type on the title-page; this shows how much the importance of the revolutionary improvement of quality in illustration technique was to the forefront. It is true that this book has a freedom and pithiness which had not been attained very often, either before or later. However, the readers were not yet in a state where they could sufficiently appreciate these qualities to continue to demand them. The results that had been achieved with royal support were partially lost again. Careful publishers gave their drawings to Belgian and French, rather than to Dutch engravers, particularly to E. Vermorcken in Brussels.

Lithography became all the more popular, certainly for the bigger illustrated works such as the *Traité de Fauconnerie* of A. H. Schlegel and A. H. Verster van Wulverhorst, a beautiful folio work, published in 1844–53 by the German lithographer Arnz in Leiden and Düsseldorf, a typical enterprise from the same court circles around William II, who had launched the Society. In the university town of Leiden, Arnz specialised in illustrated scientific works (in which Trap also would soon excel). He printed amongst others: *Verhandelingen over de geschiedenis der Nederlandsche overseesche bezittingen* of C. I. Temminck in 1839 (letterpress by La Lau), which, except for the paper, is not inferior to good English work, and the *Fauna* and *Flora Japonica* of Ph. Fr. von Siebold, the first one edited together with Temminck, Schlegel and De Haan from 1833, the second one from 1835, and a *Bibliotheca Japonica*, together with the sinologist J. J. Hoffmann, lithographed by the Chinese Ko-tsing-tsang, from 1833 (plate 8).

The recording of these large and handsome publications should not give the impression that the Netherlands printing industry already showed a modern trend after 1840. It is true that there were active and well-equipped enterprises and that the readers were moved by a new spirit. The number of political, technical and natural-scientific publications rapidly increased. However, mechanisation and a large-scale approach, with higher capital investment and aggressive sales policy, had yet to come. Former possibilities and new needs struggled together: 'on the one hand firms which continued to exist by their formerly obtained glory and which stuck to the accepted practices; on the other young, energetic sturdy men, who, where necessary, desired changes, improvements and progress', this is how J. W. Enschedé describes the 'forties. But those young people coped with financial difficulties. Investments had to be provided from retained profits, for borrowing money was considered unsound, the more so to borrow from strangers, and there were hardly any credit banks. It goes without saying that with this system the level of wages was at the extreme minimum, the labour conditions were hard, the labourers poorly skilled and not interested, and technical equipment was based on unlimited available manpower. There existed neither comprehension of cost prices nor long-term financial policy to prepare for the coming industrialisation. (An addition of 10 to 100% on wages was calculated as the hourly price. 50% for material, tools, interest, general overhead, etc., plus 25% for profit was already a lot. People had no idea of writing-off periods; for the calculation of earning capacity, in case the introduction of cylinder presses, steam-engines or gas-engines was considered, one was obliged to rely on the experience of colleagues. Lack of space often prevented mechanisation. However, the low Dutch prices checked foreign competition. In about 1860, for a sheet of big octavo in ten point type with thirty-seven lines of twenty-two ems width per page, the price of composing and printing was f 6,70 per 500 copies and f 1,75 for each 500 copies run-on. *Journal für Buchdruckerkunst* III, 48, 30 December 1863.)

1850–1890: TECHNICAL IMPROVEMENT AND AESTHETIC REGRESSION

The Netherlands started the second half of the century with a new constitution, a new king and a new ministry. In the first twenty years of this period conditions were created for the breakthrough to a modern industrial society, which was consolidated in the next two decades. These twenty years form a period in which the western 'bound' (i.e. not free) arts reached the lowest point of shapelessness and emptiness. The 'bound' or applied arts are, namely, all those arts which are governed directly by the requirements of society, consequently not only arts and crafts, industrial art and architecture, but also the academic, official art. Where society and culture disintegrated, these arts lost their firm foundations. As far as mention of the number of top achievements is concerned, this paragraph can therefore be brief: there was no book art; there was typography, but no fine typography. At the most it need be indicated how bad things were, and how technical and economic foundations were laid on which today's book typography developed from the 'nineties.

The World Exhibition of 1851 at the Crystal Palace in London had far-reaching consequences in all branches of industry, trade and industrial art. It opened a perspective on unknown technical possibilities and also showed how far one had fallen behind these possibilities. (The press gave a detailed report of the exhibition: the *Algemeen Handelsblad* even had engravings—something extraordinary for a newspaper.) A trial of strength took place there; those who were clever and energetic took to heart the lessons they could learn. Fortunately, a number of Dutchmen did so. Our country had made a bad showing at the exhibition. Anyone who looks at the book that, published for the occasion, was meant to raise our reputation, will understand why. It had nothing of its own, except its many shortcomings. (H. W. Bentinck, *Journal of the extraordinary embassy of his Excellence the Earl of Portland in France*, plate 9.)

And yet the most capable people had co-operated in producing it. However, the type matter had been made-up wretchedly: pieces had been cut from the wood blocks to make room for the text. In his report on the typographic department of the exhibition the official reporter Ambroise Firmin-Didot paid honour, in melodious phrases, to the Dutch typographical past, but not one word is mentioned about the current achievements which, except for the scientific publications, were on a level with the French routine work. Four years later, at the Paris Exhibition of 1855, our country showed its complete book-production for one year; the volume and average standard of it from a country with about three million (1850: more than 1500, 1851 and afterwards more than 1800 titles a year) gave more reason for satisfaction than such a hasty effort to vie with the handsome French and English publications, as was the Bentinck publication.

If, in 1850, the well-to-do middle classes still lived in Abraham's bossom, without much criticism of their own achievements and without any idea of social problems, this changed quickly in the following years. The London Exhibition had been an eye-opener, as were in their respective fields, Sue's *Mystères de Paris*, Harriet Beecher Stowe's *Uncle Tom's Cabin* and Büchner's *Kraft und Stoff*, soon followed by Murger's *Vie de Bohême*, by Darwin, and by Multatuli (the Dutch Nietzsche). (In the decades between 1841 and 1890 the average annual extension of the railway system in the world was, according to Sombart, respectively three, seven, ten, sixteen and twenty-four thousand kilometres.) Foreign book imports in our country nearly tripled between 1850 and 1870. People learned to compare their own results with those offered by other countries, and were consequently induced to discard some of their self-complacency. From now on a restless urge for improvement, and a consciousness of the duty to improve, would characterise the really moral man.

Mechanisation of book-printing (as distinct from newspaper-printing) truly makes a start now. In 1850 the publisher Kruseman set up a printing-office with still only two hand-presses and a calender-press. In 1853 A. W. Sijthoff bought his first cylinder-press at Reichenbach's in Augsburg (later merged with Maschinenfabrik Augsburg-Nurnberg) and two years afterwards, when buying a second one, he became the agent of this firm for the Netherlands. A specialised dealer in printing machinery and equipment did not yet exist here; the typefounder N. Tetterode was the first to take on agencies for machines and other requirements after his establishment in Amsterdam in 1857. In 1855 the printer G. J. Thieme in Arnhem accepted an agency for Klein, Forst & Bohn (later named Johannisberg); in 1862 he had delivered twenty-five of their presses. Steam power for printing presses was first introduced in Amsterdam in 1852. In 1867 Sijthoff installed, I think as the first, a composing and distributing machine made by Delcambre, Cruys and Co. in Brussels. In those years the advantages of the different composing machines (working with single foundry-type) were widely discussed in professional circles, but only the biggest and most advanced book-printing plants dared to have them. (As the standard output of a compositor with a fixed weekly wage Sijthoff gives in 1879: 1000 to 1200 characters per hour; distribution three times quicker than composition; correction seven to ten minutes per 1000 characters. The Hattersley composing machine of 1866 promised 3000–4000 characters per hour; the Young & Delcambre 6000, the Rosenborg 8000–10,000; the Mackie and Kastenbein 10,000–12,000; the composing machine independently developed by Young 12,000–15,000, and his distributing machine 14,000–18,000.) In the 'seventies H. C. A. Thieme in Nijmegen followed with the efficient Fraser composing machine, which, however, achieved little popularity.

All paper was still moistened and printed with soft cylinder-covering; calendering required fair-sized equipment. It lasted until the 'nineties before presses of heavier and more precise construction with hard tympans permitted good-quality printing on dry paper.

As for illustrations, some workshops continued to use copper- and steelengraving for art reproductions until well into the century, but this was replaced by the increasing use of photogravure and collotype, beginning with small sizes. Lithography, slowly extended with chromo after 1850, remained superior to letterpress illustration in versatility and freedom of expression and provided it with an example, but the necessity to insert lithographically-printed plates separately between the text sheets, limited, of course, the possibilites of its application.

For the most beautiful wood-engravings one had still to rely on foreign countries; the Dutch workshops provided the everyday work. The toiling of the wood-engravers on simple line drawings soon inspired the, technically, very progressive Binger to apply 'glyphography', that is the process by which drawings were scratched in the wax coating on a metal plate, from which, after applying graphite, an electro was formed with lines in high relief. He showed the first great application in his monumental edition of the Dutch poet Vondel, published from 1855 onwards. This work arose entirely from the influence of the London Exhibition in 1851; also in English style as far as the type was concerned. Poorly printed on a horrible glazed and yellowish machine-paper, with its wiry ornaments, feeble, widely-shaded drawings which emphasise the scratching in wax, this book completely breaks with what was still left of strength in the Franco-Belgian style. Twelve years after Brown's *De Nederlanden* it already represents an entirely different world; although it can be appreciated as a new and consistent design in its period, it already summarises everything that in the further development of the century will inevitably lead to the great movement of artistic renewal in the 'nineties.

The etched line block (the 'zincography') patented in 1850 by Gillot, but kept secret for a long time, was not applied in the Netherlands until more than twenty years later; more generally the process was applied just before the development of half-tone engraving, which appeared for the first time in our country in 1883, a year after Meisenbach's invention.

The urge for harder and better work, however fruitful in the technical and commercial fields, could only have fatal consequences in the aesthetic field, since sound principles of form had not yet been developed. The book designers were either the publishers themselves, commercially trained, or compositors or printers, only technically trained. Training courses for industrial arts and crafts, aimed at the development of original creative powers, did not exist; when after 1870 something like that appeared, it continued to seek safety in showing beautiful examples. (This example was looked for in history or in other countries. What had to be 'beautiful' came from abroad: all articles or luxury were imported. And France by preference held the monopoly of taste in Dutch public opinion. However, France did not think in industrial, but in artisan terms, in contrast to England, but especially to the United States, *see* J. Lessing, director of the collection of the Berlin Kunstgewerbemuseum in his *Das halbe Jahrhundert der Weltausstellungen,* Berlin 1900. That example delayed the development of industrial design; insofar as Germany, because of her activity and of the lesser linguistic difficulties, exercised an influence here with industrial products and text-books, the situation was no different, for in that country also handwork was venerated as a yardstick for industrial quality.)

In a period which, as already mentioned, thought it possible to force beauty by diligent and accurate work, this had to lead to imitation instead of authenticity, ingenuity instead of art, and splendour instead of power. The artistic crisis after 1870 expresses itself as meticulous niggling work with *ersatz* materials; the opposition against monochrome classicism covers everything with a flood of soft colours in matt finish. In the interior design, because of net curtains, drapes and deep window-recesses, a twilight reigns which blends the richness of colours and details with a pleasant atmosphere of rest and harmony. That which seems overdone in our hard light, must have then made a grand impression of phantasy and artistic sensibility. Georg Hirth, leader of the Munich trend in typography and *arbiter elegantiarum* of the German industrial arts, thought it justified to consider the inhabitants as the decoration of a room just as forty years later the architects of the decorative 'Amsterdam School' regretted that the living needs of the people in the house interfered with their façade plans. In this spirit also the text became a pretext for book decoration. (*See* for this period, Dolf Sternberger's excellent cultural historical study, *Panorama, oder Ansichten vom 19. Jahrhundert*. Hamburg, Claassen 1955.)

1890–1940: REVIVAL OF TYPOGRAPHY
AND ITS CONSOLIDATION

It was so evident that the applied arts had lost their sense of direction after the middle of the century that the best people had already searched for a long time for a new basis on which an art could be founded, as vital, coherent and sharply defined as one of the great historical style periods. A leading thought was necessary—in terms of the nineties: the Idea—which would also comprise the moral foundations of society, for the social origin of many of the artistic troubles was clear to many of the reformers. Such an Idea, a closed and simple system, but deeply founded was in the possession of the man who stood head and shoulders above the others in the 'applied' arts of the preceding period: the architect of the Rijksmuseum in Amsterdam and restorer of the Mainz Cathedral, Dr. P. J. H. Cuypers (1827–1921). It comprised in fact 'Christian or Pointed Architecture' of his roman-catholic, co-religionist Pugin, rounded off with the ideas of the anglican Ruskin and the Voltairian Viollet-le-Duc, to whom he used to refer; in other words it sought to effect a rescue by a revival of the spirit and application of the principles of mediaeval art, being technically suitable for the needs and means of its own time, and because of its christian nature also exemplary from a social and artistic viewpoint. In spite of the stress which Cuypers and his followers (as well as supporters from abroad) laid on the desirability to follow the spirit, rather than the concrete forms of gothic, it came in practice to an exploitation of the whole arsenal of gothic motifs. However, Cuypers' personality was so strong, he knew so well how to get what he wanted, and his output was so extensive, that among those who devoted themselves to the cure of the art profession and industrial art, only a few could evade his suggestive influence. And they were primarily the artists born between 1856 (Berlage) and 1869 (De Bazel and Thorn Prikker), who at the age of about thirty, had to take over the torch from Cuypers. On his seventieth birthday in 1897 it became clear that everybody knew how much they owed to him.

In typography and calligraphy Cuypers and the pupils of his workshop practised, of course, gothic models with, where necessary, renaissance motifs, just as he did in his secular building works. Since he made pen-drawings for photo-chemical reproduction, as also did Otto Hupp in Munich, his letter applications miss the power and crispness which the wood-cut gave Morris' designs. But then in principle he was not against application of modern division of labour techniques as was Morris. Until today his style has haunted those pieces of work which must make an ecclesiastical, heraldic, Old-Dutch or any other solemn impression on the man in the street (plate 11). Of more importance was what Cuypers did for the promotion of professional skill, and even more for the revival of the principle of strict unity in conception and severe earnestness in art practice. Mention must also be made of what he did in our country with its distinct protestant signature to force recognition for the work of roman-catholic artists, who express in their work their specific world of feelings and thoughts. Anybody who pursued the social and artistic revival, anybody who knew his job and wished to handle things with energy, was welcome in the circle of the enthusiastic young reformers. The axiom that roman-catholicism is equal to obscurantism, to emotional stupefaction, mental coercion and conservatism, and liberalism, on the contrary, to reason, freedom, openness and progress, had at least become a disputable thesis. The boundaries were shifted for a time.

All this is of importance for typography, because it is difficult to understand the origin of the typographical principles of the period without knowing the ideas and human relationships. If one identifies a Cuypers or Morris with neo-gothicism and mediaevalism, with catholicism or socialism, one misses the reason why they were nevertheless the inspiring examples for a younger generation or for members of the other camp. In general, dividing lines between various ideas of art or generations are often less clear than later generations suggest in their (inevitably simplified) historical school-systems.

The weakness of Cuypers and Morris was the retrospective nature of their motifs—they were, however, too creative to fall into a slavish copying manner. Their power was in the recovery of lost professional knowledge (for which they went back into history as far as necessary), independence towards the suggestion of indispensability and inevitability of the results of modern science and technique, and their urge for unity of conception, arising from a harmony between aim and means, between principal, designer, craftsman and user, between art and society. The mediaeval, retrospective side could be taken out of their system and replaced by another fundamental idea, which also defined a place for all components of applied arts. For Berlage it was a pan-humanistic socialism; for Toorop, Thorn Prikker, and Roland Holst for a time, the rosicrucianism of the phantastic Frenchman, Sâr Mérodack Joséphin Péladan; for De Bazel, Lauweriks, and Joh. B. Smits theosophy, oriental wisdom and eternal laws of harmony based on numerical systems; for the younger catholics a renewed christianity in a *rerum novarum* spirit; for the reformed protestants neo-calvinism. Between these divergent directions co-ordination was necessary. Pre-eminently this was provided by Jan Veth, who, enthusiastic but maintaining a suitable distance, exact but also on broad lines, governed the arts of design by reviews and essays in which he followed closely the events in the entire art world. He exercised his greatest influence as a member of the editorial staff of the cultural monthly magazine *De Kroniek*, which appeared from 1895, at the end of the literary revival of the 'eighties, which was completed then. Its appearance marks the breakthrough among young artists of an aesthetic and social idealism which had been strange to the—in a neutral sense—amoral and asocial glorification of beauty of the artists of the 'eighties. The *l'art pour l'art* principle could be explained in the sense of Théophile Gautier: 'Il n'y a de vraiment beau que ce qui ne peut servir à rien—Tout ce qui est utile est laid'; in any case the literary movement of the 'eighties was neither in theory nor in practice interested in a revival of the 'applied' arts. What these arts could in fact adopt from the literary principles of the 'eighties was the requirement of a unity of content and form, of purity of means and way of expression, and of art as passion.

The first expression of the new spirit among younger artists was a contribution to typography. It was an effort towards a 'Gesamtkunstwerk', made through the co-operation of artist-specialists, who, in doing so wanted to give beauty to the whole population by means of a simple, clear language of form:

this was Vondel's *Gijsbreght*, with music of Bernard Zweers, decors of Berlage and book illustration of Derkinderen, published by Erven Bohn in 1893 as the opening work for J. L. Springer's new Amsterdam Theatre. An ugly book with beautiful elements, but precious because of its originality and idealism and their effect on the world of art. (The resounding effects of the *Gijsbreght* can be found in Pol de Mont's very informative essay on typography of the Low Countries in *Die neue Buchkunst*, Studien im In- und Ausland, ed. Rudolf Kautzsch, Weimar 1902.) Of them Derkinderen was farthest on the way to-wards an 'art of the sign', then the formula with which the symbolic, monu-mental or 'community art' opposed itself to the 'art of the image'; towards a powerful, closed and simple decorative style filling the plane and working with solids. What in the work of the architects Cuypers, Springer and also Berlage (who still built old-Dutch inns for Bols Distilleries in those years) is sharp-lined and hard-coloured, is in Derkinderen's work dull, smooth, matt and tonal. He too, however, is still under the spell of the *horror vacui*. The ten-sion of the emptiness, which Van de Velde already applied so well, never got a real grip on the Dutch, just as Japanese art served less as an inspiration here than the much more detailed and linear Javanese art.

The *Gijsbreght* is a serious manifestation, heavy with exalted intentions. The vocation, the desire to testify to a new art and society, which animated young artists and intellectuals, are found in it. More clearly even than in the *Gijsbreght* the difficult conversion from the mighty suggestive Cuypers to the Art Nou-veau, and new community art, is expressed in Derkinderen's binding design for the biography: *J. A. Alberdingk Thijm by J. A.* and his lithographed title-pages and text typography of the *Gedenkboek Keuzetentoonstelling van Hol-landsche Schilderkunst uit de jaren 1860–1892* (plate 12). When one imagines the degree of spiritual kinship between Derkinderen and Cuypers, it is obvious what was necessary to convert Cuypers' Gothic-with-French-renaissance in frame-composition into fluent Art Nouveau style with large solids. The boxes remained and also the lombardic capitals (albeit in a somewhat dripping form) but the spiritual background changed. From Wagner we have come down somewhere between Franck and Debussy.

Dutch designers have always had a great need for a solid construction (for example with what is now called a grid), as a solid theoretical (and preferably also 'weltanschaulich') foundation is a condition for all actions that are to be taken seriously. This was the case with the young servants of community art. Hard creative work, pure thought and chaste life had to be the rule of those who, with their art, wanted to assist in preparing a new community.

Art and Community—the terms have already been used several times; it was also the title under which Jan Veth edited, in Dutch, Walter Crane's *Claims of Decorative Art*, a book which was also published in 1893 by Scheltema and Holkema, with illustrations by G. W. Dijsselhof. It was one of the first results of a co-operation which K. Groesbeek, director of both the above-mentioned publishing firm and of the art shop Van Wisselingh had with all those young Amsterdam decorative artists and painters, which became of great importance in this period. The relationship between Dijsselhof, C. A. Lion Cachet and Theo Nieuwenhuis was very close; on Groesbeek's initiative they made, besides book ornaments, the famous diplomas of the Dutch Booksellers' organisation and a beautiful series of calendars from 1898 to 1900, designs for Van Wisselingh's workshop of furniture and decoration, of which Nieuwenhuis took the leadership later. *See* for this period: L. Gans, *Nieuwe Kunst—De Nederlandse bijdrage tot de 'Art Nouveau'* (Utrecht 1960) and the catalogue of the exhibition *Nieuwe Kunst rond 1900*, Gemeentemuseum, The Hague, 1960–1961.

From Groesbeek's relationship with the painter-etcher Marius Bauer, whose dealer he was and remained, resulted first of all a vile piece of book-making *Akëdysseril* by Villiers de l'Isle-Adam (1894), with inserted etchings by Bauer; an example of the decadent side of the 'nineties, in outlook and level infinitely inferior to the Crane. Four years later *La jeunesse inaltérable et la vie éternelle* appeared, a Rumanian folk-tale with many etchings of Bauer and ornaments of Dijsselhof; it was much finer and showed more unity.

Groesbeek also provided the means with which Henriette van der Schalk's first volume of poetry, *Sonnetten en Verzen in Terzinen* (1895) could meet the requirement of a suitable form for beautiful content, in which the poetess' fiancé, Richard Roland Holst (later director of the Royal Academy of Art in Amsterdam, but at that time still trying to find his way in monumental arts) wished to put it. For months he worked hard on it; for advice and criticism he often consulted his older fellow-artist Derkinderen who had specialised most in this field and whose hand can clearly be recognised: the same worm-like lombardics and the same gothic filigree mixed with fluent, lobed-plant ornaments and pithy, hard woodcut decorations; the whole anchored down with red lines in the page format.

No acceptable examples were available to start from, at least no Dutch ones, and none executed with the typographic materials available here. *Akëdysseril* was an example of how not to do it, with its small text lost in the sizing of smooth paper; the Belgian volumes of that period seemed to be too free, too little based on an Idea. In the third number of *De Kroniek* (13 January 1895) Holst had given his opinion, in clear terms, about the magazine of the young Flemish *Van Nu en Straks* and about Belgian artists in general. Although he had co-operated in the Van Gogh issue of this magazine in 1893, just as had Toorop and Thorn Prikker, he thought its principle impure and illogical from a viewpoint of exterior design. Apparently the general opinion in this circle of *De Kroniek* was that the Belgians took things too easily. In the first number (1 January 1895) Frans Coenen had expressed himself in the same way, rather patronisingly, about Verhaeren's Almanac, designed by Théo van Rysselberghe. Real earnestness reigned in England, particularly, according to Holst, in William Morris's books and the publication of *Daphnis and Chloe* and *Hero and Leander* by the Vale Press—in London, Holst had been greatly impressed by his personal encounter with Morris, Crane, Ricketts, and Shannon (work of the latter two was shown by Van Wisselingh in Amsterdam in 1895, probably at his suggestion). There, in terms of Veth, community art, static and epic; in Belgium individual art, fluent and lyric, which, it appeared, was too easily considered here vapid and fickle. The difference in temperament between north and south strongly manifested itself and not always for the north in a favourable sense; even less the air of superiority which one permitted traditionally towards Flemish culture.

A proof of Veth's greatness is that he continued to weigh-up critically those products of Dutch solidity, which he could excusably have embraced as expressions of the real spirit. Reviewing Berlage's *Gedenkboek van de Delagoabaaispoorweg* in *De Kroniek* of 21 July 1895, he blames the disproportions between the values of type and ornament; it happens too often that 'one sees first the emblematic filling ornaments, and notices only afterwards that there are types in between, which then also are difficult to read', a criticism which could also apply to Derkinderen and Holst. Such practical suggestions, which limited the riotous ornamentations (leaving, however, enough room for a legitimate urge to reform) had gradually to be collated into a code which the enthusiastic artists could accept, since they came from highly-esteemed colleagues.

For typography this work was in particular to be done by Jan Kalf (1873–1954) and J. W. Enschedé (1865–1926), who was a half-brother of Charles Enschedé, author of the well-known *Fonderies de Caractères*. They made the division between what Radermacher Schorer called so aptly, 'decorators' and 'typographers'. Kalf and Enschedé both had a hereditary interest in typography, were both capable authors on this subject, but as a result of their functions (in government supervision of monuments and library work respectively), they did not work in the printing industry. However, in the beginning, when no professional typographers yet worked in their spirit, they designed publications themselves, here and there, for societies of which they were members and for printing and publishing business connections. Their influence on the development of our typography, partly also exercised behind the scenes, was nevertheless very important.

Kalf's critical work appeared regularly in *De Kroniek*, the remarkably good typography of which he probably directed himself; there should be mentioned in particular his lecture on 'The Book' for the 'Genootschap Architectura et Amicitia' in 1898 and published in its magazine *Architectura* of that year.

In this circle the young K. P. C. de Bazel and J. M. Lauweriks (who, trained by Cuypers, managed together a workshop for architecture and decorative arts and crafts) were the leading figures. They rediscovered the significance of space, that is to say the rhythm of the optic values of spaces which arise from subdividing a given plane; the same held good for three-dimensional space. De Bazel and Lauweriks sought the foundations for harmony in simple numerical proportions (analogous to what is called today 'module systems') and in so doing they consulted old Greek, Egyptian and Indian systems. This, however, did not bring them to the thin air of the Mondrianesque stratosphere; they continued to make fine virile woodcuts as well.

In Kalf's lecture all effort and experience from the 'nineties until the youngest architectonic ideas were summarised:

1. The idea of unity under a leading Idea, starting from Pugin and his two branches via Ruskin/Morris and via Viollet-le-Duc/Cuypers with socialist and roman-catholic gradations, ending in a community art with a serving character. Hence follows, for the sake of general understanding and an efficient use of energy, an acceptance and conscientious passing-on of approved traditions.

2. From the French-romantic literary school through the 'eighties: the inspiring force of art as passion; necessity of mutual fitting of form and content, and the specific task of the artist as an owner of formative power, who can create content and form from a single principle.

3. Rejection of the negative sides of the different trends of thought mentioned before, namely the retrospective attitude of the one, opposed to industrialisation, and the individualism of the other. Kalf expected good results from the machine. 'Only—and this is what gave rise to that wrong opinion—this will be a new beauty, of an original kind which we—used to an art of an entirely different nature—shall be able to appreciate, probably after long reflection only.' And, quoting an unmentioned industrial designer: 'The fact that with

the newest machines one does not succeed in making something beautiful is also due to the conservatism of artists who do not accept the machine free of any prejudice, but who want to force it to an imitation of what only another method could achieve—who consequently do not become acquainted with the machine in its essential nature and who do not believe in a not yet existing beauty.'

As for individualism, Kalf said about Morris 'whose actions were not equal to his words in this respect': 'Don't allow yourself to be seduced by the tempting example of such men as Morris and Cobden-Sanderson who, whilst giving way too much to their own artists' ideals, did create beautiful things, but owing to the way in which they did it, kept them unattainable by the public.' (Even stronger L. Simons in his otherwise highly admiring commemorative article on Morris' death in *De Gids*, 1897, I: The Kelmscott Chaucer and one volume each in Golden and Troy types is all we need... 'in our daily bookmaking we will never obtain results along that slow and archaic way.')

4. Emphasis on the functional requirements of the text with which implicitly the neglect of this by the 'decorators' is regretted. These requirements are:

a. suitability and durability of materials;

b. right proportions, for which reference is made to Lauwerik's theories (however, he does not yet connect format with category of text, bulk of the book, weight of paper, etc.);

c. legibility, regularity and adequate boldness of the type; the nineteenth-century types are too sharp, have too much contrast between thick and thin and do not give closed word-forms;

d. reduction and equal division of the spacing; thinner spaces, more use of abbreviations, if necessary hyphens to be placed on the following line(!); no indenting paragraphs because they lead to an ugly toothy dentation of black and white, hence in general closed text blocks;

e. no mixture of type styles;

f. double-page as unity for layout;

g. good impression on matt paper; avoidance of too deep an impression avoiding relief marking on surface;

h. in conformity with Cobden-Sanderson's definition, the bookbinding should keep the sheets of the book together in good order and protect it, and facilitate its use; the case-binding is only acceptable as provisional measure, awaiting a binding sewn on cords or bands.

Some details not mentioned here (and for example the last-mentioned point about bookbinding) show how much Kalf still stuck to veneration of mediaeval handwork, in spite of his forward vision on mechanical production; it is amazing that he as an amateur succeeded in drawing up these rules. He must have extracted them from studies of old printings and from the good and bad examples of his own time; technical literature of a similar outlook did not yet exist.

His ideas on its practical application appear in his typography for Jan Veth, *Jozef Israëls en zijn kunst* (1904): forming blocks in a few big units, simple and strong, just lightened with a vignette and some colour accents. As types Kalf chose the best 'old styles' he could acquire; the Fleischman which others in that period used as the most beautiful available on imitation hand-made paper, was not strong and simple enough for him.

The printing firm of Ipenbuur & Van Seldam was managed by Berend Modderman. Immediately after he settled down he joined the young artists with their aims and not only did he involve his then brother-in-law, J. W. Enschedé, but also the brothers Theo and Antoon Molkenboer as decorative artists. The latter wrote, designed and illustrated a symbolic fairy-tale *Mincelijn* (1897) which with its tight construction and multi-coloured ornaments was a prestige piece of work for the rejuvenated firm. Extending rapidly it dared to publish in 1902 a series *Notes on the art of the book*, edited by J. W. Enschedé; a piece of printer's publicity which also advanced the profession as a whole.

This merit held good even more for the four *Printer's Annuals* which Modderman and Enschedé published in 1906, 1907, 1908 and 1911. Although they did not become popular among printers and publishers, their influence on the leading typographers of the following generation was considerable. The books contained thorough typographical instructions, now here, too, with a taste, knowledge and international orientation which the criticism of free arts had already possessed since the 'eighties. The difference from Veth's and Kalf's essays of the 'nineties was a change in direction: then stimulation of decorative artists and art-lovers, now education of professionals; then the renewal was done—to use Schorer's terms—by decorators, now by typographers.

Kalf's lecture (1898) already marked the re-orientation. The efforts so far to develop a typography of its own epoch, had proved that the text as the basis was still feeble, however much artistic idealism was spent on the book as a whole. Without a good, well-composed type, decoration had to remain a mere addition; or rather: good composition together with the unprinted paper should be able to make a strong and harmonious structure, which made further decoration unnecessary. The same development showed itself else-

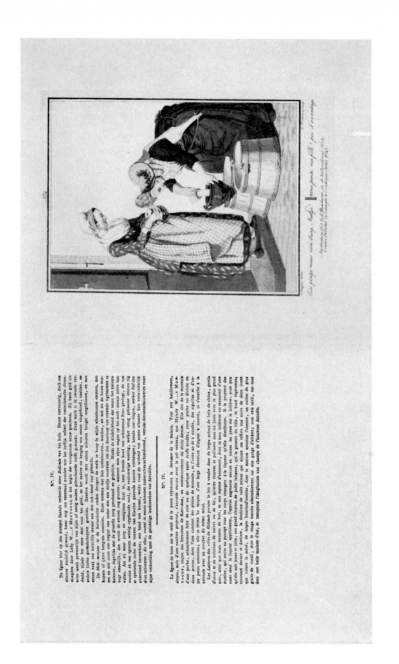

1. E. Maaskamp: *Afbeeldingen van de kleeding, zeden en gewoonten in de Bataafsche Republiek* (1803–7). Two-page opening

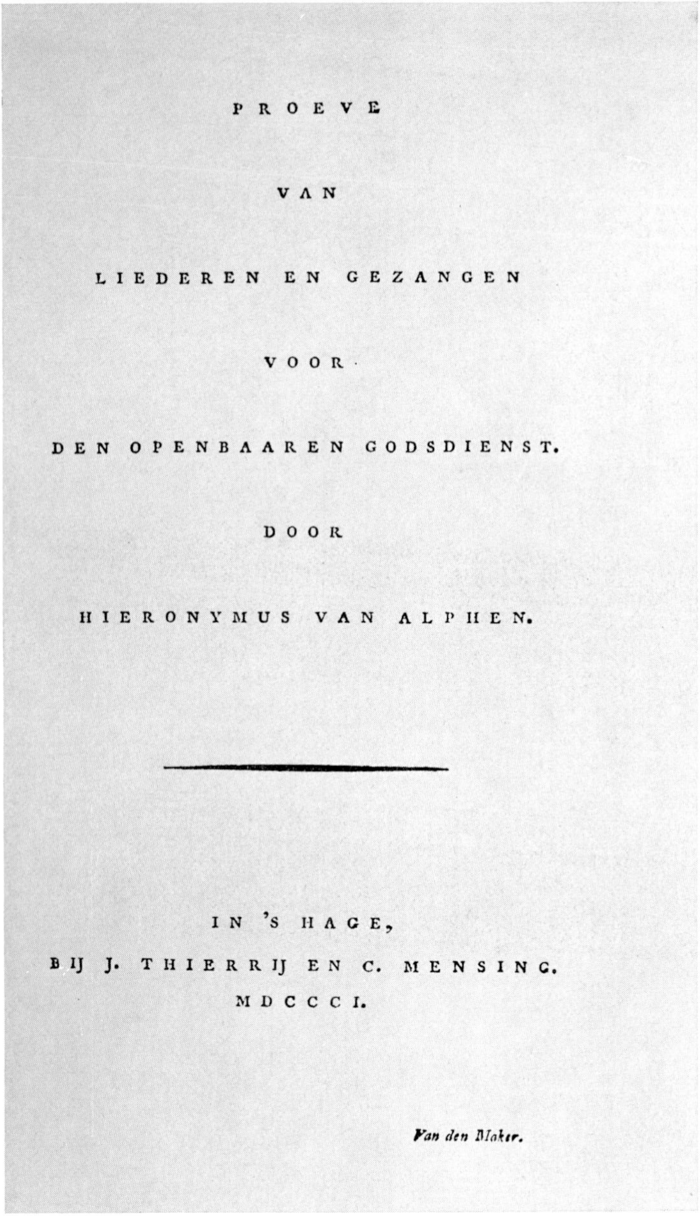

PROEVE

VAN

LIEDEREN EN GEZANGEN

VOOR

DEN OPENBAAREN GODSDIENST.

DOOR

HIERONYMUS VAN ALPHEN.

———

IN 'S HAGE,
BIJ J. THIERRIJ EN C. MENSING.
MDCCCI.

Van den Maker.

2. H. van Alphen: *Proeve van Liederen en Gezangen, etc.*, J. Thierry and
C. Mensing, The Hague (1801). Title-page

Soit: L'Azimuth de l'objet terrestre Z.
La Latitude de la station .... L.
Le demi diamètre du soleil.... $\eth$

PREMIER CONTACT.	SECOND CONTACT.
La déclinaison du soleil.....D.	La déclinaison du soleil......D'
L'Angle horaire..............P.	L'Angle horaire..............P'
L'Azimuth ....A.	L'Azimuth...................A'
La hauteur vraie ....H.	La hauteur vraie.......... ..H'
La hauteur apparente.........h.	La hauteur apparente ....h'

a. *Premiere partie.*

$$\text{Soit : Tang. } p = \cot. \tfrac{1}{2} \, P \times \frac{\sin. \tfrac{1}{2}\,(L-D)}{\cos. \tfrac{1}{2}\,(L+D)} \quad (1)$$

$$\text{Tang. } q = \cot. \tfrac{1}{2} \, P \times \frac{\cos. \tfrac{1}{2}\,(L-D)}{\sin. \tfrac{1}{2}\,(L+D)} \quad (2)$$

$$\text{Alors } A = p + q \dots\dots\dots\dots\dots\dots\dots \quad (3)$$

$$\text{Cos. } \tfrac{1}{2}\,H = \text{Cos. } \tfrac{1}{2}P \times \frac{\sin. \tfrac{1}{2}\,(L-D)}{\sin. \, p} = \text{Cos. } \tfrac{1}{2}P \times \frac{\cos. \tfrac{1}{2}\,(L+D)}{\cos. \, p.} \quad (4)$$

$$Z = A \pm \frac{\sin. \, \eth.}{\cos. \, h.}$$

b. *Seconde partie.*

$$\text{Soit : Tang. } p' = \cot. \tfrac{1}{2} \, P' \times \frac{\sin. \tfrac{1}{2}\,(L-D')}{\cos. \tfrac{1}{2}\,(L+D')} \quad (1)$$

$$\text{Tang. } q' = \cot. \tfrac{1}{2} \, P' \times \frac{\cos. \tfrac{1}{2}\,(L-D')}{\sin. \tfrac{1}{2}\,(L+D')} \quad (2)$$

$$\text{Alors } A' = p' + q' \dots\dots\dots\dots\dots\dots\dots \quad (3)$$

$$\text{Cos. } \tfrac{1}{2}H' = \text{Cos. } \tfrac{1}{2}P' \times \frac{\sin. \tfrac{1}{2}\,(L-D')}{\sin. \, p'} = \cos. \tfrac{1}{2}P' \times \frac{\cos. \tfrac{1}{2}\,(L+D')}{\cos. \, p'} \quad (4)$$

$$Z' = A' + \frac{\sin. \, \eth.}{\cos. \, h'}$$

J'ai fait à la station d'*Amsterdam* 89 observations du passage des deux bords du soleil par les verticaux des objets mentionnés ci-dessus ; j'en ai calculé 53, dont 5 ont été rejettées, à cause de leur trop grand écart, qui m'a fait soupçonner quelque dérangement dans la position de la lunette. Les résultats des 48 autres, toujours rapportées au centre de la station d'*Utrecht*, sont exposés dans le tableau suivant:

G

LEERREDENEN

VAN

N. SWART.

*

TE AMSTERDAM, BIJ

G. J. A. BEIJERINCK,

1822.

4. N. Swart: *Leerredenen*, G. J. A. Beijerinck, printed by C. A. Spin, Amsterdam (1822). Title-page

where. The flaming, whirling and waving of the Art Nouveau and Jugendstil, which had come to a last desperate explosion at the Turin Exhibition in 1902, fell flat. In its place the complete contrast appeared: a hard, static form precisely calculated. The jungle of the olive-green stems was followed by the staccato mosaic of small black and white squares.

(In Holland, apart from Toorop, the leading works of Art Nouveau hardly showed the languid, satiated forms which are characteristic elsewhere. Probably also under the influence of Indonesian batik styles, nervous tentacle and flame motifs dominated here, and further, a pre-occupation with all transitions of long, flowing, round forms into compact square ones. For instance, Dijsselhof's end-papers of *Kunst en Samenleving* with the trailing tentacles which end as squares—a motif which is frequently used by him, as also with Berlage. Very popular also is the round disc, cut in four segments, as a screw-head with cross-slits.)

Before 1890 the lack of artistry of the craftsman had been apparent; after that the lack of craftsmanship of the artists, many of whom found it beneath their dignity to study techniques and questions of costs—they thought that those craftsmen should be forced to do what beauty required. In the further growth of the idea of community art no place was left for craftsmen as a poor, skilled industrial proletariat which could only copy tasteless models, nor for artists as individualists who had beautiful dreams which somebody else had to try and realise. Synthesis asked for craftsmen in whom artistic creative power had been awakened and for artists who could be humble enough to first master craft techniques before striving for beauty. When to date artists were forced to deliver piecework (partly because they had no opportunity for more than adding ornaments, partly because they lacked ambition and persistence for revising all components of an object of industrial art), now after 1900 artists developed who, working within a production firm, could create the total product from one form principle. The slogan became: serving the public (i.e. beauty-starved, suffering mankind), with a generally valid, comprehensible, efficient and solid construction; form necessarily resulting from the function; complete unity of form in all its parts; decoration only to soften the hardness of the purely functional form.

The artist who then, prepared to accept a function in the printing industry and to work from industrial techniques, had the capacity to create an original, efficient and beautiful form, was S. H. de Roos. More about him later.

The printing industry had reached a state of fermentation in the course of the 'nineties because the rapidly increasing need for printed matter involved a faster mechanisation, which could be obtained from the progress in techniques. The traditional manual work fell into disuse in many places, with all inherent economic and social consequences. The demand seemed so unlimited that the number of new establishments rapidly increased. In 1880 there were already 425 book-printing firms with 740 cylinder-presses and 650 hand-presses (besides this 183 lithographic printing offices with 125 cylinder- and 700 hand-presses), in 1890 the first mentioned number increased to 683 and in 1909 there were already about a 1000. Too quick an expansion led to fierce competition; mechanisation required investments which poor prices could not balance and customers exploited this weakness. At the same time employees, organised long since, made ever-higher wage demands, all too justified. The letterpress printers organised themselves in 1909; the initiative came from the real book-printers, who doing a similar kind of work for a small group of publishers, thus knew their real costs better, realised their weaknesses better, and who could do more about it because of their federation. For the time being they had one aim only: a fixed price scheme, the Tariff; it would, however, take a long time before the printing industry had a solid economic basis. It is a pity that this price war and technical re-orientation weakened the drive behind the movement for artistic revival.

The bookbinding industry followed the development of the printing industry: mechanisation of the production of cased-bindings; activity of artistic bookbinders who put individual books in beautifully decorated bindings truly 'sewn on string', and of artists who were allowed to make designs for factory bindings now and then. Jan Mensing, J. A. Loeber and Joh. B. Smits should be mentioned as art bookbinders. They belonged to the society 'Kunst toegepast op boekbanden', founded in 1896, which, inspired in particular by Cobden-Sanderson, published a monthly magazine *De Boekband*. The high expectations for a flourishing of the decorative arts could not be fulfilled in the Netherlands. Just as Van de Velde, De Praetere, Thorn Prikker, Zwollo and Lauweriks, also Loeber and Smits accepted jobs in industrial art teaching in Germany and Switzerland: Smits followed De Praetere to the Kunstgewerbeschule in Zurich, from which he returned later to become director of the Amsterdam School of Arts and Crafts. The three did good work around 1900; however, the relatively high standard of the publisher's binding in the Netherlands and the lack of a strong group of wealthy bibliophiles never provided a reasonable living to independent hand bookbinders and thus prevented the development of a national binding art.

Publishers engaged artists for the design of their bindings and covers early in the 'nineties and after the turn of the century, for the same reasons that today artists are entrusted with book-jackets rather than with book typography: external appearance is more important for sales than the inside. Not a good situation, but it gave the reading public at least some new ideas. Nearly all decorative artists in that period made bindings and cover designs. Besides a simple colour stamping, the batik technique was frequently used—as in interior decoration—on parchment, leather or textiles. Batik became popular following the Colonial Exhibition in Amsterdam of 1883, and provided, as already mentioned, another reason for the Dutch Art Nouveau to display hairy, spiky motifs rather than the bulbous ornaments popular elsewhere.

In Holland it was several years after the turn of the century before sturdy modern types were available which could harmonise with the vigorous drawings of the new book artists—it is one of the reasons why they liked so much to design types themselves. This lack of type faces was felt all the more, of course, in the bookbinding industry, for the brass type for gilding suffers chronically from bad designs and a limited choice. In 1898 Kalf rightly warned against the wrong effect which designs conceived in dark-on-light have when they are executed in light-on-dark, and the other way round. It happened too often that designs were created independently without calculation of the effect in the final colours and materials.

J. G. Veldheer and W. O. J. Nieuwenkamp together made a picture book, remarkable for the period in its boldness and openness, *Oud-Hollandse Steden aan de Zuiderzee*, 1897; towns were followed by a similar one on villages, three years later, in which for the first time a sans serif was used as text type to harmonise better with the illustrations. The use in an art book of what was then considered a vulgar advertisement display type was a pioneering act which, however, was not followed up for some time. The elevation of the sans serif to an ideal of simplicity, purity and direct expressiveness begins with the constructions for architectural use by Berlage, De Bazel and Lauweriks; for the sans serif as text letter only appeared with Lauweriks' magazine *Der Ring* at the end of his Düsseldorf teaching period in 1909, if one omits the German poet Stefan George. (He first used the sans serif as a text letter in 1890, but, as Schauer says rightly, his preference for Melchior Lechter's excessive ornamentation does not justify considering this early effort as the beginning of its systematic use, since 1907, of the Akzidenz Grotesk of the Berthold foundry which had been altered to Stefan George-Schrift, according to the poet's hand-writing. This use is so much subservient to George's own way of expression that Lauweriks' later application may be called the first programmatic one.)

The publisher Van Dishoeck in Bussum (being from Zeeland stock he was much attracted to Flemish art and culture) entrusted from 1903 onwards the young Belgian medico-philologist-writer Herman Teirlinck, who also acted as an illustrator, with binding designs: pure and early examples of the decorative trend which united the mobility and the decadent-precious elements of the 'nineties with the tight, linear constructions which constituted the reaction to them. Many characteristics of this way to combine elegant play of lines with solid, closed construction can still be found in the work of advertising artists until the 'thirties.

In these same years after 1900 several efforts were made here too to give children's books an illustrative and typographic design which would be more beautiful and more expressive. Walter Crane was the starting-point in this, but also Caldecott, Boutet de Monvel and Ernst Kreidolf were admired. In January 1906 the Society 'Kunst aan het Volk' held an exhibition *Kind en Kunst* in the Stedelijk Museum in Amsterdam, where with much foreign material could be shown work of national origin. However, as far as this field and the school-book are concerned, it has to be stated with regret that they have always suffered from the publisher's axiom that the Dutch price level does not allow anything better than third-rate mass-produced work and that the Dutch public does not deserve more. It seems that only recently a change has been possible, but now the art of design results only exceptionally in poetic children's drawings.

De Roos designed his first book in 1903: some essays of William Morris under the title *Kunst en Maatschappij*, curious because of the early application of the Grasset type, which Modderman's printing firm Ipenbuur & Van Seldam had just bought through the German foundry of Genzsch & Heyse which cast it by arrangement, because J. W. Enschedé, a great francophile, expected much of it, as appears from his brochure (the second in the series of *Notes on the art of the book* mentioned before). It was De Roos' first and only product in an Art Nouveau style, albeit simple, open and solid; it had a unity, new for Holland, but not one which really agreed with De Roos' spirit. He found what he wanted in the here still unknown D. B. Updike and Bruce Rogers, and consequently afterwards also in Carl Ernst Poeschel, who, too, admired the two American master-printers and did not follow them in the letter but in the spirit. From England it was the visual simplicity and sense of quality of the Doves Press (not the high-priest manner of Cobden-Sanderson) which De

Roos admired; but with these all those foreign typographers he ever looked up to have been mentioned. He venerated Morris's attitude and principles, and naturally Berlage, Veth, Roland Holst, Kalf and J. W. Enschedé influenced him also with their broad culture, their idealism and Morrisian way of hard and sober work based on thorough craftsmanship.

This influence of Morris, denuded of its mediaevalism, reached the Amsterdam circle via Antwerp, where in 1904 Emmanuel de Bom, co-founder of the literary magazine *Van Nu en Straks*, had given a lecture at the Museum Plantin-Moretus on Morris and his influence on the book, the occasion being the opening of an exhibition on this subject. For this De Bom had got the support of the Swedish printer Waldemar Zachrisson from Göteborg, who contributed from his own work to it. Zachrisson's work, 'all so youthful, so open and airy, so new' showed how, outside the English private-press atmosphere, a commercial firm could realise Morris's principles in a national manner. Through J. W. Enschedé this became known to Modderman. It provided the inspiration for an exhibition of foreign typography in the Haarlem Museum of Arts and Crafts (summer 1907, with works of the Doves, Ashendene and Essex House presses, Vienna and Berlin Government Printing Offices, and of Buschmann and Zachrisson); inspiration, too, for the publication of the *Drukkersjaarboeken* (Printers' annuals), which to a much larger extent than the *Notes* could stimulate the understanding for a new Dutch typography.

The purchase of the Grasset type proved to be a failure: the public had had enough of Art Nouveau; the next new book type of Ipenbuur & Van Seldam was the useful but dry Romaans which was also used for the first *Drukkersjaarboek* of 1906, which gave a musty appearance to fresh contents. However, in the meantime Zachrisson had stimulated Genzsch & Heyse to produce a new book type which would be a contemporary version of Plantin's text letter, in other words a modern Garamond or Granjon. It was designed by Genzsch's artistic assistant, the excellent craftsman Friedrich Bauer, and made available as Nordische Antiqua (renamed Genzsch Antiqua afterwards) in 1906. With Benton's Century and Goodhue's Cheltenham it is the only new book face prior to 1910 which has remained in use until today, and deservedly so.

De Roos, who then had to work for his living as a lithographer in a tin-can factory, but who remained in constant touch with Modderman and J. W. Enschedé, was commissioned to produce the second *Drukkersjaarboek* in the new type. It was the start of a new phase in Netherlands book typography, for at one stroke De Roos proved that he possessed everything necessary to develop the modern national style which everybody wanted. As a result he was immediately appointed as designer at the Typefoundry 'Amsterdam', by good luck, for the management had no clear idea what to do with him; they only knew that he was a man who could set up and execute a sound and sensible artistic policy.

The *Drukkersjaarboek* 1907 (plate 13) is the first sound twentieth-century Dutch book. In spite of the efforts to achieve a strong text block—see also the two title-lines filled up with small ornaments—the page is open, sunny, sparkling, thanks to the fine effect of the text type and the soft colours of the initial on the tinted, calendered paper. In the reprint of De Bom's lecture in Antwerp, produced by the same team three years later, on hard, yellow laid paper, the same type was used more forcefully with the colour in a powerful red, which proved how De Roos carefully attuned choice of type and composition to format and kind of paper. No mere accumulation of components, beautiful separately but not forming a unity together; no forcing of the text into tight blocks (as Kalf still did) or in decorative schemes and ornamental frames; these books show a born typographer with a capable hand and splendid style.

There are sound reasons for confining the history of Dutch book typography from De Roos' start until the Second World War to that of a few leaders and their general principles. They have been dealt with in detailed studies so fully and often that here only the main lines are drawn. (Biographical and bibliographical material has been included in A. A. M. Stols, *Het Werk van S. H. de Roos*, Amsterdam 1942, a revised edition in English is in preparation; De Roos' number of *Halcyon* 9–10, The Hague 1942; G. W. Ovink, *S. H. de Roos en J. van Krimpen*, *Het Boek* XXXIII, 1958; A. M. Hammacher, *Jean François van Royen 1878–1942*, The Hague 1947; John Dreyfus, *The work of Jan van Krimpen*, Haarlem-Utrecht 1952; G. W. Ovink, *Jan van Krimpen*, Jaarboek van de Maatschappij der Nederlandsche Letterkunde, Leiden 1962; J. Engelman, R. L. Doyon, A. Witte, *In memoriam Charles Nypels*, Amsterdam 1953; Ch. L. van Halsbeke, *L'Art typographique dans les Pays Bas depuis 1892*, Brussels 1929. A catalogue of the works of A. A. M. Stols with biographical survey will appear in the course of 1966).

The year 1907 has proved rich in new starting-points for the visual arts: Jaffé and Sandberg devoted an exhibition to it in the Amsterdam Stedelijk Museum in 1957. At first glance it may seem strange to view De Roos' *Drukkersjaarboek* in relation with Picasso's studies for *Les Demoiselles d'Avignon*, but considering the natural differences in 'progressiveness' between free and bound or applied arts one can find a parallel between both series.

In 1907 not only Art Nouveau had been conquered, but also the first reactions to it; the first new means for expression of the new sense of life were available. The fact that neither in his free art of painting nor in his typography, De Roos had anything in common with the Fauves, cubists and expressionists, is of no consequence in this connection; important is the certainty of aims which broke through everywhere, the foundations of a personal objective after a choice had been made from the possibilities which were presented after 1890. Common to the artists who began their development around 1907 is the veering toward abstraction: the move developed feeling for the independent expressive value of lines, colours, space and materials apart from their possible function as components of well-known objects from the visible world. In typography this is instanced in a sensitivity for the proportion in optical weight between the lines of text and the field of unprinted paper they govern, or for the natural proportions between such different elements as a type-form, a colour, a space and a surface structure.

In the following period of Dutch book typography (apart from typography of periodicals, advertising and social printing) two different trends were gradually emerging, finally represented in the purest way by S. H. de Roos and J. van Krimpen, also because as designers in the two Dutch typefoundries, they could, with their own types, create the means for a complete realisation of their intentions.

Of the two, De Roos was the socialist industrial designer who, with his contemporaries, hoped for a just, peaceful and happy society, with beautiful people and objects; Van Krimpen was an accomplished man of letters with aristocratic outlook, who found satisfaction when a clever text stood neatly on the page or when the elusive type-form was once again for a moment precisely captured in such a way, that cultured people could read more quickly and more comfortably. De Roos was basically a pictorial artist who did not concern himself with the text; Van Krimpen a literary promoter who wanted to have a fair battle of wits between author and reader, and therefore refused with indignation, and protest, any attempt to affect the reader's mood, as an unfair influence.

For his aims De Roos obtained the co-operation of all those who desired sound and elegant typography, gay and broad in manner, showing the will to create a new world. His masterpiece, the Dutch Medieval of 1912, provided him with the means, long looked for, to give this ideal a perfectly appropriate form. It is a type of energy and cheerful enjoyment of life, not one of consideration or intuition. The first large book texts composed in it, Stijn Streuvels' *De Vlaschaard* and *Morgenstond* (L. J. Veen, both 1912, plate 14) also Van Looy's

Nieuwjaarsdag (Vereeniging Joan Blaeu, 1919) did every justice to the type, but Baudelaire's *Les Fleurs du Mal* (De Zilverdistel, 1913) fitted singularly badly its generous undulating style.

It can be understood that the three poets who together wanted to make good books—Jan Greshoff, Jacques Bloem and P. N. van Eyck—did not think of De Roos as the right person to serve them as their guide in typographical layout of lyric poetry. For this he was too much the frank painter who boldly cast the text in a fixed mould, and too little a text-taster who listens to intonation, rhythms and tempo, and tries to render them purely rather than to give them well-attuned and visually captivating compositions. Perhaps, too, apart from typographical considerations, the difference in mental climate diminished mutually the need for closer collaboration, just as it did develop with the more 'literary' Van Krimpen some years later. Greshoff and Bloem—Van Eyck came in later—began their bibliophile series in 1910, under the name De Zilverdistel—typographically designed by themselves on broad lines only, the actual layout was done by the printer Joh. Enschedé & Zonen. Up to 1912 four titles appeared, in the older types of Fleischman and Claesz.

The choice of these types is at once an expression of their own aims: against pictorial, let alone decorative arty typography, but—according to Van Eyck (1912)—for 'pure, non-ornamental book typography'; limited circulation because of necessity only, but large circulations and low prices as soon as practicable: 'a luxury of beauty, not of rarity, is what we need!' 'There is one aim: inwardly and outwardly the perfect harmony. There is one danger: snobbism, dilletantism, affection, combining in caddishness.' This was a programme which, except for fundamental rejection of decoration, De Roos could very well have affirmed, just as the following rule: 'If examples are to be followed, they firstly would be less German, more English, and among these less the works from the Kelmscott or Vale presses, but from the Doves Press.' The real difference lay in the preference of good text reproduction rather than attractive book-form; De Roos put that accent differently. Van Krimpen's principles of later years can already be found in the first phase of De Zilverdistel.

Greshoff started in 1912 a small monthly for book-lovers, under the name *De Witte Mier* (The White Ant), the inspiration for which came from Hans von Weber's *Zwiebelfisch*. The second volume is remarkable because of the prompt change from Genzsch Antiqua to the brand new Dutch Medieval and its fine title-page (plate 15), which is probably Van Krimpen's first work, including the vignette. *De Witte Mier* wished 'to try and work continuously for the generalisation of pure concepts of the demands of beauty of form which can be made and therefore must be made for the book.' A recent communication from Greshoff to the present author says: 'In that initial period both Van Krimpen and I were very orthodox. We detested everything which resembled symbolism or ornament. We wanted to make a beautiful book entirely apart from the connection with the text. This appears clearly from the book series 'Palladium', for which Van Krimpen designed a uniform layout for the most divergent texts. From the very beginning I myself pressed him in that direction as much as I could.'

Van Royen was a typical representative of that generation, in the Netherlands and elsewhere, who in their development were struck by the ideals of the 'nineties. The fervency of their idealism, the purity of their intentions and their anti-materialistic and firm attitude caused them great difficulties in the pro-materialistic society before 1918. It ruined some of them and mentally injured others for the rest of their lives; however, the struggle shaped the strongest—among them Van Royen—into leaders and reformers of an exceptional status. They combined a natural capacity for leadership and the urge for action with a universal artistic interest and almost aggressive spirituality, that weighed every human being, every object or event for ethical and aesthetical values to extremes. Such inexorably high aims and scrupulous criticism of details resulted in obtaining the best from their collaborators, if these did not take flight because of the scrupulous philosophic consideration given to the most normal things. In our days such reformers would be accepted even less. We find people such as Cobden-Sanderson, or Edward Johnston, egocentric, tyrannic phantasts (with every respect for the purity and power of their work), because they did not have the least consideration for the reality of society or for the human rights of their immediate assistants. (In 1914 Van Royen paid a visit to Cobden-Sanderson who was then seventy-four years old, 'a small, old man in a blue linen clerical garment embroidered with cream-coloured silk flowers.' The encounter increased his admiration for the man who, disregarding Emery Walker, he considered as the real leader of Doves Press, just as most did, and not the least Cobden-Sanderson himself. His credo, 'The Ideal Book or Book Beautiful' finds in phrasing an echo in 'Over Boekkunst en De Zilverdistel', Van Eyck's and Van Royen's programme of 1916, the first work composed in the 'Silvertype' which De Roos designed for the press and which itself owes a great deal to the Doves-type.) Van Royen was great because he combined an idealism such as those English people had with the 'Weltgewandtheit' of his activities as a very able and productive secretary-general of

PTT (the Dutch Post, Telegraph and Telephone Service), whose influence covered the whole government policy as regards living art.

Van Royen's ideas made a Herculean labour of design work. He had the ability to do it and to get it out of his assistants, but the propagandistic effect of his declaration of principles would have had a negative effect outside this circle. In this De Roos's influence was much greater, first of all because in his type specimens and the house journal of the Typefoundry Amsterdam he gave immediately-imitable models and understandable observations; he also lectured to craftsmen's typographical study groups. Furthermore he organised suggestive exhibitions of which the one for the society *Art for the People*, showing good and bad typography, in the Stedelijk Museum in 1913, was one of the best examples. It could convince the practical man that he, too, had tasks and opportunities.

From 1913 on Van Royen gradually took the greater part in the production of De Zilverdistel; from 1916 on he printed himself on the hand-press and in 1919 the last products appeared. An interruption followed, also because he wanted to be entirely his own master; in 1923 he began again on his own under the name of Kunera-press, the last printing of which he achieved shortly before his martyr's death in the concentration camp in Amersfoort (1942).

If one surveys Van Royen's production in Zilverdistel and Kunera, prepared and achieved with immense care and effort, the question arises whether these efforts had a proportionate effect. Was it fully realised by the satisfaction it gave the makers and a small circle of like-minded people? As has been stated, Van Royen had an esoteric and over-strung artistic side—that of his declaration of principles, of his printings in Lucien Pissarro's Disteltype, of his drawn titles, initials and vignettes (which are much wilder than De Roos—castigated 'decorative'—ever considered proper). With that he retreated so far from reality and into defensive positions within which nothing but harmony with the universe would reign, that others necessarily felt themselves excluded. The ordinary man (and not only the dumb) could answer similar claims to beauty only with a 'well, if this has to be art of the book it is not for me'. It is not accidental that for their private presses Van Royen and De Roos used the names of 'Zilverdistel' (Silver Thistle) and 'Meidoorn' (Hawthorn, literally in Dutch, May-thorn), and in doing so protected the charm of Silver and May with thistle and thorn. This was partly self-defence, partly revenge towards the wicked world. Van Krimpen, whose typography only allowed of an olympian rest, could unfortunately sublimate neither disappointment nor asperity in his work.

It can be put thus: the in a dual sense exclusive printing in Disteltype and Maythorn were the conditions under which Van Royen could realise the limpidity of Van Schendel's *Maneschijn* in Silvertype (1927, plate 18) and the dynamism of his numerous interventions in art, and De Roos both the pure happiness in his drawings of landscapes and the answers to the demands of typefoundry practice. As books they had sometimes many, sometimes few merits; as models in a period when one had to produce with machine paper and machine composition on cylinder presses with automatic feeding, they were valueless. What they represented in use of material and layout could in no way be translated into terms of normal publishers' practice. Only as examples of striving after beauty without compromise could they inspire those who, as practical printers and publishers (principally by mechanical means), hoped to raise the standards of the commercial book.

It was not so much an ideal but an economic necessity which led to the acceptance of the machine in Holland. What Francis Meynell (at the Nonesuch Press) in England pursued (and achieved), remains stuck here in contempt of, and fright for, the machine, partly based on Morris tradition, partly on real deficiencies. About 1920, when after the war Van Krimpen, Nypels and Stols and many other designers, printers and publishers wanted to work with fresh impetus and courage, the idea of 'machine' meant nothing positive. Ideologically the machine was the inhuman principle, that had just caused immense war-disasters and in the themes of art had now taken the place once occupied by the devil. In the course of the 'twenties this concept was more and more connected with an apparently brutal demolition by embittered communists and nihilists, who wanted to reject beauty in favour of such idols as efficiency (behind which nothing else seemed to be hidden than the opportunism of the fastest mass-production to appease the proletariat), or Dada, the 'Umwertung aller Werte', from which, along mysterious ways, a new beauty of honesty would have to grow—for people such as De Roos and Van Royen almost a personal insult: was this the artists' gratitude for every noble thing that had been pursued since 1890? The machine, that also meant smooth, characterless paper; ugly types composed too widely; grey half-tone blocks from vulgar photos; cylinder presses which did not leave time for good inking and even printing, and were capable of handling paper only if it were dead.

It is nevertheless significant that the youngest generation did not start off with hand-presses, private type faces and hand-made paper, but with cylinder-presses, trade types and stock papers, albeit with the ideal purpose of producing something which was good enough for the élite, hoping it would also become usual to the public. In the van stood Jan van Krimpen (1892–1958), Charles Nypels (1895–1952) and Alexander Stols (born in 1900).

Van Krimpen had paid homage in his initial period to the German neo-Biedermeier and had, of course, also been influenced by De Roos; however, with his choice of the workmanlike Caslon type for the series of 'Palladium' which he produced with Greshoff, Jacques Bloem and Jan van Nijlen as editors from 1920 onwards, his attitude towards De Roos and Van Royen was determined: the reader might not notice the typographic design; at the most he might wonder afterwards why he just had been able to read so pleasantly. With this, directives had been fixed (since then also popularised by Stanley Morison and Beatrice Warde) to which Van Krimpen stuck, except when the splendid historical types of Joh. Enschedé & Zonen at his disposal tempted or compelled him to produce something which was not only to be read but also to be seen. However, he gradually denied himself even that. Starting from a tacit supposition Van Krimpen, within its limits, almost achieved perfection. He died at the peak of his ability, his fame and his influence, embittered and disappointed, also as craftsman, because he had not succeeded in realising all his ideals, and because he saw them infringed all the time—as he thought, through misunderstanding. This tacit supposition was that the typographer makes books from good texts for interested and educated readers. However, if one of these conditions is lacking, an 'invisible typography' is no longer efficient and then even Van Krimpen's extreme concession—decorative lettering, for a single heading—can only rarely save the day.

The simplicity which is the outward characteristic of Van Krimpen's deft equilibrium between format, kind of paper, type area, choice of type and other book components, suited very well the desire for the cheapest mass-production which is natural to every publisher; the development of some foolproof formulas for a smooth automatic production is in fact included in Morison's, Warde's and Van Krimpen's rules for book typography. On the basis of these rules they would not be able to maintain that a standard typography of say Baskerville 9/10 point, 20 ems wide, could not be used for three-quarters of all books. Fortunately Van Krimpen himself added a number of types to all the available good ones and he made something different of each book. However, opposed to the beneficial influence that Van Krimpen exercised on Dutch book typography, there is the suggestion of his simplicity for the easy-going who think the inconspicuous, the acceptable things, suffice. Amongst people with taste this is a safe standard; what is ugly hits them and is consequently unfit for purpose. Outside the élite it makes people surrender to insensibility;

the rule has no built-in regulator which, when standards are lowered, opens the valve for a higher quality of form.

With this we already deal with the final phase of the development which started with Kalf. What as 'inconspicuous, acceptable' imitation of Van Krimpen shows dangerous aspects in our time, is exemplary compared with the routine work of around 1920. In those intermediate forty-five years enormous work was done of a missionary character internally, with exhibitions, lectures, articles, trade schooling, professional study groups (union organised for craftsmen), competitions, model publications and so on; many good-willing designers and producers made great efforts to advance bibliophilic and trade publications, the organisational work (the establishment of joint employer-employee and special interest groups) was intensified and extended in order to lay a foundation for a sound economic, social, technical and aesthetic development. De Roos had convinced all those involved of the fact that a Dutch book typography could exist again; the point was whether each individual thought he already practised that art, still had to pursue it, or could neglect it as not being applicable to him. Everybody was compelled to take sides and examine their position. It also meant that besides De Roos other trends appeared, and even opponents. For twelve years he had been the indisputable key figure who embodied *the* improvement of typography; now he had supporters, but also adversaries who wanted to break away from his style to enter new ways. De Roos must have felt this (although never mentioning it) as a desertion in the middle of the battle, as is the case with all pioneers who have to experience insubordination before the army is well exercised and the victory has yet to be won. Whilst the people still lacked much for their primary needs, the architect Wijdeveld arrived (Frank Lloyd Wright's paladin in the Netherlands) who, in his magazine *Wendingen*, brought decoration *ad absurdum* and with his expensive, spectacular typographic constructions turned the heads of the élite. This unreadable, wilful typography brought the whole printing art into discredit with the ordinary, reasonable public, so the reformers had reason to fear. Then there was a Van Doesburg in his magazine *Stijl* making fun—or so it seemed—of everything that good principles of construction, pure use of material and harmony in form required. His dadaistic nonsense—and those crazy chairs of Rietveld—were a stab in the back, at the moment when, with all hands on deck, a start had to be made with the reconstruction after the catastrophe of 1914–1918. The evil did not bring its own destruction. Van Doesburg was followed by hotheads such as Piet Zwart and Paul Schuitema, who, without a good typographical education, plunged in and made crude and

269

noisy things for Kabelfabriek and Van Berkel. All architects with bold façade plans and ideas about art and technics, but unable to do simple detailed work; nothing of theirs seemed to be of use to the normal publisher's book.

Now we know that Wijdeveld's typography and the whole 'line-movement' (excessive use of brass rules) expired of its own weaknesses; that Zwart's and Schuitema's ideas in a mellower and suppler form resulted in a happy reform of picture books (for looking at rather than 'reading') and of advertising typography, and, refreshing good book traditions, in a revival of the book as such. However, in the beginning it seemed that the very principles of typography would be affected; it stiffened De Roos in his purpose. He did not realise—and did not, humanly speaking, have to welcome such opposition—that Zwart, Schuitema and Kiljan tried to fill gaps which his own sound and happy typography left open on his left wing, just as Van Krimpen was to do for the right wing. The fermenting post-war years could not only be sound and happy. With his Dutch Medieval typography De Roos had started a style phase which he maintained until the beginning of his Heuvelpers prints (1928). This form system expressed an ideal, but this ideal could not remain valid for all those who, in the 'roaring twenties' searched for their own truth. Finally, it could not longer remain valid for De Roos himself; he rounded it off and corrected it with printing from his own press in the bitter-sour Meidoorn type; work which just lacks all joyous certitude. However, it remained an excellent expression for everything which was human and reasonable, gay, serious and hopeful at the time.

A printing firm which really took the trouble to produce exemplary work was then still an exception. The printer did not see any profit in this, or pretended not to, when in reality fear of his apparent lack of ability made him afraid of collaboration with exacting designers. It is all the more remarkable that two master-printers' sons of Maastricht decided, the one shortly after the other, to concentrate on book typography: first Charles Nypels, who started as an apprentice with De Roos in 1917 and who soon began to publish. Five years afterwards Alexander Stols, also five years younger than Nypels, who started his publisher's career as a student in Amsterdam, also initially with the types of De Roos, later leaning towards those of Van Krimpen. They were both highly cultured and passionately interested in books and authors, from the middle-ages up to the current experimental authors; moreover, born in Limburg in the deep south of Holland, they had a special affinity for Belgium and France. Because of this they emphasised the belles-lettres element in our book typography on the level set by the founders of the Zilverdistel. As they

were in contrast to De Roos, Van Royen and Van Krimpen, the only independent businessmen, they ran the greatest financial risks as well; they had to pay
for their ideals, suffering many losses and personal distress. If Nypels' production for some decades is already respectable, Stols's output is even much
larger. If one adds this to the output of Zilverdistel, Kunera and Van Krimpen,
one finds in thirty years a number of well- to excellently-executed books
from Dutch and foreign literature which is unique in our history—though we
can also boast of a glorious record in the seventeenth and eighteenth centuries.

The main thought in appraisal of Stols' production today, and of his four
colleagues when they died, is the doubt whether it had a positive influence. In
general the remarks about Van Royen's production again apply, but on a larger scale. The literary refinement of the texts and the financial difficulties inherent in the production did not encourage other printers and publishers to
jump on the bandwagon. However, it bred the idea that good printers and
publishers should do something for the beautiful book, if possible. This is the
basis on which book typography could develop after 1945.

Nypels, a mercurial bohemian, who with all his irresponsibilities never denied his origin, was the more impetuous; he shows the greater differences in
quality, but also produced most of the new discoveries. That is why he looked
more to De Roos, who himself differed from Van Krimpen in the above way.
He flirted, in Maastricht aided by his devoted master-printer J. W. Veltman,
with Dada in witty follies, plunged into Flemish expressionism and came
back again to De Roos's quietest pages; soon after he underlined the non-
conformism of the twenties with further bold ventures. In the publishing firm
'Het Spectrum' he was able to launch many good things in his later years; he
also trained Aldert Witte there and imbued him for ever with something of
his own enthusiasm and audacity.

Stols was a dare-devil in the size and level of his publishing production, less
in its typography, which he intentionally kept within the limits of simplicity
and optimal readability. But this simplicity always strikes a friendly note,
often emphasised by an initial in fresh red or blue. Also in the twenties (for Van
Krimpen, Nypels, and Stols, the most lively years, in harmony with the spirit
of time and their own youth) Stols remained more measured than Nypels, as
appears from a comparison of two of their illustrated works (plates 16 and 17).

After thirty years of constructive activities the results of the new Dutch
book typography could be seen, and from 1920 onwards exhibitions could be
constantly held. In 1925 for the first time a selection of the fifty best produced
books was made (repeated in 1926, 1929 and 1930/31, after that annually from

1948). In England, whence the impulse for a revival of Dutch book typography had come, a survey by De Roos of what had been achieved appeared in *Modern Book Production* (*The Studio*) and in the Printing Number of *The Times*, both in 1929 and by Van Krimpen in *The Fleuron VII* in 1930. In the same year, the First Edition Club held an exhibition in London 'One hundred Dutch books'. Other surveys by De Roos were published in *Imprimatur I*, 1930, *Buchkunst I*, 1931 and *The Dolphin I*, 1933.

However, in the meantime the economic crisis had developed which reduced bibliophilic production to a minimum, or made it completely impossible. The Kunera and Heuvel presses were stopped; Nypels left the family business and kept going, much as did Stols, with all sorts of work in or for Dutch, Belgian and French combinations. The positive side of this crisis is a not superfluous re-orientation of the mechanically produced trade-book, which in fact had formed the centre of Stols's activity from an early stage. Furthermore the rise of the dynamic, functional typography, associated with Stijl and Bauhaus and working with sans serifs, photographs and smooth paper of standard sizes, had a lasting effect on the more traditional trend and its use of mild, hand-composed garaldes (old styles), printed for a small circulation on imitation hand-made paper, and illustrated with a variety of graphic ideas. This also broke the driving force of the idealism of the 'Big Five' and their following. After the Second World War it came to life again in the Foundation 'De Roos', a bibliophile publishers' society, founded by Ch. Nypels, Chr. Leeflang and G. M. van Wees, and named after the great pioneer. The publications of 'De Roos', however, are handled on purpose as a correction to the sliding scale of quality of commercial book production, and in order to maintain standards, and the link with manual graphics, encouraging experiment; not necessarily as an ideal for every right-minded publisher to pursue.

The link between S. H. De Roos' mild, traditional typography on the one hand and the ardent, dynamic typography of the Zwart group on the other, was only established by their pupils after the war; personal incompatibilities and differences in outlook prevented an earlier approach between the mutual leaders and their work.

The years of occupation 1940–1945 resulted in a not insignificant addition to book art, arising from very different reasons: the desire to defend mental freedom and beauty, to support artists materially and to offer them possibilities for expression, and partly also as an investment of money for which there was no use and which was in danger. Suddenly the situation arose that the book had to be expensive (supporting artists of the resistance movement, covering new risks, manual work, graphics, expensive materials, small circulations), but also could be expensive because there were enough buyers. Illustration had never flourished in Holland. The thrifty Dutch nature is inclined to consider it as an extravagance—for one can just as well understand and enjoy the literary text without 'an explanatory picture'—and it is soon thought that illustration has been added to make the appearance of the book more attractive in order to increase sales. This is an insult to the literary reader for whom the text is paramount. Nor had the three eldest of the Big Five stimulated the use of illustration. De Roos, because, acting on his principles of unity, only accepted two-dimensionally conceived letterpress-illustrations, complementary with letterpress-text, (so, no lithography, etching or metal engraving with relief effects); neither did he practise illustration himself. Van Royen's demands for visual and mental harmony between illustration and aspect and content of text were so high that there was hardly any graphic artist in Holland who could and would meet them, and certainly not in the period when designers rejected the community art of the 'nineties as dull, symbolic nonsense and really wanted again the individual autonomy of ardent expression. Van Krimpen rejected pictorial illustrations entirely in favour of a 'pure typography', which should not dare to introduce subjective interpretation of text between author and reader. Nypels on the contrary liked to illustrate his books, but according to De Roos's principles almost exclusively with woodcuts and drawings as line-blocks; Henri Jonas, Josef Cantré, W. J. Rozendaal, Otto van Rees, Charles Eyck, Hermann Paul, Victor Stuyvaert amongst others worked for him. Stols threw his nets even wider, over all graphical techniques and national and international artists; for example the work of Alexandre Alexeieff and John Buckland Wright placed his Dutch publications in the Paris 'éditions de luxe' and the London 'fine books' categories; they enlarged the horizon for our book producers and readers, insofar as they had not yet been informed and influenced as a result of the relatively high interest of the Dutch public in foreign books.

The flame which Nypels and Stols had kept alive in the 'twenties and 'thirties, burned more strongly in the years of occupation. A new generation of draughtsman and graphic artists had a chance; older artists gained new impulses from the battle of the resistance, but in illegal publications also the opportunity to realise ideas freely, which previously had found little response and consequently no financial backing.

The Groningen painter-printer Hendrik Nicolaas Werkman (1882–1945) completed work in the years of war which, started twenty years earlier in an expressionist and dadaistic circle, partly unknown, was partly classified as in the lunatic fringe of national printing art. A few prints and one big work, such as *Het Boek van Trijntje Soldaats* (1928, plate 19) had also been appreciated in broader circles. His most daring (free graphics almost) pamphlets and prints such as *The Next Call* (separate issues since 1923) and the resistance publication of *De Blauwe Schuit* (from 1940 onwards) were too exclusive (Werkman himself hid them under the bushel for too long) to exercise, during his life, the great influence they had after 1945. The fact that they got a world-wide reputation is due to Sandberg, who devoted an exhibition to them at the end of 1945, shortly after his appointment as director of the Amsterdam Stedelijk Museum. 'There is no question of disregarding Werkman in the usual sense of the word; however, for years he was judged wrongly and partly underestimated. Sandberg and the Rev. F. R. A. Henkels were the first to fully understand the value of the printer's hobby, actually: the purely individual character of his creative power', to quote his biographer Hans van Straten. (*Hendrik Nicolaas Werkman, de drukker van het paradijs*. Amsterdam, Meulenhoff, 1963.)

Van Royen and Werkman, both of a gentle but firm character, who in the margin of their profession exercised the art of printing, in order to be able to communicate their highest ideals; both killed by the occupier, not so much because they committed acts of sabotage for which there was the heaviest penalty, but put out of the way (and then sacrificed by executioners) because their very nature so clearly opposed every mental and moral corruption; each of them representing, however, the pole of another cultural activity. These are the poles which Dick Dooijes chose as title for his survey of the ten years of Dutch typography, 1945–1955, as 'Tradition and Renewal' (*Traditie en Vernieuwing, Tien jaar Nederlandsche drukkunst 1945–1955*, The Hague 1959). Here one term summarises the protection and further development of the good things in our cultural heritage, and the other one the creation of new values and truths for those needs which the progress of mankind creates. Maintenance of what had been acquired and preparation of what was new against powers which menaced both, were principles which of course one was all the more strongly aware of in the years of occupation. Tradition with Van Krimpen in his designs for the Five-pound press of the publisher A. A. Balkema and the linguist W. Gs. Hellinga with classic texts in the finest classical arrangement. Renewal by Sandberg who with the Amsterdam printer Frans Duwaer (executed later) made the first series of his 'Experimenta Typografica', in which the type, now stripped of its sense, appears as a surprising figure or, super-charged, acquires an unknown power of expression. His post-war museum catalogues exercised a greater direct influence because of their nature and large circulation. With his choice of materials and colours and his virtuosity in contrast of photographs, text blocks and of paper, he showed completely new ways to book design.

Another tradition and renewal was imported by refugee artists from Germany: Henri Friedlander, Susanne Heynemann, Helmut Salden, Otto Treumann. They brought a tradition of conscientious craftsmanship and experience of what a pursuance of ideals can achieve, particularly in commercial publishing; in their new country they assisted in the struggle for a restoration of cultural values which had suffered under nazism or directly from the same mentality that had promoted the growth of national-socialism. In doing so they brought renewal as well: by a strong injection of inspired professional skill founded on well-considered principles. The occupation had also increased the tendency to look for what binds rather than what separates. The younger generation of designers was less personally involved in the emotionally coloured convictions which pre-war leaders had elevated to axioms in their period of battle; of these leaders, now having the status of 'grand old men', one admired everywhere the principles which had appeared to be fruitful and their general merits contributing towards the art of Dutch printing. The war had taught the traditionalist how necessary renewal was; revolutionaries how essential maintenance of good cultural achievements was for an early attainment of a better art and society. Questions such as symmetry versus asymmetry, romans against sans serifs, manual graphics versus photography, manual work versus machine-production, appeared to have lost their sense for the greater part; the answer was simple: both, according to circumstances.

It is not yet easy to describe the twenty years of post-war book typography, and certainly not within the scope of this essay. The large increase in number and standard of consciously and competently designed publications, the great number of people involved in them and the multifarious solutions they found —which result together in a series of continuous variants between the extremes of tradition and experiment—make it extremely difficult to draw some broad conclusions. Dooijes's study mentioned before describes the most important tendencies and personalities up to 1955 and one can continue on these lines up till now; the illustrated catalogues of the selections of the 'fifty best books' provide facts about top production, together with judgement on each book separately, and about total annual production.

Dutch book typography after 1945 as a whole is distinguishable from that of before the war by the much larger scale on which specialised book designers are engaged, and thus by the much more purposeful and conscientious application of the type. If formerly a commission to a professional artist was something which the publisher only permitted for prestige editions, which could not be attained by use of photographs, coated papers, format or artistic binding, whereas the publisher only 'discussed' his other books with the printer, nowadays artistic and especially commercial considerations often cause professional designers to be charged with the entire production. Ultimately it is cheaper for the publisher, because he can spend his time more usefully, and printer, engraver and binder do not want to be left with all the difficulties which the publisher formerly omitted to solve; production goes more smoothly and moreover the result is better. Competition forces one not to lag behind in this respect.

The book designer does not limit himself to choice of type, format, type-size and area, paper, material, blocking and title-page (with possible addition of ornaments). He also prepares the copy, does the page make-up and gives detailed composing instructions. He covers every detail down to a thin space, for he does not seek his beauty (as did private-press printers to a considerable degree) in impressive sizes, uncommon types and precious materials, but mainly in the provision of an absolutely uninterrupted course of the reading process in which no irregularity may hinder the reader. It means that he chooses types which in practice prove to be very clear and familiar, pithy and harmonious in form, and allowing mechanical composition with a full range of sorts. There are not so many types which meet these requirements; therefore, the limited choice leads to a certain monotony, unless the designer introduces variety in type-size, length of line, leading and number of lines—something in which Van Krimpen was a master (plate 21). From his ideas, developed independently but refined and consolidated as a result of contacts with typographers in and around Monotype—in particular Stanley Morison—our book designers learned much. Also with his fine calligraphy based on models of Italian Renaissance and Dutch baroque he formed a school. These elements—dry, precise typography and calligraphic elegance for titling and lettering on binding—were supplemented by Salden with a clever choice of material from the tradition of Insel-Verlag, S. Fischer and Jacob Hegner, and with here and there, a grotesque flourish inspired by Schneidler's obsessive letter phantasies. Having combined

276

these in a personal style, he created a new genre: the small thin-paper editions of collected works for publisher G. A. van Oorschot (plate 20).

The point on which many designers do not agree with Van Krimpen is the strict inconspicuousness of composed matter as a whole. For continuous matter, stories, declarations and so on, his method is gladly accepted, but all elements which do not belong to these, or which can be separated from them, are used as contrast to enliven the page and to support optically the development of the text. If there are no titles, introductions, marginal or footnotes which are suitable, any other elements such as page numbers, are emphasised in opposition to the solid text. The fact that then their optical value is no longer in proportion to their significance in the context, is considered less harmful for the reader than the boredom which would arise otherwise (and which Van Krimpen, being of the opinion that he worked for interested people, did not fear).

The sacred margin proportions are maintained as long as there are no objections, but if a practical insertion of elements added to the text makes it preferable, the text areas are placed in a page where it happens to suit and where a new balance can be created. For example Dick Elffers drew up a layout scheme for *Hundred years of typefounding in Amsterdam* (1951) which has become very popular: the text in two columns at the centre foot of a double-page, so that in the broad head- and side-margins remaining illustration, marginal notes, etc. could always find a place if they occurred. But no matter if they were there or not, the composition remained firmly founded on the text areas (plate 22).

In short, book typography became much richer in contrast than before; the effects are applied intentionally according to the functional requirements of the book—by whom, or for what purpose, they were originated does not matter. A designer works at one time in a classical, symmetric, sober, intellectual way, or in a dynamic, asymmetric way, all stops out, for the visual and even emotional effect, at another time. All specific effects are strongly emphasised because it is thought that, if an absolute unity cannot be maintained, an effort to diminish disharmony by reducing the differences, is senseless; in such cases it is better to increase contrasts and to harmonise in a higher unity.

The army of typographic designers, under pressure from the post-war speed of reconstruction and the wish to test its talents in new conquests, searches continuously for objectives from which something different can be made. The idea from previous generations that each of their few achievements should be able to serve as a model for everyone and thus require time to mature, has made way to scepticism about the duration of the life of printed matter, and consequently also to a state of unrest which needs to seize opportunities before it is too late—or somebody else makes use of them. This has not yet made the design work superficial—although that happens of course—but it does make it more intense, which again increases the violence of expression; if it is not possible to obtain an outlet for this aim inside the book, it tackles its exterior, or else publicity and advertisement typography.

Printers and publishers offer designers more opportunities for spectacular work: for the pleasure of adventuring among so much printed matter which cannot bear more than a cheap standard typography; for the prestige value as well, which the brilliant pieces bring with them in the struggle for national and international market expansion. Printers and process-engravers set off typographical fireworks annually in the Christmas numbers of *Drukkersweek-blad-Autolijn*, which is intended to be regarded with respect also in export markets; in any case it gives a number of designers and producers the urge to do their utmost. It gives print-buyers (more than formerly, a selection from the top achievements of the pioneers) the notion that printed matter can be something comfortable and beautiful; also something better not designed by themselves, but better left to professional designers. Making these ideas acceptable to the public was the aim pursued by printing trade organisations through still other means, such as the bibliographic atlas *Copy and print in the Netherlands* by W. Gs. Hellinga and others (1963, plate 28), in which Alexander Verberne, with Joh. Enschedé & Zonen, offered real models of the art of composing to the national and international world of publishers and scientists. It is typical of our time that Verberne, who here orders the most complicated text with an almost superhuman self-discipline, extreme artistic subtlety and technical precision, could at the same time evoke the most phantastic and evocative images in the house-magazine *Range* of Philips Tele-Communication Industries. In so doing he reaches the extreme possibilities, but others also vary static book typography with dynamic advertising design. The feeling developed for the specific nature of word and image (in the way in which the public receives them and in which typography has to respond to that) has particularly enriched the layout of picture books in Holland: of illustrated books for popular-scientific, art-historical and public-relations purposes, of anniversary books, museum catalogues and other publications in which the reader's attention has to be engaged, directed and retained. With the growth of this genre, which with all the means of design and printing techniques and clever psychological understanding, compels the reader to think, feel and wish in the way the authors want, a field has been opened to the art of printing of which Derkinderen with his *Gijsbreght* still only saw the possibility. A good example of such a means to an end, in which the reader from stage to stage is carried along with just what he can and must absorb, is offered by Hans Barvelink in his typography of *The Netherlands Grow* (1936, plate 27). There it appears, as fits in with the nature of the book, in a rational, disciplined form. Elffers (besides Sandberg the first who mastered problems of scale, depth, horizon, tone-value, etc., forced by the combination of heterogeneous illustrations, see his *The World of Van Gogh*, 1953) produced—just like Jurriaan Schrofer—several of such books which force an immediate sensation on the reader in a much stronger way.

Now that since 1945 so many publishers, printers and individuals promote the art of the book by commissioning many able designers, and by the way these books are actually executed, bibliophily is not impaired to such an extent that there is a reason for a revival of either the private-press movement or of bibliophilic societies in the old-fashioned sense. That is why the 'Vereeniging voor Druk- en Boekkunst' ceased its activities; it considered that the original aim, if not fully attained, was sufficiently promoted by commercial book producers, and this with financial means which a relatively small group of idealistic booklovers cannot provide. Some other bibliophile societies and private presses stopped as well, or produce at longer intervals. If they still exist it is mainly because an amateur has pleasure in doing things himself. They do not now produce any pioneering examples. Only the Foundation 'De Roos', now directed by Chr. Leeflang and C. J. Asselbergs, continues to produce some books regularly each year for its 175 members. They emphasise what an active graphical industry necessarily neglects if it specialises in strictly industrial production methods, namely, manual work in paper, illustration, printing and binding. If everything that is unusual and rare is excluded from graphic materials, and everything that requires individual care for each copy is rejected by production departments because national and private economy cannot tolerate any disturbances in its effort for a maximum production, it would make us a lot poorer. In order to be able to understand and to accept in the trade-book, smooth paper, plain types, slick photographs and sober binding, we must be able to see and to feel in strongly concentrated form the converse from time to time. Commercial and industrial production sometimes creates these compensations—thanks to the artists, who are the guardians of our mental health—with its own means of mass production, but the limitation is just there. It is not the same whether one prints rough woodcuts directly on rough paper, or reproduces such prints on smooth paper. For that reason this manual work should continue as an indispensable correction on the verge of the industry, paid for by those who realise that it is of vital importance to industry and who will not romanticise it, from nostalgia or as a protest, as the only real art. In this sense a bibliophilic organisation such as the Foundation 'De Roos' retains its right of existence. The fact that it does not always attain perfection can also be ascribed to the overburdening of the good designers and producers; that it does not open up more new horizons is not only the fault of the members who long for the old-time glory of the Big Five, but is also due to the great experimental activity of the industry itself.

However, one danger has to be mentioned which menaces both manual work and industry: a mixture of the two principles. If a Foundation 'De Roos' has to accept less than the best because industrial equipment cannot provide it with hand-finished quality any more, it loses its right of existence. On the other hand: if the printing trade only three-quarters industrialises itself, and is left with undigested phases of manual work in its organisation and technique, quality undoubtedly decreases—the handwriting has already appeared on the wall.

Nevertheless, is it not a good thing that normal trade practice already produces so many splendid things, and searches so actively for new possibilities, that the few idealists can hardly find something still needing to be done, which trade practice has not yet discovered and taken up? He who shows too openly this satisfaction is soon called a superficial optimist. But it is ungrateful and unwise not to dare to say that Dutch book typography is in a period of prosperity that has not occurred for two centuries. It is as dangerous to rest on one's laurels as to deny that the good things are good.

There is a field in which typographical forms are maintained, which no longer conform with either the way in which the reader absorbs the text in reality or the typographical possibilities which have been developed in other fields for similar problems. It is the field of those text books, the material of which is a chain of short, relatively independent arguments or explanations, whether or not with notes as deviations from the main line of the text, and with pictures as the text, or as an explanation of the text. This kind of book could be absorbed in a much easier and more assimilable way if the principles were applied of a freer form of make-up, in such a way that the student grasps those elements one by one with ever fresh attention (but with the correct feeling for their mutual values)—and in so doing does not read in words what he can see in pictures or get from pictures. In short, it is an optical pre-fabrication—or pre-digestive operation.

This necessary typographical re-thinking is hindered by two difficulties—apart from blind conservatism or laziness: such books have to be written with that typographical form in mind (there is not yet a publisher or designer who does teach this to an author) and furthermore, such typographical editorial work requires an expenditure of time and money in preparation and execution, which is not considered worthwhile because these books can be more easily produced, and sold, with the present cheap, straightforward typography. However, the idea is penetrating that an efficient use of public money for education requires that the method of teaching or learning be no longer left to the accidental capabilities and goodwill of teacher or student. This idea will also open the eyes to the fact that the traditional school- and text-book too often obliges each individual reader to systemise and grade for himself, whereas the author and publisher should have done this beforehand. The fact that abroad little or nothing has been done yet in this field (except something in American 'self-tutoring devices') does not exempt Dutch book typography from tackling the task soon.

It has been a long journey from Hieronymus van Alphen on the hand-press to the pocket-book which comes from the automated production equipment in ten thousands of copies, and from Maaskamp's hand-coloured engravings to the electronically corrected and engraved four-colour prints. This progress —for it is a progress if new needs can be met in such a way—has been fought for by printers, publishers and readers who impressed upon themselves and each other that it could still be done better, but who could draw force in doing so from the recognition of what they had already achieved. It is to be hoped that those real book-lovers in the Netherlands remain so active that the results will be worth describing again in 150 years' time.

Willy Rotzler

BOOK PRINTING IN
SWITZERLAND

The history of a country's printing is never simply that of a trade which soon turns into a profession and, in our own time, a great industry that is an important part of our economy. Printing has always been closely connected with other developments, and its history can only be understood in these wider terms. The essence of printing is that it is both the servant and the disseminator of words, and as a result its fate is intimately tied to the vagaries of the intellectual climate. The word has always been an intellectual and a political weapon, and so printing has often been very directly linked with political developments. It has proved an effective weapon in the fight for material and intellectual freedom, and has been used to suppress freedom; it can disseminate lies as easily as truth.

Ever since its invention, printing has justly been regarded as an art and not merely a trade, and its times of greatness and its doldrums can usually be seen to have a close correlation with the general state of the arts. It is usually possible to tell from any single book not merely at what point in the history of book technology it was produced, but also the cultural climate, the political conditions and the current taste of the time. All these are reflected in the type, composition, ornaments in the form of initials or illustrations, and the cover. In other words, the history of printing of any town or country is part of its general history, throwing light on it, and unintelligible without it. Conversely, the history of printing and the appearance of print differ from place to place. This is still true today, in spite of the general pressure towards conformity; there are good reasons for it—books are produced by men, in spite of all rationalisation and mechanisation. And because even today printers see their books as more than characterless mass-products, they continue to impress them with the stamp of their individual personalities, both consciously and unconsciously. Though there is no merit in indulging a sense of identity that verges on chauvinism, an attitude that is out of date in an age of international alliances, it is worth preserving the local and regional differences that still survive: they show the individual's refusal to have his work ironed out to anonymity.

The history of printing in Switzerland reflects the fortunes of that small country in the heart of Western Europe. Switzerland's place as a point of contact between the North and the South, the East and West, her participation in the life of widely varying cultures, and her repeated role of providing a refuge for the forces of the spirit, for freedom and progress, can be seen embodied in her print. In every age, foreign printers, publishers, punch-cutters, book designers and, above all, authors have gone there to live. Their work, too, has combined fruitfully with native talent. Any nationalistic appraisal of Switzerland's book production would be absurd: she owes much of the best that she has produced to the fact that she was able to take—in order to give.

The invention and the spread of printing, especially book-printing, depended on a number of prior conditions; in Switzerland's case special circumstances have given her printing history its particular character.

In the first place, Switzerland is an amalgam of many small peoples and regions, each with its own culture and language. This amalgamation began with the founding of the Swiss Confederation in 1291. Further alliances and accessions resulted in the founding of the Federal State in 1848. If the varied—and, in the first centuries, bloody—history of Switzerland has to be expressed in a single formula, it is this: freedom-loving peoples from various valleys and small towns joined forces in order to remain outside the struggles and clutches of the great European powers. This meant that the Federal State never had a ruling sovereign's residence to act as a focal point and disseminating centre for its culture. On the contrary—one of the chief maxims of Swiss political thought is that in the Federation the individual need not give up his individuality. Thus both the communities and the twenty-two Cantons that constitute the Federation have preserved their autonomy to a great extent. The autonomy of individual communities is virtually the keystone of the country's political philosophy, and for that reason many spheres of public activity, such as culture and education, are regulated not federally, but by the cantons and the communities. The justification for this is that autonomy is the best guarantee in preserving the ethnic, religious, linguistic and cultural individuality of the various regions. Multiplicity within a wider uniformity is the basis of Switzerland's greatest achievements.

Switzerland has no metropolis, no single economic, political and cultural centre which draws all the talents towards itself and then re-disseminates it into the 'provinces'. The idea of the 'provinces' is alien to Swiss thinking. A number of large and small independent cultural centres exist side by side. Switzerland's culture in general is rooted in the monastic and city culture of the Middle Ages. A few important monasteries and a number of craft cities with their distinctive guilds shaped the cultural pattern, which is still perceptible today.

The monasteries were the places at which most books were written, and it is their methods of making books, and their need for books, that determined the origin of printing. The most important Swiss monastery, in this context, is St Gallen. It was founded by Irish missionaries in the seventh century, and in Carolingian times it was already famous as an educational centre and for its writing school. Its library still holds a notable collection of some 2,000 medieval manuscripts. But scriptoria and excellent libraries were also to be found elsewhere in Switzerland. The exchange of manuscripts between monasteries produced a considerable cultural flowering. Monastic learning produced not only philologists and literary scholarship, translators and authors, but greatly increased the demand for the handwritten book: a number of monasteries in Switzerland are among the first centres of printing, and some are known to have had presses within the monastery walls. The most interesting of these was at the Chorherrenstift at Beromünster; books dating back to 1470 survive from it. Another press appears to have operated at a Dominican monastery at Zurich c. 1480. But book production in the Middle Ages was not exclusively determined by monastic culture: the gothic tradition of chivalry also had a certain influence. The *Manessische Lieder-Handschrift* (Song MS), commissioned by the Zurich knight Rüdiger Manesse c. 1300, is a fine example of this other aspect of medieval culture.

The fact that printing took root early in Switzerland and rapidly led to major achievements must be kept in mind when considering the general heritage of the country's printing, for some of the most important centres of printing are still situated where the earliest printing offices stood. A number of them have some sort of direct or indirect link with an early printing workshop. Moreover, a consciousness among Swiss printers of their own fine heritage has had a stimulating influence on them at times of new departures and improvements in book design. When examining the beginnings of printing it is easy to become so preoccupied with the technical aspects of such a momentous invention that one ignores its cultural and economic determinants. Inventions may be the work of bold or brilliant individuals, but they usually come about as the result of far-reaching cultural and material circumstances. Printing was virtually an inevitable result of the great upsurge of economic and intellectual activity from the fourteenth century onwards and the increasing democratisation of the ownership of material riches and cultural necessities in the countries of Western Europe, of which the Rhine roughly formed the axis. Apart from monastic culture, which had a strong democratic element, it was in the cities that the desire for knowledge grew fastest, and with it the need for an independent, critical appraisal of the Church's traditional views of God and the world: in the cities of the late Middle Ages the intellectual freedom of the individual was being won. Craftsmen and, to a growing extent, merchants were bringing about an economic rise in the cities which not only made them increasingly independent of the aristocracy and the lords of the Church, but also boosted their self-confidence and developed the need for middle-class education on a broad basis, resulting in the founding of city schools and universities. This widespread and active desire for education corresponded to a growing need for educational tools—a demand which could hardly be met by laboriously produced handwritten books.

Attempts to expedite the manufacture of identical books in large numbers long preceded Gutenberg's invention. They began with the rationalisation of the writing-workshops, which were virtually turned into writing-factories. The principles of textile printing, practised in the Rhineland for centuries, pointed the way to new methods. The first half of the fifteenth century witnessed a great many attempts to mass-produce books—more than we know from the sparse evidence in surviving documents. Wood-block printing for devotional pictures, playing-cards and wallpaper embodies the principle of the block-book, which probably made its appearance around 1440 and survived for some time side by side with books produced with moveable type. Block-books were produced at Basle and the monastery of Einsiedeln. The use of punches too, long known to bell founders, mintmasters and goldsmiths, may have led to several attempts to produce books in various places. There is no doubt that around 1450 many inventive individuals were trying to develop ways of meeting the demand for books by rationalising their production. Book-printing was in the air, else Gutenberg's invention would not have been able to spread with such lightning speed through the Rhine towns in the face of all attempts to keep it a secret. By 1470 printing was already an established new craft in many places.

Switzerland's first printed book was probably produced at Basle, though the oldest known book, dated 1470, comes from Beromünster. Printing began at Basle in 1467–8 and developed so quickly that within a few years the Rhine town became one of the earliest centres of printing. There were two important reasons for this, still applicable by the time Basle had become an important publishing centre; firstly, the old cathedral town and free city on the elbow of the Rhine had for centuries played an important role. The Ecclesiastical Council that had taken place within its walls between 1431 and 1448 had given it a metropolitan allure. With the support of one of the participants in the Council, Enea Silvio Piccolomini, who had in the meantime become Pope Pius II, it was able to found a university in 1460. This young centre of learning, which soon gained international repute and attracted scholars and students from everywhere, gave the principal impetus towards the establishing of printing in Basle. The second factor, an economic one, was that that papermaking was begun during the Council's period. It soon became a formidable industry, and is still active today. It became not only one of Basle's economic keystones but also a predisposing factor for the flowering of printing in Basle between 1480 and 1530. The books themselves in turn became a major export for the rising merchant town. All the processes, from papermaking to publishing, rapidly took typical early capitalistic forms, and as a result Basle's publishing soon outstripped all competition from other towns, less well provided with funds for this purpose, with the exception of Paris and Venice. Basle's first book is a *Biblia latina*, printed *c.* 1468 by Berthold Ruppel of Hanau. This is the first book known to be printed with moveable type in Switzerland. It is set in a gothic-roman, the face initially used by Basle printers, based on the face used by Peter Schöffer of Mainz. One of the reasons for the rapid growth of printing in Basle was that compulsory guild-membership was abandoned. The names of seventy printers and journeymen between 1470 and 1500 are known. The city records even note a strike of journeymen in 1471. During the last decades of the fifteenth century, Basle with seventeen known and seven to eight anonymous printing workshops, became one of the leading centres of early printing. The contents and style of its incunabula show the influence of German printing on the one hand, and French and, most of all, Italian printing on the other. It was on these solid foundations of craft and style that the fine work done by the city's printers in the sixteenth century was based.

Not long after, other printing centres began to appear in Switzerland; some of them lasted only briefly; others became a permanent part of the long tradition of printing and publishing down to the present day. One of these is Geneva, which from 1478 onwards became a centre of printing and publishing second in importance only to Basle. Most of the early work here is devoted to theological and popular books in French. Zurich followed in 1480, though her printing only began to flower during the sixteenth century.

The second great era of printing in Switzerland began with the age of humanism and the Reformation—that is from the second decade of the sixteenth century onwards. In Basle the transition from the early printers to the humanist printer-publishers was almost imperceptible. Leading printers, authors and illustrators worked together in harmony, backed and stimulated by an international circle of scholars at the university; their cooperation resulted in some of the finest work in the history of printing. When Sebastian Brant, who taught in the faculty of law, published his famous *Stultifera navis* (Ship of Fools) with the printer Johannes Bergmann von Olpe, the latter was able to call on the young Albrecht Dürer to illustrate the book with his woodcuts. Johannes Amerbach, who had learned his trade with Koberger in Nuremberg, worked in Basle from 1475 and became the nucleus of a formidable circle of scholars. An important thinker, whose correspondence forms part of the basic doctrine of humanism, he developed the elegant roman type faces that replaced the gothic faces at Basle. He died in 1514, by which time his press had produced some seventy works of major importance in both design and content. Johannes Froben, who had come to Basle from Franconia, carried the work forward another step. The beauty of his books, in which he used magnificent types, earned him the reputation of a second Aldus Manutius, and 'a prince among printers'. Froben's books bear evidence of the importance of high-quality paper. Like Amerbach, Froben was at the centre of intellectual activities in his day. He printed the works of Erasmus of Rotterdam, who lived in his house, and he had connections with Hans Holbein the younger, whose woodcut designs, initials and title-pages contributed to the high artistic standard of Basle's books. Everything combined to make the town one of the leading centres of humanism north of the Alps, and later, of the Reformation. Adam Petri and his son Henrik worked at Basle contemporaneously with Froben, and after him. The printing office of the publishing house of Schwabe, direct descendant of Henrik Petri's press, still uses his device. Basle's printing tradition was continued well into the sixteenth century by Petri, who issued Sebastian Münster's *Cosmography* in 1541 and the work of Cratander, Oporin and others. Oporin's edition in 1543 of Vesalius' *De Humani corporis fabrica* is an outstanding achievement of mid sixteenth-century printing.

In the meantime, after several false starts, printing had established itself at Zurich, too. It got under way properly when the Bavarian Christoph Froschauer settled there. A follower of the Zurich Reformer Ulrich Zwingli (Luther's Swiss counterpart), Froschauer became the real printer of the Reformation and of humanist learning. His greatest achievements are the folio Bibles, numerous editions of which appeared within a few years. Between 1524 and 1564 he published no fewer than twenty-seven complete editions of the Bible and fifteen of the New Testament in various languages. He received print orders from as far away as England. With the publication of the profusely illustrated *Swiss Chronicle* of Johannes Strumpf, 1548, he continued the tradition of the manuscript Swiss chronicles of the Late Middle Ages, decorated with illuminated pen drawings. The writing manual of Urban Wyss, published in 1549, is highly thought of by students of calligraphy and the alphabet. The natural history books of the Zurich scholar Conrad Gessner also brought international fame to Froschauer's press. After his death the press gradually lost its standing; chiefly—as at Basle—as a result of competition from printing-centres of the Counter-Reformation.

Switzerland's third early centre of printing, Geneva, catered to the French-speaking part of the country. Its first press was founded by Adam Steinschaber c. 1478–80, one of Gutenberg's circle of printers; and right away intense competition ensued between Geneva and Lyon. The emphasis of much of Geneva's early printers (some of whom came from France) was on liturgical and attractively illustrated popular works. After 1500 political writing came to the fore —from 1520, largely that of the Reformation. Calvin's work gave a special tone to Geneva's printing. The town provided asylum to religious refugees from France, among them many printers. One of them, the Parisian Robert Estienne, lived in Geneva from 1550, where he published his fine Latin and Greek Bibles. Many of Geneva's printers were scholars, like the philologist Henri Estienne, son of Robert. The town's lively book-trade called for a printers' edict, and one was issued by the government on 15 February 1560—the *ordonnances touchant l'imprimerie*. It is one of the oldest ordinances on printing privileges, censorship, master printers, journeymen, apprenticeship and other matters concerning the trade, such as pirate editions. Geneva played an important part as the centre of anti-Roman-Catholic publishing in France, the Netherlands, and even Scotland.

Among many towns without a sustained—or with only a short-lived—output, Bern produced fine books during the Renaissance: Matthäus Apiarius, a Bavarian, like Froben and Froschauer, founded the town's first press in 1537, having in all probability learned the trade in Basle. His first books are musical works, and he continued to specialise in music printed with moveable type.

His sons' printing offices produced some fine books after the mid-sixteenth century. Towards the end of the century this activity gradually ceased. An interesting point about Bern is that it is the only Swiss town ever to have instituted a *Hochobrigkeitliche Druckerei* (1599)—a state printing office, which survived until 1831.

It is no mere curiosity that Romansch, the country's fourth official language since 1938 (the other three are German, French and Italian), began to appear in print during the Reformation as early as 1560, particularly in editions of the New Testament produced in villages at Graubünden—usually on obscure presses set up by Italian Protestant refugees. If in addition to this special case of a linguistic minority with its own printing history one remembers that there were numerous other groups (some of whom remained Catholic) from the sixteenth century onwards, one can see the pattern of emergence of the culturally and economically self-contained communities that have survived in Switzerland to this day, particularly in the printing trade.

After the mid-sixteenth century, printing began to atrophy in Switzerland. The appreciation of beautiful books seems to have dwindled rapidly during the Counter-Reformation and its religious and political disputes. Cultivated, well-balanced books with fine type and woodcuts of a high artistic quality were ousted by a baroque pomp that fails to disguise the low quality of paper, type, composition, presswork and ornamentation. The gusto, the bold, searching quest of the humanist and Reformist epoch, vanished, and was replaced by rigid doctrine. Though many printers remained active everywhere, their work was of little more than local significance. On the whole, the only country to produce books of a high standard was the Netherlands. In German-language Swiss books particularly, a sometimes unbridled indulgence in bombast manifests itself in the choice of type faces (textur and fraktur predominate), initials, and title-pages packed with words and forms, and a general uncertainty with regard to illustration. From the end of the sixteenth century onwards copper-engravings, considered up to date, and rich in nuance, increasingly replaced the woodcut as the accepted medium of book illustration, so that the concept of the printed book as a unity was lost. As a result many seventeenth century books show an unpleasant dichotomy between heavy fraktur setting and fine copper-engraved illustration.

The copperplate was plainly Switzerland's creative achievement in the seventeenth century. It found expression in prints, engraved frontispieces, small and large pictures, and particularly in geographical, medical and scientific works. The Zurich engraving and publishing dynasty of Meyer demonstrates this most clearly. That the relatively high standard of engraving had no printing trade to match it in quality and thus make an impact on the outside world, becomes clear from the fact that the greatest Swiss engravers had to work outside Switzerland. Thus Matthäus Merian of Basle, who had learned his trade with Dietrich Meyer at Zurich, worked as an engraver and publisher in France, the Netherlands and finally Frankfurt, where he made his name in 1642 with his *Topographia*. No less famous was his daughter Maria Sibylla, painter and naturalist, whose flowers, caterpillars and insects make her one of the great naturalist illustrators of the seventeenth century. She died in Amsterdam, where her work on Surinam was published.

While the German parts of seventeenth-century Switzerland were submerged by narrow-mindedness and petty censorship, and the centres of culture and publishing shifted to the Netherlands, Nuremberg and Frankfurt, Geneva was able to keep her book-trade alive until late into the seventeenth century, in spite of sharp competition from Lyon. The repeal of the Edict of Nantes (1685) brought a fresh flood of Huguenot religious refugees, who gave a new impetus to the town, particularly to its printing trade.

A characteristic of the book-trade of the seventeenth century is that everywhere the originally self-assured activities of the Renaissance printers began to function in ever more well-defined channels. Beside the great fairs, which had hitherto provided the chief outlet for the book-trade, middlemen now began to play an increasing part. Economic competition, in which the Dutch printers held the lead, began to rationalise the trade, though sensible and equitable regulations were to follow very much later. In Switzerland, at any rate, the religious strife and intellectual restrictions on the one hand and the demand for popular, sensational works or edifying tracts on the other was not a very glorious time for the book trade.

The low point reached by the Swiss book-trade during the Counter-Reformation was left behind with amazing speed and completeness during the age of Enlightenment. Contact with the ideas and personalities of the Enlightenment, the feeling of relief at entering a new era, everywhere fostered new talents and released fresh impulses. The first new work was done in the natural sciences. One of the first pieces of evidence of the new spirit is the *Beschreibung der Naturgeschichten des Schweizerlandes* (Account of the Natural Histories of Switzerland) by the Zurich scholar Johann Jakob Scheuchzer (Zurich 1706). The formal design of this and other works produced at the beginning of the eighteenth century continues largely to adhere to the baroque, though there are already traces of a more simple approach and some tautening-up in style. The Füssli family began to take the place of the engraver Meyer at Zurich, and printer-publishers once more became more typical than the engraver-publishers. A striving after better technical quality and design is evident even in the earliest works of the Enlightenment proper.

An interesting fact about the history of book design in Switzerland is that the scientific works of the Enlightenment throw back a bridge—spanning the rank typography of the baroque book—to the clear, rational typography of the humanist epoch. Switzerland's contributions towards the scientific Enlightenment are considerable; there are, for instance the mathematicians Jacob and Johann Bernoulli of Basle. Jacob Bernoulli's *Positionum de seriebus infinitis* (Basle, J. C. Mechel, 1698) is an excellent example of the attempt in scientific books to return to the use of roman and italic and a tauter composition. Daniel Bernoulli's *Hydrodynamica* (Basle, J. H. Decker, 1738), a treatise on the kinetic theory of gases, is another such work. The influence of the printers of the Enlightenment in France and Switzerland now began to make itself felt very strongly. The tendency was not confined to the subject matter of the books, but also affected design, choice of type, composition, title-pages, ornaments, frontispieces, vignettes and other copperplate work. It was strongest in French-speaking Switzerland. Thus the great Basle mathematician Leonhard Euler's *Introductio in analysin infinitorum*, published at Lausanne in 1748, is not only an epoch-making contribution to higher mathematics, but a noble example of Swiss book printing; it is undoubtedly French-influenced. Books like this showed that the age of Caslon and Fournier had arrived.

Geneva, especially, profited from the intellectual and aesthetic influences from France, and from the fact that bold thinkers preferred to publish their texts away from Paris, in whose atmosphere of absolutist dogma they were not exactly popular. Several editions of Montesquieu's *Esprit des Lois* were published by Barillot at Geneva from 1748 onwards. Around the middle of the eighteenth century Voltaire who had settled in the neighbourhood of Geneva, was closely connected with the printing and publishing family of Cramer, active publicists of Rationalism. His complete works were published by Cramer in 1775. In 1776 Jean-Jacques Rousseau, a citizen of Geneva, wrote his *Contrat social*, which was, however, printed in Holland and publicly burned in Geneva. His *Confessions* and *Rêveries* were published later at Geneva; an elegant first edition of 1782 has a title-page that shows the growing effort to return to some sort of typographic discipline.

One of the customs of printers and publishers, particularly in the eighteenth century, was to publish advanced and daring works anonymously, not only omitting the author's name, but also the publisher's. This protected the author but also sometimes served to conceal pirate printing. I have a duodecimo edition in several volumes of Montesquieu's works, with the imprint 'Londres 1787'—probably printed in Geneva. Similarly, editions of *Le Droit des Gens*, by Emerich Vattel, one of the founders of international law, were printed by the Imprimeurs du Journal Helvétique at Neuchâtel in 1758, but bear a London imprint and no publisher's name.

Another characteristic of Swiss printing and publishing in the second half of the eighteenth century is that at several places, such as Bern, Neuchâtel and Yverdon, printers and intellectually and aesthetically inclined patricians got together to form 'typographical societies'. These produced many bibliophilic treasures, but also made valuable contributions to thought. As mouthpieces of the democratic élite, the typographic societies of the eighteenth century are in a sense the forerunners of today's societies of bibliophiles, whose service to the art of the book is outside the field of commercial publishing. Neuchâtel's typographical society was the focus of forces opposed to the spirit of absolutism at that time. But the most important achievements in Switzerland in the eighteenth century—both culturally and from the point of view of book production and publishing—may be summed up in the single word 'encyclopedia'. This was in keeping with the universalism of the Enlightenment, when attempts were made to gather together and make up a balance-sheet of all available knowledge. We can justly call this epoch the 'encyclopedic age', during which the political death-blow was dealt to the *ancien régime*, and, still more important, the world of rigidly stratified intellectual ideas was shattered and the 'modern' world born.

The most important single achievement of the age was the great *Encyclopédie* of Diderot and d'Alembert, which was published under difficult circumstances at Paris between 1750 and 1772, and definitively concluded in 1780.

Taking the French encyclopedia as its model, the *Société typographique* of Neuchâtel published its own *Description des arts et métiers* in 1771–83, in nineteen quarto volumes. It is not only editorially a great achievement, but also the finest piece of bookwork produced in Switzerland in the eighteenth century. Matters did not rest with this one work, produced in imitation of the French encyclopedia. The Neapolitan philosopher, physicist and mathematician Fortunato Bartolomeo de Félice had settled in the little town of Yverdon; through its *Société typographique* he published some 300 works between 1762 and 1789.

The greatest of these is the *Encyclopédie ou dictionnaire universel raisonné des connoissances humaines*. With his small circle of collaborators he produced an improved and extended variant of the Diderot encyclopedia, published between 1770 and 1780, comprising forty-eight quarto volumes of text and ten of copper engravings.

A similar encyclopedic venture was undertaken at Geneva in the same years; so Switzerland, only a short while after the appearance of the French prototype, produced three encyclopedias—enormous editorial achievements—in less than thirty years. What is remarkable about this is not so much the courage required to tackle such a task with limited finances, as the determination of small intellectual élites to create these great tools of knowledge and education.

After 1789 the upheavals of the French Revolution brought another wave of French intellectuals to Switzerland. Prominent among these was the young Madame de Staël, daughter of the Geneva-born financier Jacques Necker, who had incurred the displeasure of the French court with his proposals for reform as Minister of Finance to Louis XVI, and who lived and wrote as a political exile in Château Coppet on Lake Geneva. Madame de Staël made Coppet the meeting-point of the free literary and philosophical world of her day, particularly after her break with Napoleon. Her own writings and those of her friends, such as Benjamin Constant (born in Lausanne) were largely published at Geneva. Through Madame de Staël's connections with Germany Coppet became the real link between the German and French romantic movements. The printing trade of French-speaking Switzerland profited greatly from this intellectual activity. The role which its centres of printing played in promoting intellectual activities inside France was equalled by Zurich as the centre of the German Enlightenment. It was the personality of Johann Jakob Bodmer that gave it its chief impetus. As a poet, literary critic and translator, Bodmer, together with Johann Jakob Breitinger, had a decisive influence on the movement. Their instrument was the moralistic weekly, *Discourse der Mahlern*, which had appeared in Zurich since 1721. The two Zurich men freed the literature of the Enlightenment from its sterility, and in doing so ushered in German classicism. Germany's intellectuals looked to Zurich, where a new cultural and literary climate was beginning to set in. Klopstock, Kleist, Wieland, Fichte and Goethe came to Zurich, whose printing and publishing trade profited from, and at the same time contributed to, this activity. The focal point was the printing office of Orell, Gessner & Compagnie. Goethe said of it: 'This company has served true literature better with its excellent products than half the book-trade of Germany.'

As early as 1762–6 Wieland's Shakespeare-translation was published by Orell-Gessner—the first, and for long time the only, authoritative German translation. The same house published Bodmer's Homer translation from 1776, and at his initiative Wilhelm Heinse's Tasso translation was published in 1782, again by Orell, Gessner, Füssli. As far as book design is concerned this work seems to have brought to an end the spirit of the rococo: the circle that had initiated classicism in the field of thought now furthered it typographically too. The Zurich *Tasso* was the first evidence that the age of Bodoni had arrived in typography. The classic roman faces in the spirit of Bodoni and Didot admittedly remained the exception rather than the rule among the printers of Zurich and other German-speaking centres until well into the nineteenth century. Gothic or fraktur remained the dominant faces. It can, in fact, be claimed that the contradiction between the spirit of classicism and of fraktur is only a seeming one, for at this very time some excellent fraktur faces were being designed in Germany: apart from Breitkopf-fraktur, which dominated German printing in the eighteenth century, there is for instance the late rococo fraktur by the printer and form-cutter Johann Friedrich Unger (1793), or that of the punch-cutter J. G. J. E. Walbaum, which appeared about 1800, probably the last historically pure fraktur. It is also worth remembering that as early as 1718 the form-cutter Wilhelm Haas brought the Nuremberg typeface, Schwabacher, to Basle, where he founded the Haas'sche Schriftgiesserei at Münchenstein. The *Epreuves de caractères* issued by the Haas foundry in 1772 clearly show that the roman type face, and the italic which went with it, in a sense shared the work of fraktur and Schwabacher.

In its late eighteenth-century books, the Zurich printing and publishing trade reflect the cultural life of the town: they are a curious amalgam of Enlightenment, rococo and classicism, of cosmopolitanism and parochialism. The Bodmer-Breitinger circle exercised an enormous influence on German intellectuals; the translations being published gave rise to the idea of a 'world literature', emanating from Zurich. But at the same time national and even local characteristics attained new standing and significance. It is no coincidence that as early as 1758 Joh. Georg Zimmermann, doctor and popular philosopher, achieved success with his patriotic *Von dem Nationalstolze* (National Pride).

Salomon Gessner's *Idyllen* are still very much rococo, both in content and from the point of view of book production. This talented, versatile man had a great reputation as a poet, and even in the eighteenth century his work was translated into more than ten languages. He was a prolific copper-engraver, etcher and painter as well as an accomplished publisher. His chief contribution towards the publishing house of Orell, Gessner, Füssli & Compagnie was in the way of book decoration. He produced graceful copper-engraved title-pages and vignettes which gave the many books the firm published a magic that imperceptibly changed from playful rococo to amiable classicism. A large circle of artists, copper-engravers and art publishers formed around him. His work is a significant contribution towards the flowering of the book in Zurich, both with regard to style and aesthetic form, and content. At that time Zurich was producing not only books that satisfied the popular demand, but also had a weighty influence on contemporaries and posterity. The physiognomist Johann Kaspar Lavater and the educationist Johann Heinrich Pestalozzi are but two whose works were published in Zurich.

Printing in other Swiss towns cannot compare with that of Zurich at the time. Nevertheless, a major work in German literature was published at Bern: *Die Alpen*, by the doctor, naturalist and poet Albrecht von Haller. The Bern typographical society published a particularly beautiful French edition of this book in 1795. The last years of the *ancien régime* were not everywhere in Switzerland conducive to progressive or even nationalistic thinking, and narrow-minded censorship made the printer's work hard. This may be seen by the fact that *Die Geschichten der Schweizer*, a work inspired by the national passion and the Enlightenment, written by the historian Johannes Müller, was printed at Bern in 1780, but had the fictitious imprint '*Boston, bey der neuen typographischen Gesellschaft*' to evade the censors. Basle's main achievements, apart from works of a purely local character, were in the realm of books with plates. Christian Mechel became well known as a printer and publisher of topographic and naturalist works. Thurneysen, a publisher's printing house, was trying like the Zurich printers to achieve a break-through to elegant classicism. Friedrich Wilhelm Haas, briefly mentioned earlier, worked not only as a printer-publisher and typefounder, but also tried for technical improvements on the printing press: evidence of the awakening interest in technical aspects of printing which was to become widespread during the nineteenth century.

The turn of the century was a time of change in Switzerland, as elsewhere. The old Swiss Confederacy, a form of state that had been reconstructed and modified over hundreds of years, finally went under in the wake of the French Revolution. For a time Switzerland became a theatre of war for foreign armies. Napoleon's troops occupied the country. These uncertain times left their mark on the political, social, economic and cultural life of Switzerland. The individual and the country as a whole strove to cast off old bonds, though opinions differed as to what was the most desirable course this change was to take. A constitution on the French model was drafted, but the Swiss unitary state had great difficulty in establishing itself with the people. Tensions grew between federalists and centralists. It was only at the Congress of Vienna, which, after the fall of Napoleon, also took up the problems of Switzerland, that the country acquired a new federal treaty, comprising twenty-two independent cantons. On this foundation the concept of the Swiss Federal State gradually and laboriously evolved, coming to fruition in 1848. The after-effects of the French Revolution, the international tensions and disputes of the Napoleonic era—the difficult task of creating a new age out of the ruins of the *ancien régime* and the now unacceptable patriarchal conditions—made great demands on individuals and the whole community. Political, military, religious and, most of all, social tensions and disputes did not ease the task of creating the New Man and the New Society long outlined by the Enlightenment and finally brought about by the revolution. In Switzerland, as elsewhere, it became apparent that progressives may vie with each other when postulating and demanding a new ideal, but when the time for action comes it is almost impossible to put into a generally acceptable, practical form, ideas which suddenly prove to differ widely, and to reconcile special interests.

The fundamental difficulties, and perhaps even more the petty local squabbles, brought to an end the intellectual rigour which had given Switzerland's printing and publishing its cosmopolitanism in the eighteenth century. Her centres of printing lost their international reputation. In spite of France's changing fortunes, Paris again became the focal point of cultural life during the romantic era, and so French-speaking Switzerland declined into provincialism. Germany, rapidly turning into a major state, became a powerful competitor to German-speaking Switzerland, both culturally and economically.

The creative forces of a society manifest themselves in different fields at different times, according to general conditions. In early nineteenth-century Switzerland the best creative minds were concerned chiefly with politics, or with economic, technical or social problems. Everywhere state institutions were being created or perfected; in particular, the state school was introduced. Educational theory, going back to Rousseau and given expression by the great educationist Pestalozzi, was the chief concern of part of the intellectual élite. But the chief preoccupation was with economic and technical problems. In Switzerland, particularly, the early nineteenth century was a time of rapidly expanding industrialisation. The intellectuals either participated actively in political and economic affairs or withdrew into purely academic activities, the most popular of these being the nation's history.

The populace at large, however, longed for peace and a normal social life after the turbulence of the Napoleonic era. Thus while the more active spirits were busy building the new age—the industrial age—society as a whole retired into peaceful privacy. The greater and bolder the advances in technology and the economy, the more modest and intimate became the cultural interests of middle-class society. While the new class of industrialists worked away at great new ventures, the middle classes and the *petite-bourgeoisie* of the towns lived in their snail shells.

The elegance of classicism which had manifested itself in architecture and the applied arts—particularly that of the book—was now replaced by the romantic, bourgeois Biedermeier, with his partiality for the intimate, the small, the dainty and the sentimental. These traits show clearly in Swiss books of the time: the great intellectual and scientific works have been supplanted by amiable, intimate books. This is the age of small and diminutive book formats, whose physical dimensions correspond with the modest contents. It is the age of almanacs, pocketbooks, ladies' journals, popular science annuals, sentimental light fiction, and uplifting children's books. Sharp competition from France and Germany kept this intimate art completely within national boundaries. Though in many towns printers and publishers continued to produce books—among them some of the old, renowned presses—their work lacked verve, and was aimed at meeting a very limited demand.

Typical of the Swiss printing trade in the early nineteenth century is the way in which the field is not dominated by a few giants: a great many small ventures share a multiplicity of small tasks between them. Such a situation is not conducive to a high level of creativity. Advertising literature became the new bread-and-butter line, sponsored by flourishing industrial and commercial firms. This type of work grew in importance as technology and industry expanded, one of the inevitable results of industrialisation being the transformation of a hierarchically ordered social structure into a modern, anonymous, industrial society.

The mass-production of goods by machine must be commensurate with a mass-society which absorbs them, and the media of communication must in turn be tailored to such a mass-society. Print is the most important of these media.

The mass-production of promotional literature was soon rivalled by another mass-medium—the Press. Newspapers and magazines began to flourish after the French Revolution, and subject to the rules of the early industrial era, the Press too was determined by the principle of unlimited competition. The age of the newspaper advertisement had not yet arrived, so for a time the chief competition was for readership. Newspapers and magazines soon began to replace books as a medium of communication.

Switzerland had been a tourist country ever since the Enlightenment. A growing interest in nature on the part of city-dwellers nostalgic for unspoiled rural places made the country a major attraction. The tourist industry, which was to become an important factor in Switzerland's economy, grew rapidly with the improvement of the hotel trade, the laying down of a dense railway-network, and the opening up of mountain regions by means of a series of bold-ly constructed mountain railways. This tourist industry had directly and in-directly influenced Switzerland's graphic trades ever since the early nineteenth century. In the eighteenth century a special kind of publishing had begun, producing pictures of landscapes, costume, historical and traditional scenes. Copper-engravings, virtually mass-produced in every format, and often col-oured, were a popular form of souvenir for the foreign visitor.

As travel became more general, so this branch of printing and publishing grew.

In addition to illustrations of landscapes, costume, etc. grew up a demand for topographical printing, and, stimulated by a growing interest in historical processes, for historical descriptions of particular personalities and regions. An ever wider range of popular, popular-scientific, and specialised scientific works and textbooks was produced. In the first decades of the nineteenth cen-tury these were designed in the classicist style, though they gradually grew less elegant. Grace was supplanted by triviality, and carefully chosen type, meticulous setting and high-quality paper and presswork deteriorated into routine, slovenly workmanship. Roman type faces disappeared entirely from German-speaking Switzerland, to be replaced by a few good, but more often unsatisfactory, fraktur faces. At a first glance the books produced in the first half of the nineteenth century seem to have a certain magic, reflecting the charm of an apparently tranquil era, but closer inspection will reveal their poor design and presswork.

For a time copper-engraving was the most favoured illustration technique for the Biedermeier era, for frontispieces, title-pages, vignettes, full-page plat-es, tables, maps and general decoration; but around 1820 there was a radical change. A good deal of experimenting with illustration techniques had been going on from the beginning of the century. There was the aquatint; in contrast with gravure, with its clear lines, which are suitable to depicting facts and lend themselves to colouring-in, it had a picturesque quality and was popular for landscapes, etc. Lithographic techniques were being experimented with in Switzerland soon after 1800, and Senefelder's method was in use well before the publication of his manual in 1818, and even before the illegal publication of *Das Geheimnis des Steindrucks* by the German publisher Gotta in 1810, which aroused the interest of printers and artists. A remarkable document has survived, entitled *Kunstgeheimnis auf Steinplatten zu zeichnen und Abdrucke davon zu ziehen* (The secret of drawing on stone plates and making prints from them); a manuscript report of instructions in lithography at Zurich in 1807, which was circulated among a number of gentlemen. Their names are known: most of them were leading painters, engravers and printers who wanted to learn the secret of lithography. The breakthrough in Switzerland was due mainly to the possibilities which the new process offered in terms of technique and economic advantages; not, as in France, the exciting new scope it gave the artist. The economic ground for lithography was prepared by a number of jobbing and commercial printing firms working for industry and the tourist trade. Thus it was undoubtedly business interest that led the copper-engraver Heinrich Schoch to found Zurich's first 'lithographic printing workshop' in 1810.

During the next few years the number of lithographic workshops grew. Some of the old printing and engraving establishments changed over to lithography for work for special occasions and, to some extent, book illustration; a number of new workshops also sprang up, most of them short-lived. Nevertheless, a number of new firms that were founded between 1820 and 1840 did survive, and have made decisive contributions towards the high standard of lithographic printing in Switzerland. Some of the leading early lithographic printers soon went over to printing illustrations for scientific works; others, to a field that was later to become a Swiss speciality—cartography. In the first and well into the second half of the century this branch of lithography, with its severe demands on skill and craftsmanship, was confined to a few firms. Most of the smaller firms were content to mass-produce indifferent jobbing work.

Wood-engraving, introduced by Thomas Bewick in England late in the eighteenth century, found no active following as an acceptable new form of book illustration—with a few small exceptions. Even in the latter years of the nineteenth century, when the purely reproductive technique of xylography spread as a form of book illustration, most Swiss printers and publishers bought their blocks from Germany; only very gradually did they engrave their own, first with the help of German xylographers. The same is true of steel-engraving, which Charles Heath had been practising in England since about 1820. The first Swiss books used plates made in England. About 1850 a number of steel-engravers established themselves in Switzerland. A number of excellent engraved and printed works were published, such as the splendid *Die Schweiz in Bildern* by the landscape painter J. J. Ulrich (1856). Steel-engraving gradually disappeared again, superseded by the steel-covered copperplate.

To sum up the history of printing in Switzerland in the first half of the nineteenth century: the demands of industry and commerce for jobbing printing formed its extensive material basis. This work was mainly done by small firms. Books, monographs and periodicals were largely for local consumption. Only a few publications stand out from the mass of books in the late classicist, Biedermeier and romantic tradition. Among them are the products of the house of Orell, Füssli & Compagnie at Zurich, at that time one of Switzerland's leading publishers. Examples of some good work are the *Lyrische Anthologie* in twenty volumes (1803–7), edited by the poet Friedrich Matthisson; the delightful little book *Die Badenfahrt*, by David Hess (1818); *Voyage de Zurich à Zurich*, by Henri Meister, 1826 (being in French, it was, significantly, set in roman); and the German edition of Molière's comedies, translated by Heinrich Zschokke (published by Heinrich Gessner, 1805). Among the major publications were a number of scientific works, such as Clairville's *Helvetische Entomologie* (1798–1806) and Gaudin's *Flora Helvetica* (1828), in seven volumes, to name but two of a number of works with fine plates—frequently hand-coloured copper-engravings.

As so often in the past, Switzerland again became a refuge for those who sought relative intellectual freedom, or for those who were not able to publish their work elsewhere. The thirties and forties once again showed how Switzerland's politics and culture were enriched by fresh waves of immigrants. Until 1800 it had been chiefly Frenchmen—Montesquieu, Rousseau, Voltaire, and others; from 1830 onwards the majority of those who sought refuge or published their work in Switzerland were Germans. Foremost among them was the poet Georg Büchner who came to Zurich in 1836 and lectured in Natural History at the university, but died of a fever in 1837; then there was a group of German democrats and revolutionaries, such as Follen, Freiligrath, Froebel (the founder of kindergartens), Georg Herwegh, Hoffman von Fallersleben, and others. Between 1840 and 1848 they published their writings—political dynamite, and confiscated in their homeland—at the 'Literarisches

Comptoir in Zürich und Winterthur', the 'Literarisches Institut in Herisau' and with various other publishers. A few Swiss publishers backed these German revolutionaries with great ardour, and thus contributed directly to the workers' cause and the education of the working classes. Such activities landed many a publisher in trouble with the authorities.

Similar refuge was offered to Italy's freedom fighters, who used the facilities of the printing trade in Southern Switzerland, in the Tessin. Vanelli, at Lugano, published not only the Italian classics, such as a Dante edition in the typographical tradition of Bodoni, but also political and historical writings. The Tipografica Elvetica in Capolago, close to the Italian border, published Carlo Botta's *Storia d'Italia* and other works that formed the intellectual background of the Risorgimento.

As the century advanced, one aspect of the graphic trade became ever more important: the growth and supremacy of technology. Not much had altered in the technique of printing since its invention. The 'black art' had retained its craft character until the beginning of the nineteenth century; though its traditional processes had been improved in small details, the general principles of book-production had remained the same. Printing is a good example of the principle of mass-production: the idea of making a great number of similar copies with as little labour as possible is, after all, at the root of the invention of printing. It is therefore not surprising that the achievements of the age of technology were quickly and successfully taken up by the printing trade. At first Switzerland did not contribute actively to this mechanisation, but was content to profit from it. Mechanisation in the printing trade speeds up production by replacing—or at least complementing—human labour with mechanical labour, whether by steam or electricity. The mass-society demands from its printers ever greater quantities of identical products in a short time. Through mechanisation it not only becomes possible to produce larger editions at greater speed, but also to lower the price. This in turn leads to increased consumption. Printing shows this process of mutual activation and consumption particularly well. Printing was changed not only by technical inventions such as the steam engine and the development of heavy industries that followed from it: the rapidly growing demand for information of growing classes of readers was a further and equally important result. This is most clearly seen in newspaper printing. Speed, cheapness and availability in large editions—these were the obvious pre-conditions. Prominent stages in this development are the invention of the high-speed printing press, the rotary press, the composing machine and, last but not least, the papermaking machine. But

1. Shakespeare, Orell, Gessner & Co., Zurich (1762). Etched copper
title-page by Salomon Gessner

L E S
A L P E S.

P A R M. A L B. D E H A L L E R.

BERNE, CHEZ LA SOCIÉTÉ TYPOGRAPHIQUE

1 7 9 5.

2. Albrecht de Haller: *Les Alpes*, La Société Typographique, Bern (1795).
Copperplate engraved title-page by Duncker

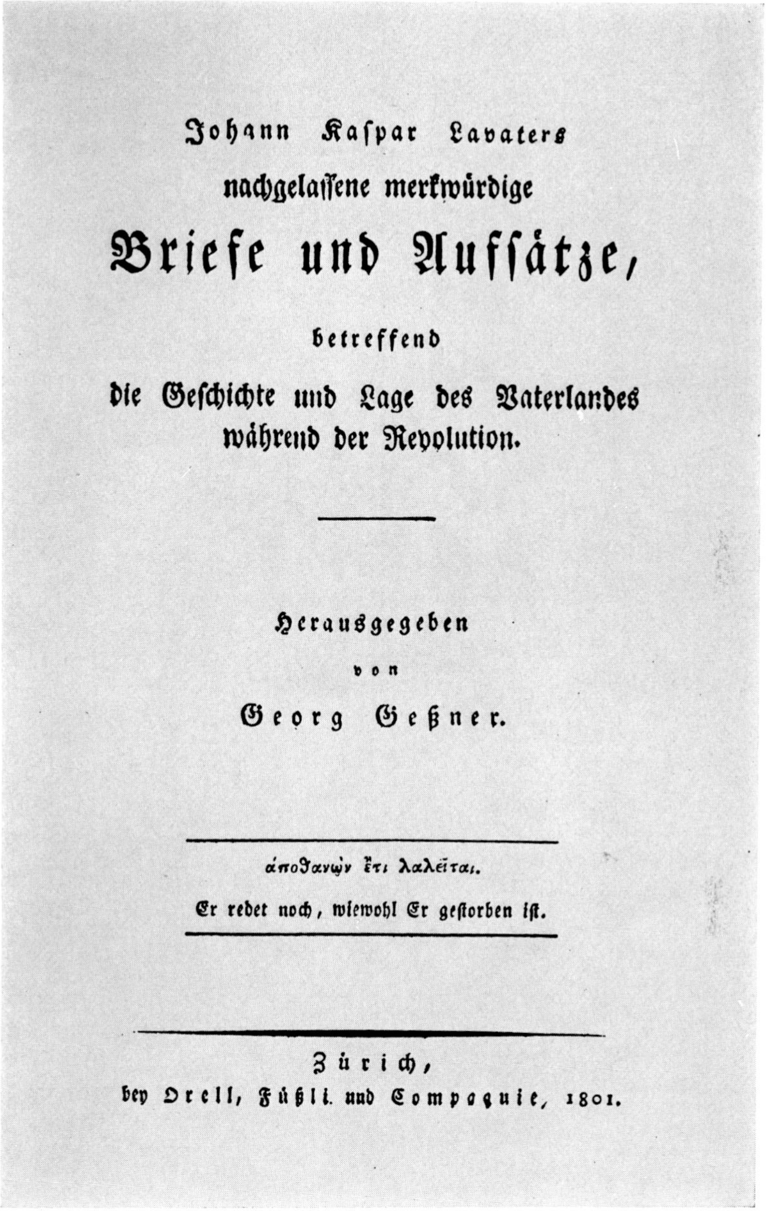

Johann Kaspar Lavaters

nachgelaſſene merkwürdige

Briefe und Aufſätze,

betreffend

die Geſchichte und Lage des Vaterlandes
während der Revolution.

———

Herausgegeben

von

Georg Geßner.

———

ἀποθανὼν ἔτι λαλεῖται.

Er redet noch, wiewohl Er geſtorben iſt.

———

Zürich,
bey Orell, Füßli und Compagnie, 1801.

———

3. J. K. Lavater: *Briefe und Aufsätze, etc.*, Orell, Füssli and Co (1801).
Title-page set in blackletter

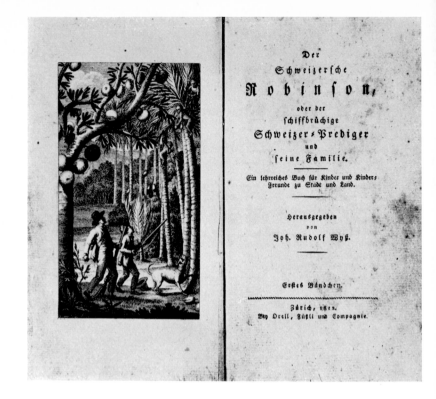

4. *Der Schweizersche Robinson*, Orell, Füssli and Co (1812). Frontispiece and title-page

LA COMMEDIA
DI DANTE ALIGHIERI

ILLUSTRATA

DA UGO FOSCOLO.

MERUIT DEUS ESSE VIDERI
CARMINE COMPLEXUS TERRAS MARE SIDERA MANES

PERENNIS
ET
FRAGRANS

LUGANO
DAI TORCHI DI G. VANELLI E COMP.
M. DCCC. XXVII.

5. Dante: *La Commedia*, Lugano (1827). Title-page

STORIA

D'ITALIA

DAL 1789 AL 1814

SCRITTA

DA CARLO BOTTA

TOMO II

CAPOLAGO
Cantone Ticino

Tipografia Helvetica

MDCCCXXXVII

6. Carlo Botta: *Storia D'Italia*, Tipografia Helvetica, Capolago (1837).
Title-page

Leiden und Freuden

eines

Schulmeisters.

~~~~~~~~

Erster Theil.

~~~~~~~~

Bern, 1838.
Wagner'sche Buchhandlung.

7. *Leiden und Freuden eines Schulmeisters*, Wagner, Bern (1838). Title-page

XI.

Die Schlacht bei St. Jakob und ihre Folgen.

Schrecken ergriff die Stadt Basel und die in ihr tagenden Väter, als 1439 ein 12,000 Mann starkes Heer des rohesten Kriegsvolks, welches das Volk nur die Schinder nannte, in das Elsaß einfiel, mit dem Zwecke, wie es hieß, die aufrührerische Kirchenversammlung zu Basel auseinanderzutreiben. Noch größer war die Bestürzung, als 1444 die gleichen Feinde, aber dreimal stärker an Zahl und angeführt von dem Sohne des Königs von Frankreich, Karls VII., sich der Stadt näherten, unter ihren Mauern an den Ufern der Birs

8. *Die Stadt Basel* (1855). Illustrated with wood-engravings

UN SOUVENIR

DE

SOLFERINO

PAR

J. HENRY DUNANT

Ne se vend pas

GENÈVE

IMPRIMERIE JULES-GUILLAUME FICK

—

1862

Tous droits de reproduction et de traduction réservés

---

9. J. H. Dunant: *Un Souvenir de Solferino*, J. G. Fick, Geneva (1862). Title-page

UNSER SCHWEIZER STANDPUNKT

CARL SPITTELER

Vortrag, gehalten in der Neuen
Helvet. Gesellschaft, Gruppe
Zürich, am 14. Dezember 1914

1918
VERLAG VON RASCHER & CIE IN ZÜRICH.

10. Carl Spitteler: *Unser Schweizer Standpunkt*, Rascher & Cie, Zurich (1918).
Title-page

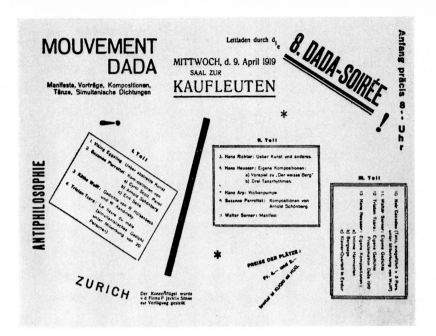

11. From a Programme for a Dada-Soirée, Zurich (1919)

12. *Die Kunst-ismen*, Zurich (1925). Binding cover designed by El Lissitsky

man seine Werke am besten telephonisch, vom Bett aus, bei einem Anstreicher bestellt.

SIMULTANISMUS

Die Gleichzeitigkeit der Farben, die gleichzeitigen Kontraste und alle aus der Farbe sich ergebenden ungeraden Maße, entsprechend ihrem Ausdruck in ihrer darstellenden Bewegung: dies ist die einzige Realität zum Aufbau des Bildes.   DELAUNAY.

DADAISMUS

Der Dadaismus hat die schönen Künste überfallen. Er hat die Kunst für einen magischen Stuhlgang erklärt, die Venus von Milo klistiert und „Laokoon & Söhnen" nach tausendjährigem Ringkampf mit der Klapperschlange ermöglicht, endlich auszutreten. Der Dadaismus hat das Bejahen und Verneinen bis zum Nonsens geführt. Um die Indifferenz zu erreichen, war er destruktiv.   ARP.

PURISMUS

Das Gemälde ist eine Maschine zur Übertragung der Gefühle. Die Wissenschaft bietet uns eine Art physiologischer Sprache, welche uns ermöglicht, beim Beschauer eindeutige physiologische Empfindungen hervorzurufen: hierauf ist der Purismus begründet.
OZENFANT & JEANNERET.

NEOPLASTIZISMUS

Der Neoplastiker gewinnt durch die horizontal - verti-

---

mieux faire que de commander ses œuvres téléphoniquement du lit, auprès d'un peintre en décors.

SIMULTANISME

La simultanéité des couleurs, les contrastes simultanés et toutes les mesures impaires issues de la couleur, selon leur expression dans leur mouvement représentatif: voilà la seule réalité pour construire la peinture.
DELAUNAY.

DADAISME

Le dadaïsme a assailli les beaux-arts. Il a déclaré l'art d'être une purge magique a donné le clystère à la Vénus de Milo et permis à «Laocoon & fils» de s'absenter enfin après s'être tourmentés dans la lutte avec la serpent à sonnettes pendant des milliers d'années. Le dadaïsme a poussé l'affirmation et la négation jusqu'au nonsens. Afin d'arriver à l'indifférence il était déstructif.   ARP.

PURISME

La peinture est une machine pour la transmission des sentiments. La science nous offre une sorte de language physiologique qui nous permet de produire chez le spectateur des sensations physiologiques précises: ce qui forme la base du purisme.
OZENFANT & JEANNERET.

NÉOPLASTICISME

Par la division horizontale-verticale du rectangle le néo-

---

can do better than order his works by telephone from his bed, by a common painter.

SIMULTANISM

Simultaneousness of colour, simultaneous contrasts and all uneven measures issuing out of colour, conform to their expression in their representative movement: this is the only reality to construct a picture.   DELAUNAY.

DADAISM

The dadaïsm has assailed fine-arts. He declared art to be a magic purge gave the clyster to Venus of Milo and allowed "Laocoon & Sons" to absent themselves at last after they had tortured themselves in the millennial fight with the rattlesnake. Dadaïsme has carried affirmation and negation up to nonsens. In order to come to the indifference dadaïsme was distructive.   ARP.

PURISM

The picture is a machine for the transmission of sentiments. Science offers us a kind of physiological linguage that enables us to produce precise physiological sensations in the spectator: thereon purism is founded.
OZENFANT & JEANNERET.

NEOPLASTICISM

By the horizontal-vertical division of the rectangle the neo-

13. *Die Kunst-ismen*, Zurich (1925). Text page by El Lissitsky and Hans Arp, designed by El Lissitsky

Ernſt Groſſe

OSTASIATISCHES

GERÄT

1927

Kunſtgewerbliche Abteilung der

Gewerbeſchule Zürich

14. Bibliophile edition, Kunstgewerbeschule (School of Applied Art), Zurich (1927). Title-page from this special printing, layout by Walter Kaech

Lo, with thine eyes I see a sweeter light,
Than I with eyes of blindness e'er behold.
And what my lameness never can uphold,
With thy limbs — see — I lift the mighty weight.

Withdraw thy wings, and pinions have I none.
Thy spirit's ardour me to the skies doth hale.
Thou mak'st me hectic and thou mak'st me pale,
Seared i' the frosts or frozen i' the sun.

Within thy will my will is compasséd.
My thought created is within thy heart.
Into my words thy word its life hath breathed.

Methinks the moon is my true counterpart,
Which men may watch illumined overhead
When borrowed sunlight round her sphere
                                        is wreathed.

15. Michelangelo: *Poems*, Johannespresse, Zurich (1941). Text page designed
by Hans Vollenweider, set in Frederic Warde's Arrighi

Garamond-Antiqua

Eine besonders wichtige Entwicklungsstufe der «klassischen Antiqua» («Mediäval»), benannt nach dem bedeutenden französischen Stempelschneider Claude Garamond, der in der ersten Hälfte des 16. Jahrhunderts lebte. Die Versalien (Großbuchstaben) gehen auf die Meißelform der alten Römer zurück und haben Serifen (Füßchen), die weich in den Grundstrich übergehen. Die Gemeinen (Kleinbuchstaben) sind von der handschriftlichen Form der Antiqua des 15. Jahrhunderts abgeleitet, jedoch, zumal in den unteren Serifen, den Versalformen angeglichen. Die Versalien (wie B) sind etwas kleiner als die Gemeinen mit Oberlängen (wie b): BbBb.

ABCDEFGHIJKLMNOP
QRSTUVWXYZ
abcdefghijklmnopqrsſtuvw
xyz ct ff fi fl ffi ſs ſt Qu &
1234567890

Eine heilige Sparsamkeit der Worte gibt
mehrenteils eine günſtige Vermutung für
eine Barschaft der Gedanken und für einen
verborgenen Schatz des Herzens ab; weil
Reichtum und Verschwendung, Tiefsinn
und Schwatzhaftigkeit schwerlich mit-
einander beſtehen können.

JOHANN GEORG HAMANN
1730 – 1788

16. *Gute Schriftformen*, Basle (1941). Page designed by Jan Tschichold

LES
MAÎTRES
D'AUTREFOIS

BELGIQUE · HOLLANDE

PAR

EUGÈNE FROMENTIN

———————

LES ÉDITIONS HOLBEIN

BÂLE

17. E. Fromentin: *Les Maîtres D'Autrefois*, Holbein, Basle (1947). Cover designed by Jan Tschichold

NACHT.
In einem hochgewölbten engen gothifchen Zimmer.

FAUST unruhig auf feinem Seffel am Pulten.

Hab nun, ach! die Philofophey,
Medizin und Jurifterey
Und leider auch die Theologie
Durchaus ftudirt mit heiffer Müh.
Da fteh ich nun, ich armer Tohr,
Und binn fo klug als wie zuvor.
Heiffe Docktor und Profeffor gar
Und ziehe fchon an die zehen Jahr
Herauf, herab und queer und krumm
Meine Schüler an der Nas herum
Und feh, daff wir nichts wiffen können:
Das will mir fchier das Herz verbrennen.
Zwar binn ich gefcheuter als alle die Laffen,
Docktors, Profeffors, Schreiber und Pfaffen,
Mich plagen keine Skrupel noch Zweifel,
Fürcht mich weder vor Höll noch Teufel.
Dafür ift mir auch all Freud entriffen,
Bild mir nicht ein, was rechts zu wiffen,
Bild mir nicht ein, ich könnt was lehren,
Die Menfchen zu beffern und zu bekehren;
Auch hab ich weder Gut noch Geld
Noch Ehr und Herrlichkeit der Welt:
Es mögt kein Hund fo länger leben!
Drum hab ich mich der Magie ergeben,
Ob mir durch Geiftes Krafft und Mund
Nicht manch Geheimniff werde kund,

5

18. Goethe: *Ur-Faust*, Johannespresse, Zurich (1949). Designed by Hans Vollenweider, set in Rotunda specially designed by him for this edition

Inclination and Reason

Our inner imagination is essentially influenced by what we have inherited, by all that counts as beautiful on the basis of tradition and can be made to coincide with this traditional conception, by everything that we have been educated to consider as objectively given. Even if it is more difficult to make an inner image of what we wish to give visible form to, in the last analysis it is the union of inclination and obligation which leads to the content of consciousness. To make inclination alone the basis of artistry would amount to working at haphazard. Obligation however, taken alone, would lead to imitation of traditional forms.

Imre Reiner: *Plant, wood engraving, 1947*
Imre Reiner: *Flowers, drawing, 1947*

"The texture of this world is made up of necessity and chance; Human reason takes up its position between the two and is able to dominate them. It treats necessity as the foundation of its being; it can steer, guide and use chance. Only when this quality stands firm and unshaken can a human being be said to be a god of the earth. Woe to him who has accustomed himself to see a kind of caprice in necessity and a kind of rationality in chance, the pursuit of which he would raise to the level of a religion. What would this be save the denial of one's own reason and the unbridling of one's inclinations?" (Goethe, *Wilhelm Meisters Lehrjahre*.)

Vanity

Vanity is a means to an end. And the end is success. To make a reality out of appearances, to move our fellows without making any movement ourselves, to achieve an effect without a deed—that is the meaner kind of vanity. In art there is a higher, more virtuous kind of vanity. Its aim is to make sure that the beautiful is seen in the right light. This is vanity that befits even the modest who may look upon it as their duty.

"Would to God that all men were vain, but were consciously so, with moderation and in the right sense. Then we should be the happiest creatures in a cultivated world." (Goethe, *Wilhelm Meisters Wanderjahre*.)

The meaner kind of vanity in art seduces the artist into snatching for effect, to be dramatic, to make what is banal, instead of giving a moving subject in a dramatic way. Drama and tragedy are genuine, they are the result of a natural event in life in which violence and pity are in conflict with one another. Dramatization, on the other hand, is something that has been distorted by vanity, artificially produced, theatricalized and staged. The dramatic is to be found in poetry as well as in painting. In the one case it is worth, in the other forms and colours that make the infinite finite.

19. Imré Reiner: *Creative Desire*, Verlag Zollikofer, St. Gall (1949). Layout and wood-engravings by the author

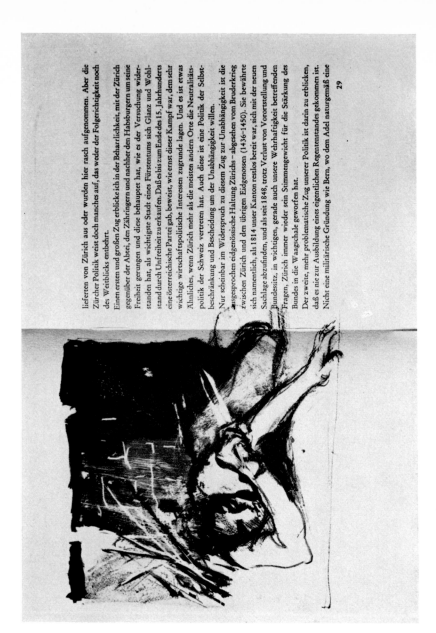

20. Max Huber: *Drei Reden*, Buchdruckerei Fretz, Zurich (1953). Layout by Walter Diethelm with lithographs by Hans Falk

die Geschichte vom bösen Kater

gesucht:

† gestorben: Daddy

Tatsachen

150

151

21. Markus Kutter: *Schiff nach Europa*, Teufen (1957). Two-page opening for a novel by Karl Gerstner

THE SUN IN ART
DIE SONNE IN DER KUNST
LE SOLEIL DANS L'ART

Sun Symbolism, from the Past to the Present, in Pagan and
Christian Art, Folk Art, Fine Art and Applied Art

Sonnensymbole aus Vergangenheit und Gegenwart in der vorchristlichen
und christlichen – in der freien und angewandten Kunst

Symboles du soleil du passé à nos jours, paiens ou chrétiens,
tirés du folklore, des beaux-arts et des arts appliqués

Editor / Herausgeber / Réalisé par:

WALTER HERDEG

AMSTUTZ & HERDEG, GRAPHIS PRESS, ZURICH, SWITZERLAND

22. *The Sun in Art*, special edition of *Graphis*, Number 100, Graphis Press,
Zurich (1962). Title-page designed by Walter Herdeg

FRITZ ERNST

—

BILD UND GESTALT

Aufsätze zur Literatur

Verlag Hans Huber Bern

und Stuttgart

23. Fritz Ernst: *Bild und Gestalt*, Verlag Hans Huber, Bern (1963). Jacket layout by Max Caflisch

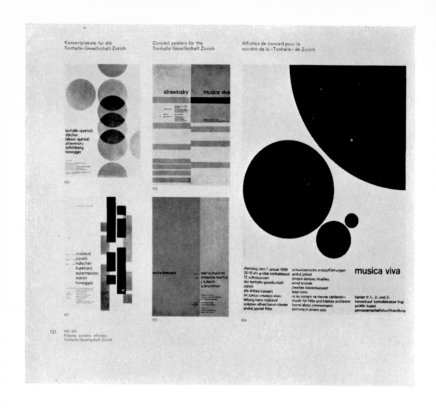

24. J. Müller-Brockmann: *Gestaltungsprobleme des Graphikers*, Teufen (1961).
Text page with reproductions of posters by the author

changes in working techniques also had their effect upon those engaged in the process: workers were obliged to adapt not only to the speeding-up of the processes themselves, but also to acquire the skills needed to use the increasingly complicated machines in their work. As the technical revolution got under way, human, hygienic and social problems grew more acute, the proletariat was born. The nineteenth century is not only the age of great technical progress: it is the age in which the worker began to establish his rights and to improve his standing in an industrial society. On the one hand the workers formed themselves into political or trade unions, on the other the employers formed their own federations. In Switzerland technical and social problems dominated the printing trade in the nineteenth century. As far as can be seen, it was newspaper-printing that was responsible for the major innovations in printing, and in Switzerland a native characteristic played an important part: the strong consciousness of communal autonomy and regional differences resulted in a newspaper industry with extraordinary ramifications. Newspapers established themselves in not only the big cities. There is scarcely a sizeable village or region that did not have its own paper. This diversification of the Press had a salutary effect on national politics. It served democracy well in that it stimulated political education and prevented strong economic or political groups from imposing their politics on the population. The diversification of the Press has remained characteristic of Switzerland to this day.

The Schweizerische Typographenbund was founded in 1858. It was originally conceived as an association of all printers—employers and employees—and was meant to lead to 'improved earnings' and 'mutual association as a barrier against unbridled competition'. The first statutes of the Typographenbund invited employers to 'reach agreement with the public and the authorities on a uniform definition of the so-called percentage'. It soon became clear that the interests of employers and employees could not be represented in a single association. In 1869 the Schweizerische Buchdruckerverein was formed by the employers. The two groups have since then attempted, by mutual agreement, to improve industrial law in the country's printing industry.

The most important achievements of the two federations—usually arrived at by negotiation, but sometimes by strikes and lockouts—has been the establishment of collective pay agreements and minimum wages, which led the employers to seek a fixed price tariff. Other important subjects have been vocational training and the control of the number of apprentices, based on the number of journeymen employed in each firm. The history of the Schweizerische Buchdruckerverein, the Schweizerische Typographenbund and, later, the Schweizerische Faktorenbund (technicians) shows that usually the demands made at various times by union-organised labour were generally first voiced and solved (usually after sharp disagreements) in the printing industry, which was considered a model for other industries. This applies to working hours, wage differentials, holidays, and many other social claims. Towards the end of the nineteenth century an analogous development took place in another branch of the industry: the Schweizerische Lithographenbund was formed in 1888, and in 1894 the employers formed the Verein Schweizerischer Lithographiebesitzer.

Compared with the great technical and social changes that took place in the second half of the nineteenth century, advances in design and publishing were very modest. There was no great intellectual and artistic stimulus. The industry was decidedly provincial and confined its output to daily and local demand. This is borne out by the fact that Switzerland's most outstanding men (of whom there were many in the nineteenth century) were obliged to develop their talents abroad or use foreign publishers for their most important works.

The French-speaking literary and scientific élite looked to Paris, the Italian to Milan, and the German to Germany. The works of the great Zurich poets Gottfried Keller and Conrad Ferdinand Meyer were published by German publishers. Eminent scholars like Jacob Burckhardt and J. J. Bachofen did some of their work in Germany, felt themselves to be part of Germany's culture, and had their books published in Germany. One reason for this was the rapid growth of Germany's publishing trade in the nineteenth century, and the founding and growth of large publishing concerns that were able to guarantee authors a greater circulation than their Swiss counterparts, who could not compete with them.

In 1849, one year after the introduction of the Federal Constitution, the Swiss book-trade, which for the most part was in German hands throughout the century, formed the Schweizerische Buchhändlerverein. In Switzerland, as in Germany, one of the greatest problems, apart from prices and politics within the industry, was the fight against pirated editions, and for the establishment of copyright. Germany's copyright law of 1871 was a useful precedent. In 1886 the Bern Convention for the protection of works of literature and art took place. This is a multilateral agreement between states. With various revisions it has remained the basis for the international regulation of copyright questions.

Aesthetic taste did not keep pace with technical advances in the printing industry and the mass production of printed matter. On the contrary; the more production was speeded up, the lower the standard of type, setting, make-up, paper, presswork and binding. In the French- and Italian-speaking parts of Switzerland a certain tradition that might be called the legacy of Bodoni's and Didot's classicism managed to survive. But in German-speaking Switzerland the standard fell as low as in Germany. The decline began in the 1850's and got worse during the second half of the century. It is not an isolated phenomenon, but the reflection of an era without style. Industrialisation had brought the development of historical styles to an end. Then a reaction set in against technical and economic progress, a reaction which might be explained psychologically as a compensatory impulse—namely, Historicism: the undiscriminating arrangement of irreconcilable elements from different stylistic epochs. This could not conceal the creative impotence of its practitioners, whether in architecture, interior décor, useful or ornamental objects, or print. It was true of all printed matter, from advertising leaflets to books, of ephemeral literature and popular magazines, and even of scientific works and editions of the classics. Thus the nineteenth century's enormous intellectual achievements were presented to contemporaries and posterity in a physical form that manifests an almost inexplicably low standard of taste. Just how great is the discrepancy between subject-matter and form in these books becomes clear when we compare them with those of the age of humanism and the Enlightenment. The latter, in the style valid for their time, have a satisfying balance between content and presentation that has stood the test of time.

Those who had aesthetic sensitivity were aware of this low standard. Towards the end of the century attempts were made in various countries to remedy it with a new, up-to-date style. In retrospect it is possible to see that the turn of the century was the time when the foundations for the Art Nouveau were laid in all fields of creative art. The initial impetus to this renewal was given by artists. Two main departures can be discerned. In the fine arts a bold advance was made in the way of representing things seen: the work of the Impressionists in France bears witness to this. In the applied arts a consciousness of good forms was first recaptured in England. But the new, Art Nouveau, which departed so completely from previous forms, did not affect manufactured things directly. It was the artist, not involved with industry or manufacture, who spread the new gospel and put it into practice in his own work, thus bringing about a change in taste. The result was that, particularly in the field of printing, it was not a case of the manufacturers taking a risk in producing something new, but of the consumers demanding it. This development shows clearly in Switzerland.

It is strange that the impetus to the renewal of creative printing in Switzerland did not come from the lively group of artists and intellectuals within her own borders, particularly if it is remembered how at previous times of cultural and scientific renewal the influence on the trade had always been so beneficial. The discrepancy was most marked in German-speaking Switzerland, though the explanation for it may be found there, too: all the eminent men of learning and literature in Switzerland—the historian Jacob Burckhardt, the poets Gottfried Keller and C. F. Meyer, and later the art historian Heinrich Wölfflin—had German publishers. Cultural ties between Switzerland and Germany were closer than they had ever been; like their counterparts in Germany authors tried to reach the entire German-reading public by means of German publishers. The 'moral obligation' to publish Swiss works with Swiss publishers did not exist, the more so since superior competition from Germany had driven Swiss printers and publishers into provincialism.

Thus the impetus came neither from Switzerland's own cultural élite nor from the numerous and for the most part small publishing houses. In Switzerland it was also the artists who tried to extend the new spirit and style in the applied arts. One of the characteristics of the Art Nouveau movement of the 1900's is that the artist acknowledged his obligations to society and tried to contribute to a 'social art' by designing for all branches of the applied arts. While some of the Art Nouveau artists worked mainly in furniture, textiles and jewellery, others, particularly painters and other graphic artists, preferred to work in media closer to print. Looking back, we can see that the painter Ferdinand Hodler (1853–1918)—with Van Gogh, Gauguin and Munch, one of the fathers of expressionism in Europe—who gave the impetus in Switzerland to a new style in the applied arts with a number of poster and other designs shortly after 1900. The discovery of this new art medium drew the attention of Hodler's contemporaries to the spectacular possibilities of the illustrated poster and other pictorial forms of applied art. This became the basis of the high standard of printing in Switzerland today. The first to start were a number of lithographic printers who, with Hodler and his successors, set the new trends in advertising design as early as 1900. This in turn had its effect on book-printing, though at first it only showed in commercial and other printed products. But the reform begun here took an ever firmer hold during the first decade of this century.

In this great reform the letter, in all its forms and applications, played an important role. It is scarcely an exaggeration to say that the design of letters and their related ornaments was the real effective medium in which the concepts of Art Nouveau found expression. In Switzerland, too, print was the chief medium for the new style.

The artistic revival in Switzerland was stimulated by a number of outside influences. Both Germany and Switzerland were influenced by the revival of book design begun in England by William Morris and the Kelmscott Press, and J. Cobden-Sanderson's Doves Press. Nowhere else (perhaps not even in England) did the English renaissance of the printed book find a readier response than in Germany, where the first private press books appeared from 1905 onwards.

Apart from the direct influence of England's new book design, which went together with a renewal of interest in printing types—in fact a return to the best sixteenth-century type faces—it was German book design that affected Switzerland most strongly. The work of Edward Johnston (whose impact was greatest in Germany), and that of German type and book designers like Otto Eckmann, Peter Behrens, Anna Simons, Walter Tiemann, E. R. Weiss, F. W. Kleukens, F. H. Ehmcke and Rudolf Koch, and the work of the excellent private presses in Germany, were carefully studied in Switzerland. In addition it was now possible to make use of the rapidly expanding and improving programmes of type design that were being undertaken by the leading typefoundries. For a time Switzerland had to use German types. The 'artistic types' in vogue at the time were as useful as the attempts of Rudolf von Larisch and others to develop type design artistically. But in the long run the greatest hope seemed to lie in that sector of type design which concentrated on the renewal of good traditional faces and on trying to rediscover the basic laws of typography. This was made possible by the recutting of historical roman types, that is both the roman faces of the fifteenth century and later ones. The pioneer work of the German private presses—their choice of type, careful composition, well-proportioned pages, etc., found a wide following among the leading publishing houses. Swiss printers and publishers, always in sharp competition with Germany, could not afford to ignore these developments, and some of them took them up quickly and of their own will. They did this the more readily since a lively circle of artists and letter-designers in Switzerland championed the new style.

An examination of Swiss book production around 1900 reveals attempts— at first hesitating and then increasingly firm—to re-enliven the design of books and other printed matter, which had grown rigid, boring and formless. To begin with, bad typographic make-up with bad type faces was adapted to the new style with *Jugendstil* ornaments.

This mere external adaptation was by no means restricted to ephemeral literature or commercial printing. Even in historical and scientific works, in children's magazines and school textbooks, attempts were made to use the new style. The results may have been modest and in many cases of dubious value, but these attempts did stimulate a more general interest in style and prepare the way for a true renewal. And so it came about that 'outsiders', particularly type-designers, individual firms not always in the printing trade, and art schools soon set an example to other printing firms. This provoked a general competiveness which was to have excellent results, particularly in recent times. Developments in Swiss printing since 1900 can be broken down into several categories; technical, economic, social and stylistic. Each of these has a real influence on quality. Within each category there are discernible developmental stages, with parallel developments in the other categories. Another way of analysing developments during the twentieth century is in terms of, say, tasks to be solved; or of the repercussions of world and local politics on the country's printing trade; or general cultural and artistic changes. Here too, reflecting greater or even world-wide developments, definite stages are discernible in the limited sphere of printing. Since we cannot elaborate on every change that took place from every point of view, we shall concentrate on design (i.e. formal) and technical aspects. A few general remarks are necessary if we are to understand the situation that exists today.

The economic backbone of the Swiss printing industry since the nineteenth century has been threefold, and in the first place the Press in the widest sense (since the consolidation of Press freedom in the new Federation in 1848). As a result of the federalistic structure and the multi-lingual population of Switzerland, and as an expression of the anti-centralist and often individualistic and separatist attitude of the Swiss, the country has an amazing number of daily and weekly papers in relation to its population. Apart from a few great newspapers published in the largest cities—*Neue Zürcher Zeitung, Tages-Anzeiger* (Zurich), *National-Zeitung* (Basle), *Basler Nachrichten, Bund* (Bern), *Gazette de Lausanne, Journal de Genève*, and others—there is an immense number of medium-sized, small, and very small papers for the regions, towns and villages. In 1928, for instance, 406 political papers were published; of these 282 were in German, 105 in French, and nineteen in Italian or Romansch. Today there are 340 newspapers in all four languages. In addition to these papers, which express regional and local religious and economic views, there are innumerable trade and special-interest newspapers and periodicals, ranging from local club bulletins to international scientific, technical and cultural magazines—again in all four languages. It is true not only of the large papers, but also of the provincial, local press, that the newspaper is the most important economic factor in large and small printing concerns.

The second category is advertising print, which chiefly supplies the needs of industry and commerce. Switzerland's economy and industry have evolved towards the modern industrial state since the late nineteenth century, and the demands made on the printing industry have increased tremendously as a result. As with newspapers, it is not just a few mammoth concerns that dominate the country's industry and economy. Apart from a few large firms of world status, there are an enormous number of medium-sized and small firms in all fields. It is unlikely that any other country, in relation to its size and population has so many, often small and decentralised, manufacturing units. There are few printing firms, whether old-established or newly founded, that do not owe the gratifying growth of their turnover to industry and commerce. Their influence is not only material: the printer has to comply with the wishes of his customers, whose demands with regard to design and technique have affected all printing. This influence has been beneficial in Switzerland. Since the early twenties Swiss graphic design has reached a standard that has earned it an international reputation. As it passes through the printing works it has stimulated the taste and interest of everyone concerned with the production of a well-designed piece of print. In this way designers have to a great extent taken over the educative function from their clients.

The third category is book-printing. As the oldest branch of the printing industry book-printers—particularly in Switzerland—can look on their history with pride. Many of the leading printing firms in Switzerland were once publishers' printers, and many of them still are today, whether working for their own publishing houses or outside ones. Here the possibilities of development largely depend on cultural developments. But here it is also possible to compare one's own work with the great achievements of the past, and with the real starting-point from which the typographic designer can affect the standard of printing.

Naturally, things are more complex than that; neither the large, medium-sized, nor small firms that comprise Switzerland's 1600 book-print workshops today can be fitted into simple categories; in fact, in no other country do conditions vary so much from firm to firm. But all Swiss houses have a number of characteristics in common.

Switzerland's geography splits her into many separate parts, many of them with quite different cultures. There are radical differences between individual regions, dating back to migratory movements long ago and further diversified by the accessions of new groups from outside. All this makes it impossible to speak of a typical Swiss, with distinctive Swiss characteristics. Nevertheless certain traits have emerged—due to whatever causes—which seem typically Swiss to the outsider. These happen to have particular bearing on printing, and have had some beneficial effects. Thus one characteristic of the Swiss is their bent for precise, painstakingly finished work, and a pre-occupation with high-quality craftsmanship. The Swiss, unlike some more light-hearted and carefree peoples, are as a rule not content with expending a minimum of effort and material on a job. They find this 'minimalism' contemptible. Indeed, they try to do any job as perfectly as possible, spending too much time and effort on it rather than not enough, and exploring every possible way of doing it just right. This feeling for quality is a heritage of Protestantism as preached by the great Swiss reformer Ulrich Zwingli: an ethos which does not measure work by material results but by the inner satisfaction which working as such bestows. This Zwinglian or Calvinistic spirit, has been given repeated fillips by the refugees who made Switzerland their second home. In an age like ours, in which economic prosperity is the ultimate good, that is where the quickest possible turnover is required, this Protestant attitude towards work is of course overlaid by considerations of utility. Nevertheless, even today everyone who comes into contact with the printing trade in Switzerland is aware that the old printer's pride in his work, and the Protestant attitude towards work, still survives—even in the Catholic regions of Switzerland. There is still a willingness to do more than the basic minimum if this will result in a superior product.

This attitude is still a prerequisite for the high-quality workmanship for which the Swiss are renowned. This tradition, rooted in the old peasant and craft culture, springs from the fact that Switzerland is a land-locked country, poor in raw materials, and can only survive (particularly in an age of high industrialisation) by producing high-quality goods from the raw materials she has to import. This applies to all her industries. It is therefore no coincidence that one of the most pressing problems is how to preserve high quality at a time when there is sharp competition and a shortage of labour.

This pre-occupation with quality also has its drawbacks, which become apparent where there is no reasonable balance between the quality of work and material on the one hand, and the practical usefulness of the product on the other. In printing, particularly, there are countless instances of products in which the use to which they are put hardly justifies the effort and care that have gone into them, particularly in commercial printing—short-lived prospectuses, packaging, and the like. Here quality has become an end in itself. But both client and printer would be deeply hurt if criticised for using expensive wood-free paper and light-fast printing inks on a poster that is likely to be covered over in a few weeks' time; or for printing a job in four colours where three would have been perfectly adequate; or for wasting high-quality art paper on a hand-out.

Though sometimes excessive, this insistence on high quality is a useful prerequisite for good design. Where there is a tendency to make the cheapest things as cheaply as possible, there is a danger of treating valuable and lasting things in the same way. Where, on the other hand, there is a feeling that even the most modest and ephemeral thing must be well-made, more exacting tasks stand a better chance of receiving careful attention. It is not possible for one and the same firm, using the same personnel and machinery, to turn out both shoddy mass-products and high-quality goods.

Closely allied to the preoccupation with quality is the fact that since the beginning of this century, and particularly in the last twenty years, printing and other firms in the graphic trade have tremendously improved their equipment. Whenever financial circumstances have permitted it they have been prepared to install the most up-to-date machinery. It can be claimed that it is possible to get good results with old and even superannuated machinery if the will is there, but it is characteristic of the Swiss to have only the best possible tools, in order to achieve the best results. They have always bought the best equipment internationally available, though since the Second World War they have been able to rely increasingly on machinery made in Switzerland. Today printing firms of all sizes are extremely well equipped; this has enabled them to achieve the rationalisation made necessary by the shortage of manpower. Typical of this constant modernising of plant has been the introduction of new type faces, particularly over the last two decades.

To the foreigner another characteristic of the Swiss is their pre-occupation with education, which is of course a reflection of their pre-occupation with quality. It is not presumptious to claim that the country which produced Pestalozzi and Rousseau has long enjoyed a high standard of education, which has always been furthered with the best means available. This also shows a specifically democratic principle: every man, regardless of his financial or social standing, is entitled to the best education that the community can provide. On the pattern of its carefully worked out primary and secondary school system, which is financed and controlled by the individual communities and not the Federation, Switzerland made an early start at organising vocational training, again on the principle that everyone is entitled to a thorough training in the trade of his choice, and, once trained, to fair remuneration for his skills. Since the second half of the nineteenth century various trades have been attempting to organise vocational training—usually at the behest of the employers. From this the regulations, long since fixed in Federal law, have slowly evolved. They guarantee a sound training in every vocational field. In the printing trade it was the Schweizerische Buchdruckerverein (the employers) and the Schweizerische Typographenbund (the unions) who established vocational training. According to regulations that have been generally binding since the late nineteenth century, school leavers are apprenticed as compositors or printers for four years. The employer undertakes to give the apprentice a thorough training in his subject, and is obliged to make sure during that period that the apprentice's training is properly carried out. The apprentice has to attend a cantonal or municipal training college one day a week, where he is given further training. In the larger towns these courses are given by special departments at the art schools. At the end of the course pupils have to pass a national examination. In addition to this compulsory training, which, often based on the Swiss model, is compulsory in most Western countries today, there is further vocational training, the idea of which began to be mooted at the beginning of this century. The need for further education was strongly pressed by the unions. It is largely the technical colleges and art schools that offer opportunities for such training. Their printing departments grew into fully fledged independent printing schools at Zurich in 1910 and at Basle in 1915. Once the employers had recognized its importance and began to give it their moral and, sometimes, financial support, advanced education in the printing trade was able to develop. To some extent world political events have helped it: before 1933 the sons of employers and others who wanted advanced training used to attend one of the leading German schools, such as the Staatliche Akademie für graphische Künste und Buchgewerbe at Leipzig. From 1933 these German schools rapidly came under the influence of the Nazi régime, and substitutes had to be found for Switzerland's younger generation of printers. Today there are so many opportunities for further education in Switzerland that there is no longer any need to go to Germany for it.

Advanced training, thanks to a great extent to the high standard of design and technique in many firms, can be both technical and artistic. Both are necessary for the training of qualified personnel. Vocational training has also profited by a few decades of industrial peace, during which most financial and social disputes have been settled by arbitration.

Let us return to the influence that the new style, which began at the turn of the century, has had on printing and design in Switzerland. At first it was practised by a few painters, but soon there came into existence a new kind of artist, who called himself a '*Schriftkünstler*' and, from about 1920, a '*Graphiker*'. This new profession subsequently divided into further specialised fields. The idea of a new age in design was accepted by the Swiss printing trade as early as the first decade of the twentieth century, and various types of printed product show its direct and indirect influence.

The outbreak of the First World War radically changed conditions in Switzerland. In many spheres of cultural life the Swiss—particularly the German-speaking ones—had to ask themselves whether they wished to dissociate themselves from a Germany with whose views they were no longer able to identify themselves. The poet Carl Spitteler, in a speech entitled '*Unser Schweizer Standpunkt*' (The Swiss Point of View), set the course for Switzerland's subsequent attitude. For Swiss publishers this was the signal to emerge from their provincial isolation and to play once more the role of mediators for German-speaking countries. This development was helped by the cultural and artistic life that was able to flourish in Switzerland—the 'island of peace'. The countries at war competed with each other in mounting cultural events on neutral soil for propaganda purposes. But, more important, freedom-loving, pacifist writers, artists and intellectuals from everywhere found refuge and a forum for discussion here. The presence of this lively, mixed company of European intellectuals, acted as a cultural and artistic stimulus. There was an upsurge of literary, political and other activity, particularly at Geneva, Bern and Zurich; which was reflected in printing. A few examples will suffice. The author Romain Rolland and the woodcutter Frans Masereel lived and worked at Lake Geneva; their pacifist daily, *La Feuille*, was published at Geneva from 1916 to 1920. At Bern and Zurich, apart from the real revolutionaries, of whom the most notable was Lenin, it was principally pacifist German writers, such as René Schickele, Annette Kolb, Leonhard Frank, Fritz von Unruh and many others, who carried the banner for internationalism. The Zurich house of Rascher published Schickele's pacifist periodical *Die weissen Blätter;* the books in their *Europäische Bibliothek* reflect these cultural trends. Nearly all Swiss publishing houses played some part in the cultural life of that period.

The most powerful influence—though off-putting to many—was exercised by the group that founded Dadaism at Zurich in 1916: Hans Arp, Hugo Ball, Marcel Jacno, Tristan Tzara and Richard Huelsenbeck. Dadaism came as a further influence in addition to expressionism, which had already found a response in Swiss art. The Dadaists produced a number of pamphlets and invitations and the periodicals *Dada, Cabaret Voltaire* and *Der Zeltweg* (published at Zurich), which were a radical departure not only because of their unusual contents, but also their free design. The anti-logical element in Dadaist design represented the circle's picture of the mad world of their time, but also expressed a deeper aesthetic feeling. In these publications, which are collectors' items today, there are already traces of the 'new typography' that was still to come. In order to be able to develop the stringent new language of design which came about in 1918–20, it was first necessary to reject all existing rules and concept of the 'beautiful' in the graphic arts. One of the pioneers of modern typography was the painter, sculptor and poet Hans Arp, as may be seen from some of the Dadaist publications. The role which Dadaism played in typography is often overlooked by those who see the movement only in terms of the influence it had on Surrealism.

The early twenties, which witnessed a general revival of the arts and intensive international exchange, were a productive period. It was generally felt that after the dismal years of the war humanity was at last on the threshold of a new age, which creative artists must help to further. The most characteristic movement of the age was—in the widest sense—'constructivism'. In Holland the movement was called *De Stijl* (The Style); in Germany, it was expressed through the Bauhaus; in Russia, by the Constructivists; and in France, by the 'Purists'. A 'constructive ethos' developed in many fields of artistic endeavour, characterised by clarity, simplicity and regularity. It was generally considered possible to solve all problems by rational means and a geometric approach; by working in accordance with the logical consequences that flow out of the 'function' (or what was thought to be the function) of a thing. In printing this new spirit found expression in what for the first time ever consciously called itself 'typography'. Jan Tschichold formulated this new kind of design in the late twenties, in his primer *Die neue Typographie* (Berlin, 1928). This advocated a radically reduced range of permissible type faces—ideally only sans serif faces—and the asymmetric arrangement of lines and pages, achieved by simple geometric grouping.

The chief Swiss exponents of these new ideas were the art schools, the new generation of graphic artists, and a few go-ahead publishers and printing houses.

Advertising design was in its nature best suited to experiments in the new typographical style, on posters, newspaper advertisements, prospectuses and various other kinds of commercial print. Print design in German-speaking

Switzerland at that time shows a marked decline in the use of fraktur faces; the extravagant *Künstlerschriften* in vogue in the early twentieth century were no longer popular. Designers concentrated on a number of more and less good, mostly modern, roman faces, combined with heavy rules. There was an interesting revival of Bodoni Light, Medium and Bold, which appealed to the rationalism of the era. One of the pioneers of the modern book, both in content and design, was Eugen Rentsch, who built up a lively publishing house in Erlenbach-Zurich. The best-known of his books is *Kunst-ismen* (Art-isms— 1925), by El Lissitzky and Hans Arp, with typography by Lissitzky. This was also the time of new techniques in photography; some interesting experiments in the form of *Schaubüchern* (picture books), which concentrated on optical aspects, were published by the house of Orell Füssli. The new, severe typographic style developed almost exclusively in the German parts of Switzerland. French-speaking Switzerland continued in the traditional style that also remained dominant in France. An exhibition of printed works in the new style, *Neue Typographie*, at the Gewerbemuseum, Basle, in 1927, was a definitive demonstration of the application of modern principles of design.

And then a curious thing happened. Around 1930 the crest of the new wave in design had suddenly passed. The intellectual and artistic impetus began to wane, and in many fields traditional and increasingly reactionary forces regained the ascendancy. The artistic *avant-garde* became a small group of conspirators. The modern form played a small role in the generally lively printing trade. Political developments in Germany from 1933 began to have an inhibiting effect on Switzerland's intellectual and artistic life. Having seen a Fascist dictatorship in operation for some time south of her borders, Switzerland now had to witness the growth of an even more calamitous régime in Germany, in the North. The threat which these constituted to freedom of thought triggered a growing desire in the Swiss to look to the basis of their own existence. The idea of a 'spiritual defence of the country' manifested itself in many fields of culture. An examination of the basic idea and history of the Swiss state was perforce retrogressive in many fields. Essential though it was, it impeded forward-looking, modern ideas and activities.

But the danger of complete retrogression and shutting out of the external world was lessened from the onset of the Nazi régime and throughout the 'thirties by the gradual growth of counter-forces. Political developments in the outside world presented Switzerland with enormous cultural responsibilities, particularly in the field of publishing. It was these new responsibilities which initiated a renaissance in the volume and quality of publishing and printing.

Switzerland was increasingly forced to publish her own books—school-books, technical and scientific literature as well as fiction and *belles lettres*. Publishing in Germany had until 1933 supplied a considerable part of Switzerland's book demand. It was now being brought into line with Nazi doctrine—a development which stopped short at neither encyclopedic nor scientific work. To protect herself against this infiltration, Switzerland had increasingly to satisfy her own needs in all fields of publishing. This forced her, for instance, to go into medical publishing; and to produce within a relatively short time, and without any experience or tradition in this field, a *Schweizer Lexikon* (Swiss Encyclopedia) that had to summarise the present-day body of knowledge democratically and objectively. Thus Germany's National Socialist totalitarianism had the salutary effect on Switzerland of forcing her to be on her guard against the thousandfold dangers that threatened her freedom and culture; it enabled her to become self-sufficient by keeping her eyes on the fundamental principles of freedom and supplying her own demand in books.

This demand soon proved to go beyond mere national interests. The more Germany's totalitarian might increased, the greater became the Swiss publishers' responsibility towards the German-speaking free world everywhere. It was this responsibility which gave it the strength it needed for its difficult tasks. The latter were magnified, though in many respects eased, by the fact that once again Switzerland became a haven for those persecuted for their convictions or race. She became an emporium of free thought.

The time of the war and the years immediately preceding it have been called a fateful hour for Swiss publishing. The fact is that all existing Swiss publishing houses and a number of newly-founded ones were producing books at a rate never known before. Swiss publishing opened out into a number of new fields, including the systematic production of scientific works.

In response to international tensions, there arose a rich political literature which was concerned with examining Swiss and European problems. To many emigrant authors from Germany, Austria and Czechoslovakia, Swiss, Dutch and Swedish publishers offered an opportunity to get their works into print. One of the more important functions played by Switzerland's publishers was the publication of German translations of foreign authors, especially those of the English-speaking world. In addition to contemporary literary and scientific writing, there were the classics, particular care being taken to produce critical, scholarly complete editions. The Artemis-Verlag's Goethe edition is one of many examples; Schwabe's edition of the complete works of Johann Jakob Bachofen is another.

Statistics bear out the growth of publishing in Switserland. The increase in the total number of books published in various years makes impressive reading:

year	no. of titles	year	no. of titles	year	no. of titles
1914	1470	1925	1748	1941	2510
1918	1764	1938	2162	1943	3358
1921	1332	1940	1705	1946	4001

Since then, in spite of the recovery of publishing in Germany, Switzerland has been able to stay at this high level. In 1962 5,086 titles were published. Two-thirds of these were in German, the rest chiefly in French, with some Italian, Romansch and a fair number of foreign and multilingual works. Publishing, previously a modest factor in the country's economy, grew in importance as a result of developments in the thirties and forties, particularly as an export trade. In 1912 book exports were worth 3.5 million francs, compared with imports worth 18.5 million. By the end of the twenties book exports and imports were about even. After 1945 exports considerably exceeded imports: 25 million francs as against 10–12 million. The figures for 1962 are: 51.9 million francs for exports and 52.3 million francs for imports of books and periodicals. Thus the export figures for books and periodicals today considerably exceed those for traditional Swiss export products—chocolate and shoes.

The material and spiritual recovery is of course only one aspect of Switzerland's book-trade. The other question to be asked is: Did design keep pace with this development? This is not a simple question to answer.

It is worth mentioning here that the growth of publishing and other branches of the book industry—particularly reproduction techniques—comes at a time when advertising art has improved considerably. Economic growth in the 'thirties, and in particular the Swiss Landesausstellung (National Exhibition) in 1939 gave the profession a great boost. A degree of cooperation developed between designers and printers that had never existed before. Designers became better acquainted with printing techniques, while printers became aware of the possibilities and problems of design. This reciprocal relationship has been beneficial. The great number of new tasks confronting printers and publishers has led to a fundamental reappraisal both of traditional printing and the work of contemporaries in other countries.

It was a stroke of luck for Switzerland that the typographer Jan Tschichold emigrated from Germany in 1933 and settled in Switzerland. He has done

319

much to improve the state of Swiss typography, both with his work and as a publicist and teacher. It is no exaggeration to say that it was Tschichold's direct and indirect influence on printing in Switzerland that has generally brought about an understanding of the true function of typography. Designers, typographers and printers who had previously put all their efforts into furthering the art of the book found new encouragement in his work. His own typographic work as art director of Schwabe and Birkhäuser and the Holbein-Verlag at Basle demonstrated in practice what he meant by the considered choice of type faces properly attuned to the task in hand, what he understood by unexceptionable composition and harmonic typography. Tschichold communicated his theories in specialist publications. His *Typographisches Gestalten*, published by Schwabe at Basle in 1935, had a decisive influence on vocational training. *Gute Schriftformen*, published by the Erziehungsdepartement (Education Department) Basel-Stadt in 1941–2 has run to several editions. Intended as a primer, this collection of samples has had far-reaching effects on printing-houses and designers. The revival of the printing trade provided the material conditions for renewing and enlarging the stock of type faces in many printing-houses, and Tschichold's teaching made it an absolute necessity. The fact that most firms today dispose of a large and ever-renewed range of type faces, both for machine (Linotype, Intertype and, particularly for book-work, Monotype) and hand composition, can largely be attributed to the groundwork put in by Tschichold twenty-five years ago.

In 1931 the Hungarian type designer and illustrator Imre Reiner came to live in Switzerland—another stroke of luck for the country. He, too, greatly influenced book design with his work for many Swiss publishers and his writings (e.g. *Typo-Graphik*, 1944; *Modern and Historical Typography*, 1948—both published by Zollikofer, St Gallen). While Tschichold worked chiefly for typography that serves its purpose 'anonymously', Reiner's field was more the artistic, personal and exclusive. Apart from his work as artistic adviser with Schwabe at Basle, Zollikofer at St Gallen, and other publishing houses, Reiner enriched the trade with a number of fine books for bibliophiles; in many of them he proved his talent as a pioneer and master of modern wood-engraving.

A number of Swiss typographers of the older generation also contributed to the re-awakening of the art of the book in Switzerland. The most important of these is Hans Vollenweider, who was art director first for Fretz and later for Orell Füssli at Zurich, but continued to devote himself to his Johannespresse—a private press which he had founded in 1919, and which produced superb pieces for bibliophiles in small and very small editions. These were largely the work of young authors or classical texts. He used the best hand- and machine-set types. One of his major works was an English edition of Michelangelo's poems, set in Arrighi; another was Goethe's *Ur-Faust*, for which he designed Rotunda, which Walter Schneider cut in 14 point.

Since the twenties, private-press work has flourished in Switzerland. Bibliophiles, whether printers, publishers, typographers or dilettanti, kept up an output of fine books, either singly or as part of a series. This work is usually motivated by idealism, and commercial motives have seldom played a part in it. The main stress has been on original illustrations. In this particular field the most distinguished work has been done in the German, and even more in the French parts of Switzerland. The de-luxe editions of the brothers Gonin at Lausanne, mainly classics, are illustrated by some of the great modern masters. The illustrated book, both private-press and commercial, which is also once more showing some interesting and handsome new developments, has its own norms, which often direct the attention away from purely typographical qualities.

A large circle of bibliophiles contributes towards the continued cultivation of the beautiful book, particularly in the form of private-press work. The *Schweizerische Bibliophilen-Gesellschaft* has played a leading role in this work. It has some 700 members and its own carefully designed periodical (formerly *Stultifera navis*, and now *Librarium*—designer Heinrich Kümpel), concerns itself with old and modern book design, and makes its own contribution to the art of the fine book in the form of its annual gifts. The *Schweizerische Gutenbergmuseum* has a similar function. It is the organ of an association that supports a centre of that name for collecting and fostering all aspects of printing and newspaper history. It is housed in the Gewerbemuseum, Bern. A number of printers, publishers, and firms outside the trade have cultivated the admirable practice of regularly sponsoring the publication of annual gifts, which are often fine examples of Swiss printing. Among these are the *Zürcher Drucke* of the Zurich printing house of Fretz (which have been coming out some twenty-five years and were for a long time under the care of Walter Diethelm, the designer of Diethelm-Antiqua), and the New Year gifts of the Buchdruckerei Winterthur, which have for several years been edited by Walter Kern. Happily, there are quite a number of projects of this kind, thanks to the country's prosperity. They have a stimulating effect on normal book production.

Another form of competition is the annual award for the best books of the year, similar to those in various other countries. In Switzerland it was started by Jan Tschichold, who proclaimed the ten best books of the year in 1943. The award, given to about twenty-five books each year, is organised by the Schweizerische Buchhändler- und Verleger-Verein. Its thirteen-man jury consists of representatives from all fields of book production, and the winners are publicised in a pamphlet and in shop-window displays.

In the work of this jury and in the many verbal and published discussions of the form of the modern book a dichotomy becomes apparent, which has been affecting the entire book-production of Switzerland—as indeed of other countries. This is the argument of 'traditional' versus 'modern'. The discussion, heatedly and repeatedly pursued in Switzerland, and cropping up annually in the award for the best books, faces every publisher and designer with each project. It, too, goes back to Jan Tschichold. When Tschichold came to Switzerland he was generally known as one of the pioneers of the 'modern' or 'new' typography. But his work in Switzerland has ever more clearly been in the service of 'classical' typography, which he defined very precisely in numerous publications and essays (the most recent was in *Zur Typographie der Gegenwart*, published in *Druckspiegel*, 2, 1958, and later privately printed by the Monotype Corporation at Bern, 1960). Tschichold found many followers with this theory in Switzerland. The most distinguished of this younger generation of typographers is Max Caflisch, for many years art director of the house of Benteli at Bern-Bümpliz, and at present head of the graphic section at the Kunstgewerbeschule, Zurich. But Tschichold's creed of 'classical' typography has also encountered some formidable opposition. Its spokesmen feel that typography—choice of type faces and composition—ought to be part of the contemporary vocabulary of forms. They have tried to find a link with the typography of the twenties, whose tradition has continued most strongly in commercial design. Apart from the original pioneers of the new art in Switzerland (foremost among them Max Bill), a large circle of progressive designers and typographers has taken the side of modern typography. Emil Ruder, one of its most eminent advocates, and head of the printing classes at the Kunstgewerbeschule, Basle, has called it '*ordnende Typographie*' (typography which creates order).

These two extreme positions are both evident in the Swiss book today, and between them there are various attempts at a conciliatory golden mean. These strive to become timeless by means of contemporary design, or contemporary by means of timeless design. A more or less distinctive 'classical' style is the general rule in literary and learned books, while subjects in their nature contemporary—such as technical publications and the wide range of illustrated books, particularly those involving photography—are usually given the 'modern' typographic treatment. In this contemporary field the real experiments in typography take place: typographic exercises, such as those at the schools which aim at familiarising young trainees with contemporary design, and experiments with books that lend themselves to this treatment. These advances are valuable because they show the possibilities and limits of typography as 'art' and act as counter-forces to the danger of routine, to which traditional typography is particularly exposed unless constantly re-examined with a critical eye. In Switzerland today the 'progressive' forces are powerful enough to be able to jog the traditional ones out of their equanimity. Conversely, the forces of inertia are great enough to safeguard against the danger of tradition being sacrificed on the altar of modernism for its own sake. This does not mean that the answer lies in characterless compromise. Both forces are strong enough to permit successful interaction. By far the greatest danger lies in the increasing industrialisation of the printing and publishing trade, aggravated by the difficulty of finding enough newcomers prepared to work for an industry with a great tradition.

James M. Wells

BOOK TYPOGRAPHY IN THE UNITED STATES OF AMERICA

In the year 1800 printing in the United States had barely begun to demonstrate independence of English modes and English material. Ever since the establishment of the first press in the colonies, in Cambridge, Massachusetts, in 1638–39, American printers had imported their paper, type, and presses from Europe, mainly from England. They naturally imitated the books to which they had been accustomed there. During the succeeding century, when most books were still imported, they continued to produce books which resembled English work. These were scarcely inspired days in English typography, nor could one expect printers with limited resources, working under great handicaps, to improve upon their models. Nevertheless, the best of the colonial American books were sound, sober, and well made, decently printed and plainly bound. Some, like John Eliot's Indian Bible (1661–63) represent significant scholarly achievement as well as a remarkable technical accomplishment.

The colonial press was primarily a utilitarian affair. Its product consisted mainly of theological and legal works, school books, commercial and legal forms, and the like. As in most young countries, the emphasis was on necessities, among which literature apparently ranked low. There were families, especially in the South, which prided themselves on their links with England and which brought sizeable libraries along with their furniture, silver, and family portraits. These people continued to read and buy English literary works, either through London agents with whom they maintained accounts or from the booksellers who soon established themselves in the Colonies. But the average colonist, whether he had left because of religious principle or because he saw a bright economic future as an emigrant, had little interest in belles lettres. The printer's staple during the eighteenth century was not the

327

novel or the poem, but the legal acts of the local assembly and the provision of the multitude of forms and certificates required to keep government going. It is no accident that in each colony the first press was usually established in the capital. Early in the eighteenth century (the Boston *Gazette* was established in 1704), journalism joined commercial printing as the prime source of revenue.

The printing-office in the colonial small town was its centre for the distribution of news and information; it was natural for the printer to combine his trade with other related ventures. He was often the postmaster, since he was the greatest user of the postal system; he might well keep a general store, stocking medicine, stationery and books; since there was a shortage of skilled craftsmen, he often doubled as bookbinder. The colonial printer was, until mid-eighteenth century, a small tradesman, with few apprentices or journeymen and little equipment.

By the time of the American revolution, however, it had become possible for a successful printer to become a considerable man of affairs. Such men as Benjamin Franklin or Isaiah Thomas were astute businessmen, who realised that larger editions meant lower costs, and that larger sales meant greater profits. This was difficult to achieve in the small, slow-growing colonial towns. Both Franklin and Thomas achieved their goals by finding and training bright, hard-working young men who were sent out as partners to manage a network of branch offices.

Franklin (1706–90), who learned his trade as apprentice to his brother James, in Boston, moved at seventeen to Philadelphia, where he soon demonstrated his abilities and readily made friends. One of these, Governor Keith, offered to set him up on his own and in 1724 sent him off to London to buy equipment, promising letters of credit which never arrived. In London Franklin supported himself by working in the shops of Samuel Palmer and John Watts, both printers of above average ability and taste. Palmer, best known for his history and grammar of printing, had definite notions on book design and its component elements, page layout, spacing, leading, and evenness of colour. Watts was one of a trio of printers who in 1720 had loaned William Caslon £500 to set up his foundry, and who were among the first to use his types. From his experience as a compositor under such masters Franklin improved both his taste and his mastery of his craft; as a result of his observations in London he was able, on his return to Philadelphia in 1727, to make a mould, strike matrices in lead from types, and fill in sorts when his new master, Samuel Keimer, ran low. At twenty-four Franklin established his own shop, which he developed into a chain of offices throughout the colonies, so that in

1748 he could afford virtually to retire from printing and devote himself to other interests. Ultimately he had eight branches, for which he acted as banker and supplier of ink, paper, and equipment. David Hall, who became his partner in 1748 and directed the firm of Franklin and Hall until its dissolution in 1766, could purchase in bulk as well as exchange stock of books and periodicals among a number of vigorous outlets.

Benjamin Franklin, despite his attainments as a scientist and inventor, made no significant contribution to the technology of his craft, nor did his books reveal any innovations in typographic design. His best pages are competent, rarely more, with good margins and close setting. He never progressed beyond the standards he brought back from London at the beginning of his career; as Lawrence Wroth says, in his essay 'Benjamin Franklin: The Printer at Work' (in *Typographic Heritage*, New York, 1949), 'He was interested in printing as a means of earning a living, not as a means of artistic expression.'

Isaiah Thomas (1749–1831), leading publisher of his day, followed the classic American pattern of rags to riches. He entered a printing-office at the age of six, with but six weeks of formal schooling, and by the time he was seventeen had become an excellent printer. In 1770, with a partner whom he soon bought out, he established in Boston *The Massachusetts Spy*, which continued publication until 1904. Thomas was so outspoken a champion of popular freedom and American independence that he was forced from Boston by the British occupation. He secretly moved his material to Worcester, where he was appointed official printer to the colony, publishing on his own account as well. Eventually he employed 150 persons, and besides his printing-shop, with seven presses, ran a paper-mill and a bindery. Thomas kept a close watch on his apprentices, choosing the likeliest as partners in branch shops or newspapers. At one time he had eight such branches, with his own messenger service connecting them.

Thomas was a highly successful publisher with a keen sense of the needs of a rapidly growing country. His more than 400 volumes included the first folio Bible in English printed in the United States, the first Greek grammar, and the first American dictionary, William Perry's (of which he sold 54,000 copies). He also published, in 1789, William H. Brown's *The Power of Sympathy*, the first American novel, as well as many children's books, among them the first American *Mother Goose*. By 1802 he could retire and devote the remainder of his life to scholarship, particularly to the writing of *The History of Printing in America* (1810), a pioneer work still of great value. Much of his source material came from his own large library, from which he gave books to Harvard, Dartmouth, and the American Antiquarian Society; he founded the latter in 1812 and became its first president.

Thomas was a plain, careful printer of conservative taste. He relied primarily upon English types, generally from Caslon, as his 1785 specimen-book shows. Franklin called him 'the Baskerville of America', not too high-flown a compliment, as an examination of his output reveals.

Among other, less spectacularly successful printers of note during the early years of the republic were Robert Aitken, of Philadelphia, who printed the first American Bible, in 1782; Christopher Sauer II, who imported moulds and matrices from Germany about 1770 and with them produced types of his own manufacture in his *Ein Geistlicher Magazin* the next year, 'der ersten schrift die jemals in America gegossen worden'. Two of Sauer's journeymen, Justus Fox and Jacob Bay, learned casting in his foundry and went on to design and cut their own roman letter, used in the first issue of the Philadelphia *Pennsylvania Mercury* on 7 April 1775. The earliest roman type designed, cut, and cast in the colonies had been that of Abel Buell, of Killingworth, Connecticut, in 1769, a crude piece of work which achieved slight success.

After the revolution American printers began to strengthen their own sources of supply, a matter of necessity, since the new nation was obliged to conserve its foreign exchange. Typefounding, paper, ink, and press manufacture all grew rapidly. As domestic industry increased, so did the place of the United States in the improvement of printing technology. At the beginning of the nineteenth century there had been no important American contribution to the art or craft of printing; by mid-century, when the industrial revolution had almost transformed printing, there had been many; by the beginning of the twentieth century American invention and engineering had played a leading role in changing printing from handicraft to mechanised mass production. Less significant was America's contribution to aesthetic and design. The nineteenth century cannot on the whole claim a high place in the history of the book for the beauty or the quality of its work; American books, still largely derivative in style, were no better than their models.

In 1800 the United States consisted of sixteen Eastern states with a population of approximately four million persons. It was just about to start its geographical expansion across the continent. The first major territorial acquisition, the Louisiana Purchase, from France, would take place in 1803. The centre of the book trade was Philadelphia, replacing Boston, which had led throughout the colonial period. By mid-century New York had achieved the leadership in publishing it has never since relinquished, although economic

By 1850 he was a successful bookseller-publisher, who had issued a number of magazines and periodicals, a series of popular school-books, many almanacs, and a few books of genuine substance, notably Henry Schoolcraft's *Notes on the Iroquois*, a pioneer work in linguistics and ethnology. He was firmly committed to a publishing programme which eventually included books on local and family history; reprints of scholarly Americana, a field in which he was an early leader; works for historical societies and bibliophile clubs; and catalogues and bibliographies for other scholarly booksellers and publishers who shared his interests. Munsell was particularly interested in the history of printing and books about books. As early as 1839 he printed an edition of 100 copies of a pamphlet called *Outlines of the History of Printing*, based upon Thomas, which he later tried to recall and suppress, ashamed both of his plagiarism and his typography; in 1865 he issued a thirty-eight page *Catalogue of a Bibliographical Library*, offered for sale *en bloc* and purchased by the New York State Library, which included a copy of Moxon. In 1868 a *Catalogue of Books on Printing...* offered Bodoni's *Manuale Tipografico* and the 1764 Caslon specimen-book. His *Bibliotheca Munselliana* (1870) listed and discussed the more than 2,000 books and pamphlets he had printed, with details of size, of edition and descriptions of format, the first detailed record of the output of any American printer. Munsell's own writings and printing, besides the early *Outlines*, include numerous short articles for printers' magazines and newspapers; *Typographical Miscellanies* (1850), made up of such pieces; and *A Chronology of Paper and Papermaking*, first published in 1856 and reprinted four times, a pioneer work that is still useful.

Munsell's growing interest in the history of printing and in early printed books is reflected in his own output. His youthful work, mostly jobbing printing, shows the fashionable mixture of ornamented faces and stock cuts. By 1850 he had begun to form his own style and had progressed to the point where the *Scientific American* would say, 'Mr. Munsell is one of the best printers of this or any other country.' Within the limits of his purse he did the best possible work. In 1871 he wrote, 'The only desire I have to be rich is to print books much better than I do, and not to take anything for them. I could do that, if I did less of them.' Munsell was so particular about paper that he had three lots made for his 1874 printing of Thomas's *History of Printing* before he found one that suited. He counselled against beginning to print before all copy was in hand, because it was impossible to keep even colour over a long period and because the edges of long-stored sheets would yellow. In a letter to De Vinne he complained about unreasonable customers:

'I have printed more than one monstrosity to the *order* of the author or publisher... the woefullest of all woes I suffer, arise from authors who come to me understanding that I am competent to print books, and when we have entered upon their works, insist upon so wrong impertinent and blasted idiosyncrasies of their own, as to damn the workmanship in the eyes of all good judges and expose the printer to the strictures of the critic, who stands in wait to show off his own nice perceptions in the matter.'

Munsell closely followed changes in fashion and technique, especially in England. He subscribed to foreign magazines and imported books, both for his own library and for stock. While he first objected to the Caslon revival of Pickering and the Whittinghams as being reactionary rather than progressive, by 1855 he had changed his mind and attempted to lay in a supply of old-style types. He found that Farmer, Little and Company, the only foundry to show them, had but two sizes of roman and no italic, so that he had to order a font of Caslon from the foundry in England. His 1856 *Papers relating to the Island of Nantucket* was the first American book in the nineteenth-century old-style revival. Munsell went on to add head- and tail-pieces in the Chiswick style, which he used frequently; to his more pretentious books he added a rubricated title-page; those of which he was proudest bore his dolphin and anchor mark with the motto: 'Aldi discipulus albaniensis.'

The nineteenth century produced a distinguished line of scholar-printers: Blades, Reed, Firmin Didot in England and Europe; Thomas and Munsell in America. Theodore Low De Vinne (1828–1914) belonged firmly in this tradition. He was one of six sons of a Methodist minister, of whom four became printers and the others binders (perhaps a result of their father's friendship with the Harper brothers, all active Methodists). On finishing his apprenticeship De Vinne moved, in 1848, to New York City, where two years later he became a journeyman in Francis Hart's shop. Hart quickly recognised De Vinne's qualities and made him foreman; in 1858 he became a partner. Hart's will stipulated that De Vinne be allowed to purchase the business on his death.

De Vinne was neither a great artist nor a great innovator. Rather he was a man of much natural talent; good, if not original, taste; an enormous capacity for hard, sustained work; keen business sense; and high standards of craftsmanship. One sees these qualities in his writings as well as in his printing. It is not insignificant that his first published works should be *The Profits of Book Composition* (1864) and *The Printers' Price List*, nor that the De Vinne Press's specimen-books should display the proprietor's historical writings. He was no mere dilettante historian, however, writing copy to sell his wares. *The Inven-*

tion of Printing (1876) is a work of original scholarship based upon close observation and study of early printing, much of it from his own library, to whose method of production he had applied his own great knowledge of printing and typefounding methods; it is a seminal work in the scientific study of incunabula. De Vinne taught himself French, German, and Italian so that he could pursue the wide reading his scholarship demanded, and introduced to many of his colleagues who knew only English the findings of continental research. He built up a considerable and valuable library for his own use; the 6,000 volumes in the 1920 auction of his estate constituted one of the finest typographic libraries ever offered in the United States. His other historical works included *Plain Printing Types* and *Historic Printing Types*, used and praised by Updike and Morison: an annotated edition of Moxon's *Mechanick Exercises*, its first reprint; and *Title-Pages as Seen by a Printer* and *Notable Printers of Italy during the Eighteenth Century*. The two latter were published by the Grolier Club, which he helped to found in 1884, its twin aims the advancement of bibliophily and the raising of printing standards. De Vinne's writings on the practice of printing were equally valuable, especially *The Practice of Typography*, a four-volume printers' manual which combined his own experience with the fruit of his wide observation and research.

De Vinne's work was the first in the long line of manuals ultimately derived from Moxon which dealt with the modern typesetting machines and their intelligent use. The Linotype and Monotype machines, patented in 1884 and 1887 respectively, were rapidly improved technically. Unfortunately the early faces cut for them were mediocre copies of nineteenth-century favourites, themselves weak and ugly letters. Not until after the First World War (except for the English Monotype Imprint) was there any real effort to bring the aesthetic quality of the types up to the same standards of excellence set for the mechanical performance of the machines. De Vinne, even though he was incapable of getting good faces for machine composition, did realise the possibilities. As Lawrence Wroth has said, *The Practice of Typography* 'is an original, creative study of the printing craft, informed by knowledge of the past and enlightened by faith in modern mechanical methods and by the conviction that through their thoughtful use the great traditions of typography might still be carried on.'

De Vinne's printing, like his written work, is sound and well made, notable for its craftsmanship rather than its inventiveness or its beauty. It is far above the level of American work of its period, but not as good as that the next generation, inspired by Morris and the arts and crafts revival, would produce. De

337

Vinne himself was too practical a man to admire Morris or be deeply influenced by him. His standards were high, but at the same time he was a successful businessman, with a large staff, a great capital investment, and the need to charge competitive prices. He was not only among the first of his generation to accept new machines and materials, but among the few to attempt to get as good or better results from them. The De Vinne Press was particularly successful in printing wood-engravings, from which he extracted remarkably high quality. In 1872 he began printing *Saint Nicholas*, a children's magazine whose standards of literary and artistic excellence made it one of the most successful and influential ever published in the United States. He also printed *Scribner's Magazine* and the *Century Magazine*, for which he devised clean, traditional typographic styles utilising old style types and ornaments, the first American magazines to revive their use. When process-engraving began to replace wood blocks, De Vinne quickly experimented with its use and, in collaboration with S. D. Warren and Company, developed coated papers for half-tone reproduction. His work is conservative in design, spare in ornamentation, and superior in workmanship. Among the best are his Moxon; the *Century Dictionary*, an able and intelligent piece of bread-and-butter scholarly printing which he regarded as his best book; a number of Grolier Club publications, among them, appropriately, Arthur Warren's *The Charles Whittinghams, Printers;* and *Investigation and Studies in Jade*, the two-volume elephant folio catalogue of the Bishop collection, of which 100 sets were printed for presentation to libraries and museums. This shows almost every variety of colour printing known at the time; De Vinne's skilful use of multi-colour wood blocks is a remarkable achievement.

De Vinne's books, as has been noted, took into account the enormous changes in printing technology which occurred during the late nineteenth century. These were a result of the constant effort of the printer to produce faster and cheaper, in order to satisfy the constantly growing appetite for his wares—a process which began with the industrial revolution and has by no means stopped today. It is a continuum, in which it is difficult to isolate the contributions of any one man or any one process; as one bottleneck was resolved, another was created: first paper shortage, solved by the fourdrinier, the development of wood pulp fibres for paper manufacture, and related chemical and mechanical innovations; then the invention of power presses, which created a new problem, the inability of compositors to work fast enough; the invention of mechanical typefounding and composing machines, which both necessitated and depended upon the invention of punch-cutting and engraving tools. The invention of photomechanical reproduction, itself a result of the discovery of photography, caused the development of new coated papers; the rapid increase in offset printing brings about a new emphasis on photo-composition. One cannot isolate the work of individuals, nor even of nations, in these, which belong perhaps to the history of technology rather than of book-printing, but the work of some American inventors certainly must be noted, since it changed the whole course of printing history.

We have already recorded the work of such men as George Clymer in developing the hand-press in America, and of Isaac Adams with the flat-bed book press. The most important innovations in press-production in this country are associated with Robert Hoe and his successors, mainly in the de-velopment of high-speed newspaper presses. Established in New York in 1805, the firm has always been in the van in improving press construction, its most notable contribution the 'Hoe Type Revolving Machine' of 1847, one of the earliest successful cylinder presses. Another American press-builder whose name has become internationally known was Robert Miehle, whose 'Miehle Vertical' appeared about 1886.

America's most significant technical contributions have been in the field of typesetting and casting machinery. One of the pioneers in the develop-ment of composing machines was Dr. William Church, a native of Vermont who emigrated to England, where in 1822 he patented a casting and a com-posing machine which anticipated many of the features of modern com-posing machines, including distribution through the melting-pot. The search for efficient and economic typecasting and composing machines continued through the century until, within a few years of each other, the German-born Othmar Mergenthaler patented his Linotype in 1884 and Tolbert Lanston his Monotype in 1887. Neither machine could have succeeded without the panto-graphic boring machine, which made possible the required large-scale pro-duction of punches and matrices, patented by Lynn Boyd Benton in 1885.

Among the group of younger printers influenced by De Vinne's example was Walter Gilliss (1855-1925), who began printing as a partner with his brother on a toy press with a 6″ × 9″ chase. The boys solicited small jobs from neighbouring businessmen with such success that, after two years, they de-cided to try their fortune at printing for a living; they invested their joint savings in a larger Gordon job press on which they turned out a variety of small ephemera. Their industry; reliability (they often stayed up several nights running to meet a deadline they had promised, not realising a job was beyond their capacities); and rapidly improving skill brought them a number of

339

steady customers, among them Columbia University and the Metropolitan Museum of Art, for whom they executed a great deal of unpretentious and intelligent printing. The Gilliss Press also printed regularly for the Grolier Club and for a number of well-to-do collectors, among them Robert Hoe and J. Pierpont Morgan. Gilliss's most pleasing books were those he produced for William Loring Andrews, a book collector who must have been an almost ideal customer—Andrews combined considerable means with unusual taste and originality, high standards with a willingness to pay for their maintenance. The twenty-six little books Gilliss printed for Andrews are among the most charming of their day: modest, with meticulous inking and presswork, even black colour, and excellent proportions. Andrews was especially fond of copper-engraving, and commissioned the work of a number of well-known artists, including Sidney L. Smith and E. D. French. He enjoyed the luxury of hand-made paper, and of second or even third colours. Perhaps the best of the Andrews-Gilliss books (for customer and printer worked so closely that one must consider them joint ventures) was *New York as Washington Knew It After the Revolution* (1905), which in its modest but sure typography, its immaculate presswork, and attention to detail represents the best in American book technique of its era.

The eighteen-nineties are a difficult decade to characterise, as one can learn from the vast number of books which have attempted the task. Two parallel— or, more properly, intertwined—movements, both romantic, both rebellious, reached their zenith during that era: the arts and crafts revival and *fin de siècle* aestheticism. Both were international movements which appeared in the United States almost as soon as in Europe, so powerful was the *Zeitgeist* and so rapid the speed of international communications.

It is almost impossible today to comprehend the impact of William Morris upon his contemporaries, whether in literature, the decorative arts, or politics. Printing was one of his last and briefest enthusiasms—he died but six years after founding the Kelmscott Press—but his books influenced a whole generation of young printers throughout the world. They were imitated in America, usually badly, in the early work of such sincere admirers as Updike, Rogers, and Rollins, who outgrew their borrowed mannerisms as they acquired styles of their own; they were imitated even more badly by those who plagiarised Morris's ornamentation and types without comprehending his genuine passion for the best possible material and workmanship or his genuine belief that handicraft was the only possible solution for the drabness and ugliness of modern industrial life. The most successful (economically) of these pseudo-Morrises was Elbert Hubbard (1856–1915), who debased the Morris style in printing, in decoration, and even in prose, and yet who transmitted to tens of thousands an inkling of Morris's ideas that they would never have had otherwise.

Hubbard, born in Bloomington, Illinois, came as a lad to Chicago, where he spent four years as a reporter, after which he became an advertising agent and salesman. In 1892 he retired with a modest fortune and decided, at the age of thirty-nine, to enroll as an undergraduate at Harvard. He soon found the discipline irksome and the company of the young boring and withdrew, turning to travel instead. He paid a call upon Morris and immediately determined to become his American disciple and champion. On his return he founded at East Aurora, New York, the Roycroft Shop, a publishing firm, printing-shop, school, inn, furniture factory, and amalgam of various other activities which at its peak employed some 500 men. The Roycroft Shop published Hubbard's journal, *The Philistine*, written almost entirely by himself, which had 225,000 circulation; and his books, including the series of *Little Journeys* to the homes of the great (the first was to Kelmscott House) and the phenomenally successful *A Message to Garcia*. The Roycroft books were printed on heavy, rough paper, in ugly and eccentric types surrounded by distorted Art Nouveau borders; their de-luxe bindings were of that extremely soft and cheap suede known in the trade as 'limp ooze'; in their pretentiousness and lack of taste they reflected their flamboyant creator, with his long locks, soft hat, and flowing tie.

Yet, poor as Hubbard's design and craftsmanship might be (and they were vulgar and meretricious indeed) they awakened in thousands of Americans a deep dissatisfaction with the mass-produced objects, including books, they could find in the shops, and a desire to improve both what they made and what they used. Among those who admitted to having been influenced by Hubbard, and started on their careers by his example, were Will Ransom and Dard Hunter.

The aesthetic movement appeared in America, as in Europe, considerably before the *fin de siècle*; Oscar Wilde had made his famous American lecture tour in 1882, and *Patience* had scored as resounding a success in New York as in London. During the 1890's it reached its peak, quickly going out of favour as an aftermath of the Wilde scandal; during its heyday in the '90's it made up in intensity what it lost in longevity. Like the arts and crafts revival, the aesthetic movement attracted its *poseurs* and imitators, but it also numbered among its young and enthusiastic members a number who showed genuine originality and talent. Among these were the publishing firms of Stone and Kimball, Way and Williams, and Copeland and Day, all of which published small books of great originality and charm, bearing a certain family resemblance, and yet each with its own house style and originality. More significant, perhaps, was Thomas B. Mosher, literary pirate and publisher, of Portland, Maine. The most original figure to emerge from the aesthetic stream was Will Bradley, a versatile and prolific artist equally at home in illustration, type design, posters, book and magazine design, and advertising typography.

Herbert S. Stone and Ingalls Kimball founded their firm at Cambridge, where both were Harvard undergraduates, in 1893. Stone, whose father edited a Chicago newspaper, had some money of his own, as well as family backing; a number of foreign languages and a love for foreign literature, especially French, acquired during several trips abroad; acquaintance with a great many Chicago writers, friends of his father; and a flair for discovering and encouraging new talent. His partner had less original taste, but was willing to experiment; he contributed to the firm a knowledge of printing practice, acquired as business manager of the Harvard paper, and an ability to handle finance. After graduation the partners moved the firm back to Chicago, then enjoying a literary and cultural boom sparked by the 1893 World's Fair. Their first lists included books by Eugene Field, Hamlin Garland, and Joaquin Miller, all widely known writers who were friends of Stone's father. In 1894 they launched *The Chap-Book* which, despite its mere five years' existence, was one of the most influential journals of its era. Reflecting the taste of its editor, *The Chap-Book* printed the work of Verlaine, Mallarmé, and Rimbaud in French and in translation, often for the first time in the U.S.A.; it helped to create the poster craze in the country with its posters by Toulouse-Lautrec, Beardsley, Will Bradley, and Claude Bragdon, among others; its small oblong format, its informal elegance, and its art-for-arts' sake tone made it not only the typical but the best American little magazine of the 'nineties.

Stone and Kimball dissolved partnership in 1894; Stone remained in Chicago, where he founded Herbert S. Stone and Company, and Kimball moved to New York to establish the Cheltenham Press. Kimball applied his bookish taste and typographic training to advertising, creating a new school of 'literary' copy and layout which scored a quick success; the most lasting monument of the Cheltenham Press was the family of types named for it, devised by Kimball and drawn under his direction by Bertram Goodhue, a young Boston architect who also designed types and ornament for Updike.

Herbert Stone, whose taste was responsible for the design and appearance of most of the books which appeared under his imprints, admired small, comfortably held books like those of Pickering. He took great pains with their bindings, frequently using light-coloured cloths with heavily blocked over-all patterns in gold; or poster-like illustrations from the text extending over both covers. Paper, water-marked with one of half-dozen emblems devised by Bragdon, Bradley, or Joseph Leydendecker, was usually deckle-edged and soft in colour. Title-pages were simple, although Stone occasionally allowed himself a second colour or a fleuron. Important enough books might merit an illustrated or lettered title-page; George Santayana produced a highly successful one for his *Sonnets and Other Verses*, issued from Cambridge in 1894. During the Cambridge days Stone generally used the University Press of John Wilson and Company, a staid and highly respectable firm which was much favoured by the Boston literary world; in Chicago he preferred the Lakeside Press, during the 'nineties, as at present, one of the city's best printers. He was a demanding customer, who chose his printers with care and got their best work in return for his interest.

The books of Way and Williams, another short-lived Chicago firm, and Copeland and Day in Boston resembled those of Stone in style and general flavour. They shared his predilection for English and French writers; for small, pocketable volumes in gay bindings, and for light, clean, uncluttered pages. They all employed the same printers and artists, sold their books to the same readers, and quit publishing at about the same time, just after the close of the century.

Thomas Bird Mosher (1852–1923), who lived far off the beaten track in Portland, Maine, shared the literary and aesthetic ideals of these young *avant garde* publishers even though he was much their senior—moreover, unlike them, he made aestheticism pay. Mosher was the son of a sea captain who took the boy out of school at fourteen to accompany him on his travels. Captain Mosher bought young Tom a set of John Bell's *English Theatre* to keep him amused during the long intervals between ports. The boy read all thirty-four volumes avidly and developed a life-long addiction to good writing and decent printing. On his return to Portland in 1870 he became a clerk in a publishing house and, by 1882, had saved enough to become a partner in McLellan, Mosher, and Company, dedicated to producing 'beautiful books at low cost'. Mosher was completely by-passed by Morris and the Kelmscott cult; he preferred the small, cheap, classic eighteenth-century formats, which he used with great success. Although his taste was far superior to his means, he

343

was unembarrassed by any feelings of guilt or shame; resolved to print only the best of modern writing, and unable to pay for that, he unabashedly stole without royalty books unprotected by American copyright, rewarding their authors with letters of admiration, packages of prettily printed books, and (very rarely) a cheque. Many of Mosher's authors were amused by his effrontery; others, like Andrew Lang, considered him a thief and a blackguard, and refused both his cheques and his plaudits.

Mosher printed more than 500 books, all of which he designed and saw through the press himself, using local printers almost entirely and getting from them first-rate work. He liked hand-made papers, which he imported himself regularly; and paper-on-board bindings, simple and lightly ornamented, which were pleasant and cheap. His typography was chaste and elegant, with a minimum of decoration. Mosher's books were pioneering efforts in providing the best in literature, printed with equally high standards, at low prices.

Of the many talented young artists who worked for Stone and Kimball, Will Bradley (1868–1961), was the most influential. Self-taught, he began work as printer's devil in a jobbing printshop where he had all-round experience in setting type, making layouts, and writing copy. He moved as a young man to Chicago, where he became part of a congenial group of young artists which included Fred Goudy and Will Ransom. In 1893 Bradley set up his own studio and quickly made an international reputation with his posters for the World's Fair, which brought him to the attention of Herbert Stone, who commissioned posters, title-pages, and typographic ornamentation for *The Chap-Book*. His most important Chicago work was a series of twelve covers for *The Inland Printer*, the first American magazine to change its cover design monthly, done at Bradley's instigation. One of these displayed a style of lettering so distinctive that it was copied and cut into type by a German and four American foundries. A.T.F. paid him a small commission for their version, which they named 'Bradley'.

In 1895 Bradley moved to Springfield, Massachusetts, where he founded the Wayside Press to do general advertising design and job printing. His first important commission was a sample book for the Strathmore Paper Company, using the Caslon types and crude chap-book ornaments which he liked and which he had studied closely in the Barton collection of colonial printing at the Boston Public Library. He concluded that they represented 'the most direct, honest typography America has ever known'.

To publicise his Wayside Press, Bradley wrote and issued *Bradley: His Book*, whose seven issues are among his best work. He was almost too successful. His press could not handle all the work he had attracted; his solution, moving it to Cambridge where it became part of the University Press, did not work out and after three years he gave up printing to become a full-time designer, mainly for A.T.F. and such magazines as *Collier's* and the *Ladies' Home Journal*. For A.T.F. he designed twelve *American Chap Books*, which displayed to best advantage his types, ornaments, and cuts, which attained a considerable vogue. Bradley also worked as art director for William Randolph Hearst's magazines and films. Although he retired in 1930 he continued designing; as recently as 1954 he developed another portfolio for the Strathmore Paper Company which displayed the same lively ingenuity and unhackneyed freedom as his early work.

Will Bradley typifies a new development in typography, the free-lance designer working for many clients rather than within a single organisation. Until late in the nineteenth century books and other printed matter were generally designed by the printer himself, frequently at the case. With industrialisation and its attendent proliferation of processes, types, and high-speed machines, the division between printer and designer, between craftsman and artist, was widened. The Linotype or Monotype keyboard operator followed a layout furnished by the designer, working for either publisher or printer; choice of type face, imposition, design of title-page and other preliminaries were all specified for him.

The turn of the century saw the emergence of a new generation of American book designers who were to achieve international reputations. Chief among them were Daniel Berkeley Updike, Bruce Rogers, Frederic Goudy, W. A. Dwiggins, Carl P. Rollins, and T. M. Cleland. Most of them were first inspired by Morris's example; all quickly outgrew such imitativeness and as they matured developed their own styles. They came from all parts of the country but converged, at a particularly formative period, on Boston which for a brief period regained its pre-eminence as the centre for graphic experiment and design.

D. B. Updike (1860–1941) was a New Englander by birth, by training, and by choice. Born and educated in Providence, Rhode Island, he was forced at eighteen, by the death of his father, to forego the college education he anticipated and start to support himself. After a brief period working at the Providence Athenaeum, where he had ample leisure to read, to handle many books, and to study their appearance, he moved to Boston, where he became an errand boy for Houghton Mifflin Company. He was soon given a more responsible post, clipping notices of the firm's publications from newspapers from throughout the country—a task which trained his eye in the quick recognition of type faces and house styles and their assignment to their respective owners. Next came the preparation and layout of advertising copy, at which Updike proved himself so adept that he was transferred to the firm's printing plant, the Riverside Press, in Cambridge. His new surroundings proved less congenial, and so Updike resigned to found his own shop. He was fortunate in having friends with sufficient confidence to give him commissions during his early years, for he had little capital of his own. Updike had other valuable assets, however: a good mind, sound taste, the desire and ability to work hard, and a natural talent for business.

Updike founded the Merrymount Press in 1893, although it was not christened until three years later. He first intended merely to design fine printing and have it executed by others. He gave up that idea when he found that he was unable to satisfy his own exacting standards: 'to make work better for its purpose than was commonly thought worthwhile, and by having one's own establishment, be free to do so'. He was inevitably forced to buy his own type and press and hire his own workmen, who could be made to realise that their goal was not to satisfy the customer but the proprietor.

Updike's early work was very much in the Morris mode. His first major book, commissioned by a friend, was an *Altar Book* for the Episcopal Church —an appropriate work for one who was throughout his life a devout and dedicated Christian and who believed firmly in the need for working within a framework of conviction and faith. The book, which took three years to make, was set in a type designed for it by Bertram Goodhue, who also provided borders and initials in the Kelmscott style. Updike's Boston shop set and locked up the forms, which were shipped to New York, where De Vinne printed an edition of 350 copies. The book, despite its imitativeness, shows signs of Updike's greatest strength: the solution of complicated problems in spacing and the arrangement of a difficult text in a logical and functional manner.

Updike, who never shared Morris's bias against machines, soon abandoned his medievalism. His first press was a Colt Armory, powered by electricity. When he felt that he could get acceptable type faces for machine composition he installed Monotype. His next phase after the medieval, inevitable in a man with his passion for order and his historical bent, was a close study and emulation of Renaissance book styles. Among the best books of this period are those he printed and published under the series title of 'The Humanist Library'. The

346

first four, issued 1905–08, were all designed by Herbert Horne, who also designed the Montallegro type, based on early Florentine models, in which they were set. The next four, also in Montallegro, had title-pages by T. M. Cleland and W. A. Dwiggins. They were in larger format and were published at half the price of the earlier series, in an unsuccessful attempt to make them more attractive to buyers. It is an odd comment on book collectors that they refused to buy better-made books at half the price!

As Updike attracted a steady clientele he gave up publishing, for he disliked the routine of bookselling. His customers, most of whom became regular clients, included trade publishers, who realised that he consistently produced books superior to the norm in design and manufacture; book clubs and institutions willing to pay de-luxe prices for work of the highest obtainable quality; ecclesiastical and educational bodies, whose work he enjoyed because it posed difficult problems to be solved efficiently, economically, and handsomely; and private individuals seeking anything from a lavishly produced family history to a Christmas card or book plate. He complained in his *Notes on the Merrymount Press* that he got too little routine and ephemeral work, since many thought he was above it. Updike was a true professional: 'Over and over again we have said that all kinds of work are done here and no piece of printing, no matter how small, is neglected—much less despised... The reiterated statement that labels for biscuit boxes would be a welcome job is supposed to be the amusingly exaggerated but unconvincing product of a whimsical mind.'

The Merrymount Press's steady increase in business forced Updike to add slowly both to his equipment and his personnel. Soon after leaving Houghton Mifflin he was fortunate in being able to hire as foreman John Bianchi, whom he made his partner in 1915. Bianchi possessed a knowledge of machines lacking in Updike, who was uninterested in them, as well as an equally useful ability to estimate and control costs; Updike confessed he was never able to deal with figures. It proved an unusually successful collaboration, in which Updike's taste and knowledge were buttressed by Bianchi's craftsmanship and sound business sense. The firm never grew large—at its peak it numbered but thirty employees, carefully selected by the partners, who took a paternalistic interest in them. Updike's interest in types, which led to the publication of *Printing Types* in 1922, had a solid basis, the selection of a limited and economic stock for his own shop. Like most printers who developed from the private-press tradition he commissioned his own types: Horne's Montallegro and Goodhue's Merrymount. He soon got over his fondness for both and rarely used them again. Instead he employed the best faces from the historical reper-

347

tory, often tracking down the original punches and matrices so that he might order authentic types. His most frequently used types were Caslon; Scotch; Oxford, a favourite, from the original Binny and Ronaldson cutting held by A.T.F., which he used for *Printing Types;* Mountjoye, discovered at the Riverside Press, traced back to the English foundry holding the matrices, and subsequently found by Stanley Morison to have been cut by Richard Austin for John Bell; and Janson, used in a number of Updike's best books, including the 1930 *Book of Common Prayer*, considered by many his masterpiece. He had few contemporary types, but those he chose will probably be among the small group of modern faces which will survive. He was the first American printer to stock Times New Roman and one of the first outside Holland to buy Van Krimpen's Lutetia. As he bought his types Updike extended his knowledge of their history and makers; he built an excellent library of type-specimens and finely printed books which he bequeathed to the Providence Public Library. In 1911 the Harvard Business School asked him to lecture on the subject of typography, which he continued to do until 1916. It is typical of Updike's thoroughness and meticulous scholarship that it took him six more years to prepare the lectures, already thoroughly conceived and written, for press. *Printing Types*, like all his works, reveals a man steeped in scholarship yet devoid of pedantry, with the ability to comprehend and synthesise great masses of complicated materials so that they seem simple, as well as a man possessing abundant wit and a high sense of style.

Updike's printing mirrors the man: respect for tradition and reason; abhorrence of vulgar display; a preference for understatement; a keen eye for harmony and proportion. He was never revolutionary, nor often original. His books were so well and honestly made that, as Stanley Morison said in a posthumous tribute to an old friend, they 'reached a higher degree of quality and consistency than those of any other printing house of its size, and period of operation, in America or Europe'. Updike belonged in the line of modern scholar-printers which included Blades, Reed, Enschedé, and De Vinne, of whom he may well have been the greatest. It is difficult to see how, when printing has become so increasingly complicated, specialised, and concentrated into a few large houses requiring huge capital investments, such men can be expected again—a loss which will be felt by the wider world of letters as well as the printing industry.

If Updike was the greatest printer America has yet produced, Bruce Rogers (1870–1957) was its greatest book designer. Born in Indiana, he was taught to draw by his father, an artist. At sixteen he entered Purdue University, where he studied applied art, one of two boys in an otherwise all-feminine class, and began his typographic career turning out title-pages, decorations, and illustrations for college publications. He sold his first professional work, some lettering for T. B. Mosher, while still an undergraduate. On graduation Rogers moved to Indianapolis, where he became a newspaper illustrator. J. M. Bowles, editor of a new quarterly called *Modern Art*, introduced him to the work of William Morris and the new French painters and gave him several commissions. When Bowles moved, with the magazine, to Boston he was soon followed by Rogers. In Boston he worked briefly for L. Prang and Company, who took over the magazine, and did free-lance work for Stone and Kimball and Way and Williams. He thoroughly enjoyed the stimulating atmosphere of Boston, where he readily made friends with such kindred spirits as Updike, Goodhue, Will Bradley, and Carl Rollins. He was able to work at his own pace and to spend a great deal of time at painting.

In 1896 Rogers met George Mifflin, junior partner in Houghton Mifflin and Company, who offered him a job at the Riverside Press. Four years later Mifflin gave him the opportunity of setting up a department for the production and sale of limited editions, with full responsibility for editorial, design, and production policy. The next twelve years were among the most productive and happiest in Rogers's life. Mifflin gave him extraordinary support—he was allowed free access to any of the plant's facilities, he could work as slowly as he liked, he was allowed to budget for perfection rather than profit, and he was allowed to re-do a job until it satisfied him. He did some of his best work during this period: *Geofrey Tory*, in which he redrew all the borders to strengthen the weak inking and impression of the sixteenth-century originals; *The Love Poems of John Donne*, with its splendid architectural title-page; *The Compleat Angler*, small, compact, amiably readable. Rogers's books, unlike Updike's, are not easily recognisable by style—he was an eclectic, whose 'allusive' period typography was used to mirror the text and reinforce it. Binding, types, and paper varied from volume to volume, the only unifying thread Rogers's desire for perfection and his steadily surer taste.

By 1911 Rogers had begun to be bored with the Riverside Press, while his employers were beginning to tire of a bargain which was profitable only in prestige. He resigned, determined to be his own boss, so that he could allow himself ample time for reflection and travel. Next year he made his first voyage to England. He felt at home at once, and made there a number of life-long friends, particularly Emery Walker. On his return he settled in New York, where his clients included the Museum Press of the Metropolitan Museum of

Art, directed by H. W. Kent, who became one of his staunchest supporters. When Kent saw the new type face on which Rogers was working, freely redrawing enlarged characters from a copy of Jenson's *Eusebius*, he commissioned several sizes of capitals for the Museum's posters and case labels. Rogers went on experimenting with the type and by 1915 felt ready to try it in a book —a translation of Guérin's *The Centaur*, for which he named it. His wife was the compositor. The book was printed at the Montague Press, housed in an old mill owned by his friend Carl Rollins.

In 1916 Rogers returned to London for a brief partnership with Emery Walker in the Mall Press, whose one book was Dürer's *On the Just Shaping of Letters*. Working in war-time London was difficult (Rogers, who shared Updike's distaste for machines, had to act as press-man himself for part of the job) and life was uncomfortable, so that he was glad to accept an invitation to act as advisor to the Cambridge University Press. During his two years in Cambridge he produced only a few books, none of any consequence; far more important was the report he drafted on the typographic equipment of the Press, which was used as the basis of a complete overhaul when the end of the war made this possible.

In 1919 Rogers was appointed advisor to the Harvard University Press. At about the same time a casual meeting with William E. Rudge, a successful New York printer, led to an invitation to join forces with him in his Mount Vernon, New York, plant just being opened. Rogers' eight years there were among his most fruitful. Working conditions were almost as ideal as at the Riverside Press. Rudge was a good printer, an enthusiastic patron, and a superb salesman. He had assembled an excellent staff, including a group of bright and hardworking young men attracted by the excitement of the place who would go on to make their own names in printing—Joseph Blumenthal, Peter Beilenson, Frederic Warde, among others. Rogers was always kind to the young, enjoying both their stimulation and their admiration, and his work at this period reflects something of the gaiety of the atmosphere. The 'twenties were an excellent period for selling expensive limited editions, most of them not worth the money, as an examination of either the books or their current prices will indicate. Rogers's books for Rudge were rarely in this category—they were witty, usually understated rather than overdressed, charmingly decorated. This was the period in which he was most interested in type ornament, combining fleurons and rules with great originality and style. *The Pierrot of the Minute* and *The Symbol and the Saint* typify these conceits.

1928–32, spent in England again, mark the high point of Rogers's career.

The noblest and most majestic of his works fall into these years. It may be that the tradition and the calm of English life made it possible for him to produce work of a monumental beauty that he never produced in his native land. Whatever the explanation, the Oxford lectern *Bible;* T. E. Shaw's translation of the *Odyssey*, which he published in association with Wilfred Merton and Emery Walker; and the Grolier Club edition of his friend Stanley Morison's *Pacioli*, printed at Cambridge, are all books of incomparable assurance, dignity, and strength. Rogers was sometimes accused (especially by himself) of being a 'typographic playboy', in Carl Rollins' phrase. These books of his maturity reveal that he had intellectual power and discipline as well as wit.

Rogers spent the rest of his life at his home in New Fairfield, Connecticut, where he continued to paint, carve, write, and design books almost to the day of his death. His health prevented his going to New York often, and so October House became a magnet for typographic pilgrims from all over the world. Among the books of this later period were many major works; the Limited Editions Club Shakespeare; the Boswell Papers; the great Frick catalogue, which he took over after Porter Garnett's death; and the World *Bible*, which he (but few others) preferred to his Oxford *Bible*.

Rogers's best work is distinguished for its clarity, its strong sense of style, its lack of pedantry, and its superb rightness in detail. He will rank among the best American graphic designers, but not among the most influential, since his qualities were too individualistic to be readily imitated. Period typography can be copied—and frequently was—but not the tact and skill with which Rogers used it. The best of his work, the classic simplicity and dignity of such books as the Oxford *Bible* and the *Odyssey*, demands a discipline and an intelligence which are so rare as to be inimitable.

Carl P. Rollins (1880–1962), already frequently mentioned, was a modest man whose thousands of books, produced mainly for the Yale University Press, demonstrated that scholarly books need be neither ugly nor shoddily made. Rollins attended Harvard for three years, helping to support himself by printing menus for the student dining-table; he quit during his last year, having decided that he wished to be a printer and might as well begin. He showed his work to Updike, who gave him encouragement but no job, and to Will Bradley; the latter offered an introduction to Carl Heintzemann, who took him on as an apprentice compositor. Heintzemann was a generous and warmhearted man, a bibliophile, musician, and admirer of Morris, whose shop was one of the most modern and best run in Boston. Here Rollins met W. A. Dwiggins, another newcomer to Boston, J. M. Bowles, Rogers, and a number of other young men who shared his enthusiasm for the Kelmscott books and the prospects for a revival of fine printing; while he soon outgrew his imitations of Morris's style, he never changed in his unswerving admiration for the man and his ideals. In an article in *Printing and Graphic Arts* (June, 1958), he said:'I am sure that I was influenced by Morris to a greater or less degree in everything that I ever did... I think that it was probably because of Morris that I became a printer!... Nobody could resist it (his work) nor could anybody resist the ebullient personality of the man.'

In 1903 Rollins moved to Montague, Massachusetts, where he became printer to New Clairvaux, a socialist community which attempted to revive handicraft as a way of life. When the community dissolved he bought the Dyke Mill and installed the Montague Press, which became inactive when he was invited in 1918 to join the Yale University Press. Two years later he was made Printer to the University. During his thirty years at Yale Rollins established a reputation for intelligent design, high quality production, and respect for scholarship which won him the admiration and affection of the learned world as well as the graphic arts community.

Henry Watson Kent was another who did much to improve the level of institutional printing in the United States. Trained as a librarian, Kent spent several years as an assistant at the Grolier Club, where he knew and was influenced by such men as De Vinne, Gilliss, and W. L. Andrews. In 1905 he became Assistant Secretary to the Metropolitan Museum of Art, a few years later succeeding to the secretaryship. In this post he was responsible for much of the routine administration of the Museum, including the provision of all its printed matter: labels, posters, stationery, catalogues, monographs, all the wide array of printing required by a large and active institution. Kent, who had an innate respect for craftsmanship, a good eye, and a natural talent for design thoroughly enjoyed this work. He established in the Museum a printing-office, and set about imposing upon the Museum's printing a form and beauty worthy of its collections. Whether as head of the Museum Press or as the employer of such printers and artists as De Vinne, Gilliss, Updike, Rogers, and Rollins, Kent insisted that any Metropolitan Museum publication—whether a simple case label or an elaborate *catalogue raisonné*—be functional, handsome, and distinctive.

The most prolific, as well as the most articulate, of American type designers was Frederic W. Goudy (1865–1947). The son of a teacher in Bloomington, Illinois, Goudy had no formal art training. He amused himself as a child by copying pictures from magazines, and developed a precocious skill at letter-

MAMUSSE

WUNNEETUPANATAMWE

UP-BIBLUM GOD

NANEESWE

NUKKONE TESTAMENT

KAH WONK

WUSKU TESTAMENT.

Ne quoſhkinnumuk naſhpe Wuttinneumoh *CHRIST*
uoh aloowefit

JOHN ELIOT·

CAMBRIDGE:

Printeuoop naſhpe *Samuel Green* kah *Marmaduke Johnſon.*

1 6 6 3.

1. John Eliot: *Indian Bible*, Cambridge, Mass (1663). Title-page of the first
Bible printed in the American Colonies

The Printer to the Reader.

THIS Verfion of CICERO's Tract *de Senectute,* was made Ten Years fince, by the Honourable and Learned Mr. LOGAN, of this City; undertaken partly for his own Amufement, (being then in his 60th Year, which is faid to be nearly the Age of the Author when he wrote it) but principally for the Entertainment of a Neighbour then in his grand Climacteric; and the Notes were drawn up folely on that Neighbour's Account, who was not fo well acquainted as himfelf with the Roman Hiftory and Language: Some other Friends,

)(2 how-

2. Cicero: *Cato Major*, Benjamin Franklin, Philadelphia (1744). Opening page

THE NEW
TESTAMENT
OF OUR LORD AND SAVIOUR
JESUS CHRIST:
Newly tranflated out of the
ORIGINAL GREEK;
And with the former
TRANSLATIONS
Diligently compared and revifed.

PHILADELPHIA:
PRINTED AND SOLD BY R. AITKEN, BOOKSELLER,
THREE DOORS ABOVE THE COFFEE-HOUSE,
IN MARKET-STREET.
M.DCC.LXXXI.

3. *The New Testament*, Philadelphia (1781). Title-page from the first complete
English Bible to be printed in the United States of America

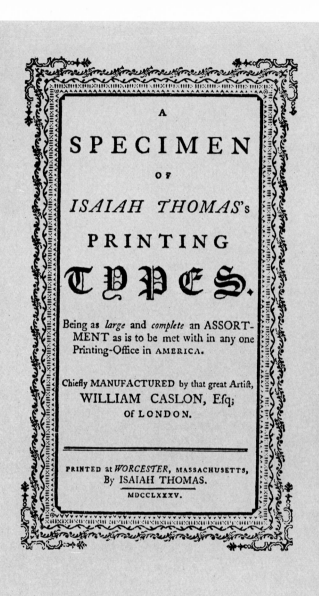

4. Type Specimen Book of Isaiah Thomas, Worcester, Mass (1785).
Title-page

PARADISE LOST,

A

P O E M,

IN

TWELVE BOOKS;

By JOHN MILTON,

WITH

A BIOGRAPHICAL AND CRITICAL ACCOUNT

OF THE

AUTHOR and his WRITINGS.

WASHINGTON:

PRINTED FOR MATHEW CAREY,

MARKET-STREET, PHILADELPHIA.

1801.

5. Milton: *Paradise Lost*, Mathew Carey, Philadelphia (1801). A typical
example of this publisher's books

THE

COLUMBIAD.

BOOK VI.

But of all tales that war's black annals hold,
The darkest, foulest still remains untold;
New modes of torture wait the shameful strife,
And Britain wantons in the waste of life.
    Cold-blooded Cruelty, first fiend of hell,
Ah think no more with savage hordes to dwell;
Quit the Caribian tribes who eat their slain,
Fly that grim gang, the Inquisitors of Spain,
Boast not thy deeds in Moloch's shrines of old,
Leave Barbary's pirates to their blood-bought gold,   10
Let Holland steal her victims, force them o'er
To toils and death on Java's morbid shore;
Some cloak, some color all these crimes may plead;
Tis avarice, passion, blind religion's deed;

6. Joel Barlow: *The Columbiad*, printed by Fry and Kammerer, Philadelphia
(1807). Text page from the first American edition–de–luxe

WAPELLA.

WAPELLA, whose name signifies the *Prince*, or the *Chief*, is the head man of the Musquakee, or Fox tribe. He was one of the delegation led by Keokuk to Washington in 1837, and made a favourable impression by the correctness of his deportment on that occasion. In stature he is shorter, and more heavily built than most of the Indians, and has the appearance of great strength and activity.

In the council held by the Secretary of War, for the purpose of reconciling the Sioux with the Sauks and Foxes, Wapella spoke next after Keokuk, and acquitted himself well. Although he possessed not the fine form and striking manner of Keokuk, many thought his speech not inferior to that of the principal chief. It was well digested, sensible and pertinent. We remarked that, in the opening of his harangue, the authority of Keokuk was distinctly recognised, as well as the identity of interest of the tribes represented respectively by these two chiefs. "My father," said Wapella, "you have heard what my chief has said. He is the chief of our nation. His tongue is ours. What he says we all say—whatever he does we will be bound by it."

Having concluded their visit at Washington, the delegates were conducted to several of the principal cities of the Atlantic states, where they excited much curiosity, and, we are happy to say, were treated with uniform kindness and hospitality. Unfortunate as are the relations between our government and the Indians, imposed by a train of circumstances for which, as a people, we are not accountable, there is evidently no lack of generous sympathy towards that race in any part of our country.

The reception of these Indian delegates at Boston was conducted with more ceremony than at any other place, and must have been highly gratifying to them, as well as interesting to numerous assemblages of citizens, most of whom saw for the first time the American savage in his native costume. It is said that so great a multitude was never assembled in that city to witness a public spectacle. In the morning, from ten to twelve, the chiefs held a levee at Faneuil Hall, for the reception of ladies exclusively, when it might doubtless have been said of the Boston ladies, as a New England poet wrote, long ago.

"All longed to see and touch the tawny man."

7. McKenney & Hall: *A History of the Indian Tribes of North America*, Philadelphia (1838–44). Two-page opening from one of the finest nineteenth-century American illustrated books

THE

TYPOGRAPHICAL MISCELLANY.

BY J. MUNSELL.

ALBANY.
JOEL MUNSELL, 58 STATE STREET.
1850.

8. Joel Munsell: *The Typographical Miscellany*, Albany (1850). Title-page showing influence of Chiswick Press style upon his work

Sectional view of the Cliff Street building.

9. Jacob Abbott: *The Harper Establishment; or How the Story Books Are Made*, New York (1855). Illustration with schematic plan of the Harper plant, the most modern at that date

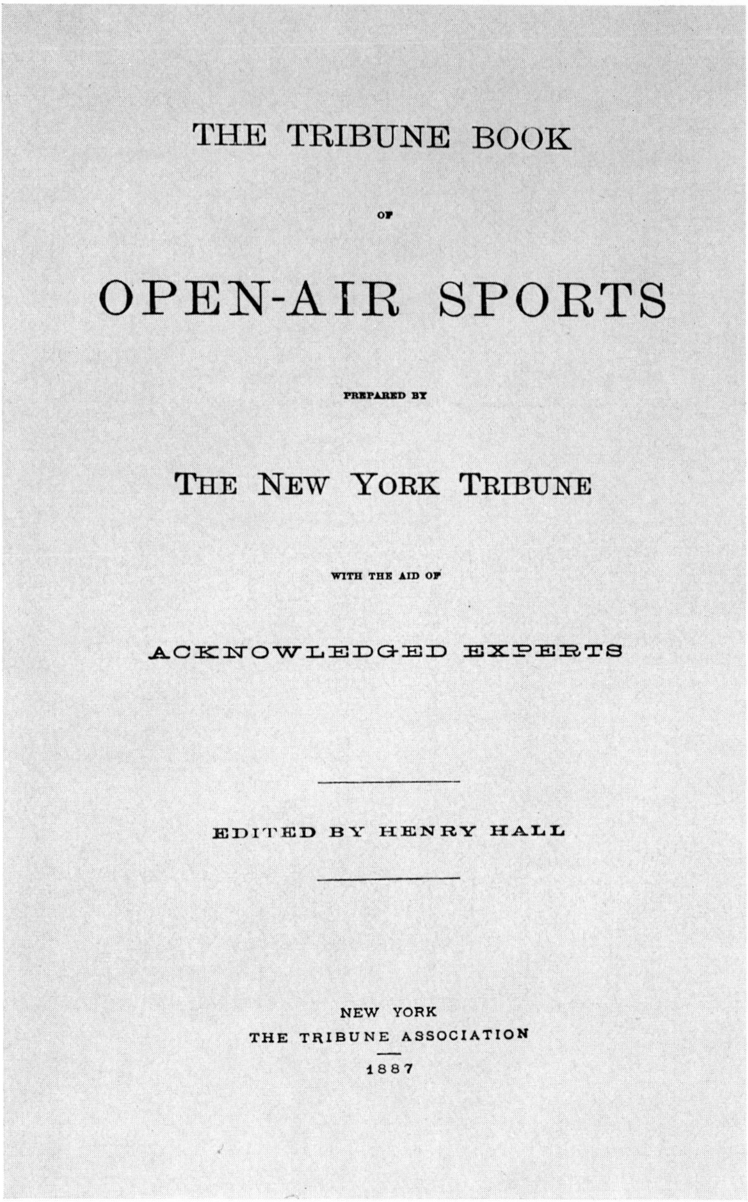

THE TRIBUNE BOOK

OF

OPEN-AIR SPORTS

PREPARED BY

THE NEW YORK TRIBUNE

WITH THE AID OF

ACKNOWLEDGED EXPERTS

EDITED BY HENRY HALL

NEW YORK
THE TRIBUNE ASSOCIATION
1887

10. Henry Hall (*ed.*) : *The Tribune Book of Open-Air Sports*, New York (1887). Title-page of first book to be set on Linotype keyboards

POEMS

OF

Paul Verlaine

TRANSLATED BY
GERTRUDE HALL

PICTURED BY
HENRY McCARTER

CHICAGO
STONE & KIMBALL
MDCCCXCV

11. Paul Verlaine: *Poems*, Stone & Kimball, Chicago (1895). Title-page typical of this printer's style, the tree is in a soft green

RIP VAN WINKLE

A Posthumous Writing of Diedrich Knickerbocker.

By Woden, God of Saxons,
From whence comes Wensday, that is Wodensday,
Truth is a thing that ever I will keep
Unto thylke day in which I creep into
My sepulchre.—CARTWRIGHT.

WHOEVER has made a voyage up the Hudson, must remember the Kaatskill mountains. They are a dismembered branch of the great Appalachian family, and are seen away to the west of the river, swelling up to a noble height, and lording it over the surrounding country. Every change of season, every change of

12. Washington Irving: *Rip Van Winkle*, New York (1897).
Double-page opening: decorations by Will Bradley

PRINTING

RINTING, in the only sense with which we are at present concerned, differs from most if not from all the arts and crafts represented in the Exhibition in being comparatively modern. For although the Chinese took impressions from wood blocks engraved in relief for centuries before the wood-cutters of the Netherlands, by a similar process, produced the block books, which were the immediate predecessors of the true printed book, the invention of movable metal letters in the middle of the fifteenth century may justly be considered as the invention of the art of printing. And it is worth mention in passing that, as an example of fine typography, the earliest book printed with movable types, the Gutenberg, or "forty-two line Bible" of about 1455, has never been surpassed. ❦Printing, then, for our purpose, may be considered as the art of making books by means of movable types. Now, as all

b

13. William Morris & Emery Walker: *Printing* (an essay), Village Press, Park Ridge, Illinois (1903). Designed, printed and bound by F. W. Goudy and Will Ransom, set in Goudy's Village type

CHAPTER III

HE first bright little gamin one meets on Wall or Nassau Street, crying the daily papers, can tell the stranger " seeing New York " that Washington's installation as President of the United States, took place in the balcony of Federal Hall, on the thirtieth of April, 1789,—for has he not read and pondered, time and again, the story inscribed on the granite base of the heroic-sized bronze statue of the " Father of his Country " which, on the steps of the Sub-Treasury, stands sentinel over the spot where

39

14. William Loring Andrews: *New York as Washington knew it after the Revolution*, printed by Walter Gilliss (1905). Designed by the author and printer, with copperplate engravings by Sidney L. Smith

JADE

I

GENERAL INTRODUCTION

HE name Jade has been popularly given to several distinct kinds of ornamental stones, although it is scientifically restricted to the minerals *nephrite* and *jadeite*, including in the latter term *chloromelanite*, a variety of jadeite rich in iron, of dark color and high specific gravity. The qualities and distinctive characteristics of these minerals are fully discussed by competent authorities in the Mineralogical Part of the book and need not detain us here. But it should be premised that scientific accuracy is hardly to be expected from the older writers on the subject, who lived in an unscientific age, nor even from the modern Chinese, who rank jade as the most precious of materials for artistic work and for personal decoration, although they know nothing of its chemical constitution or microscopic details.

There is no word of jade in European literature before the discovery of America by Columbus in 1492. The earlier Spanish navigators brought back specimens of green stones which were highly valued by the natives of Central and South America, and were worn by them as badges of rank or as amulets against certain diseases. For this last reason it was given the name of *piedra de hijada*, "hypochondriac or colic stone," which first occurs in the works of Monardes, a physician of Seville, in 1565. He describes it as of emerald-green tint mingled with milky white, the darkest being the best, and dilates on its occult curative properties. He also alludes to its synonym *piedra de los riñones*, or "kidney-stone," and to its reputed value in renal diseases. Hence the name of nephrite, from νεφρός, the kidney, and that of *lapis nephriticus*, which is so frequently used by the older writers.

Sir Walter Raleigh is said to have been the first to bring the stone to England. He always refers to it in his books under the Spanish name of *hijada*.[1]

The *Discoverie of the Large, Rich and Beatiful Empire of Guiana*, Raleigh, Knight, Captaine of her Maiesties Guard, Lo. Warden of the with a Relation of the Great and Golden City of Manoa (which the Stannaries, and her Highnesse Lieutenant generall of the Countie of Spaniards call El Dorado), etc. Performed in the yeare 1595, by Sir W. Cornewall. Imprinted at London by Robert Robinson, 1596. (p. 24.)

15. *The Bishop Collection: Investigations and Studies in Jade*, New York (1906). Text page opening from De Vinne's most ambitious book

TWENTY-ONE POEMS
WRITTEN BY LIONEL
JOHNSON : SELECTED BY
WILLIAM BUTLER YEATS

PORTLAND MAINE
THOMAS B MOSHER
MDCCCCVIII

16. Lionel Johnson: *Twenty-one Poems*, Thomas B. Mosher, Portland, Maine
(1908). Title-page showing both the printer's literary taste and typographic
style

THE CENTAUR. WRITTEN BY MAURICE DE
GUÉRIN AND NOW TRANSLATED FROM THE
FRENCH BY GEORGE B. IVES.

Was born in a cavern of these mountains. Like the river in yonder valley, whose first drops flow from some cliff that weeps in a deep grotto, the first moments of my life sped amidst the shadows of a secluded retreat, nor vexed its silence. As our mothers draw near their term, they retire to the caverns, and in the innermost recesses of the wildest of them all, where the darkness is most dense, they bring forth, uncomplaining, offspring as silent as themselves. Their strength-giving milk enables us to endure without weakness or dubious struggles the first difficulties of life; yet we leave our caverns later than you your cradles. The reason is that there is a tradition amongst us that the early days of life must be secluded and guarded, as days engrossed by the gods.

My growth ran almost its entire course in the darkness where I was born. The innermost depths of my home were so far within the bowels of the mountain, that I should not have known in which direction the opening lay, had it not been that the winds at times blew in and caused a sudden coolness and confusion. Sometimes, too, my mother returned, bringing with her the perfume of the valleys, or dripping wet from the streams to which she resorted. Now, these her home-comings, although they told me naught of the valleys or the streams, yet, being attended by emanations therefrom, disturbed my thoughts, and I wandered about, all agitated, amidst my darkness. 'What,' I would say to myself, 'are these places to which my mother goes and what power reigns there which summons her so frequently? To what influences is one there exposed,

17. *The Centaur*, Bruce Rogers, Montague Press (1915). Text opening set in
Centaur designed by Bruce Rogers and named for the book

There is a theory tenable about the place of the earth in the cosmic scheme that scientists do not exploit, the assumption, namely, that the world is a discontinued pattern. This is as reasonable a deduction from the evidence in hand as the assumption that the machine is a success and pays dividends. And (in a way) it is more respectful to a

18. Hermann Püterschein (W. A. Dwiggins): *Paraphs*, Alfred A. Knopf, New York (1928). Illustrated and designed by the author

THE BOOK OF
COMMON PRAYER
and Administration of the Sacraments
and Other Rites and Ceremonies
of the Church

ACCORDING TO THE USE OF THE
PROTESTANT EPISCOPAL CHURCH
IN THE UNITED STATES OF AMERICA

Together with The Psalter
or Psalms of David

PRINTED FOR THE COMMISSION
A. D. MDCCCCXXVIII

19. *The Book of Common Prayer* (1928). Designed and printed by Daniel B.
Updike, it is perhaps his finest book

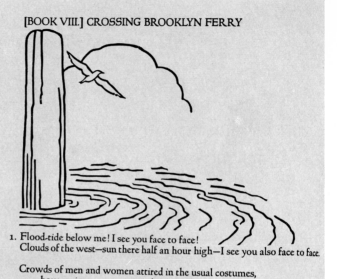

[BOOK VIII.] CROSSING BROOKLYN FERRY

1. Flood-tide below me! I see you face to face!
Clouds of the west—sun there half an hour high—I see you also face to face.

Crowds of men and women attired in the usual costumes,
　　how curious you are to me!
On the ferry-boats the hundreds and hundreds that cross, returning home,
　　are more curious to me than you suppose,
And you that shall cross from shore to shore years hence are more to me,
　　and more in my meditations, than you might suppose.

2. The impalpable sustenance of me from all things at all hours of the day,
　　The simple, compact, well-join'd scheme, myself disintegrated,
　　　every one disintegrated yet part of the scheme,
　　The similitudes of the past and those of the future,
　　The glories strung like beads on my smallest sights and hearings,
　　　on the walk in the street and the passage over the river,
　　The current rushing so swiftly and swimming with me far away,
　　The others that are to follow me, the ties between me and them,
　　The certainty of others, the life, love, sight, hearing of others.

126

20. Whitman: *Leaves of Grass*, The Grabhorn Press (1930). Text page with
woodcut by Valenti Angelo

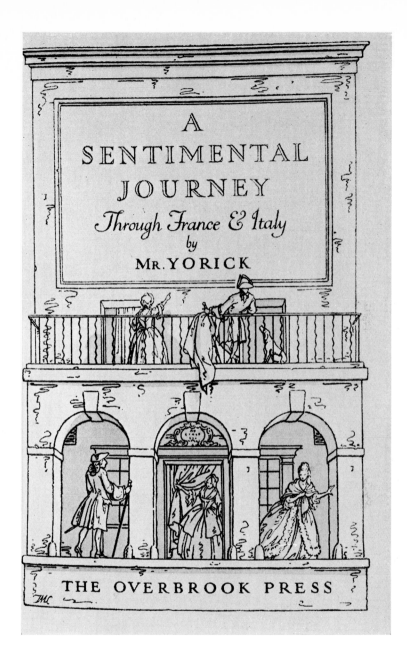

21. *A Sentimental Journey*, The Overbrook Press (1936). Title-page designed
by Thomas M. Cleland, an excellent example of his skill at pastiche

JOHANN CHRISTIAN FRIEDRICH HÖLDERLIN

MDCCLXX — MDCCCXLIII

GEDICHTE/ENTWÜRFE ZU GEDICHTEN UND
BRUCHSTÜCKE

AUS DEN JAHREN MDCCXCVI — MDCCCIV

22. J. C. F. Hölderlin: *Gedichte*, Victor Hammer, Stamperia del Santuccio,
Aurora, New York (1949). Title-page with metal-cut by the printer

Comforted years will sit soft-chaired
    In rooms of amber;
The years will stretch their hands, well-cheered
    By our lives' ember.

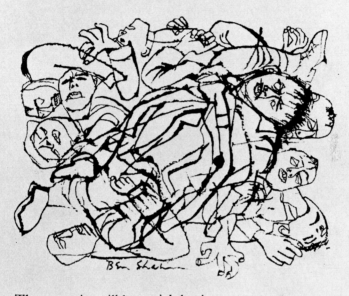

The centuries will burn rich loads
    With which we groaned,
Whose warmth shall lull their dreaming lids
    While songs are crooned.
But they will not dream of us poor lads
    Lost in the ground.

23. *Thirteen Poems by Wilfred Owen*, Leonard Baskin, Gehenna Press, Northampton, Mass (1956). Text page illustrated by Ben Shahn

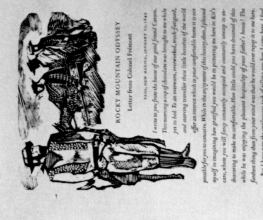

24. Jessie Frémont: *A Year of American Travel*, Saul & Lillian Marks, Plantin Press for the Book Club of California (1960). Two-page opening

ing. In 1890 Goudy moved to Chicago, to become a book-keeper; he moved through a succession of clerical jobs, some of which gave him a chance to dabble with designing and laying-out advertising and printing. A great deal of his spare time was spent at McClurg's Bookstore, where he avidly studied the books of the new private-press movement. A friend offered to lend him the money to start a small printing shop, the Camelot Press, which survived its proprietor's inexperience and lack of capital long enough to print *The Chap-Book* and other Stone and Kimball ventures; for it he designed his first type face, Camelot. In this, as in all his subsequent ventures, he was assisted and supported by his wife, Bertha, who acted as compositor, binder, or in whatever capacity required, and who proved herself a first-rate craftsman in all.

Goudy sold the Camelot Press just before it failed and retired to the security of book-keeping. He kept up his type designing, turning out a number of advertising faces which sold easily and provided welcome extra money. Encouraged by Mrs. Goudy he returned to commercial art, and did lettering for Stone, Irving Way, and Mosher, among others. He also taught at the Frank Holme School of Illustration, a shortlived affair which turned out a number of highly gifted lettering artists, including Dwiggins, Will Ransom, and Oswald Cooper.

In 1903 Goudy again decided to run his own press, supported by Will Ransom, who contributed all his own available funds as well as loans from a friend. The Village Press was domiciled in Park Ridge, a Chicago suburb. The Village type, which Goudy had cut for it by Robert Wiebking, was a re-working of an advertising face rejected because the client considered the 250 dollars needed to engrave matrices and cast type too much. The face was a freely-drawn letter based upon Italian fifteenth-century types, mainly Jenson's. Ransom withdrew from the press when the Goudys decided to move it to Hingham, Massachusetts, lured by a magazine article on the Boston Arts and Crafts Society Center there. When Boston proved inhospitable they again moved, in 1906, to New York, where Goudy eked out a living as a free-lance designer. In 1908 a studio fire destroyed his press, type, and books—almost all his possessions.

Soon after the fire, Goudy, whose types (by now numbering about thirty) were becoming widely known, was invited by the Lanston Monotype Company to design a new face for *Life* magazine. The connection with Lanston lasted almost until his death and produced some of his best work. The resultant financial security made it possible for him to travel, and to move from the city to a small estate, Deepdene, near Marlborough, New York; there he built the second Village Press, also destroyed by fire in 1939. In 1910 Goudy made his first trip abroad, during which he studied and became enamoured of Roman inscriptions, especially those on Trajan's column. Much of his work thenceforth was an effort to rationalise the art of the anonymous stone-cutters and to re-create it in type. The Trajan lettering was the subject of *The Alphabet*, first issued in 1918, and of *The Capitals from the Trajan Column* (1936); it is the basis for several of his shorter pieces and for *The Elements of Lettering* (1922); it inspired several type faces, notably Forum and Trajan Title. Goudy, besides being a prolific writer, edited two journals, *Typographica* and *Ars Typographica*, devoted largely to propagandising his views on printing and letter design. The Village Press printed and published many of its proprietor's works.

Goudy's methods, which he described thoroughly, were unlike those of the early printers or, for that matter, most other type designers. He was a letterer rather than a calligrapher, a man who drew rather than wrote. His letterforms reveal a certain stiffness, perhaps the result of overworking them in a search for perfection. Goudy learned the technique of matrix engraving from Wiebking, so that he could cut his own. After drawing his letters he incised them upon large metal patterns which he used to guide the pantographic tool which engraved the matrices, reduced to proper size mechanically. Goudy's lack of formal training and discipline is mirrored in many of his more than one hundred type faces. Most are novelty advertising designs, already badly dated. Even his book faces often suffer from mannerisms and eccentricity which call attention to the type rather than the text; of these Goudy Modern and Old Style hold up best.

Will Ransom (1878–1955), who came to Goudy's aid in his early, difficult days, was one of the most modest and appealing of his generation of designers and printers. As an earnest and impressionable youth in Washington, he wrote out and illuminated manuscripts, copied Morris and Beardsley indiscriminately, and learned to print as a newspaper odd-job man. In 1903 he arrived in Chicago to attend the school of the Art Institute, armed with a letter to Goudy, whom he joined in the Village Press. When the Goudys moved, he became a book-keeper but in 1911 decided to try art again, urged to do so by his wife. He was primarily a commercial artist, with a desire to produce fine books; this led him in 1921 to establish his own press, which turned out a number of limited editions, mainly of contemporary poetry, none of which were successful. He soon had to return to commercial art, keeping up an interest in fine printing which led to the publication, in 1929, of his *Private Presses and their Books*, still the best bibliography in its field. Ransom left Chicago in 1930, to become art director for the firm of Leo Hart, in Rochester, N.Y., where he produced a number of limited editions, the best being Dwiggins's edition of *The Travels of Marco Polo*, a pleasantly printed and designed book. After five years in Rochester Ransom held a number of minor jobs until, in 1941, he became designer for the University of Oklahoma Press, where he remained until his death. Ransom was a competent printer, a meticulous bibliographer, and a man of extraordinary warmth and generosity, who never hesitated to encourage and assist the many who turned to him for aid or advice.

William Addison Dwiggins (1880–1956) was born in Martinsville, Ohio, a doctor's son, and grew up in various midwestern small towns. At nineteen he entered Frank Holme's school in Chicago, where he studied lettering under Goudy; five years later he followed the Goudys to Hingham, where he remained the rest of his life. For the next decade he did advertising and lettering in Boston, experience which led to his *Lay-out in Advertising*, published in 1928 and reissued twenty years later—an unusual occurrence in a field where few books remain valid for two decades. Dwiggins, although unusually successful in advertising, where his industry, intellect, and talent were all far above average, was dissatisfied with the ephemeral nature of such work. A man of wide reading who also wrote well, he was far more interested in book design; his deeply considered ideas were sharpened by discussions with Updike and Rollins, who encouraged him to make his views more widely known. In 1919 he began to issue *The Transactions of the Society of Calligraphers*—an organisation of which he was founder and secretary, as well as president, under the pseudonym of Hermann Püterschein. 'Extracts from an Investigation into the Physical Properties of Books', written by Dwiggins and his cousin, L. B. Siegfried, is a satiric attack upon so-called 'scientific' research techniques and upon current standards of book production, which had fallen sharply during the war. Dwiggins had had some recent experience in book production as acting Director of the Harvard University Press for a brief period during the war. Chester Lane, its regular director, encouraged him to try for more publisher's work and gave him letters of introduction to several New York firms. He used these in 1923 during a visit which resulted in a number of jobs, among them one from Alfred A. Knopf, just beginning to build his list and willing to gamble on new talent in design as well as in literature. Their association, which lasted until Dwiggins's death, was among the most influential in modern American tradebook design; from it resulted a long series of handsome, thoughtfully designed, and well-printed books which did much for the general level of book design. Dwiggins's main concern was to produce books easy to read which also revealed clearly and emphatically the author's intent; he was adept at solving the problems of difficult scholarly works, with their complex apparatus of footnotes, bibliography, indexes, tables, and the like, which he managed to resolve into pages both handsome and functional. Dwiggins had a natural talent for decorative design, which he used to great effect on bindings, jackets, and chapter headings. He was particularly fond of small, repetitive units, fleurons or geometric shapes which he cut into stencils or on stamps for experiment; he used these with great vigour and originality, especially for binding spines. A row of Dwiggins bindings, mechanically made and blocked, the designs carefully planned within the limitations of machine and material, are effective in the same way as a shelf-full of eighteenth-century handtooled leather bindings—as wall decoration as well as individual volumes.

Dwiggins also designed many de-luxe editions, mainly for George Macy's Limited Editions Club, founded in 1929. These, like his trade books, were made to be read rather than merely admired—they showed the same clarity, logic, and lightness of touch, avoiding the all too frequent pretentiousness and vulgar display of bibliophile publications. In these he could indulge his love of colour, choosing unusual combinations that yet were highly pleasing, applied in large expanses of flat, low-keyed tints. *Tartarin of Tarascon* (1930); *The Tales of Edgar Allan Poe* (1930) and *The Travels of Marco Polo*, (1933) are among the best of these.

It was inevitable that Dwiggins, trained as a letterer and with a free and natural talent in calligraphy, should be asked to design types. In 1929, after the appearance of *Lay-out in Advertising*, in which he had commented on the legibility of various type faces, he was invited by the Mergenthaler Linotype Company to design one. He adapted the stencil technique he had invented for decoration to the production of letterforms, so that he could experiment with fit, proportion, and evenness of colour. When satisfied with these experimental letters he did finished drawings which were sent to the company for cutting. Dwiggins designed eleven faces for Linotype, among them several frankly experimental ones never produced. Two of his types, Electra and Caledonia, attained great success in book work. Another, Falcon, was introduced after his death, in 1962.

Dwiggins was a modest, gentle, highly likable man with wide interests and sympathies; writing, painting, woodcarving, puppets and puppet theatres were but a few of his hobbies. He was far more interested in creating usable books than monumental ones; the improvement in the design and production of American tradebooks between the two world wars owes more to his example than that of any other designer.

Rudolf Ruzicka was born (1883) in Bohemia and brought to Chicago by his parents when he was eleven. Despite difficulty in learning English he completed seven years schooling in three, studying art at a settlement house on Saturdays; at fourteen he was apprenticed to a commercial wood-engraving studio, continuing his art training in evening classes at the Art Institute of Chicago. In 1903 the young artist moved to New York, where he worked for an advertising agency; in his spare time he experimented with wood-engraving, especially with chiaroscuro prints. A meeting with Updike in 1907 brought a commission to engrave a Dwiggins title-page, as well as an invitation to call if he ever came to Boston. In 1910, while visiting Dwiggins, he accepted the invitation. Updike was cordial to him, appreciative and critical of his work. In 1911 he began the first of a series of views of Boston sent by the Merrymount Press as New Year's Keepsakes until Updike's death—work in which Ruzicka proved himself one of the most sensitive topographical artists America has produced, and which brought him a number of book commissions, including *New York* (1915) and *Newark* (1917). While best known for his coloured wood-engravings, which display a bold line and large flat tints of colour, Ruzicka has worked in many other media: copperplate *(Fables of La Fontaine,* 1930); aquatints *(Washington Irving,* 1921); rubber plates; type metal; and wood-cuts. He has also designed many books and book jackets; a great deal of advertising and commercial printing; and a type face, Fairfield, as well as a number of fleurons for the Linotype. Ruzicka's work, like the man, is notable for its directness, its simplicity, and its integrity, shunning virtuosity for its own sake.

Fred Anthoensen, proprietor of the press that bears his name, in Portland, Maine, is one of the most skilled printers in the United States in difficult scholarly printing, particularly bibliographies. The work of the Anthoensen Press is like that of the Merrymount Press, some of whose custom it inherited: solid, unostentatious, with regard for the convenience of the reader and the intent of the author; its books are handsome, well-made, and impeccably proofread. A younger New England firm, the Stinehour Press, at Lunenburg, Vermont, shares these virtues; the small quarterly which it publishes, *Printing and Graphic Arts,* edited by Professor Ray Nash of Dartmouth College and Roderick D. Stinehour, has published a number of valuable articles on typographic and historical subjects as well as some of the best reviews in American graphic arts journals.

Thomas Maitland Cleland (1880–1965) was born in Brooklyn, N.Y., and grew up in New York City, where he attended several schools. Bored with the conventional curriculum (he preferred copying magazine illustrations and making things with his hands), he persuaded his parents to allow him to enter an art school when he was fifteen. Sketching from plaster casts or copying paintings did not interest him, but the discovery that a fellow student with a gift for free-hand design was selling his work did. Cleland tried his hand at it, and sold a border to a printer almost at once for five dollars. He spent his first fee on a copy of Walter Crane's *The Decorative Illustration of Books*, which he found in a second-hand shop. From it he learned of Beardsley and Morris, whose Kelmscott Chaucer he admired for hours in the window of Scribner's Book Store. Lewis Hatch, one of the assistants, noticed the repeated visits of the entranced youngster and invited him in to see the Chaucer and other finely printed books at close range whenever he liked—an enchanting experience which made him resolve to produce such books himself. At about the same time he found the work of Will Bradley, which he collected and studied avidly. In 1904 Cleland embarked upon a short-lived printing venture, the Cornhill Press, in Boston, which failed for lack of capital. There he met Rogers, Dwiggins, Rollins, and especially Updike, who took an interest in him, criticised his work frankly and severely, and gave him a number of commissions. After a brief trip to Italy, the first of many, which confirmed his love of renaissance decoration, he settled again in New York to become art director of *McClure's Magazine* and to execute a great quantity of elegant and highly decorative advertising material, in which his excellent sense of *pastiche* served him well: Toryesque borders, eighteenth-century rococo motifs, or decorative details from Adam plaster-work embellished his automobile advertisements; a series of illustrations inspired by French eighteenth-century paintings and prints adorned his work for the Strathmore Paper Company; plaques in the Wedgwood manner extolled the virtues of printer's inks.

Cleland's books, whether for trade or limited distribution, demonstrate the same sure decorative sense. They are elegant and sophisticated, with a highly individualistic sense of style. A text-book, Wentworth and Smith's *High School Mathematics* (1917) has charming little illustrations in the manner of Sebastian Le Clerc; *Tom Jones* (1952), for the Limited Editions Club, is in his favourite eighteenth-century French manner, as is his most recent work, the *Manon Lescaut* for Overbrook Press (1958). Cleland spent over six years on its silk-screen illustrations, for which he designed new printing techniques to make possible the delicacy of register required for the effect he sought. A classicist and conservative by taste and conviction, he has defended his principles with pungent wit and great power, especially in two frequently reprinted lectures, *Harsh Words* (1940) and *Progress in the Graphic Arts* (1948).

Elmer Adler (1884–1962) turned to printing relatively late in life. Son of a wealthy clothing manufacturer, he took part in the family business until 1922, when he moved to New York and founded the Pynson Printers, dedicated to the production of fine books. Among the artists whom Adler sponsored and helped to popularise were Rockwell Kent and Hans Alexander Mueller. He was also a founder of Random House, which during its early years acted as New York agent for the Nonesuch and Golden Cockerel Presses, and issued on its own account a number of limited editions with work of Kent, Lucien Bernhard, Dwiggins, and Valenti Angelo, among others. The Pynson Printers' most notable achievement was the publication of *The Colophon*, begun in 1930 and revived briefly after a wartime interruption as *The New Colophon* in 1948, the best American bibliophile journal. In 1940 Adler dissolved the Pynson Printers and moved his library and art collection to Princeton, where as a member of the University library staff he organised a Department of Graphic Arts which did much to interest undergraduates in both producing and collecting fine printing. On retiring from this post in 1952 he moved to San Juan, Puerto Rico, where he established another notable library and museum of the book.

Frederic Warde (1894–1939) was a curious amalgam of romanticism and practicality, in life as in typography. Born Arthur Frederick Ward, he became Frederick Warde during the war to distinguish himself from another Ward in his aviation training unit; Frederique Warde during a brief interval at the Princeton University Press; and finally the Frederic Warde under whose name most of his work appeared. On leaving the army Warde spent three years with Rudge at Mount Vernon, where he learned the technique of his craft and developed the meticulous attention to detail which characterised his work. A strong influence was his association with Bruce Rogers, from which resulted his *The Work of Bruce Rogers* in 1925. Warde spent the next three years as printing director of the Princeton University Press, where he planned and executed a wide variety of books. In 1924 he went abroad, as did so many young Americans in the twenties, in search of greater freedom and adventure. During his four years in Europe he met and worked with Morison and Mardersteig, both of whom influenced his thinking and his style. *The Tapestry* by Robert Bridges, which he printed himself in 1925, contains the first of his three versions of Arrighi, based on the hand and types of the sixteenth-century

Italian writing-master, eventually used as a companion italic for Centaur. In 1928 Warde returned to the U.S.A. with the idea of establishing, with Crosby Gaige, a private press for the production of limited editions. When this became an early casualty of the depression, he turned for the rest of his life to free-lance book design and advertising typography.

Warde's books, whether for Princeton, the Limited Editions Club, or his own imprint, the Pleiad, are usually sparse, lightly decorated, and classic in design and feeling. Like his great friend William A. Kittridge of the Lakeside Press, with whom he carried on a frequent and lengthy correspondence on personal and typographic matters, he preferred a grey page, light and even in colour, the result of careful under-inking and light impression. His books, comparatively few and slight, display a conscious search for clarity and a regard for perfection which make them memorable.

William A. Kittridge (1891-1945), who was Warde's closest friend and confidant, had had varied experience as a compositor, pressman, layout artist and art director in Boston and New York before he joined the Lakeside Press in Chicago in 1922. The firm had been organised by R. R. Donnelley, who came to Chicago in 1864 and in 1870 entered the Lakeside Printing and Publishing Company, which he built into one of the largest and most profitable in the country. The plant and equipment had always been, as it is today, among the most efficient in the United States, and its ambition was to demonstrate that a large and modern printing establishment is capable of quality work. Kittridge, who had a penchant for fine, hand-made Italian papers and monumental designs, often based upon those of Bodoni or Gillé, was chosen to become director of design because he was interested in producing *de luxe* books which would bring prestige to the firm and because he was equally interested in raising the standards of the enormous amount of commercial printing it handled. His most notable books were the Four American Classics published in 1930: *Moby Dick*, illustrated by Rockwell Kent; *Walden*, by Rudolph Ruzicka; *Two Years Before the Mast*, by E. A. Wilson; and Poe's *Tales*, by Dwiggins. Kittridge also designed a number of books for the Caxton Club, the Chicago book collector's society, for various private patrons, and for trade houses. His influence in Chicago and throughout the country was further intensified by the many exhibitions he organised in the Lakeside Press's exhibition galleries, and by the series of excellently written and produced booklets, books, and mailing pieces produced by Donnelley's to advertise its facilities.

California, whose printing history began with the press of Zamarano in

1834, is the one area of the United States whose work shows a strong regional character. Whether because of its geographic separation from New York and Boston, or because it has few of the large printing establishments that dominate book production in the rest of the country, California has managed to produce a steady stream of small, highly individualistic printers whose work often shows great liveliness and ingenuity. Another reason may be the presence of a number of wealthy patrons who have commissioned local work, of publishers and book shops who have sponsored it, and of such institutions as the Huntington Library and the Book Club of California which have assisted California printers with both patronage and publicity.

John Henry Nash (1871–1947) was among the first of the California printers to make an international reputation. Nash, born and educated in Canada, came to San Francisco as a journeyman printer in 1895. After the great earthquake and fire of 1906 he moved to New York for a five-year interval, where he met and was deeply influenced by De Vinne and H. L. Bullen, the founder and director of the A. T. F. Library in Jersey City. Far more influential, however, was the work of William Morris and of the fifteenth-century Italian printers whose work he imitated throughout his career, usually rather heavy-handedly. In 1916 Nash set up his own shop in San Francisco, where he prospered, printing and publishing on his own account (*The Divine Comedy*, 1929, his most ambitious venture); for book clubs, especially The Book Club of California; and for a number of millionaire clients, among them William Randolph Hearst, W. A. Clark, and C. L. Clark, who appreciated both his evangelical salesmanship and his taste for printed pomp and circumstance. His books are marked by their thick, hand-made paper, their rigidly classical typography, and their heavy inking and impression.

Far more gifted than Nash, as well as more original, is the Grabhorn Press, today California's senior private press, which combines the publication of its own books with a wide range of commercial, institutional, and private commissions. The Grabhorn brothers, Edwin and Robert, were born in Indianapolis, where Edwin was trained as a music printer. In 1917 they published their first book there, under the imprint of the Studio Press: an edition of De Vinne's *Typographical Effect*. Two years later they moved to San Francisco, where they did commercial jobs and pamphlets while accumulating capital and equipment for bookwork. Their first commission for a book came from the Book Club of California, in 1921. By 1928 they had established their reputation sufficiently to be asked to print books for the new firm of Random House; two of their best known works, an edition of Hawthorne's *The Scarlet*

Letter, in that year, and Whitman's *Leaves of Grass* (1930), with decorations by Valenti Angelo, resulted. The Grabhorns' work is lively and virile, far removed from the cult of the deckle-edge and the pseudo-medieval. They are particularly skilful in colour-printing, especially from wood-blocks. Jane Grabhorn, wife of Robert, is an excellent and witty printer in her own right, the books of her Jumbo Press and Colt Press distinguished by a freshness of approach and sprightliness of spirit. The Grabhorns encouraged and influenced a whole generation of printers who are today making their own reputations. Among them are Adrian Wilson, of San Francisco, and Jack W. Stauffacher, typographer of Stanford University Press, whose Greenwood Press has issued a number of handsome little volumes.

Other northern California firms of note are Taylor and Taylor, founded in 1896, less bohemian and commercially more successful than any of the others here discussed. Henry H. Taylor, one of the brothers who own and manage it, is a graduate of the Harvard Business School, where he attended Updike's lectures in 1912 and 1913, an experience immediately reflected in the style of Taylor and Taylor's work—plain, functional, well-made, stressing careful editing and immaculate text. In addition to a large volume of routine commercial work, the firm has printed a number of excellent books. Its type-specimen book, issued in 1939, is among the handsomest ever published by an American printer.

One would expect Southern California, symbolised by Hollywood, to produce work of ebullience bordering on vulgarity. Yet the quietest, and to a great extent the most distinguished of Southern California typography and book production is that of Saul and Lillian Marks's Plantin Press. Saul Marks was born in Europe, where he had some training as a printer, and emigrated to the United States in 1921. Late in the twenties he moved to Los Angeles, where with his wife Lillian he founded the Plantin Press in 1931. The Markses have turned their originally low capital into one of the firm's strongest assets: forced by necessity to choose their equipment and types with great care, they chose only the conservative and well-made which would wear well. They are particularly fond of English Monotype faces, their favourite being Bembo, which they space meticulously, adjusting careful machine composition by hand. Their shop has been kept deliberately small, for Marks feels that to do good work ultimate control must be kept in one man's hands. He favours restrained decoration, using an occasional second colour and fleurons; Italian papers, since he considers English hand-made paper too hard for satisfactory press work without dampening; and slow, painstaking presswork. Marks's regular customers include Dawson's Book Shop, in Los Angeles, who have done much to encourage local printers, especially with their Western Travel Series; the Huntington Library; and the bookselling firm of Zeitlin and Ver Brugge. His most elaborate books have been commissioned by the Limited Editions Club; they include *The Ring and the Book* (1949) and *Travels with a Donkey* (1957). The Plantin's best work, marked by a blend of good taste and impeccable technique, is found among the small, unillustrated books for which it can assume complete responsibility.

Anderson, Ritchie, and Simon is larger and more prolific than the Plantin Press. It dates back to 1932 when Ward Ritchie, who owned a Washington hand-press and a little type, much of it a gift from the Grabhorns, was asked by Elmer Adler to print a signature for the *Colophon*. This necessitated the purchase of an ancient power press and additional type. Ritchie, who had intended to become a lawyer, had become a printer instead as a result of reading Cobden-Sanderson's *Journals*; he then attended a trade school and worked with Schmied in Paris for a year, to prepare himself. In 1935 Gregg Anderson joined the firm. He and Ritchie had first met in 1928 at the Huntington Library, where Anderson was working part-time. After graduating from college Anderson, who had precocious taste in literature and typography, tried to work for Updike; he treated Anderson kindly but would not hire him. There followed a stint at the Meriden Gravure Company, and, on his return to California, employment and partnership with Ritchie. Anderson, a stout admirer of De Vinne and Updike and a man with an orderly and logical mind, did much to systematise the work of the firm and put it on a sound financial footing. When he was killed in the war, in 1944, his widow entered the plant; Joseph Simon, the senior pressman and a brother of Lillian Marks, was later made a partner.

Anderson, Ritchie, and Simon do commercial job printing, book production, and publishing. It is a medium-sized establishment of a sort that thrives better in California than elsewhere in the United States, with its own bindery attached. From the beginning it has had strong ties with the Huntington Library, for which it has printed many books, as well as with nearby colleges. Ritchie's own books tend to be bold, with strong colour and powerful typography; he has also printed for such *avant garde* typographers as Merle Armitage and Alvin Lustig, with whose work he has shown much sympathy.

Porter Garnett (1871–1951) was a native of California, whose taste and style of working was formed there, but his most important work was achieved in the East. Garnett was born and grew up in San Francisco, where during the 'nineties he was associated with the gay and bohemian group of artists and writers who first made that city's reputation as a centre of the arts; he was a member of the staff of *The Lark*, a short-lived little magazine best remembered as the first publisher of Gellett Burgess's famous *Purple Cow*. In 1922, both older and far more austere in taste, he was invited to the Carnegie Institute of Technology, in Pittsburgh, to conduct in its department of printing technology and management, courses in design which would help cultivate in these future printing foremen and executives a respect for the appearance and the content of the work they would produce. The Laboratory Press, established by Garnett, taught hand-composition and presswork, with emphasis on the niceties of spacing and make-ready which spell the difference between ordinary and good printing; its members were responsible for choosing texts worthy of permanent preservation and for working out experimental (usually conservative) formats which would express their meaning with clarity, force, and beauty. The Press continued its work until 1935, during which time it gave several generations of printers a sense of the dignity and importance of their craft.

Book design changed rapidly in the United States, as elsewhere, during the nineteen-thirties, as a result of the depression and of the rise of Hitler. The market for the luxurious, if often tasteless, limited edition dried up. Many designers who had specialised in limited editions were forced to turn to trade books, or to advertising. Books themselves grew more utilitarian, more economic in decoration and manufacture. The forced emigration of a great many European artists and designers brought to the United States new ideas and new talents, some traditional, some revolutionary.

Links with Europe were not a new development in American printing: such designers as Ruzicka and Saul Marks were European-born; a number of younger American artists and teachers had studied in Europe, among them Warren Chappell, who had worked in Koch's workshop in Offenbach. The new generation were mainly German, many, like Georg and Stephan Salter or Fritz Kredel, stemming from the Koch tradition, which fitted gently and easily into the prevailing mode. They obtained posts as teachers in the New York art schools, they designed jackets and books and illustrated them, and they brought new life into the American scene.

The most individualistic, and yet perhaps most influential, of the emigrés in the Koch tradition is Victor Hammer. Hammer, born (1882) in Vienna and trained in an architect's studio there, has modelled himself upon the renaissance ideal. His skills embrace not only printing, but calligraphy, painting, and sculpture as well, and he is equally proficient in all. He had already had a distinguished career in Europe, as proprietor of the Stamperia del Santuccio in Florence (1922–34) and as Professor at the Vienna Academy of Fine Arts when, in 1939, he left in order to escape Nazi control. During the next decade he taught at Wells College, in Aurora, New York, where he reestablished his press; on retirement from that post, in 1948, he moved to Lexington, Kentucky, where he was artist-in-residence at Transylvania College and where he has also taught privately. There he has continued his printing, using the imprint of the Hammer Press, and has inspired the foundation of a number of other private presses, including the Anvil Press, under the guidance of his wife, Carolyn Reading Hammer, and the Gravesend Press of the late Joseph Graves, the friend and supporter who arranged for Hammer to move to Kentucky. Hammer's work as a printer is very much in the private-press tradition; his press, like most German presses, has been influenced more by Cobden-Sanderson than Morris, although his social and political ideals and his distrust of machinery stem directly from the latter. Hammer's books are upon hand-made paper, with ample margins and leading; title-pages are classically simple, occasionally adorned with a metal-cut of his own devising; he is fond of using, as second colour, a terracotta which sets off the deep black colour of his text. Hammer's favourite type is his own American Uncial, a reworking of a face he had earlier designed in Italy. He is his own punch-cutter, having been instructed in that art by Koch's son, Paul, for he feels that the highest results can be obtained only when one man is responsible for both the written letterform and its transmutation into metal. His books are printed on the hand-press, formerly by his son, Jacob, more recently by himself and his wife. Among the best of those he has printed in America are his edition of Charles Péguy's *Jeanne d'Arc* (1943) and of Hölderlin (1949), both in the highest hand-press tradition which, although some may consider it archaic in the twentieth century, still serves as the ultimate touchstone by which the modern printer can judge his work.

Another group of emigrés was also assimilated, but not so gently nor so comfortably. While members of the Bauhaus group settled in the East, Gropius at Harvard and Albers at Yale, it was in Chicago that the school made its real impact. In 1937 Lazlo Moholy-Nagy, who had been working in England, was invited by a group of Chicago industrialists, at the suggestion of Gropius, to found a New Bauhaus in Chicago. He accepted the invitation and later that year the school began its tempestuous career in the old Marshall Field mansion on the South Side. Within a year it had run out of money; moreover the Board of Directors, all conservative businessmen, were aghast at the progressive and disturbing ideas they had imported. Moholy himself wondered why they had done it—he commented to his wife, 'I am bewildered. Do they know what they are doing?' After the school collapsed, in 1938, Moholy refounded it, giving it a new, more American name— the School of Design, staunchly supported in his campaign by one of the original directors, Walter Paepcke of Container Corporation. The students of the School of Design (now a part of Illinois Institute of Technology, and called the Institute of Design) were trained in a simplified version of the original Bauhaus tradition, adapted to American needs, but with its basic concept of the fundamentals course, emphasising free experiment with materials and techniques, unchanged.

Paradoxically, this experimentation has produced a new orthodoxy, with its stress upon asymmetrical layout, the double-spread title-page, and the use of sans serif types as the true evocation of the machine age. The new typography, as practiced by Moholy-Nagy, Georgy Kepes, and Herbert Bayer had a strong effect upon certain kinds of American books, primarily on art and architecture, which benefitted from the free handling of text and illustrations which it made possible. The high point of the movement occurred after the Second World War, when a group of members of the Trade Book Clinic of the American Institute of Graphic Arts staged at the New Art Circle in New York City an exhibition entitled *Books for Our Time*. The published catalogue of that exhibition, with essays by George Nelson, Marshall Lee, Herbert Bayer, Merle Armitage, John Begg, S. A. Jacobs, and Ernst Reichl, constitutes a manifesto of American Bauhaus typography. In books which rely more upon text than picture the effect of Bauhaus typography seems to be waning. In magazine design, in advertising, and in package design especially it has played a more lasting role.

Book printing in the United States during the Second World War was no different from that in Europe—generally miserable. Paper shortages, overworked plant, the call-up of craftsmen all contributed to the shoddy books which characterise wartime production. The only innovation worthy of note, perhaps, was the enormous success of the cheap paperback books produced in large editions for the troops, which proved that the much maligned average American would read decent literature if it were readily available at low cost; the Armed Services Editions paved the way for the post-war success of the quality paperback series, undoubtedly the most significant development in recent American publishing history. Pocket Books and Bantam Books which purveyed bestsellers on the news-stands and were inspired by Tauch-nitz and Penguin, were securely established before the war. But a intellec-tual paperback series typified by Anchor Books, the first and still a leading series, providing solid fare in well-designed and printed form, their wrappers the work of some of the best graphic artists, are a wholly new phenomenon in the American book-trade.

A new generation of book designers made its appearance after the war, as Dwiggins, Rogers, Updike and their contemporaries retired or died. Some were bright young doctrinaires like Alvin Lustig and Paul Rand, eager to transfer to books the experience they had gained in advertising or industrial design. These had their greatest influence in the paperbacks. Others were more traditional in their approach. One cannot yet gain sufficient distance to see new trends or new figures in true perspective, but there are already some in-dications of the patterns emerging in current American book-printing and of the people who will weave them. The economics of post-war printing and publishing, as of most American industry, point toward increasing stress on automation, expensive labour-saving equipment, with faster and larger runs to pay for it. Already there have been numerous mergers in both publishing and printing, for the small firm cannot afford the research to develop the new methods nor the machines which result from them. The magazine publishers, concerned for their falling circulation and expert in the technique of large-volume direct-mail sales, are increasingly turning to trade books, text-books, teaching machines, and allied ventures to replace their shrinking market. The book which depends upon its text rather than its illustration or multi-colour printing to attract readers has become increasingly the province of the university press or of the small *avant-garde* publisher, both of whom often find that they must print abroad where small editions are still economical. And yet there are new, highly individualistic artists and printers, as there always have been, who swim against the tide and who generally print and publish their own books because in no other way can they produce them in the way they wish. Among them are Joseph Low, a successful advertising artist and illustrator of childrens' books, whose basic premise is that the artist should be his own printer—that in no other way can he realise the full poten-tial of his work. Low's favourite medium is the linoleum cut, its texture modified by scraping, sanding, or etching; on occasion he uses rubber plates, or wood blocks. He is partial to hand-made or mould-made papers, particu-larly Japanese ones, which offer opportunity to experiment with colour and texture. As many as eighteen colours, with forty-five cuts, have been employed on one small portfolio of ten plates. Low's favourite subjects are animals and birds, executed in a deceptively primitive style, medieval in character, with great economy of line and with great vigour.

Leonard Baskin is another artist who has become his own printer to satisfy his own standards and to be able to experiment freely. Baskin is a successful wood-engraver and sculptor who has shown extensively in the United States and in Europe; he has had one-man shows in Paris, London, and The Hague, and has sold work to many of the country's leading museums. He began printing when an art student at Yale, where the first book bearing his Gehenna Press imprint was produced.

After leaving Yale, Baskin and his wife, Esther, who has collaborated on most of his books, continued their work in Worcester, Massachusetts, where he taught for a brief period at the school of the Art Museum; from there they moved to Northampton, where he became a Professor in the Smith College Department of Art. Here he joined forces with Richard Warren of the Metcalf Printing Company, which now produces almost all the Gehenna imprints. These have included *Thirteen Poems by Wilfred Owen* (1956), with drawings by Ben Shahn, another of the few serious American artists to concern himself with book-illustration; *Horned Beetles and Other Insects*, a collection of etchings on a selection of hand-made papers (Baskin very much enjoys experimenting with the textures obtainable from exotic papers); *Voyages*, by Hart Crane, printed for the Museum of Modern Art in 1957, with boxwood engravings utilising an extremely fine line; and *The Seven Deadly Sins*, by Anthony Hecht, a series of poems with emblematic illustrations, a preoccupation of Baskin. Just completed (1962) is a series of powerful drawings for the *Iliad*, to accompany an edition by the University of Chicago Press.

Baskin is a highly articulate and intelligent artist, who reads widely and collects books, mainly emblem books and woodcut illustration. His work, while highly personal, still shows influences of earlier artists whose work he admires, especially Blake; others of his engravings show reminiscenses of Beardsley, but with greater strength and less emphasis on decorative line.

Several of the university presses, as has been briefly indicated above, consistently produce better than average printing. The Princeton University Press, whose typography was for many years the responsibility of P. J. Conkwright, is especially noteworthy; Yale, under Carl Rollins and more recently under Alvin Eisenman; the University of Michigan Press, with George Lenox; and the University of Chicago Press, with Greer Allen, all publish books which are functional, well-made, and more often than not handsome.

While today's average American book leaves much to be desired in design and manufacture, there are a number of firms, generally the smaller ones, which attempt to maintain high standards. Among them may be noted A. Colish, Rudge's successor as Bruce Rogers' favourite printer, who has printed both low-budgeted trade books and limited editions of high quality; Joseph Blumenthal, one of Rudge's alumni, whose Spiral Press in New York City prints for the Pierpont Morgan Library, the Grolier Club, and other institutional clients who wish work showing dignity and taste; and Clarke and Way, also in New York City, printers of the great Frick Catalogue as well as much first-rate commercial work. R. R. Donnelley and Sons' Lakeside Press does comparatively little bookwork (that is, as compared with the vast quantities of magazine and commercial printing they execute) but that which they do is generally extremely good.

The emphasis in the present article has been on individuals rather than groups; one must however at least mention briefly a few of the organisations which have influenced American printing design and production. The American Institute of Graphic Arts is the most important of the American organisations dealing with printing design, as well as the only one which is truly national in scope. It goes back to 1914, when the Secretary of State in Washington received an invitation for American participation in the Leipzig International Exhibition for the Book Industry and the Graphic Arts, and was unable to find any group capable of organising the American exhibit. The request was forwarded to President Wilson, who asked the National Arts Club to undertake the job. Accordingly forty men were co-opted to select the show; from this nucleus came a permanent organisation, dedicated to the improvement of American graphic design and to international co-operation in the holding of graphic arts exhibitions. A.I.G.A. has since grown into an organisation of thousands of members, representing all phases of printing and publishing. In 1922 it held the first of its annual Fifty Books of the Year exhibitions, which mirror current taste and fashion in book design and have done much to formulate American style in design. It also holds exhibitions of children's books, text-books, commercial printing, packaging, and other types of printing, offers clinics and classes in printing and design, and has published as keepsakes, catalogues, or journals a number of valuable contributions to American printing and publishing history.

There are other regional graphic arts groups in almost every major printing centre which have also had considerable influence. The Society of Typographic Arts, in Chicago, was formed in 1927 by a group of dissident A.I.G.A.

members who felt the parent organisation was unfairly biased in favour of New York, the national headquarters. It holds an annual exhibition of Design in Chicago Printing which usually stresses advertising rather than book typography, since book design and production form a comparatively small part of its membership's interests. The Chicago Book Clinic holds a regional book exhibition which fills that gap; other regional shows are held throughout the country, the most notable being the Southern Book Exhibition and the Western Book Exhibition, the latter sponsored by the Rounce and Coffin Club of Los Angeles. Such societies and exhibitions have done much to improve local standards of design and production, and to arouse lay interest in the subject.

It is difficult, if not impossible, to summarise briefly over a century-and-a half of printing history, even when it is confined to but one country, yet one feels that some sort of generalisations should be attempted. The history of American printing is, to a great extent, the history of the printers' breathless attempt to keep up with his expanding resources. The first American printers, trained in Europe and using European materials, produced work comparable to their models. Soon after the beginning of the Republic, however, the American printer declared his independence of both his European mentors and his European suppliers. Most nineteenth-century American printing, like that of the rest of the world, was poor in design and execution, with too much decoration, wretched types, and bad workmanship and materials. A few printers, like Joel Munsell and De Vinne, swam against the tide. Most were content to go along with it, since this was profitable. The influence of William Morris and the revival of printing which followed in his wake inspired a generation of American printers, among them Updike, Rogers, Goudy, and Dwiggins, who developed their own styles and their own principles and who, in the twentieth century, placed American printing at a level where it need not feel shame at comparison with that of England and the Continent. At the moment, as printing faces a new threshold of technological change, with photo-composition and other new methods rapidly developing, the situation seems much as it did a half-century ago, when mechanical composition and high-speed presses were coming into their own. The printer must appraise the capacities of his new tools and grow accustomed to their use before he can extract from them either very original or very good work.

Index

Abbreviations used:

des / designer	pu / publisher
eng / engraver	qd / quoted
ill / illustrator	t / type face
j / journal	td / type designer
pp / private press	tf / typefounder
pr / printer	ty / typographer

373

375